FOOD&WINE

Wine Guide

2017

by the Editors of Food & Wine and Richard Nalley

Published by Time Inc. Books
225 Liberty Street
New York, NY 10281

volume editor **JOSEPH GONZALEZ**
contributing editors **PATRICK COMISKEY, LINDA MURPHY**
editorial assistant **NICOLE FISHER**
project editor **LACIE PINYAN**
junior designer **ANNAMARIA JACOB**
copy editor **ADRIENNE DAVIS**
proofreader **LISA LEVENTER**
research chief **JANICE HUANG**
researchers **MARY KAN, ELLEN MCCURTIN, PAOLA SINGER**
senior production manager **GREG A. AMASON**
assistant production director **SUE CHODAKIEWICZ**

cover photography **CHRISTOPHER GRIFFITH/TRUNK ARCHIVE**

FOOD & WINE
editor **NILOU MOTAMED**
executive wine editor **RAY ISLE**
books editor **SUSAN CHOUNG**

ISBN-10: 0-8487-4841-7
ISBN-13: 978-0-8487-4841-8

ISSN 1522-001X
Manufactured in the United States of America

FOOD&WINE
BOOKS

FOOD&WINE

Wine Guide

2017

CALIFORNIA
OREGON
WASHINGTON
NORTHEAST
SOUTHEAST
MIDWEST
SOUTHWEST

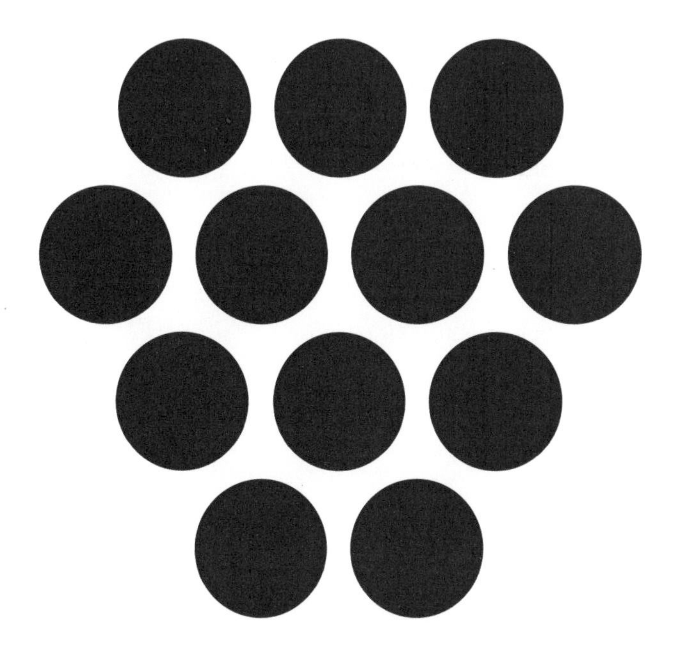

Contents

Foreword

This is an exciting time for American wine. Our country has more wineries than ever before making better wines than ever before. We're not just talking about California, either, even if that state does produce a lion's share of the wines we drink. In these pages you'll find brilliant Pinot Noirs and Chardonnays from Oregon, emphatic Cabernets and Merlots from Washington State and a plethora of wines from other regions around the US, too: the Texas High Plains, Michigan's Leelanau Peninsula, the rolling horse (and grape) country of Virginia and Arizona's high desert, where Rhône varieties have found an adopted home. And, of course, California, where we do deep dives into benchmark regions like Napa Valley and Sonoma County, as well as profile up-and-coming stars from farther-flung locations like Santa Barbara County and the Anderson Valley. The end result is an impossible-to-beat collection of the

500 best wineries in the United States, with reviews and recommendations of their top bottlings. We're confident you'll find that the 2017 F&W *Wine Guide* is an indispensable resource.

Nilou Motamed
Editor
FOOD & WINE

Ray Isle
Executive Wine Editor
FOOD & WINE

KEY TO SYMBOLS

TYPE OF WINE

● RED
● ROSÉ
○ WHITE

PRICE

$$$$ OVER $60
$$$ $30+ TO $60
$$ $15+ TO $30
$ $15 AND UNDER

Wine Terms

You won't find much fussy wine jargon in this guide, but some of the terms commonly used to describe the taste of wine might be unfamiliar or used in an unfamiliar way. References in tasting notes to flavors and textures other than "grape" are meant to serve as analogies: All the wines in this guide are made from grapes, but grapes have the ability to suggest the flavors of other fruits, herbs or minerals. Here's a mini glossary to help you become comfortable with the language of wine.

ACIDITY The tart, tangy or zesty sensations in wine. Ideally, acidity brightens a wine's flavors as a squeeze of lemon brightens fish. Wines lacking acidity taste "flabby."

AMERICAN VITICULTURAL AREA (AVA) Most US labels carry an AVA, showing the legally defined region from which the wine comes. Unlike many European designations, AVAs don't stipulate how a wine must be produced, which grapes may be used or the maximum yields allowed per vineyard. Rather, US law dictates that at least 85 percent of the grapes in a wine labeled with an AVA must come from that region. If an AVA wine lists a vintage date, 95 percent of the fruit is required to be from that year's harvest. Wines with the name of one grape, often called varietal wines, must contain 75 percent of that grape variety. Some states go beyond these requirements. Oregon, for example, mandates a higher minimum percentage for most varietal wines and for geographic designations.

APPELLATION An officially designated winegrowing region. The term is used mostly in France and the US. In Europe, a wine's appellation usually reflects not only where it's from but also aspects of how it's made, such as vineyard yields and aging.

BALANCE The harmony between acidity, tannin, alcohol and sweetness in a wine.

BIODYNAMICS An organic, sustainable approach to farming that takes into account a farm's total environment, including surrounding ecosystems and astronomical considerations, such as the phases of the moon.

BODY How heavy or thick a wine feels in the mouth. Full-bodied or heavy wines are often described as "big."

CORKED Wines that taste like wet cork or newspaper are said to be corked. The cause is trichloroanisole (TCA), a contaminant sometimes transmitted by cork.

CRISP A term used to describe wines that are high in acidity.

CRU In France, a grade of vineyard (such as *grand cru* or *premier cru*), winery (such as Bordeaux's *cru bourgeois*) or village (in the Beaujolais region).

CUVÉE A batch of wine. A cuvée can be from a single barrel or tank (*cuve* in French), or a blend of different lots of wine. A Champagne house's top bottling is called a *tête de cuvée.*

DRY A wine without perceptible sweetness. A dry wine, however, can have powerful fruit flavors. "Off-dry" describes a wine that has a touch of sweetness.

EARTHY An earthy wine evokes flavors such as mushrooms, leather, damp straw or even manure.

EXTRACT Essentially the minerals and other trace elements in a wine; sugar-free dry extract is everything in a wine except water, sugar, acids and alcohol. High extract often gives wine a dusty, tactile impression of density. It frequently serves to buffer, or mitigate, high alcohol or strong acidity.

FILTER/FINE Processes used to remove sediment or particulates from a wine to enhance its clarity.

FINISH The length of time a wine's flavors linger on the palate. A long finish is the hallmark of a more complex wine.

FRUITY A wine with an abundance of fruit flavors is described as "fruity." Such wines may give the impression of sweetness, even though they're not actually sweet.

HERBACEOUS Depending on context, calling a wine "herbaceous" or "herbal" can be positive or negative. Wines that evoke herb flavors can be delicious. Wines with green pepper flavors are less than ideal; such wines are also referred to as "vegetal."

LEES The sediment (including dead yeast cells) left over after a wine's fermentation. Aging a wine on its lees (*sur lie* in French) gives wine nutty flavors and a creamy texture.

MALOLACTIC FERMENTATION A secondary fermentation that some white wines and most reds go through. It's the conversion of sharp, citrusy malic acid into rich, buttery lactic acid (the same acid in milk), a process that helps to soften the wine.

MERITAGE Pronounced like "heritage," this category recognizes multivariety blends, often with proprietary names, made from traditional Bordeaux grapes—chiefly Cabernet Sauvignon and Merlot in reds and Sauvignon Blanc and Sémillon in whites.

MÉTHODE CHAMPENOISE/MÉTHODE TRADITIONNELLE The most traditional and costly way to make sparkling wine is by causing a second fermentation in the bottle. That's achieved by adding sugar syrup and yeast. Only wines from the Champagne region of France that are made using this process may be labeled "méthode champenoise."

MINERAL Flavors that (theoretically) reflect the minerals found in the soil in which the grapes were grown. The terms "steely," "flinty" and "chalky" are also used to describe these flavors.

NOSE How a wine smells; its bouquet or aroma.

OAKY Wines that transmit the flavors of the oak barrels in which they were aged. Some oak can impart toast flavors.

OLD VINES The US government does not regulate the term "old vines" on labels, meaning that winemakers can define it however they like. Many of them agree that vines older than 35 years qualify as old; some believe that only vines 50 years or older make the cut.

OXIDIZED Wines that have a tarnished quality due to exposure to air are said to be oxidized. When intended, as in the case of sherry, oxidation can add fascinating dimensions to a wine. Otherwise, it can make a wine taste unappealing.

PALATE The flavors, textures and other sensations a wine gives in the mouth. The term "mid-palate" refers to the way these characteristics evolve with time in the mouth.

POWERFUL Wine that is full of flavor, tannin and/or alcohol.

RESERVE Another term that has no legal definition, "reserve" can be applied to any wine regardless of its age or how it was made; how much the designation is actually worth depends entirely on the brand.

RUSTIC Wine that is a bit rough, though often charming.

TANNIN A component of grape skins, seeds and stems, tannin is most commonly found in red wines. It imparts a puckery sensation similar to oversteeped tea. Tannin also gives a wine its structure and enables some wines to age well.

TERROIR A French term that refers to the particular attributes a wine acquires from the specific environment of a vineyard—i.e., the climate, soil type, elevation and aspect.

VITIS LABRUSCA Native to North America, this hardy grape species includes such varieties as Concord and Catawba. The *Vitis labrusca* species has largely been supplanted in the US by European "noble" *Vitis vinifera* grapes (such as Chardonnay, Cabernet Sauvignon, Sauvignon Blanc and Pinot Noir).

California

Americans love California wine. The state's 4,400 wineries produce 60 percent of all the wine we drink each year, from three-liter boxes to $500 cult Cabernets. A remarkable array of European-descended grapes flourish here, many originally transplanted by 19th-century immigrants. Today, California is the world's fourth leading wine producer, and its best wineries can easily challenge the great names of Bordeaux, Burgundy and Tuscany. Top California regions like Napa Valley and Sonoma County are so prestigious now that younger winemakers are taking their ambitions farther afield, to cooler, more marginal areas, to produce exciting, streamlined wines that are an alternative to California's traditionally luscious, ripe style.

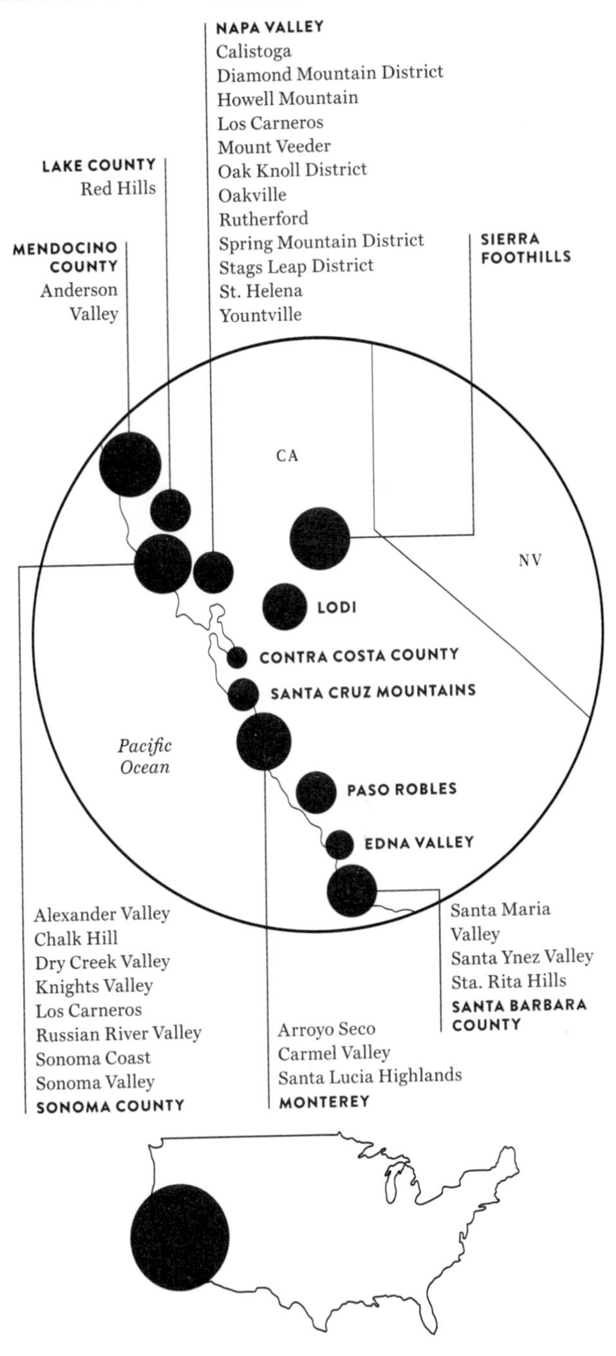
NAPA VALLEY
Calistoga
Diamond Mountain District
Howell Mountain
Los Carneros
Mount Veeder
Oak Knoll District
Oakville
Rutherford
Spring Mountain District
Stags Leap District
St. Helena
Yountville
LAKE COUNTY
Red Hills
MENDOCINO COUNTY
Anderson Valley
SIERRA FOOTHILLS
CA
NV
LODI
CONTRA COSTA COUNTY
SANTA CRUZ MOUNTAINS
Pacific Ocean
PASO ROBLES
EDNA VALLEY
Alexander Valley
Chalk Hill
Dry Creek Valley
Knights Valley
Los Carneros
Russian River Valley
Sonoma Coast
Sonoma Valley
SONOMA COUNTY
Arroyo Seco
Carmel Valley
Santa Lucia Highlands
MONTEREY
Santa Maria Valley
Santa Ynez Valley
Sta. Rita Hills
SANTA BARBARA COUNTY

Napa Valley

CLAIM TO FAME

It was in Napa Valley that Robert Mondavi kick-started the modern era in California viniculture by founding his namesake winery back in 1966. The half-century since has seen this picturesque, 30-mile-long valley, once home to prune plum orchards and cattle ranches, planted nearly wall-to-wall with vineyards that now provide grapes for more than 500 local wineries. The valley's Mediterranean climate offers warm, dry growing seasons to ripen grapes, with just enough ocean and bay influence to cool them down at night and lock in acidity. And its location affords another advantage: Just 50 miles north of San Francisco, Napa Valley draws millions of tourists a year. These visitors are often surprised to learn that California's most glamorous wine region actually produces only about 4 percent of its wine. Napa is not a high-volume, jug-wine territory, but a haven for family-owned, premium-price wineries. Though there is a little of everything planted here, the overwhelming trend in the past decades has been to push cooler climate–loving grapes like Pinot Noir and Chardonnay south toward San Francisco Bay, and to establish the warmer, more northerly Napa Valley as a bastion of Cabernet Sauvignon and related Bordeaux-style red blending grapes like Merlot and Cabernet Franc.

REGIONS TO KNOW

HOWELL MOUNTAIN Perched above the marine fog layer at 1,400 feet up in the Vaca Mountains to the east, this distinctive AVA, with its volcanic and red-clay soils, extended ripening season and small, intense grapes, is famous for producing mouth-filling, dark-fruited Cabernets with sturdy tannins that, in the top wines, soften in time into a muscular elegance.

LOS CARNEROS The first AVA to be based on climate rather than political borders, this southern area of rolling hills straddling the Napa-Sonoma county line at the foggy upper reaches of San Francisco Bay came into vogue in the 1980s with the realization that Burgundian grapes like Pinot Noir and Chardonnay flourished in cooler climes. Somewhat overshadowed by newer, even cooler coastal areas elsewhere, Carneros still produces many notable still and sparkling wines.

OAKVILLE This two-mile-wide, east–west strip in midvalley is a hotbed of influential vineyards and wineries, and a benchmark for Napa Cabernet Sauvignons, notable for their rich, black-currant fruit character.

RUTHERFORD Arguably the heart of Napa Valley, Rutherford is home to historic wineries and a major tourist nexus. These six square miles at the valley's widest, sunniest point produce rich, supple Cabernet Sauvignons, sometimes said to carry a hint of "Rutherford dust," which some perceive as an actual quality of the tannins, others simply as the overall particularity of the area's wines.

SPRING MOUNTAIN DISTRICT Tucked into the rugged contours of the Mayacamas Mountains, the vineyards here rise to 2,600 feet. The Spring Mountain District's small family producers are renowned for their high-quality wines, particularly Cabernet Sauvignon and Merlot.

STAGS LEAP DISTRICT A "valley within the valley" nestled under the cliffs of the Stags Leap Palisades, this area became world famous when a Stag's Leap Wine Cellars Cabernet won the famous 1976 Judgment of Paris. It has evolved into one of Napa Valley's most prestigious sub-regions, producing Bordeaux-style reds with the characteristic "iron fist in a velvet glove"—firm tannins wrapped in lush fruit.

YOUNTVILLE Stags Leap's midvalley neighbor, Yountville is a small but viticulturally diverse (and much-visited) AVA. It is probably as well known for its boutiques, hotels and restaurants (think the renowned French Laundry, for instance) as for its esteemed wineries.

KEY GRAPES: WHITE

CHARDONNAY Though plantings have been migrating from the midvalley floor to the south or elsewhere, Chardonnay remains the second most widely planted grape variety in Napa Valley. The region's producers turn out Chardonnays in a wide range of styles, from classically juicy, oaky palate-flatterers to leaner, more minerally bottlings from hillsides and the cooler vineyards of Carneros.

SAUVIGNON BLANC This Bordeaux-descended white variety typically prefers a warmer climate than Chardonnay does, and Napa Valley produces notable rich, New World–ripe versions. These wines are often bargains compared to Chardonnays, though Napa producers like Screaming Eagle, Vineyard 29 and Philippe Melka have introduced super-premium-priced Sauvignon Blanc bottlings.

KEY GRAPES: RED

CABERNET FRANC A small but worthy coterie here produces wines centered around this understated and often overlooked Bordeaux blending grape, which is known for its intriguing spicy-violet aromatics.

CABERNET SAUVIGNON The great Bordeaux flagship is also Napa's cornerstone grape. It is produced both on the valley floor, in versions that are—as a very broad, general rule—softer and more accessible, and from hillside vineyards like those of Howell, Spring and Diamond Mountains, which make generally more tannic, slower-evolving wines. The overall style emphasizes big flavors and richly matured fruit.

MERLOT Napa Valley's often outstanding Merlots are generally priced well below its Cabernets. This despite the fact that the qualities many value in Napa Cabernets—luscious mouthfeel, supple texture and perfumed, purely translated fruit—are offered in abundance in the top Merlots.

PETITE SIRAH Often misidentified in field blends (much of it is apparently Durif, a little-regarded workhorse blending grape in France), Petite Sirah has a small but devoted following, particularly for wines from Napa's patches of old-vine fruit.

PINOT NOIR The Los Carneros region, which southern Napa shares with neighboring Sonoma Valley, produces delicious, refined Pinot Noirs that have been somewhat overshadowed in the current wave of experimentation with colder, riskier vineyards elsewhere in coastal California (including out on the Sonoma Coast). But Los Carneros, cooled by breezes from the northern reaches of San Francisco Bay, turns out lovely wines from a cohort of skilled producers that are very much worth seeking out.

SYRAH A few high-end wineries like Colgin, Araujo and Shafer have shown Napa's potential for producing nuanced, transcendent, Rhône-rivaling Syrahs. The simpler, if sometimes mouthwatering, versions turned out by the great majority of Napa producers are part of the learning curve with this relative newcomer grape.

Producers/ Napa Valley

ABREU VINEYARDS

David Abreu is the third generation of his family to farm Napa Valley, but it is safe to say that his forebears could not have imagined the heights to which he would take the grapes under his care. In his day job, Abreu is probably the most sought-after vineyard consultant in California; his client list—including such premier names as Bryant Family Vineyard, Colgin Cellars (see p. 32) and Screaming Eagle—reads like a high-end wine auction catalogue. But Abreu began developing vineyards of his own in 1980 and now controls four obsessively farmed sites around Napa Valley, from which he produces five tiny-production, ultra-luxury-priced proprietary wines, all Cabernet Sauvignon– and Cabernet Franc–based and nearly all spoken for by his mailing list.

● **Las Posadas / 2012 / Howell Mountain / $$$$**
Foresty spice and layers of intense fruit make this Cabernet-focused red extraordinarily compelling—and it had better be, given the equally extraordinary price.

ACACIA VINEYARD

Now part of Treasury Wine Estates, Acacia was a pioneer of Pinot Noir and Chardonnay in the Carneros region back in 1979. The winery continues on its Burgundy-inspired mission, with Pinots and Chardonnays that tend to be leaner framed and more European in profile than the general run of California bottlings. Though Acacia's stars are its single-vineyard wines, in a good vintage the Carneros Chardonnay can be a steal for the quality it delivers. A newer label, A by Acacia, offers wines sourced outside Carneros, including a Rhône-style red blend, at even more affordable prices.

○ **Acacia Sangiacomo Vineyard Chardonnay / 2014 / Carneros / $$$**
From a pioneering Carneros vineyard comes this rich wine with aromas of vanillin oak and tropical fruit and ripe apple and pear flavors. The finish is clean and refreshing.

● **Acacia Lone Tree Vineyard Pinot Noir / 2013 / Carneros / $$$**
This is a deep and intensely fruity Pinot, with black cherry and briary blackberry framed by vanillin and chocolaty oak.

ADAMVS

A very-limited-production, collector-quality winery founded in 2008, this is the US project of billionaire philanthropist Stephen Adams and his wife, Denise, known in the wine world for rejuvenating Château Fonplégade in Bordeaux's St-Émilion. In Napa Valley, the Adamses bottle small quantities of three generally all–Cabernet Sauvignon wines (Quintvs, Adamvs, Téres), sourced mostly from ten biodynamically farmed estate vineyard parcels 1,500 to 2,000 feet up Howell Mountain. The dense, full-bodied, well-structured (and ultra-luxury-priced) wines are produced by a team that includes veteran viticulturist Michael Wolf and go-to winemaker Philippe Melka. The estate also turns out an even tinier amount of Sauvignon Blanc.

● **ADAMVS / 2012 / Howell Mountain / $$$$**
A bit more accessible now than the Quintvs, it still sports Howell Mountain's signature perfumed dark fruit and powerful tannins. Dense black currant and black cherry fruit is wrapped in creamy vanillin, lending suppleness to the palate.

● **ADAMVS Quintvs / 2012 / Howell Mountain / $$$$**
Volcanic and red-clay soils produced a monolithic, black-mineral wine with concentrated black and blue fruit. Its brawny tannins beg for more time in bottle.

AD VIVUM CELLARS

The single-vineyard Ad Vivum bottling, with its purple hues and perfumed aromatics, is the result of a longtime collaboration between the project's owner/winemaker Chris Phelps, whose impressive résumé includes Dominus, Caymus and Swanson, and Larry Bettinelli, owner of Yountville's superlative Sleeping Lady Vineyard. Phelps and Bettinelli worked for years with various Cabernet Sauvignon clones in the vineyard, with Phelps making experimental lots of wine along the way. For Phelps, the motivation to finally bottle this all-Cabernet wine came in two unique forms. In 2005, he was struck by lightning and lived, which drove him to get on with things (the project's Latin-derived name, meaning "to that which is alive," is a salute to the intersection of wine and life), and the singular expression of the 2007 vintage of his wine sealed the deal.

● **Ad Vivum Cabernet Sauvignon / 2013 / Napa Valley / $$$$**
Heady aromas of violets and blackberries lead to a rich palate of cassis, wild berries and vanillin, framed by sizeable tannins. Cellar for five or more years.

ALPHA OMEGA

Robin and Michelle Baggett's boutique winery, situated since 2005 along the main Highway 29 tourist route in Rutherford, has made a splash with affluent wine drinkers thanks to its extraordinary portfolio of single-vineyard Cabernet Sauvignons, many of them sourced from stellar Beckstoffer family vineyards such as To Kalon, Missouri Hopper and Dr. Crane. The cellar is under the care of Swiss-born winemaker Jean Hoefliger, formerly of Newton Vineyard (see p. 63), and the world-striding French consultant Michel Rolland. The densely packed, intense but elegant, top-end reds are the image makers here, but the team also turns out estimable Chardonnays in both oaked and unoaked styles.

○ **Alpha Omega Chardonnay / 2013 / Napa Valley / $$$$**
This is as voluptuous and deeply oaked as Napa Chardonnay gets, with crème brûlée, butterscotch and baking spice front and center, and citrus, green apple and pear taking a back seat.

● **Alpha Omega Cabernet Sauvignon / 2012 / Napa Valley / $$$$**
Dense in ripe black cherry and black plum fruit, this Cab gains complexity from smoky oak, licorice and cigar notes. It's full-bodied and generous.

ALTAMURA VINEYARDS & WINERY

Frank and Karen Altamura cleared land for their grapes in 1985 from a cattle ranch that Karen's family had worked since 1855. The property is located in Wooden Valley, a hidden pocket of the Napa Valley appellation cooled by summer fogs and afternoon winds that extend the growing season. The vineyards, planted at altitudes from 800 to 1,000 feet, yield distinctive grapes that make exuberant, complex wines. Best known for estate-grown mountain Cabernet Sauvignon, Altamura is also among California's top producers of Sangiovese, sourced from the estate's 28-year-old hillside Sangiovese vineyard. Fans also snap up Altamura's tiny output of much-praised Sauvignon Blanc.

○ **Altamura Sauvignon Blanc / 2012 / Napa Valley / $$$**
Fermented and aged in new French oak, this Sauvignon is a California riff on Bordeaux Blanc. The oak adds texture and depth to the citrus, yellow stone-fruit and quince fruit profile.

● **Altamura Cabernet Sauvignon / 2012 / Napa Valley / $$$$**
Black fruit—think currant, cherry and plum—is enhanced by assertive notes of forest floor, cedar, anise and herbs in this solidly structured wine that will soften with cellaring.

AMICI CELLARS

This under-the-radar producer of fine Cabernet Sauvignon and Sauvignon Blanc was founded (and is still owned) by a group of friends (*amici* in Italian) who started off making wine for themselves. Joel Aiken (longtime winemaker at Beaulieu Vineyards) was the consultant here for many years; stellar talent Tony Biagi joined the project as winemaker during the 2015 harvest. The Napa Valley Cabernet Sauvignon remains realistically priced, but much of the excitement here is generated by the three big-structured, complex single-vineyard Cabs at the top of the portfolio. Amici's sister label, Olema, focuses on Sonoma County Cabernet, Pinot Noir and Chardonnay.

○ **Amici Sauvignon Blanc / 2014 / Napa Valley / $$**
Many Sauvignon Blancs display citrus and herbal character; this one, fermented and aged in stainless steel, tends toward tropical, with peach, guava, passion fruit and a pineapple note.

● **Amici Morisoli Vineyard Cabernet Sauvignon / 2012 / Rutherford / $$$$** The vineyard is a Rutherford benchmark for high-quality Cab. This bottling shows the region's textbook expressive red fruit and refined tannins. Rewarding now, it will age superbly.

ANTICA NAPA VALLEY

The fabled Antinori family has been making wine in Tuscany for more than 600 years, but when they tried to revolutionize American Sangiovese by growing grapes 1,500 feet above Napa Valley, the venture, called Atlas Peak Vineyards, never met expectations. Undaunted, the Antinoris relaunched the project as Antica (*Anti*nori *Ca*lifornia), focusing on Cabernet Sauvignon and Chardonnay (though they turn out several other wines, including Sangiovese). Over the past decade, Antica has been producing sensational Cabs, including the top-end Townsend Vineyard bottling (made only in the best vintages), and estimable Chardonnays that pair Napa power with Tuscan food-complementing finesse.

○ **Antica Chardonnay / 2014 / Napa Valley / $$$**
Its sturdy structure belies the notion that Napa Chardonnays are soft. There is plenty of rich pear, apple and citrus fruit here, plus brisk acidity, subtle oak and sparkling minerality.

● **Antica Cabernet Sauvignon / 2013 / Napa Valley / $$$**
The estate vineyard's soils produce a black-stone character in this Cab, which offers firm tannins, savory black olive, cedar and Christmas-spice notes, and a palate rich in black cherry, dark plum and bittersweet chocolate.

ARAUJO ESTATE WINES

When longtime owners Bart and Daphne Araujo sold their estate in 2013 to Groupe Artémis (Château Latour), this elite property began yet another chapter in its history, which goes back to 1884. Centered on the Eisele Vineyard, renowned for its Cabernets since Napa Valley's revival in the early 1970s, this is one of the New World's premier wineries, with prices to match. In addition to its famous Cabernet Sauvignons, Araujo produces some of the state's most complex Sauvignon Blanc and Syrah, all from the biodynamically farmed Eisele Vineyard. A second-label Bordeaux-style blend, Altagracia, made partly from purchased fruit, can be outstanding in its own right.

○ **Araujo Eisele Vineyard Sauvignon Blanc / 2014 / Napa Valley / $$$$**
Layers of lime, pineapple, mango and grapefruit unfold in this mouth-filling wine with a pleasantly tannic bite on the finish.

● **Araujo Eisele Vineyard Cabernet Sauvignon / 2012 / Napa Valley / $$$$** Luxuriantly concentrated black-fruit ripeness and an intensely fruity yet refreshing finish mark this stunning Cab.

ARIETTA

This winery is the creation of Fritz Hatton—pianist, passionate music lover and arguably (along with Ann Colgin) America's most famous wine auctioneer—and his wife, Caren. Winemakers Andy Erickson (see Favia, p. 42) and Morgan Maureze craft Arietta wines, applying traditional Bordeaux winemaking techniques—fermentation with indigenous yeasts; no fining or filtering of the red wines—to long-ripened, luscious California fruit. The ultra-premium Arietta roster includes the acclaimed H Block red, a right bank Bordeaux-style Cabernet Franc–Merlot blend; and Variation One, a Syrah-Merlot blend. The Sauvignon Blanc–Sémillon On the White Keys bottling is one of the New World's top expressions of Bordeaux-style whites.

○ **Arietta On the White Keys / 2014 / California / $$$$**
Sauvignon Blanc gets a textural lift from Sémillon in this rich, full-bodied wine, with juicy white peach, citrus and a hint of vanilla and an exotic, viscous pineapple note at the finish.

● **Arietta H Block / 2012 / Napa Valley / $$$$**
The Hudson Vineyards Cab Franc–Merlot blend opens with smoky oak, moves to dark fruit accented by herbs, licorice and bittersweet chocolate, and closes with a brisk snap.

BARNETT VINEYARDS

Hal Barnett was in the real estate business, and he and his wife, Fiona, had an eye for property. The one they chose—40 acres' worth, back in 1983—was 2,000 feet up at the top of Spring Mountain. They have been bottling limited quantities (8,000 cases total) of highly regarded wines up there ever since. Winemaker David Tate's signatures are the luxury-priced, mountain-grown, estate Spring Mountain District blends and Rattlesnake Cabernet Sauvignon. But the winery also produces a range of more moderately priced Pinot Noirs, Chardonnays and a rosé from top cool-climate vineyards elsewhere, including Savoy in Mendocino County and Sangiacomo in Carneros.

● **Barnett Vineyards Merlot / 2013 / Spring Mountain District / $$$$**
This is a voluptuous Merlot with Cabernet-like weight, plump plum and black cherry fruit and a palate-whisking finish.

● **Barnett Vineyards Rattlesnake Cabernet Sauvignon / 2013 / Spring Mountain District / $$$$** Muscular tannins frame the black currant and black cherry core of this intense red, with a thread of minerality running through it. Aging will soften its tannins.

BEAULIEU VINEYARD

Founded in 1900, this landmark winery, known as BV to its fans, survived Prohibition by supplying the booming market for Communion wine. Beaulieu's Georges de Latour Private Reserve, a Bordeaux-inspired red, helped define world-class California Cabernet Sauvignon for decades. The winery passed from family hands in 1969, ultimately becoming the property of international wine industry giant Treasury Wine Estates. Today BV fields a sprawling range of wines sourced from vineyards in Napa Valley and other areas of the state. The Napa-sourced wines in particular constitute a very solid line, including the entry-level BV Napa Valley Cabernet and the pricier Tapestry blend; the Georges de Latour can be exceptional.

○ **Beaulieu Vineyard Reserve Chardonnay / 2014 / Carneros / $$$** Yeasty banana and tropical aromas lead to a voluptuous palate of vanillin oak, ripe pear, caramel apple and citrus. A full-bodied yet refreshing white.

● **Beaulieu Vineyard Georges de Latour Private Reserve Cabernet Sauvignon / 2012 / Napa Valley / $$$$** Don't let the 15.5 percent alcohol fool you: This is a supremely balanced wine with toasty oak, ripe dark cherry/berry fruit and supple tannins.

BEHRENS FAMILY WINERY

Les Behrens and Lisa Drinkward's winemaking obsession, which started as a sideline to their (now-sold) Northern California restaurant, took root as a professional endeavor in 1993 up on Spring Mountain. Their exuberantly flavorful Bordeaux-style reds, hand-crafted with grapes from around the valley, have gained the winery an avid following. Produced in small quantities and sold at hefty prices, gems like the Moulds Cabernet Sauvignon, Cemetery and The Heavyweight have also made the operation a critics' favorite. New to the roster are Rhône-style reds and La Danza, a Sauvignon Blanc–Sauvignon Blanc Musqué blend.

○ **La Danza / 2015 / Sonoma County / $$$** This mouthwatering white brims with grapefruit, gooseberry and tropical-fruit juiciness.

● **Head in the Clouds / 2012 / Napa Valley / $$$$** Cabernet Sauvignon gets a kick of complexity from Cabernet Franc and Petit Verdot in this wine, boasting ripe black and blue fruit and palate-caressing texture.

BERINGER VINEYARDS

Napa Valley's oldest continuously operating winery was founded by brothers Jacob and Frederick Beringer in 1876. Today, Beringer is part of Australian-based Treasury Wine Estates, but in a neat twist, Jacob Beringer's great-great-grandson, Mark Beringer, became head winemaker in 2015. Beringer's portfolio ranges from mass-market White Zinfandel to Chardonnays and Cabs (notably the Private Reserve wines) that rival Napa's best. The sweet spot, valuewise, lies in the midprice bottlings, including those sourced from the winery's own vineyards in Knights Valley. But few large wineries anywhere match Beringer's ability to put fine value into the bottle at every price level.

○ **Beringer Luminus Chardonnay / 2014 / Oak Knoll District of Napa Valley / $$$** Nutty oak frames citrus and tropical fruit in this elegant wine, with medium-full body and a long, crisp finish.

● **Beringer Private Reserve Cabernet Sauvignon / 2012 / Napa Valley / $$$$** Grapes from Beringer's best vineyards go into this cellar-worthy red. Its lushness and concentration are countered by firm tannins and acidity.

BLACKBIRD VINEYARDS

Blackbird proprietor Michael Polenske left a financial career to follow his passions for wine, art and antiques—all combined at his wonderful tasting/viewing venue, Ma(i)sonry, in Yountville. In the heart of Cabernet Sauvignon land, Blackbird takes its cue from Bordeaux's Merlot- and Cabernet Franc–oriented right bank, and even the superb, top-end Cabernet Sauvignon–heavy Contrarian has substantial portions of these grapes. Sometimes lost among Blackbird's pricey reds is the lovely and affordable Arriviste rosé. Aaron Pott, formerly of Bordeaux's Château Troplong Mondot and Napa's Quintessa (see p. 71), crafts these boldly flavored wines from seven well-known vineyards around the valley, including Blackbird's own in the Oak Knoll District.

● **Blackbird Vineyards Arise / 2013 / Napa Valley / $$$**
Aromas of violets, fresh herbs and leather lead to a palate of black cherry, dark plum, anise and Asian spice in this great-value Merlot–Cabernet Sauvignon–Cabernet Franc blend.

● **Blackbird Vineyards Paramour / 2013 / Napa Valley / $$$$**
This classic Bordeaux right bank marriage of Cabernet Franc and Merlot is a true love affair, with creamy vanillin oak caressing the sturdy, crisp tannins and ripe dark-berry fruit.

BLACK STALLION ESTATE WINERY

Black Stallion comes by its name honestly—it is located in the old Silverado Horseman's Center. The winery was purchased in 2010 by the Napa and Central Valley–based Indelicato family, whose wine empire includes some 16 brands. At this Oak Knoll District property, the family produces an array of wines with enormous price differences. Most are small lots—including limited-release wines from top vineyards like Stagecoach and Rockpile—that are sold mainly at the winery, online or via the Black Stallion wine clubs. The well-priced (for Napa) Napa Valley Cabernet Sauvignon, Los Carneros Pinot Noir and Napa Valley Sauvignon Blanc and Chardonnay carry the brand into the national marketplace.

○ **Black Stallion Viognier / 2014 / Napa Valley / $$$**
With vivid peach and pear fruit and a hint of spicy oak, this expresses Viognier's floral aromatics and honeyed character beautifully and elegantly.

● **Black Stallion Limited Release Cabernet Sauvignon / 2012 / Napa Valley / $$$** Medium-full-bodied and tannic now, this limited-release Cab has savory truffle and cigar notes accompanying its plump black cherry and dark plum fruit.

BLANKIET ESTATE

One of Napa Valley's, not to say America's, premier artisan vintners, this well-funded, tiny producer is a true estate in the Bordeaux manner. Its scenic Paradise Hills vineyard wraps around a series of tectonic knolls in the Mayacamas foothills above Yountville. Proprietors Claude Blankiet, a French denim magnate, and his wife, Katherine, have hired a parade of all-stars, starting with David Abreu (see p. 17) and Helen Turley (see p. 89), who developed the project. Today, Blankiet offers five elegant wines from Bordeaux grapes; all are much sought-after, including the second-tier Prince of Hearts wines.

● **Prince of Hearts Rosé / 2014 / Napa Valley / $$$**
Merlot and Cab Franc grapes were fermented in new French oak barrels and aged for a year to produce this full-bodied rosé, with bright red fruit and hints of spice and vanilla.

● **Blankiet Estate / 2013 / Napa Valley / $$$$**
Don't even think about opening this Cabernet Sauvignon–led wine (if you can find it) for a decade or more, as it's tightly wound and tannic now. Patience will be greatly rewarded.

BOND

Former Pacific Union real estate mogul H. William Harlan and his director of winegrowing, Bob Levy, produce one of the New World's costliest wines at Harlan Estate (around $500 a bottle and up). But Harlan recognized that he didn't have a monopoly on Napa's great vineyard land—hence this project, also ultra-premium-priced and sold mostly through a mailing list. It has exalted five small, hillside Cabernet Sauvignon vineyards around Napa to "*grand cru*" status: The St. Eden bottling, for example, comes from an 11-acre rocky knoll in Oakville. All are given the Harlan treatment in the vineyard and cellar. The second wine, Matriarch, is blended from the various vineyards.

- **Bond Melbury / 2012 / Napa Valley / $$$$**

A single seven-acre vineyard in the hills east of Rutherford provided the fruit for this blackberry-rich, spicy Cabernet.

- **Bond Vecina / 2012 / Napa Valley / $$$$**

From the property closest to Harlan Estate, this 100 percent Cabernet Sauvignon bottling has a smoky intensity and massive tannins in 2012; cellar it for at least 10 years.

BRAND NAPA VALLEY

Is there room for another stratospherically priced, sold-mainly-through-the-allocation-list, tiny-production Napa Valley Cabernet? Former packaging manufacturer Ed Fitts clearly thought so, as he and his wife, Deb, got into the game with their first wines from the 2009 vintage. The enthusiastic reception of the wines proved them right. It didn't hurt that the land they purchased for their estate vineyard is in what is arguably Napa's trendiest subregion, on Pritchard Hill, or that they hired the esteemed Philippe Melka (see p. 61) to make the wines. And Melka has delivered, pulling three silky, elegant and defined variations of Cabernet Sauvignon–Cabernet Franc–Petit Verdot wines from the estate's red volcanic soils.

- **Brand Cabernet Sauvignon / 2013 / Napa Valley / $$$$**

More intense than the Brio yet just as generous on the palate, this offers juicy dark fruit, a mouth-filling mid-palate and a hint of spice from French oak. The finish is fresh and lingering.

- **Brio Cabernet Sauvignon / 2013 / Napa Valley / $$$$**

The Fitts estate's rocky soils and elevation above the fog line are responsible for this Cab's dense black-fruit flavors, chocolate and tobacco notes and supple tannins.

BUEHLER VINEYARDS

The Buehler family (retired Bechtel executive John, Sr., and his son John, Jr., the proprietor today) bought this remote property on a Napa Valley hillside above Conn Valley in 1971, before real estate (and wine) prices skyrocketed. The pre-Prohibition ghost winery now shares the site with a handsome French neoclassical château-style home. The estate's low-yielding, dry-farmed Cabernet Sauvignon and Zinfandel vineyards are more than 30 years old now, and they produce superb wines at very reasonable prices. Winemaker David Cronin reaches down to Carneros and west to Sonoma's cool Russian River Valley for Buehler's Chardonnay, but sticks closer to home for the signature reds.

○ **Buehler Vineyards Chardonnay / 2014 / Carneros / $$** This great-value Chardonnay offers crisp green apple, stone-fruit and pear flavors in an elegant package with a toasty finish.

● **Buehler Vineyards Papa's Knoll Cabernet Sauvignon / 2013 / Napa Valley / $$$** In Napa Cab terms, this is a steal. Grapes from an old-vine block make for an intense, extracted wine with deep black fruit and edgy tannins that beg for cellaring.

CADE ESTATE WINERY

The in-crowd behind PlumpJack Winery and the new Odette Estate—Gordon Getty, California politician Gavin Newsom and well-regarded Napa industry veteran John Conover—built this small stunner of a LEED-certified winery 1,800 feet up on Napa Valley's Howell Mountain to showcase organic grapes and a more supple style of mountain Cabernet. The first several vintages of Cade's Howell Mountain estate bottling proved that it could keep company with Napa's finest, but the Cabernet Sauvignon that winemaker Danielle Cyrot makes entirely from purchased grapes—the Napa Valley bottling—is also well worth pursuing. The estate's layered, linger-on-the-tongue Sauvignon Blanc is a sometimes overlooked gem.

○ **Cade Sauvignon Blanc / 2015 / Napa Valley / $$$** This white's mélange of aromas and flavors of grapefruit, green apple, honeydew melon and fennel stays fresh and scintillating from sniff to swallow.

● **Cade Estate Cabernet Sauvignon / 2012 / Howell Mountain / $$$$** Succulent and supple, this has the briary character of Howell Mountain grapes but without the astringent tannins they can impart. It's delicious now; no waiting necessary.

CAIN VINEYARD & WINERY

Part of the Napa Valley wave of the early 1980s, Cain consists of 550 stunningly scenic acres—90 of them planted to vineyard—carved from a historic sheep ranch at the top of Spring Mountain. Still owned by Jim and Nancy Meadlock, two of the early partners, the 15,000-case winery concentrates on three Bordeaux-style reds: Cain Cuvée, a multigrape blend from two vintages and various vineyards; Cain Five, an estate wine composed of the five major Bordeaux blending grapes; and Cain Concept, a blend of richer, lower-elevation grapes. Cain wines generally eschew a blockbuster style in favor of classical weight.

● **Cain Concept / 2012 / Napa Valley / $$$$**
A blend of Cabernets Sauvignon and Franc, plus Petit Verdot and Merlot, this is a bright wine with red fruit, forest truffle notes and brilliant acidity.

● **Cain Five / 2012 / Spring Mountain District / $$$$**
Chris Howell blends Cabernet Sauvignon with the other four major Bordeaux varieties to create this structured, precise wine with Old World black cherry, dried red cherry, forest-floor and herbal character.

CAKEBREAD CELLARS

There have been few more ardent advocates of Napa Valley wines through the decades than Jack Cakebread, a former photographer who fell in love with a piece of land in Rutherford and launched his winery with the release of a 1973 Chardonnay. The runaway success of that ripe, full-bodied wine fueled Cakebread's growth. Today the family—with the second generation well represented—owns 13 vineyard sites, with 560 planted acres, in the Napa and Anderson Valleys. These estate vineyards contribute to a broad range of reds and whites, and though Chardonnay remains a star, winemaker Julianne Laks also has a deft hand with Cabernet Sauvignon and red blends.

○ **Cakebread Cellars Chardonnay / 2014 / Napa Valley / $$$**
The winery's flagship white is barrel-fermented, rich and moderately toasty, with juicy golden apple and pear fruit and a slightly sweet finish, offset by firm acidity.

● **Cakebread Cellars Dancing Bear Ranch / 2012 / Howell Mountain / $$$$** This fruit-forward yet substantial Cab is classically styled with cassis and black cherry flavors, cedar and forest-floor notes and mocha oak in the background.

CARDINALE

This is a brand devoted to producing a single wine, a lush, full-bodied Cabernet Sauvignon-based blend priced well north of $200, if you can find it—more than half of its annual production is sold through the winery's mailing list. Because Cardinale is under the capacious Jackson Family Wines umbrella, its tasting room offers wines from other super-premium Jackson brands—Mt. Brave, La Jota Vineyard Co. (see p. 54) and the ultra-luxury-priced Lokoya (see p. 57)—all made by star winemaker Christopher Carpenter. Jackson Family's far-ranging network of vineyards allows Carpenter to choose from a wealth of Napa Valley sources (the core is typically mountain fruit from Howell Mountain and Mount Veeder) in assembling the components for Cardinale.

- **Cardinale / 2012 / Napa Valley / $$$$**
  Of all the mountain-grown Cabs Chris Carpenter makes, this is the most suave and polished. Full-bodied and concentrated, it gets its grace from supple tannins and a gentle oak influence. The finish is crisp, the complexity remarkable.

CAYMUS VINEYARDS

Caymus's hearty Special Selection Cabernet Sauvignon defined classic Napa Valley Cab in the 1970s, when it helped create the California cult wine phenomenon. The torch was passed from father to son—the winery is now in its third generation under the Wagner family—and Special Selection is still going strong. So is the family, whose holdings now include 350 Napa Valley vineyard acres and an array of brands, among them Mer Soleil, Conundrum and Belle Glos. But the Caymus name itself remains indelibly associated with full-bodied, refined reds, including two less-costly wines that offer a taste of Caymus's big, bold style: the Napa Valley Cabernet and a small-lot Zinfandel.

- **Caymus Vineyards Cabernet Sauvignon / 2013 / Napa Valley / $$$$**
  This has the personality of the flagship Special Selection Cabernet, with velvety tannins and deep, mouth-filling dark fruit that leaves a slightly sweet impression. The difference: a bit less oak and a bit more acidity.
- **Caymus Vineyards Special Selection Cabernet Sauvignon / 2014 / Napa Valley / $$$$** Full-bodied, ripe and almost viscous, the flagship Cab spotlights the winery's use of lavish oak to lend toast, chocolate and vanilla character to the soft, supple palate.

CHAPPELLET

When Donn and Molly Chappellet moved up from Los Angeles to found their winery in 1967, they had the vision to settle into a steep, terraced hillside in the Vaca Mountains. Little could they have known that Pritchard Hill would become the renowned wine district it is today (though the Chappellets *did* trademark the Pritchard Hill name). The roster of stellar winemakers who have passed through Chappellet includes Philip Togni, Tony Soter and Cathy Corison. Phillip Corallo-Titus, winemaker since 1990, keeps the Pritchard Hill bottlings in particular at the forefront of Napa Cabs. Whites—Chardonnays and a luscious Chenin Blanc—can be very good here, too.

○ **Chappellet "Signature" Chenin Blanc / 2014 / Napa Valley / $$$**
A 2004 replanting of ancient vines has Chappellet back in the Chenin game, and in an exotic, luxuriant way. The palate here is lush and juicy, the finish crisp and long.

● **Chappellet Pritchard Hill Cabernet Sauvignon / 2013 / Napa Valley / $$$$** Malbec and Petit Verdot join Cabernet Sauvignon in this sophisticated, supremely balanced wine with enticing floral aromas, intense fruit and refined tannins.

CHARLES KRUG WINERY

Founded in 1861, Charles Krug lays claim to being Napa Valley's oldest commercial winery. Under the direction of the Mondavi clan since 1943, Charles Krug long pursued a strategy of making relatively affordable wines that were sometimes a letdown, sometimes a breath of fresh air amid Napa's spiraling prices. Around the turn of this century, Peter Mondavi, Sr.—a Napa wine luminary who passed away at 101 in 2016—and his sons, Marc and Peter, Jr., initiated a nearly decade-long, $25 million investment program designed to help the winery catch up. Today, a resurgence in the quality of Krug's core Cabernet Sauvignons and blends signals that this venerable producer is truly back.

○ **Charles Krug Sauvignon Blanc / 2015 / St. Helena / $$**
This brisk, full-flavored Sauvignon Blanc flashes New Zealand–like qualities, with its pungent, pleasantly herbal aromas and flavors of lime zest, ruby grapefruit and passion fruit.

● **Charles Krug Family Reserve Generations / 2013 / Napa Valley / $$$**
This Cabernet Sauvignon–based wine is deeply aromatic with ripe blackberry, licorice and black spice. Firmly tannic now, it begs for five years of cellaring.

CHATEAU MONTELENA WINERY

Chateau Montelena rocked the California wine world when its Napa Valley Chardonnay bested an array of prestigious white Burgundies in the famous 1976 Judgment of Paris tasting. That award-winning Chardonnay was only the second vintage for the revived 1882 Calistoga estate, which had been bought and rehabilitated by Jim Barrett. Today, under the longtime direction of his son Bo, Montelena continues to bottle lovely, somewhat restrained Chardonnays, but it is certainly better known for its bouquet of fine reds: the supple, earlier-drinking Napa Valley Cabernet, the briary Calistoga Zinfandel and the cellar-worthy Estate Cabernet.

○ **Chateau Montelena Chardonnay / 2014 / Napa Valley / $$$**
Steely in structure, with a distinct minerality and a fruit character that's not yet fully developed, this Chardonnay typically blossoms with bottle aging.

● **Chateau Montelena Cabernet Sauvignon / 2013 / Calistoga / $$$**
The silky, medium-full-bodied Napa Valley Cab has bright red fruit with shades of blackberry, spice and tobacco and an admirable concentration.

CLIFF LEDE VINEYARDS

The scion of a Canadian construction company fortune, Cliff Lede put his passion and capital to work in this showplace Napa Valley floor winery, in his art-filled home on a knoll above it and in the luxury Poetry Inn on a hillside across the way. The winery's Bordeaux-style wines more than hold their own in their super-premium-price set. The flagship Poetry bottling is a benchmark of the dense, ripe-fruit Napa style, but it's wrapped up with a sure-handed Stags Leap–area elegance. At the more affordable end of the portfolio are one of Napa Valley's most estimable Sauvignon Blancs and the Claret bottling, which gives a more wallet-friendly taste of Cliff Lede's rich, suave style.

○ **Cliff Lede Sauvignon Blanc / 2014 / Napa Valley / $$**
This full-flavored, great-value white has a minerally, saline quality, with smoothly blended Meyer lemon, pear, white peach and melon flavors and a subtle creaminess on the finish.

● **Cliff Lede Poetry Cabernet Sauvignon / 2013 / Stags Leap District / $$$$** With concentrated black cherry, black currant and plum fruit and exotic spice, this Cab is a bruiser now; give it five years or more to show its true, balanced and complex self.

CLOS DU VAL

Founded more than 40 years ago by two Frenchmen, John Goelet and Bernard Portet, Clos Du Val was an early settler in the Stags Leap District, and a very independent-minded one. While the wineries around it developed Stags Leap's reputation for producing velvety, rich-but-elegant reds, Clos Du Val clung to a more austere style that its principals felt was truer to the soil. But today, sweeping stylistic changes are under way as the winery refocuses almost exclusively on estate-grown grapes, with winemaker Ted Henry and top consultant Tony Biagi aiming for a riper, lusher style that, as the winery puts it, "embraces the Napa Valleyness" of the wines.

○ **Clos Du Val Chardonnay / 2014 / Carneros / $$**
This is a lovely, Chablis-like Chardonnay at a great price, with high-acid structure and gentle hints of spice and oak. Its lemon chiffon, pear and green apple flavors are mouthwatering.

● **Clos Du Val Cabernet Sauvignon / 2012 / Stags Leap District / $$$$**
Solidly fruity yet balanced, this elegant Cab is never lacking in flavor. Oak hides in the background, enhancing the texture.

COLGIN CELLARS

One of California wine's gold standards, this is a spare-no-expense estate whose production is aimed at the pinnacle of the collectors' market. Owned by its founder, former Sotheby's wine auctioneer Ann Colgin, and her financier husband, Joe Wender, the winery is spectacularly situated on a Pritchard Hill slope at the north end of the stellar IX Estate Vineyard, overlooking Lake Hennesey. Winemaker Allison Tauziet and Bordeaux consulting star Alain Raynaud craft attention-riveting reds from grapes either tended by the estate or supplied by star vineyardist David Abreu (see p. 17), in the case of the Cariad blend.

● **Colgin IX Estate Syrah / 2013 / Napa Valley / $$$$**
This wine's earth, smoked-meat and peppery aromas recall northern Rhône Syrahs, yet the palate is fruitier and more luscious, with rich black fruit, Moroccan spice and anise flavors and sturdy tannin, oak and acid structure.

● **Colgin Tychson Hill Vineyard Cabernet Sauvignon / 2012 / Napa Valley / $$$$** This boldly fruity and firm Cabernet is exceptionally complex, with layers of violets, sage, cedar, vanillin, coffee and dried herbs adding interest to the wild berry and black cherry fruit.

CONN CREEK WINERY

Founded in 1973 by Bill and Kathy Collins, this pioneering winery on the Silverado Trail is now under the umbrella of Washington's Ste. Michelle Wine Estates. Veteran winemaker Mike McGrath continues Conn Creek's longtime focus on Bordeaux varietals, bottled here in three pricing tiers. The flagship offering is the rich, palate-flattering, Cabernet-based Anthology, a "spice-rack" blend of grapes from as many as 14 Napa sub-regions. At the opposite end of the blending philosophy are the pricey AVA Series wines, single-appellation designates meant to represent the *terroir* of their AVAs. Though reds are its image-makers, Conn Creek also produces lovely Chardonnay.

○ **Conn Creek Chardonnay / 2014 / Carneros / $$**
Creamy vanillin oak complements bright, juicy golden apple, ripe pear and yellow stone-fruit flavors. This is sourced from the famed Sangiacomo Family Vineyards.

● **Conn Creek Anthology Cabernet Sauvignon / 2013 / Napa Valley / $$$** Twelve vineyards in nine Napa appellations contributed to this wine, aged 19 months in oak. Seamless and medium-bodied, it's a textbook expression of traditional Napa Cabernet.

CONTINUUM ESTATE

Following the sale of their family's Robert Mondavi Winery (see p. 74), Tim Mondavi—who ran the winemaking end (brother Michael was president and CEO)—and his sister Marcia set up shop on Pritchard Hill to make very-limited-production, cutting-edge wine. First released in 2005, their luxury-priced Cabernet Sauvignon–based Continuum has been a smash hit. The area's volcanic hillsides provide limited yields of intense grapes that give the wine its core; a relatively high percentage of Cabernet Franc and Petit Verdot contributes gracefully layered elegance. The second wine, Novicium, typically follows a Merlot- and Cabernet Franc–dominated Bordeaux right bank model.

● **Continuum / 2013 / Napa Valley / $$$$**
This all-estate-grown Continuum bottling is the first to be produced in the new estate winery. Volcanic soils lend the wine a mineral edge, joining the savory herbs, toasty oak and solid tannins that frame its dense dark fruit. Decant before serving.

● **Novicium / 2013 / Napa Valley / $$$$**
Made from younger, still-maturing estate vines, this delicious Merlot-led blend offers buoyant ripe fruit and minerality.

CORISON WINERY

Much-admired winemaker Cathy Corison lent her talents to such producers as Chappellet (see p. 30) and Staglin Family Vineyard (see p. 82) before devoting herself to her own boutique Napa Valley label. Her small-production roster includes the Corazón Gewürztraminer from Anderson Valley, the Corazón Cabernet Sauvignon Rosé and two signature Cabernet Sauvignons: the single-vineyard, sustainably grown Kronos and the Napa Valley bottling, sourced from the benchland between Rutherford and St. Helena. In both Cabs, Corison's hands-off approach lets the vineyard shine; the results are expertly balanced wines that target finesse and harmony over sheer strength.

● **Corison Cabernet Sauvignon / 2013 / Napa Valley / $$$$**
This very flavorful, finely balanced Cab offers fresh red and black fruit, forest-floor notes, velvety tannins and a long, vigorous finish.

● **Corison Kronos Vineyard Cabernet Sauvignon / 2012 / Napa Valley / $$$$** Old, low-yielding vines produce a wine with assertive aromas and flavors of potpourri, black fruit, Asian spice and black olive and scintillating acidity.

CROCKER & STARR

In 1971, tech entrepreneur Charlie Crocker acquired the historic Dowdell winery and vineyard in southern St. Helena and began its revival as the Crocker Estate. Today, the property encompasses 85 vineyard acres growing the five red Bordeaux varieties—the top-end Stone Place Cabernet Sauvignon is made with grapes from 40-plus-year-old vines—as well as Sauvignon Blanc. Crocker partnered with noted winemaker Pam Starr (formerly of Spottswoode; see p. 81) to establish Crocker & Starr in 1997; the pair released the first of their now-acclaimed wines in 1999. Starr's way with aromatic, full-bodied wines has made the winery a benchmark not only for Cabernet Sauvignon, but notably for Cabernet Franc and Malbec, and Sauvignon Blanc, too.

○ **Crocker & Starr Sauvignon Blanc / 2014 / Napa Valley / $$$**
This white, which Pam Starr describes as "Napa style," is exotic, rich and supersmooth, with sweet tropical and citrus flavors.

● **Crocker & Starr Cabernet Franc / 2013 / St. Helena / $$$$**
Cabernet Franc's distinctive floral character is on display in this deeply fruited, big-bodied wine. Almost viscous and quite spicy, it finishes with bright acidity.

CUVAISON ESTATE WINES

Thomas Schmidheiny, who with his family bought Cuvaison in 1979, has taken the long view, reinvesting profits and building a substantial wine operation that has not been afraid to change with the times. In 2015, Cuvaison sold its original production facility and tasting room in Calistoga in order to focus the brand exclusively on the wines—Pinot Noir, Chardonnay and small amounts of Syrah and Sauvignon Blanc—from its Carneros estate. Winemaker Steven Rogstad produces both an Estate Series and a Single Block Series, which in pricey Napa can be terrific bargains. He also crafts the Cabernet Sauvignon, Zins and Bordeaux-style red blend of Cuvaison's sister label, Brandlin.

○ **Cuvaison Chardonnay / 2013 / Carneros / $$**

Cuvaison's Chardonnay style is elegant and understated—never too ripe, too oaky or plush. This Estate Series bottling fits the mold, with citrus and peach flavors lifted by bracing acidity.

● **Brandlin Cabernet Sauvignon / 2012 / Mount Veeder / $$$$**

Lavish vanillin and spicy oak complements mountain-grown black fruit in this rich though nicely balanced red.

DALLA VALLE VINEYARDS

Naoko Dalla Valle's hillside winery above the Silverado Trail burst on the scene in the 1980s, with intense Cabernet Sauvignon– and Cabernet Franc–based wines made by a succession of winemaking all-stars, including Heidi Barrett, Tony Soter and Mia Klein. The current winemaker, Andy Erickson (formerly of Screaming Eagle), is no less eminent, and is assisted by famed French consultant Michel Rolland. This is a world-class operation with prices to match. The red-soil, volcanic hillside vineyards produce three Bordeaux-style reds: the Cabernet Franc–showcasing cult wine Maya; the estate Cabernet Sauvignon; and a younger-vines third wine, Collina Dalla Valle.

● **Dalla Valle Cabernet Sauvignon / 2012 / Napa Valley / $$$$**

Concentrated blackberry and cassis, mocha oak and solid tannic structure mark this estate Cab. More accessible than Maya now, it still would benefit from more time in the bottle.

● **Maya / 2012 / Napa Valley / $$$$**

Cabernet Franc marries beautifully with Cabernet Sauvignon, with the former adding floral, herb and black spice to the latter's black currant and blackberry. Brawny tannins and toasty oak dominate now; age it for five years or more.

DIAMOND CREEK VINEYARDS

In 1968, the late Al Brounstein and his wife, Boots, created a Napa Valley winery that was the exception to every rule. In a Chardonnay era, they focused on Cabernet Sauvignon. Their wines were profoundly *terroir*-driven, at a time when that was hardly a concept in California, and crafted in a style that could be austere and tannic at first, sometimes taking years to soften and open up. Diamond Creek wines have remained true to their legacy. Al Brounstein's bedrock belief in his vineyards—Volcanic Hill, Gravelly Meadow, Red Rock Terrace and tiny Lake, whose wine is only rarely produced—has paid off by giving his winery a lasting, passionate, deep-pocketed following.

● **Diamond Creek Gravelly Meadow Cabernet Sauvignon / 2012 / Napa Valley / $$$$** True to the vineyard name, there's a crushed-rock quality to this wine. At once voluptuous and sturdy, it has berry jam character now, with more complexity to come over time.

● **Diamond Creek Red Rock Terrace Cabernet Sauvignon / 2012 / Napa Valley / $$$$** Typically the most accessible Diamond Creek wine when young, it still needs a few years in bottle to start showing the plump red and black fruit under its silky tannins.

DOMAINE CARNEROS

Founded by Champagne Taittinger, Domaine Carneros's impressive château has been a familiar sight to wine tourists on Route 12 since 1989. Under the direction of Eileen Crane from the beginning, the winery has established itself among the top rank of California sparkling wine producers, offering viable alternatives to French sparklers, particularly the attractively priced entry-level tier. The far costlier flagship Le Rêve bottlings—notably the Blanc de Blancs—echo the graceful power of Taittinger's Champagnes. Nearly all of Domaine Carneros's grapes, including those for its also estimable still wines, come from four certified sustainable estate vineyard sites.

○ **Domaine Carneros Brut / 2011 / Carneros / $$$**
Green apple, citrus and toasted almond aromas lead to a brisk, structured palate. A Chardonnay-Pinot Noir blend, this sparkler has a creamy mid-palate that adds complexity.

● **Domaine Carneros Cuvée de la Pompadour Brut Rosé / NV / Carneros / $$$** This fruity yet refined sparkling wine is named for a mistress of King Louis XV, who introduced him to Champagne. It has great depth and energy.

DOMAINE CHANDON

It was a major turning point for Napa Valley's credibility on the world wine scene when Champagne giant Moët & Chandon announced in the early 1970s that it would open a sparkling wine facility in Yountville. And with the parent company's resources at its disposal, Domaine Chandon didn't stint. It eventually acquired three substantial vineyards—the home ranch in Yountville for Chardonnay; a Mount Veeder property for a smaller-berried, mountain-grown Chardonnay; and 800 acres in Carneros for Chardonnay, Pinot Noir and Pinot Meunier. The broad range of offerings—including still wine—is generally fairly priced all the way to the top-end étoile cuvées.

○ **Domaine Chandon Étoile Brut / NV / Napa and Sonoma Counties / $$$** The producer's flagship sparkling wine is elegant and focused, with subtle toast, spice and brioche character joining crisp citrus and green apple fruit.

● **Chandon Rosé / NV / California / $$** This fun-to-drink sparkler has the acidity and carbonation to support the juicy strawberry and red raspberry fruit, yet remains dry and sophisticated.

DOMINUS ESTATE

This luxury winery's stunning yet simple, rocks-in-a-cage façade provides a confident contrast with the legion of faux-Tuscan and faux-French neighbors in Napa Valley's high-rent districts. Dominus owner and art patron Christian Moueix is one of Bordeaux's leading wine producers (Château Pétrus) and tastemakers. The estate's 124 dry-farmed acres are centered on the famous Napanook Vineyard, first planted by Yountville's original settler, George Yount, in the early 19th century. Today it yields Cabernet Sauvignon, Cabernet Franc, Petit Verdot and two world-class Bordeaux blends: the complex, structured Dominus and a more accessible, though typically superb, second bottling called Napanook.

● **Dominus / 2012 / Napa Valley / $$$$**
Made in an Old World style with New World verve, this savory Cabernet Sauvignon has sage and cedar notes accenting vivid red and black fruit, all balanced by firm tannins and acidity.

● **Dominus Estate Napanook / 2012 / Napa Valley / $$$$**
The estate's still brilliant second bottling, Napanook is a spicy and intense rendition of Cabernet Sauvignon. No weakling, it's full-bodied and concentrated, yet very drinkable now.

DUCKHORN VINEYARDS

Dan and Margaret Duckhorn founded this St. Helena winery in 1976, and struck gold with Merlot, especially their iconic Three Palms Vineyard bottling. The winery also made palate-flattering Cabs and one of Napa's finest Sauvignon Blancs, and prices soon climbed into the super-premium range. Duckhorn stayed ahead of the curve, founding a game-altering Anderson Valley Pinot producer, Goldeneye, and launching spin-offs such as Paraduxx (unique Napa Valley red blends), Migration (cool-climate Chardonnay and Pinot Noir), the less pricey Decoy line, and Canvasback (Washington State Cabernet). Now under the stewardship of a private equity firm, GI Partners, Duckhorn continues to produce this array of wines at a reliably high level.

○ **Duckhorn Sauvignon Blanc / 2014 / Napa Valley / $$**
A good dose of Sémillon, and partial barrel fermentation and aging, add texture to this wine, marked by bright citrus and lemongrass aromas and flavors and vibrant acidity.

● **Duckhorn Three Palms Vineyard Merlot / 2013 / Napa Valley / $$$$**
Rich yet focused in plum and dark cherry fruit, with black olive, vanillin, sarsaparilla and fresh-herb notes, this Merlot is perfumed, balanced and just delicious. It will age splendidly.

DUNN VINEYARDS

Randy Dunn honed his craft at Caymus (see p. 29), where he defined Special Selection—among modern Napa's first cult wines—in its early years. He and his wife, Lori, bought their own five-acre vineyard on Howell Mountain in the late 1970s and set about creating a mountain style of Cabernet: dark, big-scaled wines with massive but supple tannins. Though the family's holdings have expanded to over 200 acres (35 under vine), Dunn still produces a very limited amount of much-sought-after wine (4,000 cases), and still typically in just two bottlings: the highly structured Howell Mountain and the softer Napa Valley.

● **Dunn Vineyards Cabernet Sauvignon / 2012 / Howell Mountain / $$$$** The muscular tannins here need bottle aging to mesh with the intense wild blackberry, tar, Asian spice and toasty oak in this massive wine.

● **Dunn Vineyards Cabernet Sauvignon / 2012 / Napa Valley / $$$$**
Somewhat more accessible in its youth than the Howell Mountain bottling, this keeps to the house style of dense berry fruit, spicy oak and substantial tannins that beg for cellaring.

EHLERS ESTATE

In the mid-1980s, French entrepreneur Jean Leducq began buying parcels of land in the northern part of what is now Napa Valley's St. Helena appellation, centered on Bernard Ehlers's historic 1886 Bale Mill winery. By the time of Leducq's death in 2002, the property had expanded to include 42 contiguous acres of prime vineyard land, and was left in trust as part of his and his wife Sylviane's substantial philanthropic endeavors. Farmed organically by winemaker Kevin Morrisey and vineyard manager Francisco Vega, the property specializes in rich, expressive Cabernet Sauvignons and other Bordeaux-grape reds. Ehlers also makes an excellent Sauvignon Blanc and rosé.

○ **Ehlers Estate Sauvignon Blanc / 2015 / St. Helena / $$**
Sancerre-like in its floral aromas and palate of bracing lime and grapefruit, this is a bone-dry, structured and elegant wine, with lip-smacking acidity.

● **1886 Cabernet Sauvignon / 2012 / St. Helena / $$$$**
Named for the year the winery was founded, this juicy, full-bodied red will improve with cellaring, yet is delicious now. Chewy tannins, spicy oak and vibrant black currant and blueberry fruit close with a mouthwatering finish.

EL MOLINO

This is a tiny (under 2,000-case), high-end St. Helena–based estate with a difference—in Cabernet-centric Napa, El Molino ("The Mill") produces Pinot Noir and Chardonnay, grapes that have generally migrated south and away from mid-valley. Then again, there's a throwback aspect to this operation in general. Owned by Jon and Lily Berlin—she grew up on the property; he was winemaker at Viader (see p. 91)—El Molino is a resurrected 19th-century ghost winery. Using grapes from the family's Star Vineyard in Rutherford, the Berlins craft their Pinot Noir and Chardonnay in a juicy, full-bodied style, with New World gusto.

○ **El Molino Chardonnay / 2013 / Rutherford / $$$**
While decadently rich and lavishly oaked, this lively, citrus-laden wine remains bright and juicy with Meyer lemon, lime zest, green apple and pineapple aromas and flavors.

● **El Molino Pinot Noir / 2012 / Rutherford / $$$$**
An elegant Pinot from Rutherford, land of Cabernet, this wine charms with its vibrant cherry and raspberry character, supple tannins and accents of oak, spice and sandalwood.

ELYSE WINERY

Ray Coursen and his wife, Nancy, left Cape Cod in 1983 and landed in California, where Ray worked in vineyards, then as a cellar rat, and eventually became head winemaker at the well-regarded Whitehall Lane. In 1987, the couple bottled their own wine—named for their daughter Elyse—from Zinfandel bought from the old-vine Morisoli Vineyard in Rutherford. Today, with Morisoli still a prime source for both Zin and Cabernet Sauvignon, the Elyse label offers a range of richly styled (and under-the-radar) wines. In 1998, Elyse's younger brother, Jacob Franklin, got a label of small-production wines named after him, too (available through the winery and its website and wine club).

● **Elyse Korte Ranch Vineyard Zinfandel / 2012 / St. Helena / $$$**
A savory high note of tobacco, spice and leather accents this Zin's juicy berry, cherry and plum fruit flavors, with some chocolate on the finish.

● **Elyse Morisoli Vineyard Zinfandel / 2012 / Rutherford / $$$**
Zinfandel is joined in small rations by Petite Sirah, Alicante Bouschet, Carignane and other field-blend grapes. The result: a complex, briary wine with spice, smoke and superb balance.

ETUDE WINES

One of the West Coast's seminal winemakers and consultants, Tony Soter (who now runs his namesake winery in Oregon; see p. 218) founded Etude 35 years ago, with the primary aim of making great, straight-from-the-vineyard Pinot Noir. Soter planted numerous clones and low-yielding heirloom varieties at his Carneros estate, and they remain the basis for some of Etude's top bottlings, though the winery reaches far and wide for cool-climate Pinot grapes. Part of Australian-based Treasury Wine Estates, Etude is now perhaps just as much known for Cabernet Sauvignon as for Pinot Noir. Winemaker Jon Priest fields a consistently impressive lineup that also includes some excellent Chardonnay and a superb Pinot rosé.

● **Etude Cabernet Sauvignon / 2012 / Napa Valley / $$$$**
Firm tannic structure and mocha oak meet juicy cherry and blackberry fruit in this superbly balanced red.

● **Etude Temblor Vineyard Pinot Noir / 2013 / Carneros / $$$$**
This Pinot offers bright Bing cherry fruit with sarsaparilla, licorice and tobacco-leaf notes. Suave tannins and mouthwatering acidity make it a classy pour.

FAILLA WINES

Ehren Jordan is one of California's quieter winemaking superstars. He left his prestigious, longtime job at Turley Wine Cellars (see p. 89) to concentrate on multiappellation winemaking at Failla, which is named for his wife and partner, Anne-Marie Failla. Though the winery is in Napa, nearly all of its typically superb Pinot Noirs (plus some Chardonnay and Syrah) are sourced from the cool, foggy Pacific Coast, mostly in Sonoma County's rugged coastal range. The flagship Pinot Noirs, including the Estate and Hirsch Vineyards, are grown in marginal climates and made with hands-off, traditional winemaking techniques.

○ **Failla Keefer Ranch Chardonnay / 2013 / Russian River Valley / 2013 / $$$** From one of the most respected vineyards in Sonoma's Russian River Valley comes this Chardonnay with layers of citrus, peach and apple, gently influenced by generous oak in both the mouthfeel and finish.

● **Failla Occidental Ridge Vineyard Pinot Noir / 2013 / Sonoma Coast / $$$** Showing its cool-climate, true Sonoma Coast provenance, this is a wine of restraint and refinement. Crisp, crunchy red fruit, citrus and spice notes are kept fresh by brisk acidity.

FAR NIENTE

The late Gil Nickel purchased this 1885 National Register landmark—abandoned and run-down since Prohibition—in 1979 and lavishly restored it. The famous gardens and wine caves offer pleasant distractions, but the wines themselves are the real draw. The Nickel family and their partners have since launched sister wineries Dolce (sweet wines), Nickel & Nickel (single-vineyard wines), EnRoute (Russian River Valley Pinot Noir) and the Napa Cab specialist, Bella Union, but the parent Far Niente winery still produces just two wines: a Cabernet and a Chardonnay that are among Napa's finest wines of their type.

○ **Far Niente Chardonnay / 2014 / Napa Valley / $$$$**
This is a crowd-pleaser of a Chardonnay, with caramel oak framing juicy citrus and tropical fruit, a slightly creamy mid-palate, and a lingering, citrusy finish.

● **Far Niente Cabernet Sauvignon / 2013 / Oakville / $$$$**
At once fresh and lush, polished and stylish, this Cab has firm black cherry and blackberry flavors, creamy vanillin oak and anise notes, and a sturdy structure to counter the richness.

FAVIA

This boutique label is the passion project of superstar winemaker Andy Erickson (see Dalla Valle, p. 35, and Mayacamas, p. 60) and his viticulturist wife, Annie Favia. The pair have scouted out simpatico growers around the North Coast and produce small quantities of various wines at luxury prices. Among the prized offerings are three Rhône-style reds, including the exuberant Rompecabezas Grenache-Syrah-Mourvèdre blend; a Viognier from Amador County; and a signature vibrant, velvety Cabernet Sauvignon. But for those fortunate enough to have access, Annie Favia's particular love, Cabernet Franc, is the showstopper in blends like the La Magdalena and Cerro Sur.

○ **Favia Línea Sauvignon Blanc / 2014 / Coombsville / $$$$**

Purity of citrus and tropical fruit marks this brisk, refreshing wine from a Napa sub-appellation better known for Cabernet.

● **Favia Rompecabezas / 2013 / Amador County / $$$$**

From Ann Kraemer's multivariety Shake Ridge Vineyards (see Yorba Wines, p. 195), the spicy, vibrant Rompecabezas (Spanish for "jigsaw puzzle") GSM blend is all dark fruit, with sturdy tannins that call for cellaring.

FLORA SPRINGS

A familiar presence to Napa Valley visitors thanks to its wavy-façade tasting room near St. Helena on Highway 29, Flora Springs was an abandoned 19th-century ghost winery revived in the 1970s by Flora Komes and her husband, Jerry. Along with their children, the Komeses turned into dedicated producers and growers, farming what would eventually increase to 650 acres of vines. Grandchildren Nat Komes and Sean Garvey now run the winery. The Cab-based Trilogy—one of the original Meritage wines (see Wine Terms, p. 8)—leads the roster of reds, while the big, juicy Barrel Fermented Chardonnay and the stylish Soliloquy Sauvignon Blanc headline the white offerings.

○ **Flora Springs Soliloquy Sauvignon Blanc / 2014 / Oakville / $$$**

Aging in oak barrels and concrete "eggs" and stirring of the spent lees produced perhaps the finest Soliloquy yet, with snappy citrus and pear character and mouth-filling texture.

● **Flora Springs Trilogy / 2013 / Napa Valley / $$$$**

Petit Verdot and Malbec add depth and complexity to this elegant, composed Cabernet-based blend, offering dark fruit, black spice, creamy oak and well-honed tannins.

FORMAN VINEYARD

Ric Forman is a Napa Valley legend who has done it his way since 1983—with a Francophile belief in hands-on everything and a style that targets finesse over sheer power. Today Forman and his son Toby reign over their 60 acres with a passionate dedication that may see every vine touched 24 times during the growing season. Forman produces only two wines: a classically structured Cabernet Sauvignon–based blend and a Chablis-style Chardonnay that emphasizes minerality and racy purity. The prices of these wines—though not astronomical for Napa—have climbed in recent years, evidence that his maverick style is finding a sophisticated and avid audience.

○ **Forman Chardonnay / 2013 / Napa Valley / $$$**
By not allowing the softening malolactic fermentation to occur, Ric Forman keeps this Chardonnay's lemony fruit and steely texture intact, enhancing its ageability.

● **Forman Cabernet Sauvignon / 2012 / Napa Valley / $$$$**
This full-bodied Cab is loaded with luscious blackberry and black currant fruit; its sturdy tannins and crisp acidity make for a refreshing finish.

FRANCISCAN ESTATE

A fixture on the Napa Valley tourist circuit—it's the winery with a large, cascading fountain out front, on Highway 29 in St. Helena—Franciscan has devoted itself to pleasing crowds since 1973. The Napa wine world has changed around it, but Franciscan—now a 300,000-plus-case operation that's part of Constellation Brands—has kept the focus on value. Its five Napa Valley appellation wines in particular are perennial good deals. The top-end bottlings deserve at least a footnote in valley history: Magnificat was among the earliest of the Meritage wines (see Wine Terms, p. 10), and Franciscan's all-out Burgundy-method Cuvée Sauvage Chardonnay is said to be the first Napa Chardonnay fermented with native yeasts.

○ **Franciscan Estate Cuvée Sauvage Chardonnay / 2014 / Carneros / $$$** "Sauvage" references the wine's wild-yeast fermentation. Offering tasty ripe tropical and pear fruit, a lemon custard note and spicy oak, it will gain complexity with bottle age.

● **Franciscan Estate Magnificat / 2013 / Napa Valley / $$$**
A tribute to J.S. Bach's masterpiece, this Bordeaux-style red is stylish and rich, with generous dark fruit and a supple palate.

FRANK FAMILY VINEYARDS

A long-running Hollywood inside player, Rich Frank has a résumé—it's still unscrolling in his 70s—that includes tenure as president of the Paramount Television Group and nearly a decade as president of Walt Disney Studios. His historic Calistoga winery has a notable résumé of its own—it is on the site of the old Kornell Champagne Cellars and the 19th-century Larkmead Winery before that. With veteran Todd Graff in the cellar, Frank Family Vineyards has established itself as a top producer of luscious, densely wrapped, high-end Cabernets and Bordeaux-style blends, including the much-sought-after Winston Hill red. Less well known are the small-lot, artisan sparkling wines that are often among California's very best.

○ **Frank Family Vineyards Chardonnay / 2014 / Carneros / $$$** Exotic tropical fruit and pear flavors meet vanillin oak and brisk acidity in this sumptuous, satisfying Chardonnay. It's rich and creamy, finishing with verve.

● **Frank Family Vineyards Cabernet Sauvignon / 2013 / Napa Valley / $$$** Sensibly priced for Napa, this delivers generous black-fruit flavors, textbook Cab herbal and cedar personality, and grippy tannins that promise good things ahead with cellaring.

FREEMARK ABBEY

There's a wealth of history at this 131-year-old property. Though never actually an abbey, it was the first winery on record in Napa Valley to be owned by a woman. Though Freemark is now part of the Jackson Family group, winemaker Ted Edwards has been at the helm since 1985, relying on two famous vineyards for his top Cabernet Sauvignon bottlings: Sycamore and Bosché. Inexplicably, these wines remain somewhat underappreciated—as are Freemark Abbey's graceful, midrange offerings—and while not cheap, they are still well priced for their quality.

○ **Freemark Abbey Viognier / 2014 / Napa Valley / $$$** Viognier may be an outlier in Napa, but this bottling demands notice for its honeyed aroma, juicy tangerine, white peach, pear and blood orange palate, and a richness cut by vibrant acidity.

● **Freemark Abbey Cabernet Bosché Cabernet Sauvignon / 2012 / Rutherford / $$$$** This single-vineyard wine was aged for 26 months in oak and blended with 10 percent Merlot. The result is a seamless wine with bold cassis and mulberry character, perfect ripeness and caressing tannins.

FROG'S LEAP

The onetime sole employee of Stag's Leap Wine Cellars (see p. 83)—he helped make the Cabernet that won the 1976 Judgment of Paris—veteran winemaker John Williams started his own Napa venture on the site of a former frog farm. (The brand's motto: "Time's fun when you're having flies.") Since the 1980s, Frog's Leap has set a high bar for eco-friendly farming, forgoing chemicals, pesticides and—very unusual for Napa Valley—irrigation. The sophisticated wines reflect a similar conviction, holding to a restrained, food-friendly style that has increasingly come back in vogue. Though about half the winery's production is Sauvignon Blanc, Williams also has a deft hand with reds, notably Zinfandel and Cabernet Sauvignon.

○ **Frog's Leap Sauvignon Blanc / 2015 / Rutherford / $$**
Fermentation and aging in stainless steel preserves the racy Meyer lemon and white peach character of this pure, focused wine. Perfect for oysters on the half shell.

● **Frog's Leap Cabernet Sauvignon / 2013 / Rutherford / $$$**
This competes in quality and deliciousness with Napa Cabs at twice the price. It has richness, supple tannins and savory background notes, all in a compact, fresh-tasting package.

GRGICH HILLS ESTATE

After his 1973 Chateau Montelena Chardonnay won the famous 1976 Paris tasting, Mike Grgich founded his own winery with coffee heir Austin Hills (there are no actual hills at this valley-floor winery). Grgich's first hits were creamy, full-flavored Chardonnays that helped set the California standard in the 1980s. Grgich's nephew, Ivo Jeramaz, is now in the cellar, and Chardonnays remain the headliners, but they may not actually be Grgich's best wines. Try the lively Fumé Blanc, or the graceful, medium-rich Cab or Zinfandel to understand the winery's approach to making wines of finesse. True to his convictions, Mike Grgich bottles only his own organically farmed grapes.

○ **Grgich Hills Estate Miljenko's Selection Essence Sauvignon Blanc / 2014 / Napa Valley / $$$** This magnificently structured and delicious Sauvignon Blanc offers layers of citrus and tropical fruit, minerality, high energy and a succulent finish.

○ **Grgich Hills Estate Paris Tasting Chardonnay / 2013 / Napa Valley / $$$$** A tribute to Mike Grgich's 1976 Judgment of Paris win, this Chardonnay is expressive, refined and worth a search.

GROTH VINEYARDS & WINERY

This boutique Oakville winery, established in 1981 by the former Atari executive Dennis Groth and his wife, Judy, gained fame in the 1980s for its full-on rich Reserve Cabernet. But the vineyards required replanting in 2000—Groth has now replanted 90 percent of its vineyards since 1996—and the Groth family was unable to make Reserve Cabernet again until 2005, when the new vines came into their own. Now run by the second generation of Groths and longtime winemaker Michael Weis (joined by Cameron Parry in 2014), the winery fields an Oakville Cab in addition to the Reserve and two well-priced whites, with the creamy Sauvignon Blanc particularly worthy of attention.

○ **Groth Sauvignon Blanc / 2014 / Napa Valley / $$**
An exceptional value, this delicious Sauvignon Blanc offers energetic green melon and citrus fruit and a creamy mid-palate, the result of aging on its lees.

● **Groth Reserve Cabernet Sauvignon / 2012 / Oakville / $$$$**
The richness of this seductive, stylish wine is balanced by bright acidity, supple tannins and barrel spice. It oozes flavor.

HALL WINES

Hall was launched in the early 2000s by Kathryn Hall, a former US ambassador to Austria, and her husband, Dallas financier Craig Hall. About half of the grapes for the winery's full-bodied California takes on Bordeaux-style blends are sourced from the producer's seven sustainably farmed estate vineyards, including the 19th-century Bergfeld Vineyard in St. Helena. The main offerings here are the Napa Valley Collection, four wines blended from estate vineyards, including the flagship Kathryn Hall Cabernet and a vibrant Sauvignon Blanc. But the winery also turns out a slew of smaller-production, single-vineyard Artisan Collection wines, such as the sought-after Exzellenz, a massively scaled Cabernet crafted to showcase Hall's small, mountaintop Sacrashe Vineyard in Rutherford.

○ **Hall Sauvignon Blanc / 2014 / Napa Valley / $$**
This stainless steel–fermented wine is effusively floral and solidly built, with racy lemon-lime and mandarin orange fruit and a kiss of peach.

● **Kathryn Hall Cabernet Sauvignon / 2013 / Napa Valley / $$$$**
This dense and intense Cab boasts bold black fruit, spice and supple texture. It has a long life ahead of it in the cellar.

HARLAN ESTATE

This is the jewel in the crown of former real estate executive and current Napa Valley luxury maven H. William Harlan (in addition to his Bond winery, see p. 26, he has interests in the wine-focused Napa Valley Reserve private club and Meadowood Resort). Perched above the fog line on a series of rolling hilltops in the Mayacamas Mountains, Harlan Estate produces just around 1,800 cases of what is arguably California's most famous collectors' wine. Prodigiously structured and complex, the nearly all–Cabernet Sauvignon Harlan Estate bottling has a flawless track record, and a price tag to match. The Maiden, an even smaller-production second wine (about 900 cases) selected from softer, earlier-drinking lots, has an avid following of its own.

● **Harlan Estate / 2010 / Napa Valley / $$$$**
Parsing out the aromas and flavors of a wine this potent yet nuanced is nearly impossible. Suffice it to say, this is a glorious example of what Napa Valley can offer in a good vintage.

● **Harlan Estate / 2011 / Napa Valley / $$$$**
The herbaceous note here from the cool vintage only adds to the complexity of this tautly structured, currant-scented red.

HEITZ CELLAR

It would be difficult for this producer to recapture the resonance its name carried for wine lovers in the 1960s, '70s and '80s, when Heitz epitomized a kind of newly discovered California magic: world-class American Cabernet Sauvignon, made by a hands-on family operation. But for the most part, the magic is still there, including the hands-on family. The second and third generations of Heitzes continue to make wonderful wine from their 375 organically farmed acres, including the iconic Martha's Vineyard Cabernet. Heitz also produces some delicious, less stratospherically priced wines, among them a soft, easy-drinking Zinfandel and red and rosé Grignolino bottlings.

● **Heitz Cellar Grignolino Rosé / 2015 / Napa Valley / $$**
This bright, juicy rosé has strawberry and blood orange character, a tannic edge and a refreshing finish.

● **Heitz Cellar Martha's Vineyard Cabernet Sauvignon / 2010 / Napa Valley / $$$$** This wine is always late-released, as it's tightly wound when young. The 2010 is just now unfolding, with its famous mint-eucalyptus note accompanied by savory herbs, cherry, raspberry and elegant tannins.

THE HESS COLLECTION

The Swiss mineral-water mogul Donald Hess merged two of his passions—wine and contemporary art—in his impressive 1903 stone winery on Mount Veeder. (His wineries in Argentina and South Africa also house art museums.) The Napa art collection is worth a detour on its own. Given the value they deliver, the Hess Collection wines remain strangely under the radar. The ambitious Mount Veeder bottlings, like the 19 Block Mountain Cuvée and the Mount Veeder Cabernet, compete with any Napa Bordeaux-style wines in their price range; the Hess Select line offers reliable everyday drinking.

○ **The Hess Collection Chardonnay / 2014 / Mount Veeder / $$$** Unlike most Napa Chardonnays, this one does not undergo a second, softening malolactic fermentation. As a result, it's crisp, steely, pure and complex, with honeysuckle, pineapple, peach and pear flavors, dusted with baking spice.

● **The Hess Collection 19 Block Mountain Cuvée / 2012 / Mount Veeder / $$$** The Malbec grape forms the backbone of this supple, juicy, black- and blue-fruit-flavored blend, with 30 percent Cabernet Sauvignon and 10 percent Syrah.

HONIG VINEYARD & WINERY

The struggling garage operation Michael Honig took over in 1984 has blossomed into a multigenerational family success story. The Honigs have been industry leaders in green practices, with their solar-powered winery and sustainably farmed vineyard acreage. A rare American winery that founded its reputation on Sauvignon Blanc, Honig makes three versions: the Napa Valley bottling, aged mostly in stainless steel to retain freshness; the Rutherford estate bottling, which gets some barrel aging; and a dessert wine. With acreage in the heart of Rutherford's Cabernet country, Honig also bottles very fine Cabs, including the top-end Bartolucci and Campbell single-vineyard designates.

○ **Honig Sauvignon Blanc Reserve / 2014 / Rutherford / $$** Honig's entry-level Sauvignon Blanc is a bargain, but this well-priced Reserve version is a step up in interest, thanks to aging in barrels and splashes of Sémillon and Muscat. It's a bright mélange of melon, citrus, lime peel and fresh herbs.

● **Honig Cabernet Sauvignon / 2013 / Napa Valley / $$$** This voluptuous, silky wine abounds in juicy blackberry, black cherry and toasty oak personality.

HOURGLASS

With top winemaker Tony Biagi (formerly of PlumpJack; see p. 69) in charge of the cellar—he took over from founding winemaker Bob Foley just in time for the great vintage of 2012—Jeff Smith's prized, super-luxury boutique winery continues to turn out ripe, richly flavored, massively built Bordeaux-style wines that somehow come across as seamlessly balanced. The flagship vineyard is a special piece of land at the narrowest pinch of hourglass-shaped Napa Valley. The winery's second vineyard, Blueline (named for the two streams that drain the hillsides above it and formed its mineral-rich soils), is also proving to be a stunning site for Bordeaux varietals.

○ **Hourglass Sauvignon Blanc / 2015 / Napa Valley / $$$**
A mix of vineyards, plus fermentation in stainless steel, new oak and used oak, produced a wine that is both rich and lively, with generous flavor and palate weight.

● **Hourglass Blueline Estate Merlot / 2013 / Napa Valley / $$$$**
Ripe and intense, with chocolate and vanilla undertones, this near-black red stays fresh and balanced, thanks to crisp acidity and firm tannins.

HUNDRED ACRE

A flamboyant, obsessive former investment banker, Jayson Woodbridge plunged into the luxury wine business in 2000 with zero experience and now makes and sources wine all over the world. His tiny-production Hundred Acre wines (he also owns the value-oriented Layer Cake brand) are rarefied cult reds that sell for hundreds of dollars—if you can get your hands on them. The stars are the single-vineyard, usually all–Cabernet Sauvignon bottlings from Woodbridge's own Napa Valley vineyards: Kayli Morgan, Ark and Few & Far Between. The rarest of these rarities is Deep Time, a Cabernet Sauvignon that may spend up to 40 months in barrel.

● **Hundred Acre Ark Vineyard Cabernet Sauvignon / 2012 / Napa Valley / $$$$** From the Howell Mountain estate vineyard comes this heady, extracted, plush red, with intense blackberry, plum and blueberry fruit, lavish oak and a long, juicy finish.

● **Hundred Acre Kayli Morgan Vineyard Cabernet Sauvignon / 2012 / Napa Valley / $$$$** Similar in style to the Ark bottling, the concentrated Kayli Morgan Cab floods the mouth with jammy fruit, but has a bit more spice and cedar complexity.

INGLENOOK

One of Napa Valley's foundational 19th-century vineyards, Inglenook was split up over the years and its name slapped on countless bottles of jug wine made elsewhere in the state. Enter filmmaker/vintner Francis Ford Coppola. Starting with his Niebaum-Coppola tract over four decades ago, Coppola eventually reunited the historic property, which became known as the Rubicon Estate. Renamed Inglenook after Coppola repurchased the name in 2011, the estate today produces an intriguing and generally solid roster of wines. While Cabernet Sauvignon–based reds are the core offerings, the often delicious Rhône-style white blend Blancaneaux is worth seeking out.

- **Inglenook Cask Cabernet Sauvignon / 2012 / Napa Valley / $$$$** Rich, spicy and lingering, Rubicon's little brother is full-bodied and boldly flavored without being too heavy and ripe.
- **Inglenook Rubicon / 2012 / Rutherford / $$$$** This is the winery's mostly Cabernet Sauvignon flagship. Compared to Cask, it's got more of everything—ripeness, concentration, oak influence, spice and firm tannins—that the hedonistic wine drinker could want.

J. DAVIES ESTATE / DAVIES VINEYARDS

Hugh Davies, owner of the premier sparkling wine producer Schramsberg (see p. 77), manages this twin-pronged project devoted to still red wines. The graceful, well-knit J. Davies Cabernet Sauvignon comes from the estate's own vineyards on Napa's Diamond Mountain. Unveiled in 2016, the limited-production J. Davies Jamie Cabernet is made from the cellar's top 12 barrels. Originally focused exclusively on Pinot Noir (a key component in several Schramsberg sparklers), the Davies Vineyards label turns out single-vineyard still Pinots from prestige North Coast spots such as Ferrington and Londer and, as of the 2012 vintage, three Cabernet Sauvignons as well.

- **Davies Vineyards Ferrington Vineyards Pinot Noir / 2013 / Anderson Valley / $$$** From one of the finest vineyards in Mendocino County's Anderson Valley, this bright, juicy Pinot has depth and verve and an acid structure that begs for cellaring for a decade.
- **J. Davies Cabernet Sauvignon / 2013 / Diamond Mountain District / $$$$** There is a spicy warmth to this supremely balanced and supple wine that is in stark contrast to some of the more tannic-when-young Cabs from Diamond Mountain.

JOSEPH PHELPS VINEYARDS

There are new faces on Napa's ultra-luxury wine scene seemingly every year, but few are likely to establish the glittering track record of Insignia, the world-class Cabernet-based wine introduced by the late Joe Phelps in 1974. His son Bill heads the winery today, with Ashley Hepworth as winemaker. The original Spring Valley Ranch location remains focused on Bordeaux varieties and Syrah from biodynamically farmed estate vineyards, including the famous Backus Vineyard Cabernet; some estimable dessert wines are also made here. In 2007 Phelps built a winery on the Sonoma Coast dedicated to producing Burgundy-style Pinot Noir and Chardonnay under winemaker Justin Ennis.

- **Joseph Phelps Freestone Vineyards Pinot Noir / 2013 / Sonoma Coast / $$$** The Freestone's cool climate formed this vividly floral wine that has delicate yet flavorful red cherry and berry fruit, with cinnamon and leafy herb accents.
- **Joseph Phelps Insignia / 2012 / Napa Valley / $$$$** This wine has remarkable equilibrium, with drink-now generosity and the substance to evolve for two decades. The 2012 may be its richest and most layered bottling in years.

KAPCSÁNDY FAMILY WINERY

While making plans to retire to a Napa vineyard, Hungarian-born chemical engineer and wine importer Louis Kapcsándy and his wife, Roberta, came upon Beringer's State Lane Vineyard in Yountville, a famous 20-acre parcel for sale after being ravaged by the phylloxera vine pest. The couple bought the property in 2000 with their son, Louis, Jr., and spent a year rejuvenating the soil before replanting. Under the guidance of Louis, Jr., Kapcsándy produces small quantities of four stellar, luxury-priced Bordeaux-grape wines, led by the luscious Roberta's Reserve Merlot and the multilayered Estate Cuvée Cabernet.

- **Kapcsándy Family Winery Estate Cuvée / 2013 / Yountville / $$$$** Cabernet Sauvignon, Merlot, Cabernet Franc and Petit Verdot come together for a still-developing mouthful of dense dark cherry, blackberry and plum fruit wrapped in dark chocolate and vanillin oak.
- **Kapcsándy Family Winery Roberta's Reserve / 2012 / Yountville / $$$$** This bold yet beautiful Merlot is a head-turner with voluptuous texture and intense dark fruit and chocolate character framed by toasty French oak.

KONGSGAARD

Napa native John Kongsgaard is a guru whose road to enlightenment is much-admired but difficult to emulate. He takes his sumptuous, gorgeously layered Chardonnays, for example, to the extreme edge, leaving them for months-long fermentations in a process that would cause other vintners to lose sleep. In the 1980s, at Newton Vineyards, Kongsgaard pioneered much of what is lauded today as "natural winemaking." (He has also been a mentor to such future winemaking stars as Aaron Pott, Andy Erickson, Abe Schoener and Nick Peay.) His tiny lots of Chardonnay, Cabernet-Merlot blends, Syrah and Viognier-Roussanne are snapped up by avid fans.

○ **Kongsgaard Chardonnay / 2013 / Napa Valley / $$$$**
Easier to find than Kongsgaard's The Judge Chardonnay, this is a rich, big-fruited and luscious wine made with grapes from the renowned Hudson and Hyde Vineyards in Carneros.

● **Kongsgaard Syrah / 2013 / Napa Valley / $$$$**
A New World take on an Old World, northern Rhône Valley style, this sumptuous Syrah shows blackberry fruit seasoned with roasted meat, bacon fat and white pepper.

LADERA VINEYARDS

A long-delayed trip to Napa Valley proved life-changing for Montana ranchers Pat and Anne Stotesbery. The couple went on to acquire an 1886 ghost winery and vineyard high up on Howell Mountain. Under winemaker Jade Barrett, who came on board in 2012, Ladera Vineyards remains focused on crafting concentrated, structured mountain-style Cabernet Sauvignons, made primarily from the small-berried, intensely flavored grapes grown in the red volcanic soils of the home vineyard. The winery also turns out graceful Chardonnay and Pinot Noir from Sonoma's Russian River Valley under its Pillow Rd. label.

○ **Pillow Rd. Vineyard Chardonnay / 2013 / Russian River Valley / $$$**
Napa wineries are increasingly turning to Sonoma for Chardonnay. This classic Russian River Valley version offers vibrant citrus, green apple and yellow stone-fruit character, moderate richness and mouthwatering finish.

● **Ladera Stile Blocks Cabernet Sauvignon / 2012 / Howell Mountain / $$$** Napa Cabernet at this price and quality is hard to come by. This supple wine has a thread of minerality running through its juicy black currant and blackberry fruit.

LAGIER MEREDITH

This is a name to remember, partly for the excellent wine made here at reasonable (for Napa) prices, partly for the sheer soulfulness of the project. Stephen Lagier was a winemaker at Mondavi. Carole Meredith is probably the most famous wine researcher of her generation at UC Davis (she's known as Dr. DNA for her work identifying the origins of Zinfandel and other grape varieties). The pair cleared a plot of wilderness high on Mount Veeder and produce wines they want to drink, which means no new oak to mask flavors, no super-rich extractions and no filtration. Syrah is the calling card, but the "discoverer" of Zinfandel also bottles a beauty from the 4.5-acre vineyard.

● **Lagier Meredith Syrah / 2013 / Mount Veeder / $$$**
Aromas and flavors of ripe, but not sugary, blackberry pie are laced with a minerally, saline character and licorice, pepper and cardamom notes. Give it a year or more before opening.

● **Lagier Meredith Tribidrag / 2013 / Mount Veeder / $$$**
This Zin bears the medieval name of the grape's Croatian ancestor. Tribidrag is a sophisticated, well-mannered wine with plump berry fruit, supple tannins and a hint of spice.

LAIL VINEYARDS

Founder Robin Lail is Napa Valley aristocracy. She's the great-grandniece of Gustave Niebaum, who founded Inglenook (see p. 50)—and some would say Napa's reputation—in 1879, and the daughter of John Daniel, Jr., who continued Niebaum's legacy into the 1960s. Lail's daughters, Erin and Shannon, both partners in the winery, are the family's fifth generation in the Napa wine business. Lail Vineyards produces five bottlings—three Cabernets and two outstanding Sauvignon Blancs (including the collector-priced Georgia bottling)—all with famed winemaker Philippe Melka's silky touch. The flagship J. Daniel Cuvée Cabernet stands among Napa's finest reds.

○ **Lail Vineyards Blueprint Sauvignon Blanc / 2014 / Napa Valley / $$$**
With the glorious Georgia bottling extremely difficult to find (and expensive), this partially barrel-fermented Sauvignon is a fine substitute: it's brisk and lemony, with a lengthy finish.

● **Lail Vineyards J. Daniel Cuvée Cabernet Sauvignon / 2012 / Napa Valley / $$$$** This intensely fruity, layered Cab is cloaked in a rich robe of vanillin and chocolate oak. Sturdy tannins support its first-impression plushness, suggesting time in the cellar.

LA JOTA VINEYARD CO.

Famous for its burly, tannic Howell Mountain wines under its former owner Bill Smith, this small, luxury producer—a revitalized 1898 winery—has undergone a profound shift since it came under the aegis of Jackson Family Wines in 2005. One of the group's premier winemakers, Christopher Carpenter—he also crafts Cardinale and Lokoya (see pp. 29 and 57)—has taken La Jota to new heights. Carpenter's winemaking puts a premium on tannin management, shifting La Jota wines from slowly evolving and sometimes rustic to smoothly structured. The 28 acres produce three reds: the signature Cabernet Sauvignon and often very fine Merlot and Cabernet Franc.

● **La Jota Vineyard Co. Cabernet Sauvignon / 2012 / Howell Mountain / $$$$** Attractively priced for the neighborhood, it's bold yet balanced, with buoyant red and black fruit, seamless texture and perfect tannins for drinking both now and in 10 years.

● **La Jota Vineyard Co. Merlot / 2012 / Howell Mountain / $$$$** This red has deep plum, vanilla and spice aromas, and similar notes on the lush, silky palate; it finishes with bright acidity.

LANG & REED WINE COMPANY

The sky-high potential of Cabernet Franc has made the aromatic Bordeaux grape something of a darling in Napa Valley these days, but John Skupny was among the first to put it on center stage. Since founding Lang & Reed in 1996, Skupny, in partnership with his wife, Tracey, has combed vineyards and nurseries to find the finest Cab Franc clones—including the 214 clone from France's Loire Valley that makes the Two-Fourteen bottling named after it—and the best sites around the North Coast to grow them. The resulting reds display the grape's seductive, not-over-the-top-rich character, brimming with blueberry and spice notes. On the white side, the Skupnys champion the underappreciated (in the US) Loire staple Chenin Blanc.

○ **Lang & Reed Wine Company Chenin Blanc / 2014 / Napa Valley / $$** This honeyed Chenin Blanc is full-bodied yet crisp, with flavors of ripe pear, red apple, citrus and fennel. Concentrated and complex, it's at once rich, refreshing and delicious.

● **Lang & Reed Two-Fourteen Cabernet Franc / 2013 / Napa Valley / $$$** The 214 clone produced a wine that is rich, round and spicy, with a chocolaty note to the bold cherry liqueur and dark cherry foundation. Its subtle herbal streak is classic Cab Franc.

LARKIN WINES

Scotsman Sean Larkin, a self-described "bon vivant and bona fide Napa Valley Cabernet Franc producer," is the talented vintner behind this operation. The flagship Larkin wines are produced in extremely limited amounts that sell out quickly; the mailing list is the way to go here. The label's two wines—an opulent Cabernet Sauvignon and the Cabernet Franc—are defined by their bold flavor and concentration. Perhaps confusingly, Sean Larkin's other label is called Jack Larkin, after his son. The Jack Larkin Cabernet Sauvignon, priced somewhat higher than the Larkin version, is a richer, denser single-vineyard wine.

- **Larkin Cabernet Franc / 2013 / Napa Valley / $$$$**
  In this muscular red, Cabernet Sauvignon, Merlot and Petit Verdot add color and dimension to Cabernet Franc's signature floral aromas and ripe, concentrated red raspberry fruit.
- **Larkin Cabernet Sauvignon / 2013 / Napa Valley / $$$$**
  Similar in style to the Cab Franc, this is a generous, extracted wine with rich dark-berry fruit, hints of cedar and black spice, and soft tannins that make for immediate enjoyment.

LARKMEAD

Owned by members of the Solari family since 1948, Larkmead is one of a handful of Napa Valley heritage properties operating continuously since the 19th century (even through Prohibition). Today it's a top-notch producer of Bordeaux-style reds. The 9,500 cases crafted by winemaker Dan Petroski are all sourced from the property's contiguous 120-acre vineyard in Calistoga. The offerings include some distinctive whites, but the image-makers are the luxury-priced reds: LMV Salon, Solari and the Lark. Larkmead's commitment to quality is evidenced by the fact that none of the three were bottled in the difficult 2011 vintage. The more wallet-friendly Firebelle Merlot-based blend can be superb, but it's also heading skyward in price.

- **Larkmead Cabernet Sauvignon / 2013 / Napa Valley / $$$$**
  This flashes old-school Napa Cabernet personality, with forest-floor, cigar-box and loam aromas and a savory, gentle eucalyptus edge to its well-ripened fruit.
- **Larkmead LMV Salon / 2013 / Napa Valley / $$$$**
  Cabernet Franc lends floral aromas and palate brightness to this full-bodied, mostly Cabernet Sauvignon red. Tight now, it will benefit from at least five years in bottle.

LA SIRENA WINERY

Few people in Napa Valley are more esteemed by insiders but generally unknown to the public than Heidi Peterson Barrett. Daughter of one winemaking legend (Richard Peterson), wife of another (Bo Barrett of Chateau Montelena) and winemaker/consultant to the luxury wine stars (including Paradigm and Kenzo) herself, Barrett is one of the valley's leading—and most talented—citizens. No wonder that the wines from La Sirena ("the mermaid"), her personal project, command such a following. A master Cabernet Sauvignon maker, she also crafts one of Napa's top Syrah-based blends, Le Barrettage (a play on her name and Hermitage), and her labor of love, a blue-bottled Muscat Canelli called Moscato Azul.

○ **La Sirena Moscato Azul / 2014 / Calistoga / $$**

This dry Muscat Canelli has a steely, Riesling-like quality, with vivid white-flower aromas and mouthwatering Meyer lemon, white peach and lime zest flavors.

● **La Sirena Cabernet Sauvignon / 2012 / Napa Valley / $$$$**

A subtle salted-licorice thread runs from first sniff to finish in this ripe, opulent red marked by toasty oak, spice, vanilla and cedar, with firm tannins balancing the lush texture.

LEWIS CELLARS

Founded by former Indy car driver Randy Lewis and his wife, Debbie, this well-regarded small producer (about 9,000 cases a year) made its mark with spicy, full-throttle reds. The high-end choice is the Cab-based Cuvée L, made only in top vintages. But Lewis fans also appreciate the less pricey Alec's Blend, a juicy Syrah-Merlot combo with a touch of Cabernet that showcases the winery's deep-fruit style. It is one of Lewis's four Syrahs, including a rosé version. The full-on Meursault-treatment Chardonnay (barrel-fermented, with a malolactic secondary fermentation to help soften it) also has an avid following.

○ **Chardonnay / 2014 / Napa Valley / $$$**

Unapologetically rich, creamy and buttery, this full-bodied wine remains balanced, with vanilla and baking spice adding interest to the ripe pear, peach and pineapple palate.

● **Alec's Blend / 2013 / Napa Valley / $$$$**

The base of this super-ripe, voluptuous blend is Syrah (60 percent), and it's a mouthful, with blackberry liqueur and mocha character and baby-soft tannins.

LOKOYA

The late Jess Jackson established Lokoya in 1995, with skilled winemaker Greg Upton originally at the reins. From the start, this Jackson Family Wines project aimed to push the envelope, both in quality and in price. The wines have been made for many years now by Christopher Carpenter, who also crafts the Cardinale and La Jota wines (see pp. 29 and 54) for the company. Lokoya's four stratospherically priced Cabernet Sauvignons come from mountain vineyards in four appellations: Diamond Mountain, Howell Mountain, Mount Veeder and Spring Mountain. With their massive payloads of flavor and aroma, these wines mean to knock drinkers' socks off.

● **Lokoya Cabernet Sauvignon / 2012 / Howell Mountain / $$$$**
A block of the winery's W. S. Keyes Vineyard was replanted in 2006, and those grapes appear for the first time in this dense Cab with sizeable tannins and minerality. Delicious now, it will only improve with cellaring.

● **Lokoya Cabernet Sauvignon / 2012 / Mount Veeder / $$$$**
Don't open this for five years, minimum, because it's closed and tannic now. Yet decadent wild blackberry, licorice, minerals and crunchy acidity are just waiting to emerge.

LONG MEADOW RANCH WINERY

Ted Hall's stunning, panoramically situated 650 acres are the focus of a lot of ambitions besides winemaking. Long Meadow Ranch produces superior olive oil, beef from its prized Highland cattle, heirloom vegetables, preserves made from estate fruit, honey, eggs and on and on. Every bit of the operation is committedly organic, closely integrated and sustainable to the point that solar arrays produce all of its power and its farm vehicles run on biodiesel. The wines are typically good—especially the flagship Sauvignon Blanc (sourced from the ranch's valley-floor Rutherford estate) and the estate Cabernet—and, not surprisingly, they're made to complement food.

○ **Long Meadow Ranch Sauvignon Blanc / 2014 / Rutherford / $$**
A pure, fresh, unoaked wine, it delivers zesty citrus aromas and flavors, with white peach and gooseberry in the background and a bracing finish.

● **Long Meadow Ranch Cabernet Sauvignon / 2012 / Napa Valley / $$$**
This elegant red is appreciated for its spicy black-fruit character and food-friendly, moderate 13.5 percent alcohol.

LOUIS M. MARTINI WINERY

A focus on big, bold Cabernet Sauvignons has reinvented this Napa Valley producer, which started out making jug wines in 1933, after the repeal of Prohibition. Under the auspices of Gallo, which bought Martini in 2002, the winery fashions exemplary Cabernets, topped by the triple-digit-priced Lot No.1, made in the Cellar No. 254 "winery within a winery." Better known—and more widely available—are the amazingly value-priced Sonoma County bottling and the famous flagship Monte Rosso, from the estate vineyard in Sonoma, 1,200 feet up in the Mayacamas range. Martini has a well-deserved reputation for Zinfandel, too; the Gnarly Vine version, also sourced from the Monte Rosso Vineyard, is superb.

● **Louis M. Martini Cabernet Sauvignon / 2013 / Napa Valley / $$$**
This Cab brims with juicy blackberry and black currant flavor; cedary oak and a dusting of dried herbs add complexity.

● **Louis M. Martini Monte Rosso Vineyard Cabernet Sauvignon / 2012 / Sonoma Valley / $$$$** Textbook Monte Rosso, it's red-fruited and savory, with leather, black spice and earthy notes accenting the cherry compote and red plum core. Chewy tannins add structure and cellar-worthiness.

MARK HEROLD WINES

In a place where many wineries bear the names of proprietors who embarked on second careers after achieving success in other fields, Mark Herold put his name on the marquee based on his winemaking talent. A sought-after consultant for many projects (including the superb The Vineyardist; see p. 92), Herold made a splash with his Merus cult label, which he sold in 2007. The Mark Herold wines are like a roster of their maker's joys and preoccupations: the Acha Tempranillo, the Flux Rhône-style wines and the whatever-the-vintage-suggests Collide red blend. At the top are the lusciously ripe, full-throttle Cabernet Sauvignons, made in tiny quantities for the collectors' market.

○ **Acha Blanca / 2014 / California / $$**
A ripe yet delicate blend of Albariño with 10 percent Verdejo, Acha Blanca (Spanish for "white axe") delivers bright melon, peach and grapefruit character and a long, juicy finish.

● **Herold by Mark Herold / 2012 / Napa Valley / $$$$**
The winery's top-tier "white label" Cab is a full-bodied, sweet-fruit, lavishly oaked wine that delivers mouth-coating flavor.

MARSTON FAMILY VINEYARD

This late 19th-century vineyard and orchard property on the southern slopes of Spring Mountain already had a colorful history (Clark Gable honeymooned there in 1955) by the time Michael and Alexandra Marston bought into it in 1969 (they became full owners in 1976). Over the past two decades, much of their Cabernet grape production has been sold to Beringer (see p. 24) for its Private Reserve and Marston Vineyard bottlings. But with the 1998 vintage, the Marstons, under the tutelage of star consultant Philippe Melka, debuted the intensely flavored estate-produced Cabernet Sauvignon they're known for today. In charge of the cellar since 2010, winemaker Marbue Marke also crafts a sought-after Sauvignon Blanc, Albion.

○ **Marston Family Vineyard Albion / 2015 / Napa Valley / $$$**
This Sauvignon Blanc is made in a Bordeaux Blanc style, with partial barrel fermentation adding roundness and texture to the fresh citrus, melon, green apple and tropical fruit. It finishes long and crisp.

● **Marston Family Vineyard Cabernet Sauvignon / 2012 / Spring Mountain District / $$$$** Dense in blackberry and black currant fruit, this concentrated, ripe red has hints of tobacco, anise and leather; sweet vanillin and mocha oak tie it all together.

MASSICAN

Brooklyn native and heartfelt Italophile Dan Petroski's wine project is an outpost of northeastern Italy in Napa and a kind of corrective to the full-on Cabernet-ization of the valley. Petroski, whose day job is as winemaker at Larkmead (see p. 55), produces a few hundred cases each of four white wines under the Massican label. These are true expressions of a European sensibility, generally low in alcohol, vibrant with acidity and meant to be savored with food rather than overwhelm you with richness. Given the tiny production, Massican's mailing list may be your best bet for obtaining the wines.

○ **Massican Sauvignon / 2015 / Napa Valley / $$**
This complex mélange of key lime, Meyer lemon and tropical fruit has bracing structure and a savory note on the finish.

○ **Massican Annia / 2014 / Napa Valley / $$$**
Petroski coaxes Tocai Friulano, Ribolla Gialla and Chardonnay into an integrated wine with bright citrus, chamomile, walnut skin and honey notes. It's both deep and refreshing.

MATTHIASSON

Many winemakers talk about how "wine is made in the vineyard," but Steve Matthiasson lives it every day as a hands-on farmer and much-sought-after vineyard consultant. His vineyard work gives Matthiasson on-the-ground knowledge of the grapes, both purchased and estate-grown, that go into his eclectic lineup. He is best known for Chardonnay and Bordeaux-style wines, like the top-of-the-line Red Hen Vineyard Merlot, that emphasize finesse as much as power. But Matthiasson also creates an array of wines from lesser-known grapes like Ribolla Gailla, Refosco dal Peduncolo Rosso and Schioppettino, all with his trademark intense flavor profile at moderate alcohol levels.

○ **Matthiasson White Wine / 2014 / Napa Valley / $$$**
Sauvignon Blanc–based, with lesser amounts of Ribolla Gialla, Sémillon and Tocai Friulano, this is a racy, refreshing and also complex wine, with citrus, white peach and tropical fruit, stony minerality and a spicy kick.

● **Matthiasson Cabernet Sauvignon / 2013 / Napa Valley / $$$**
Generous, yet structured, this has a core of brambly blackberry, black raspberry, cranberry and dark cherry, with fresh herbs, cedar, pencil lead and mocha notes on the firmly tannic palate.

MAYACAMAS VINEYARDS

It is a new era—again—for this venerable Mount Veeder property, with its picturesque 19th-century stone winery and grounds. In 2013, wine entrepreneur Charles Banks (Sandhi, Qupé, Wind Gap) and his wife, Ali, bought Mayacamas in partnership with members of the retail-magnate Schottenstein family—only the fourth set of owners in the winery's 128-year history. Star winemaker Andy Erickson (see Favia, p. 42) was enlisted to enhance, not alter, the estate's old-school Cabernets. Tight and sometimes lean on release like traditional Bordeaux reds, Mayacamas wines soften with time; the best age beautifully for decades.

○ **Mayacamas Chardonnay / 2013 / Napa Valley / $$$**
Expect this wine to unwind and reveal its vibrant citrus, Asian pear and gravelly character with bottle age—five years or more.

● **Mayacamas Cabernet Sauvignon / 2010 / Mount Veeder / $$$$**
This current release demonstrates the producer's long-term approach to aging wines. It offers Bing and black cherry fruit, black olive and herbal accents, sturdy tannins and a promise of aging splendidly.

MELKA WINES

Bordeaux native Philippe Melka exudes charm and confidence, a combination that's been catnip to the elite Napa properties—Dana Estates, Lail and Hundred Acre among them—that hire him as a consultant. Melka Wines is Philippe and wife Cherie's own project, comprising the reasonably priced CJ Cabernet Sauvignon, which gives you a sense of his fluid, ripe, polished style; small-production luxury wines in the Mekerra line; the top-end Métisse proprietary reds; and the Majestique label, for diverse wines from around California and the world. Though renowned for Bordeaux-style reds, Melka has a Graves-like touch that may change your take on California Sauvignon Blanc.

● **Melka CJ / 2013 / Napa Valley / $$$$**

This Cabernet is lush and layered, with juicy dark fruit, licorice, cigar and spice from French oak barrels. The tannins are sturdy enough for steak, yet polished enough for sipping.

● **Melka Métisse Jumping Goat Vineyard / 2013 / Napa Valley / $$$$**

A Cab-based blend with small amounts of Petit Verdot and Merlot, this is extraordinarily rich, weighty and viscous, yet also energetic on the finish, thanks to its bright acidity.

MERRYVALE VINEYARDS

Located along a well-traveled stretch of Highway 29 in St. Helena, historic Merryvale, once known as Sunny St. Helena Winery, dates back to the end of Prohibition in 1933. The estate has been owned by the Schlatter family since the mid-'90s but seems to have hit its stride in the 2000s, perhaps coinciding with the return of former assistant Sean Foster as winemaker in 2006. Merryvale produces a broad range of wines under its own label, led by the Silhouette Chardonnay and the triple-digit-priced Bordeaux-style Profile. The affordable Starmont label became so successful that it's been spun off as its own brand.

○ **Merryvale Chardonnay / 2014 / Carneros / $$$**

Sourced mostly from the winery's Stanly Ranch Estate, this nicely structured, medium-bodied wine brims with classic Carneros character of crisp apple and pear fruit, plus hints of tangerine, vanilla and baking spice from oak fermentation.

● **Profile / 2012 / Napa Valley / $$$$**

Merryvale's calling card is this full-flavored, mostly Cabernet blend, with 15 percent Petit Verdot imparting black olive and licorice notes. Succulent, balanced and elegant, it's a beauty.

MINER FAMILY WINERY

Miner is familiar to Napa Valley visitors for its Silverado Trail tasting room, featuring a nearly bewildering array of mostly high-quality, reasonably priced (for Napa) wines. Owner Dave Miner left the software business in 1993 to follow his vinous dreams and founded the winery in 1996. He owns some prime land but also pursues contracts with numerous vineyards around the state, with the proviso that he specifies the farming practices. The most famous result of these collaborations is The Oracle, a complex, concentrated red Bordeaux blend sourced from Stagecoach Vineyard high up on Atlas Peak. The same collaboration produces the generally excellent Syrah La Diligence and forms the basis for the Rhône-style white, Iliad.

○ **Miner The Iliad / 2012 / Napa Valley / $$**

This Marsanne-Roussanne-Viognier blend is largely barrel-fermented, which lends creaminess to the aroma and texture. It's full-bodied and supple, with soft pear and peach fruit.

● **Miner The Oracle / 2012 / Napa Valley / $$$$**

Five Bordeaux red varieties, led by Cabernet Sauvignon, make up this single-vineyard blend. Vanillin oak and substantial tannins frame a core of ripe raspberry and blackberry fruit.

MORLET FAMILY VINEYARDS

Luc Morlet, a native of France's Val d'Or, became winemaker at prestigious Peter Michael (see p. 134) before passing the torch to his brother Nicolas. Starting in 2006, Luc and his wife, Jodie, began producing their own wines, and in 2010 acquired their pre-Prohibition St. Helena winery. The acclaimed Morlet lineup has a distinctly Peter Michael look: a pan-French roster of vineyard-based, luxury-priced wines with French proprietary names (Mon Chevalier, Côteaux Nobles). Morlet's big-flavored, elegant-but-dense wines are sold mainly through the mailing list—and there's a waiting list to get on it.

○ **Morlet La Proportion Dorée / 2014 / Sonoma County / $$$$**

This rich, intense blend of barrel-fermented Sémillon, Sauvignon Blanc and Muscadelle offers ripe peach and yellow-flesh plum fruit and great floral character.

● **Morlet Estate / 2013 / St. Helena / $$$$**

Bottled unfiltered after aging for 16 months in French oak, the Estate Cabernet combines power with opulently rich fruit, smoky oak and graceful tannins.

MUMM NAPA

This winery was started as a joint venture between G.H. Mumm Champagne and Joseph Seagram under the guidance of the indefatigable Guy Devaux. Both Mumm, the French parent, and Mumm Napa have ridden a rocky corporate road since, passing through the hands of Allied Domecq before landing in the Pernod Ricard portfolio. The Napa venture lost visibility with Devaux's death in 1995 and the various corporate changes, but the quality of its sparkling wines, especially the top-end DVX bottlings, remains quite high. The entry-level wines like the nonvintage Brut Prestige and Brut Rosé can be outstanding bargains.

○ **Mumm Napa Brut Prestige / NV / Napa Valley / $$**
This great-value nonvintage sparkler has never been better. Impressively yeasty and brioche-like, it also has crisp green apple and Asian pear fruit, a hint of ginger and a lively finish.

○ **Mumm Napa DVX / 2008 / Napa Valley / $$$**
This California version of a Champagne prestige cuvée is vibrant and elegant, with white flowers, almond, white peach and baked-bread complexity. Finer in texture than the Brut Prestige, it's likely to age beautifully.

NEWTON VINEYARD

This is one of Napa's most stylish wineries, set amid formal gardens, with sweeping views of Spring Mountain. Founded by Su Hua Newton and the late Peter Newton in 1977, the winery—and its original winemaker, John Kongsgaard (see p. 52)—pioneered natural fermentations and unfiltered bottling, giving the wines a European sophistication that endures under the current ownership of LVMH. Newton Vineyard's Unfiltered Chardonnay is one of California's benchmark Chardonnay bottlings. The Puzzle, a mostly Cabernet blend, is the top expression of the home estate's vineyards in any given year.

○ **Newton Unfiltered Chardonnay / 2013 / Napa Valley / $$$**
Made with grapes from Carneros and Sonoma's Knights Valley, this was fermented in French oak and aged on the lees for a year, giving the wine its creamy texture and richness. It also boasts focused ripe fruit, nuttiness and crisp acidity.

● **Newton The Puzzle Cabernet Sauvignon / 2013 / Napa Valley / $$$$**
Sourced from among 109 estate vineyard blocks, the 2013 The Puzzle is a dense wine with boldly ripe black fruit accented by cigar-box, cedar, mocha and licorice notes.

NICKEL & NICKEL

From the Nickel family and their partners (see also Far Niente, p. 41), this is an ambitious undertaking directed at deep-pocketed wine lovers. Nickel & Nickel makes small lots of 100 percent single-varietal wines from individual vineyards. In any given vintage this may mean upwards of 20 bottlings, with fifteen or so being Cabernet Sauvignon and the rest Chardonnay, Merlot and Syrah. These are impressive, highly polished wines, leaning toward full-throttle richness, with genuine *terroir*-grounded differences across the portfolio. Two constants are the Martin Stelling Vineyard, which also provides the core of the Far Niente flagship Cab; and the John C. Sullenger Vineyard, at Nickel & Nickel's home ranch in Oakville.

○ **Nickel & Nickel Truchard Vineyard Chardonnay / 2014 / Carneros / $$$** This is a beautifully balanced and minerally Chardonnay, with juicy pear, Meyer lemon, peach and pineapple fruit supported by creamy vanilla and brisk acidity.

● **Nickel & Nickel Martin Stelling Vineyard Cabernet Sauvignon / 2013 / Oakville / $$$$** The Martin Stelling Cabernet is a superstar. Silky tannins balance rich blackberry fruit and spicy vanillin oak, all leading to a mouthwatering finish.

OPUS ONE

The late Robert Mondavi and the late Baron Philippe de Rothschild of Bordeaux's Château Mouton Rothschild modeled this groundbreaking Napa Valley joint venture winery after a *grand cru* Bordeaux, focusing squarely on a high-end Cabernet-based blend. Under winemaker Michael Silacci, Opus One has cemented its place among California's iconic reds. The second wine, a still-pricey multivintage bottling called Overture, is crafted to be more readily approachable in its youth. The sleek operation is now jointly owned by the Rothschilds and Constellation Brands (which purchased Mondavi), with the Rothschilds taking the lead in vineyard management.

● **Opus One / 2012 / Napa Valley / $$$$**
This polished and elegant red is finely textured and rich in blackberry fruit, with smoky oak, leather and tobacco notes adding complexity. A solid structure ensures ageability.

● **Overture / NV / Napa Valley / $$$$**
Well knitted and complex, this multivintage Bordeaux-style red offers ripe red and black fruit, spicy oak and supple tannins.

ORIN SWIFT CELLARS

The curious Orin Swift wine names—Veladora, China Doll, Papillon—can be traced to the restless marketing mind of David Swift Phinney, who operates this modestly sized but growing Napa Valley–based endeavor, as well as other far-flung wine projects from Argentina to Corsica. As his fans know, Phinney is a very talented winemaker who puts a lot of exuberant character into the bottles. Though he first became known for his innovative, not to say idiosyncratic, blends—most famously The Prisoner (see p. 70), which he sold to the Huneeus (Quintessa) family—his single-grape wines, like the high-end, exuberantly aromatic Mercury Head Cabernet Sauvignon, show that he also has a sure hand with the classics.

○ **Veladora / 2014 / Napa Valley / $$**
The Veladora Sauvignon Blanc is rich and weighty, with melon, peach and pear fruit, finishing with citrusy acidity.

● **Papillon / 2013 / Napa Valley / $$$$**
With its purple color and brazenly ripe black fruit, this Bordeaux-grape blend is a mouthful. Coffee bean and chocolate notes add interest; soft tannins make it easy to drink now.

O'SHAUGHNESSY ESTATE WINERY

Inky, full-bodied, mountain-grown Cabernet Sauvignon–based reds from estate vineyards on Howell Mountain and Mount Veeder made the name of this boutique Napa Valley producer. Winemaker Sean Capiaux, well known for his own Capiaux Cellars Pinot Noirs, makes these wines for Betty O'Shaughnessy Woolls and her family with a full appreciation for Cabernet's potential for depth and power. The Howell Mountain bottling is essentially a Meritage wine, with a melange of Bordeaux-derived blending grapes; the Mount Veeder is all Cabernet. Though overshadowed by the reds, O'Shaughnessy's Sauvignon Blanc and Chardonnay bottlings are also estimable.

○ **O'Shaughnessy Chardonnay / 2014 / Oakville / $$$**
A complete and elegant Chardonnay, this displays floral aromas and generous lemon and yellow stone-fruit flavors, backed by subtle oak and refreshing acidity.

● **O'Shaughnessy Cabernet Sauvignon / 2012 / Howell Mountain / $$$$** Eight Bordeaux varieties are here, with Cabernet Sauvignon and Malbec in the lead. Despite its sturdy tannins and dense black fruit, this is a supple and energetic red.

OUTPOST

This remote property high up on Howell Mountain may qualify as an "outpost," but it does have prestigious neighbors. Purchased in 2003 by Kathy and Frank Dotzler, it more than upholds the neighborhood standards. Under the direction of winemaker Thomas Rivers Brown (see Rivers-Marie, p. 138), Outpost built its reputation at first on brooding, complex old-vine Zinfandels from its high-altitude (1,600 to 2,200 feet), volcanic-soil estate vineyards. But the success of its dark, subtle, massively structured Cabernets may have overshadowed the Zin. Rhône fans should keep an eye out for Outpost's acclaimed Grenache.

● **Outpost Zinfandel / 2013 / Howell Mountain / $$$**
With its significant tannins, this requires a year or more in the cellar for the underlying blackberry, black raspberry, bramble and pepper notes to emerge.

● **Outpost Cabernet Sauvignon / 2013 / Howell Mountain / $$$$**
Mountain tannins and chocolate oak dominate now, but underneath lurks blackberry and cassis fruit that will get its star turn with age.

PAHLMEYER

The producer of impressively scaled, super-rich Bordeaux-blend reds from Napa Valley and Pinots and Chardonnays from the Sonoma Coast, Jayson Pahlmeyer began in the early 1980s with a bit of vinous roguery. He and his partner, so the legend goes, smuggled their original vines from Bordeaux, via Canada, in suitcases to avoid impoundment by the authorities. A succession of stars—from Randy Dunn through Bob Levy, Helen Turley and Erin Green—put Pahlmeyer wines on the map. In 2012, two new winemakers were brought on board: Kale Anderson (Napa production) and consultant Bibiana González Rave (Sonoma wines). Though the great 2012 and 2013 vintages clearly helped, Pahlmeyer doesn't seem to have skipped a beat.

○ **Pahlmeyer Chardonnay / 2014 / Napa Valley / $$$$**
Crème brulée rich, with mostly new French oak adding butterscotch and graham cracker notes, this large-scale wine has enough citrusy acidity to support the weight.

● **Pahlmeyer Red Wine / 2013 / Napa Valley / $$$$**
The Cab-based blend packs a punch, with 15.2 percent alcohol, intensely ripe blackberry and blueberry fruit and caressingly smooth tannins. A vibrant finish pulls it all together.

PARADIGM WINERY

Paradigm's owners are something of a rarity on the Napa scene: they're deep-rooted Californians. Ren Harris's family arrived in the 1700s; his wife Marilyn's clan has been in Napa Valley since 1890. A longtime grower that started bottling its own wines in the early 1990s, Paradigm has had the good fortune to be taken under the wing of the esteemed Peterson family: Father Dick helped get the project started; daughter Heidi Peterson Barrett is the winemaker. If Barrett has rarely produced the kinds of hits here that she did at, say, Screaming Eagle, the prices for Paradigm wines have remained within the realm of reality.

- **Paradigm Merlot / 2012 / Oakville / $$$**
  Plush and plummy, with caramel and vanilla accents and suave tannins, this Merlot gains color and structure from small additions of Cabernet Sauvignon and Petit Verdot.
- **Paradigm Cabernet Sauvignon / 2012 / Oakville / $$$$**
  This is a nicely balanced, everything-in-moderation Cab, with deep berry and black cherry fruit, firm yet supple tannins, gentle oak toast and spice, and a bright, lingering finish.

PHILIP TOGNI VINEYARD

British-born and Bordeaux-educated, Philip Togni arrived in Napa Valley in 1959, and made legendary wines for Chalone, Chappellet, Cuvaison and Mayacamas before retreating to his 25-acre retreat atop Spring Mountain to make his wine, his way. These days that means 2,000 cases of two stunning, estate-grown Cabernet Sauvignons structured to age with grace rather than for immediate gratification. The triple-digit-priced Philip Togni blend is sometimes described as Margaux-style, appropriately enough for a man who was assistant winemaker at Château Lascombes early in his career. The second wine, Tanbark Hill, is often closer to 100 percent Cabernet and very reasonably priced if you can find it—try Togni's mailing list.

- **Tanbark Hill Vineyard Cabernet Sauvignon / 2013 / Napa Valley / $$$**
  This is a bit more accessible when young than the flagship. Still, its tight tannins and linear character will unfold with age.
- **Philip Togni Vineyard Cabernet Sauvignon / 2013 / Napa Valley / $$$$** The producer suggests cellaring this for a decade or more, though a taste now reveals tremendous complexity in the form of cedar, dried herbs, licorice and graphite. When the fruit fully develops with aging, it should be exceptional.

PIÑA NAPA VALLEY

The four Piña brothers have a unique perspective on Napa Valley. They are the eighth generation of their family to farm here (ancestor Bluford Stice arrived in 1856). And they come at winemaking as farmers first: their Piña Vineyard Management is one of the valley's most prominent viticultural companies. Their offerings, crafted by Francophile winemaker Anna Monticelli, include six single-vineyard Cabernets and a single-vineyard Chardonnay, from sites the brothers own, lease or oversee. The best-known of the luxury-priced Cabs is the Buckeye Vineyard bottling from their own Howell Mountain property.

○ **Piña Cellars Low Vineyard Chardonnay / 2013 / Oak Knoll District / $$$** French oak is on full display here, with hazelnut, toast and vanilla aromas leading to a rich, creamy palate of ripe stone fruit and citrus and a slightly sweet finish.

● **Piña Napa Valley Buckeye Vineyard / 2012 / Howell Mountain / $$$$** With semisweet chocolate, mocha and toasted spice character, silky tannins, juicy black currant fruit and a modicum of acidity, this lavishly oaked Cab makes for a decadent drink.

PINE RIDGE VINEYARDS

The jewel in the crown of the Crimson Wine Group, which also owns Seghesio and Oregon's Archery Summit (see pp. 141 and 202), Pine Ridge produces wine from 200 acres spread among 12 estate vineyards in five major Napa Valley appellations. Winemaker Michael Beaulac combines fruit from these varied locations into several Cabernet and red-blend bottlings, including the top-end Fortis, Cave 7 and Tessitura. Even the generally excellent Stags Leap District Cabernet Sauvignon is blended from four estate vineyards within that single subregion. Pine Ridge turns out an extensive range of wines, across a variety of price points. For an affordable taste of the winery's style with whites, try the vibrant Chenin Blanc–Viognier.

○ **Pine Ridge Chenin Blanc–Viognier / 2014 / California / $** This great-value white delivers an off-dry ambrosia salad of bright tropical, citrus and peach aromas and flavors.

● **Pine Ridge Vineyards Cabernet Sauvignon / 2012 / Stags Leap District / $$$$** Displaying the district's "iron fist in a velvet glove" personality, this firmly structured Cab frames luscious dark berry fruit with silky, licorice-edged tannins and bright acidity. Lamb loin and steak would be great mates.

PLUMPJACK WINERY

Founded by high-profile owners Gavin Newsom and Gordon Getty in 1995, this winery burst onto the scene with full-bodied but ultra-polished Cabernet Sauvignons—a legacy of its Oakville home vineyards, which formerly produced Villa Mt. Eden in that wine's 1970s heyday. The PlumpJack Group (the name refers to Shakespeare's Falstaff) now encompasses resorts, restaurants and two additional wineries, CADE (see p. 27) and Odette. Founding winemaker Tony Biagi turned over the PlumpJack cellar to Aaron Miller in 2012, but the winery has stayed on message, turning out a small range of highly distinctive wines, including a Chardonnay and a Syrah built for serious pleasure.

○ **PlumpJack Reserve Chardonnay / 2014 / Napa Valley / $$$**
Here's a Chardonnay with no butter, moderate oak, pure pear, citrus and tropical character and mouthwatering acidity.

● **PlumpJack Estate Cabernet Sauvignon / 2013 / Oakville / $$$$**
Layers of rich cassis and blackberry cobbler unfold with each sip of this sumptuous, big-bodied wine; creamy vanillin, spice and anise seed add to the opulent impact.

POTT WINE

Who but Aaron Pott, *philosophe*, French-trained vintner and student of biodynamics, would speak of wine as "a way to tune in your spiritual radio"? The former winemaker at Bordeaux's Château Troplong-Mondot, and current consulting winemaker for high-caliber clients like Blackbird, Seven Stones and Fisher, Pott and his wife, Claire, also make tiny quantities of their own coveted wines. Pott's work around the valley has led him to several special plots, in addition to the couple's home vineyard on Mount Veeder, playfully dubbed "Châteauneuf-du-Pott." With near-neighbors Carole Meredith and Steve Lagier (see p. 53), the Potts also produce the Chester's Anvil label. Best bet for acquiring any of these wines: Join the mailing list.

○ **Pott 20M3 / 2014 / Napa Valley / $$$**
From Stagecoach Vineyard's K2B block, this 100 percent Viognier offers all of the variety's honeysuckle, poached pear and peach attributes in a richly textured, energetic format.

● **Pott Incubo / 2013 / Mount Veeder / $$$$**
The Bordeaux-style Cabernet from the Potts' home vineyard is all about restraint and elegance, with pretty red and black fruit and the structure for long-term cellaring.

PRIDE MOUNTAIN VINEYARDS

A brick stripe on the crush pad at Pride Mountain traces the Napa-Sonoma county line, which runs through this high-elevation Spring Mountain estate (called Summit Ranch when vineyards were first planted here in 1869). Family-owned Pride is known for its unctuous reds and oak-kissed whites. It's a style made famous under former winemaker Bob Foley and brilliantly executed since 2007 by Sally Johnson. She oversees a 19,000-case portfolio of a dozen bottlings in three tiers: Pride, Vintner Select and Reserve. The Pride-designated wines are often bargains for their quality (by Napa standards); the upper-tier wines compete with Napa's (or Sonoma's) very best.

○ **Pride Mountain Vineyards Chardonnay / 2014 / Napa Valley / $$$** This spice- and vanilla-accented Chardonnay was fermented mainly in neutral oak barrels, which allowed its vibrant lemon, tangerine and pear fruit to shine.

● **Pride Mountain Vineyards Reserve Cabernet Sauvignon / 2013 / Sonoma and Napa Counties / $$$$** This wine's ripe, briary blackberry flavors are cloaked in vanillin oak and enhanced by hints of violets, toffee, black tea and dark chocolate.

THE PRISONER WINE COMPANY

The Prisoner red blend became a breakout hit thanks to the fertile imagination of its creator, David Phinney (see Orin Swift, p. 65), who had the insight that a well-marketed, well-packaged and, above all, tasty wine sourced from all over could be made in sizeable quantities and sold at a reasonable, if still premium, price. The Huneeus family (see Quintessa, opposite) acquired The Prisoner and the four other Prisoner Wine Company brands in 2009, and sold the portfolio on to Constellation Brands in 2016. The Huneeuses are staying on in a consulting role, and winemaker Jen Beloz and her team remain in the cellar to ensure continuity in the wines.

○ **Blindfold / 2014 / California / $$** A kitchen-sink mix of Chardonnay, Roussanne, Viognier, Grenache Blanc and other varieties goes into this fat, juicy wine with loads of ripe-fruit flavor and a kiss of sweetness.

● **The Prisoner / 2014 / Napa Valley / $$$** Zinfandel-based, with Cabernet Sauvignon, Syrah, Petite Sirah and Charbono added for intrigue, it's a heady mouthful of ripe black fruit with inky color and crowd-pleasing sweetness.

QUINTESSA

This stylish winery was established by the Huneeus family (see The Prisoner, opposite, and Flowers, p. 113), who brought with them from Chile a cosmopolitan flair and a deep belief in natural agriculture. The biodynamically farmed, 170-acre vineyard is devoted to two wines crafted by veteran winemaker Charles Thomas with consultant Michel Rolland: the Illumination Sauvignon Blanc and the Bordeaux-style red blend, Quintessa. Composed from barrel-aged selections from the estate's various microclimate blocks, Quintessa is a wine of high refinement, notable for a layered subtlety that reveals itself over years.

○ **Illumination / 2014 / Napa and Sonoma Counties / $$$**

This vibrant Sauvignon Blanc was fermented in oak, for added depth of body; in stainless steel, to preserve the citrus and tropical fruit; and in concrete "eggs," for palate richness.

● **Quintessa / 2013 / Rutherford / $$$$**

With Cabernet Sauvignon in the lead, supported by Merlot, Cab Franc, Carmenère and Petit Verdot, this elegant red offers black and blue fruit, gentle herbaceousness and a savory finish.

RAYMOND VINEYARDS

This longtime source of solid, reasonably priced wines was rejuvenated in 2009 when international wine mogul Jean-Charles Boisset added Raymond to his portfolio (Bouchard, Domaine de la Vougeraie, DeLoach) and enlisted winemaker Stephanie Putnam, formerly of Far Niente (see p. 41). She now presides over an extensive lineup, including the affordable Family Classic line and the District, Estate and Small Lot Collections. In general, Boisset has moved Raymond steadily upmarket, with the much-respected Generations Cabernet Sauvignon at the forefront. Raymond began implementing organic and biodynamic farming practices in 2010 and received certifications for most of its 325 planted acres in 2013.

○ **Raymond Barrel Fermented Chardonnay / 2014 / Napa Valley / $$$**

This Small Lot Collection Chardonnay offers vanillin and caramel aromas followed by juicy tropical and citrus fruit. The soft, creamy mid-palate turns fresh on the finish.

● **Raymond Generations / 2012 / Napa Valley / $$$$**

Its youthful blackberry and blueberry fruit, supple yet sturdy tannins and hints of mint, graphite and mocha suggest that this Cab will age gracefully for a decade or more.

REALM CELLARS

Founder Juan Mercado all but willed Realm into being. An ICU nurse and hospital administrator with neither capital nor an enology degree, he outlasted skeptics, near bankruptcy and a warehouse fire that destroyed his entire 2003 vintage to produce ethereal small lots of wines from some of Napa's greatest vineyards. With managing partner Scott Becker handling the business end and Michel Rolland protégé Benoit Touquette as winemaker, the tiny cult winery is now soaring. Fortunately for its mailing-list fans, it still has the same superb sources, like Beckstoffer To Kalon Vineyard, whose owner, Andy Beckstoffer, was first persuaded to sell to Realm by dint of Mercado's sheer conviction and personality.

- **Realm Beckstoffer Dr. Crane Vineyard / 2012 / Napa Valley / $$$$** Fragrant florality contrasts with the full-bodied, black-fruit character of this dense and concentrated Cabernet Sauvignon. Its muscular tannins beg for time in the cellar.
- **Realm The Tempest / 2013 / Napa Valley / $$$$** This cellar-worthy Merlot-dominant red has a jammy plum, black cherry and blueberry palate framed by firm oak tannins.

ROBERT BIALE VINEYARDS

From the back porch of the Biale place in the town of Napa, you can see the bushy, old-fashioned Zinfandel and Petite Sirah vineyard planted by Robert Biale's grandfather in 1937. (He would offer customers "Black Chicken," code for homemade Zin.) Winemaker Tres Goetting ferments today's Black Chicken—the signature bottling for this old-vine Zin specialist—in traditional open-top vats but ages it in French-oak cooperage. Biale's wines are remarkable for their tongue-purpling density and exotic perfume. Also worth seeking out are the exceptional Grande Vineyard and Aldo's Vineyard Zinfandels and benchmark Petite Sirahs like the massively scaled Royal Punishers.

- **Robert Biale Vineyards Black Chicken Zinfandel / 2014 / Napa Valley / $$$** Intense and jammy at the start, it evolves in the glass into a more balanced, vibrant wine with cinnamon spice, soft brambly fruit and a vanillin finish.
- **Robert Biale Vineyards Royal Punishers Petite Sirah / 2013 / Rutherford / $$$** This has everything most Petite Sirah lovers want: brawny tannins, tooth-staining purple fruit, and leather, chocolate and black pepper complexity.

ROBERT CRAIG WINERY

At the end of a winding road 2,300 feet up Howell Mountain sits Robert Craig's eponymous winery and one of his estate vineyards. It's a perch that suits Craig well—he long ago developed a passion for concentrated, firmly structured mountain-grown grapes. With some 25 vintages under his belt, Craig has built a reputation for putting outstanding Cabernet Sauvignon into the bottle at restrained prices. These offerings include four single-appellation Cabernets—from Mount Veeder, Spring Mountain, Diamond Mountain and the home vineyard on Howell Mountain—plus the Affinity estate bottling and, as of the 2013 vintage, a Napa Valley Cabernet. Craig also releases small quantities of single-vineyard Chardonnay and Zin.

- ● **Robert Craig Affinity Cabernet Sauvignon / 2013 / Napa Valley / $$$$** The 2013 vintage Affinity is the first to be made entirely from estate-grown grapes. It's solidly tannic and minerally, yet abundant in cassis, blackberry and plum fruit.
- ● **Robert Craig Cabernet Sauvignon / 2013 / Mount Veeder / $$$$** Given its mountain provenance, the wine is remarkably balanced, with saturated black fruit and earthy tones offset by sturdy tannins. It finishes with a refreshing wild-berry finish.

ROBERT KEENAN WINERY

In the mid-1970s, the late Robert Keenan bought an abandoned 19th-century vineyard site on Spring Mountain. Now run by his son Michael, who makes the wine with an assist from consulting winemaker Nils Venge (of Saddleback Cellars), the winery has seen its quality level rise since the mid-2000s on Michael's watch. In addition to its image-making Cabernet Sauvignons, Keenan fields a stellar lineup of Merlots, ranging from the well-priced (for Napa) non-estate Merlot to the curiously named Mernet estate blend of Merlot and Cabernet. The winery's luscious Chardonnays include an estate bottling and Summer Blend, which mixes in portions of Albariño and Viognier.

- ○ **Keenan Chardonnay / 2014 / Spring Mountain District / $$$** This wine crackles with mouthwatering acidity that contrasts nicely with the lush stone-fruit, citrus and hazelnut palate.
- ● **Keenan Reserve Cabernet Sauvignon / 2012 / Spring Mountain District / $$$$** Despite its massive structure, this Cab has voluptuous dark fruit and seamless tannins. Smoke, herbs, graphite and forest-floor notes give it a Bordeaux-like profile.

ROBERT MONDAVI WINERY

The late Robert Mondavi kick-started the modern California wine industry when he created this project in 1966. After the stormy years that led to the family's loss of their iconic winery in a 2004 merger with Constellation Brands, the Mondavi ship has righted itself to an impressive extent. With the cellar in the hands of Geneviève Janssens since 1997, Mondavi wines continue to compete with Napa's best at the high end and offer terrific values on less expensive bottlings. Mondavi also retains some of Napa's most prized sources for Cabernet Sauvignon, and the winery that invented the name Fumé Blanc (for Sauvignon Blanc) deserves its fine reputation for that wine as well.

○ **Robert Mondavi Winery Reserve Fumé Blanc / 2013 / Napa Valley / $$$** This steely-structured yet rich Sauvignon Blanc from the famed To Kalon Vineyard offers aromas and flavors of acacia flowers, lemon zest, guava, lemon drop, fresh herbs and toast.

● **Robert Mondavi Winery Cabernet Sauvignon / 2013 / Oakville / $$$** Mondavi's Reserve Cabernet is a stunner, but this Oakville bottling deserves attention for its richness, silky texture and concentration, at about one-third the price of the Reserve.

ROBERT SINSKEY VINEYARDS

Free-spirit Robert Sinskey—his company bio lists his title as Daydream Believer, Vintner—left California to attend art school in New York, then later returned to assist his father, a onetime hobbyist winegrower. As he expanded his own vineyard holdings to 200 acres in Carneros and Stags Leap, Sinskey remained true to his convictions. One of California's pioneer biodynamic farmers and winemakers, Sinskey operates much of his winery via solar power and his vehicles with biodiesel (and his vineyards are now certified organic). He also has a very graceful hand with his wines, producing a small group of vineyard-based, fancifully named blends and some lovely, food-friendly Pinot Noirs.

○ **Abraxas Vin de Terroir / 2013 / Carneros / $$$** This blend of Riesling, Pinot Blanc, Pinot Gris and Gewürztraminer is full of verve and juicy peach, apple and citrus, with hints of spice and minerality.

● **Robert Sinskey Vineyards Pinot Noir / 2012 / Carneros / $$$** From its translucent ruby color to the lingering pure-fruit finish, this is a pretty Pinot Noir of great elegance and class. It brims with bright cherry and raspberry personality.

ROMBAUER VINEYARDS

Rombauer's decadent, golden Chardonnays became one of the best-known examples of the buttery, oaky style that defined California Chardonnay in the 1980s and '90s, and they remain a staple of restaurant wine lists. Today this family-run estate—founded in St. Helena in 1980 by Koerner and Joan Rombauer—enjoys a loyal following. The family has continued to make major investments in vineyard land, most recently securing a prime Zinfandel source in the Sierra Foothills and another 150 acres of Chardonnay in the Sonoma Carneros region. With winemaker Richie Allen in charge of the cellar since 2008, Rombauer's fans know that its wines will be consistently well made.

○ **Rombauer Vineyards Sauvignon Blanc / 2015 / Napa Valley / $$**
In contrast to Rombauer's viscous Chardonnays, this is brisk, bright and slightly pungent. Its grapefruit and lemon aromas and flavors gain heft from 10 percent barrel fermentation, with the rest in stainless steel to preserve freshness.

● **Rombauer Vineyards Cabernet Sauvignon / 2013 / Napa Valley / $$$**
Sometimes overshadowed by the Chardonnay's notoriety, the Rombauer Cab is an honest drink: rich, smooth and full of ripe black currant and blueberry fruit, with a hint of oak spice.

RUDD OAKVILLE ESTATE

Entrepreneur Leslie Rudd (former owner of Dean & DeLuca) bought the old Girard Winery in the heart of Oakville's Cabernet country in 1996. Rudd's deep pockets allowed him to assemble an all-star team to revitalize the 55-acre estate, whose prestige neighbors include Screaming Eagle and PlumpJack (see p. 69). The winery declassifies (i.e., sells off) up to half its wine lots each vintage, a sign of the seriousness of its intent. The enthusiasm of connoisseurs for Rudd's ultra-premium wines, such as the magisterial Oakville Estate red, speaks eloquently for itself.

○ **Rudd Sauvignon Blanc / 2014 / Mount Veeder / $$$$**
This winning white offers enticing floral and mineral aromas and a crisp, textured palate of white peach, citrus and pear.

● **Rudd Oakville Estate / 2012 / Oakville / $$$$**
Cabernets Sauvignon (70 percent) and Franc (18 percent) predominate in this red blend, which displays the latter's floral, red cherry and herbal signature and the former's rich black cherry, cedar and tobacco notes. Fleshy and seamless, it has excellent tannin and acid structure.

SAINTSBURY

Founded in 1981 by David Graves and Dick Ward, Saintsbury helped prove that Carneros wasn't just grazing land: With its warm afternoons and cool breezes, it was ideal territory for Pinot Noir and Chardonnay. Along the way, the two friends acquired a new understanding of how to handle the fickle Pinot Noir grape. Their style has always emphasized finesse and a slow, seductive reveal as opposed to blockbuster power, and the Carneros bottling remains one of the best deals in California Pinot Noir. Saintsbury's next chapter is unscrolling as the winery adds new cool-climate vineyard sources, giving Tim Colla, winemaker as of 2015, new resources to work with.

○ **Saintsbury Chardonnay / 2013 / Carneros / $$**
This great-value Chardonnay is all about elegance and understatement. It delivers zesty white peach, kaffir lime and green papaya notes and a clean, crisp, barrel-spice finish.

● **Saintsbury Lee Vineyard Pinot Noir / 2014 / Carneros / $$$$**
Replanting of Ira and Shirley Lee's vineyard to diverse Pinot Noir clones starting in the 1990s paid off in this succulent bottling with red and black cherry and Santa Rosa plum accented by cola and spice notes.

SCARECROW WINE

This tiny-production, ultra-luxury label draws its grapes from a vineyard planted in 1945 at Napa's Cabernet ground zero in Rutherford, adjacent to historic Inglenook. Long owned by MGM executive J.J. Cohn (among his successes: *The Wizard of Oz*—hence the Scarecrow name), the estate is now run by his grandson, photographer/vintner Bret Lopez. It was Lopez who decided that these pedigreed grapes, which had gone into fabled wines like Opus One and Insignia, should be bottled by the estate. With production under the direction of talented Celia Welch and well-regarded vineyardist Michael Wolf, the property's two wines sell out quickly via the mailing list.

● **M. Étain / 2012 / Rutherford / $$$$**
This lovely Cabernet is more forward and easy to drink on release than the main wine, but not remotely lacking in depth.

● **Scarecrow / 2012 / Rutherford / $$$$**
From one of the few old-vine Cabernet Sauvignon parcels in Napa Valley, this sought-after red is voluptuous, but with enough tannic structure not to be overblown.

SCHRAMSBERG VINEYARDS

Perched on a mountainside above St. Helena, venerable Schramsberg—the late Jack and Jamie Davies revived the century-old winery in 1965—has long been one of Napa Valley's most beautiful properties. And these days it just might be making its finest sparkling wines ever under the direction of their son Hugh Davies (see J. Davies, p. 50). Bottlings like the Blanc de Blancs (served by Richard Nixon on his historic trip to China) and the high-end J. Schram and Schramsberg Reserve show the result of years spent honing the craft. Any given wine may be blended from Napa, Sonoma, Mendocino and Marin County grapes, and vinified in multiple ways (e.g., barrel-fermented and/or steel-fermented) to layer in complexity.

○ **Schramsberg Blanc de Blancs / 2013 / North Coast / $$$**
This all-Chardonnay sparkler charms with its racy acidity, tight bubbles and crisp Granny Smith apple and citrus fruit. A small portion was aged in oak, lending depth to the palate.

○ **Schramsberg J. Schram / 2007 / North Coast / $$$$**
Named for founder Jacob Schram, this sparkler is complex and layered, with a pronounced yeasty character to accompany the complex apple, citrus and orange rind flavors.

SEAVEY VINEYARD

In 1979 the Seavey family purchased a friend's Conn Creek Valley cattle ranch, which had been a winery in the 1870s. They dedicated their efforts to producing Cabernet Sauvignon, Merlot and Chardonnay on the still-lovely site. Today, it is the lineup of Cabs that leads well-heeled wine pilgrims to the Seaveys' door. Under the longtime direction of esteemed consultant Philippe Melka, who works alongside resident winemaker Jim Duane, these wines have established a reputation for envelope-pushing ripeness, flavor saturation and massive, well-tamed tannin structure. The entry-level Caravina red blend provides a taste of the richness without breaking the bank.

○ **Seavey Chardonnay / 2014 / Napa Valley / $$$**
This barrel-fermented Chardonnay is both bracing and broad, with generous apple, Asian pear and citrus notes.

● **Seavey Caravina Cabernet Sauvignon / 2013 / Napa Valley / $$$**
Very approachable now and likely for the next five years, this good-value (for Napa) Cab is loaded with juicy red cherry and red plum fruit, framed by spicy oak and minty herbs.

SEQUOIA GROVE

Sequoia Grove has flown under the radar for many years—surprising, given its location on heavily traveled Highway 29, and the fine dollar-to-quality ratio of its entry-level wines. It also enjoys several advantages, including an ace winemaking team headed by president and director of winemaking Michael Trujillo and winemaker Molly Hill and two estate vineyards on the famous Cabernet soils of the Rutherford Bench, plus long-term relationships with prime vineyards such as Morisoli in Rutherford. (The Chardonnays are grown in Carneros.) The winery's impressive quality shines through in the flagship Cambium red and the single-vineyard Cabernets. The far more gently priced Napa Cabernet bottling is well worth searching out.

○ **Sequoia Grove Chardonnay / 2014 / Napa Valley / $$**
The majority of its grapes were grown in Carneros, giving the wine a light-bodied texture and flavors of citrus and green apple. Barrel aging adds a yeasty, spicy note to the finish.

● **Sequoia Grove Cabernet Sauvignon / 2013 / Napa Valley / $$$**
Delivering a big bang for the buck, this is an elegant, medium-full-bodied Cab, with pure blackberry and currant fruit, gentle tannins and notes of earth, toast and spice.

SHAFER VINEYARDS

Former publishing executive John Shafer founded his Stags Leap District winery in the late 1970s; his son Doug has run the property since 1994. Shafer's longtime winemaker, Elias Fernandez, has a talent for crafting formidable wines that maintain balance despite their power. That quality is best seen in the flagship cuvée, Hillside Select, arguably the most sought-after Stags Leap District Cabernet. Easier to find are Shafer's three other reds: the One Point Five Cabernet; an inky Merlot; and a full-throttle Syrah blend, Relentless. The winery is also known for its super-juicy Red Shoulder Ranch Chardonnay.

○ **Shafer Red Shoulder Ranch Chardonnay / 2014 / Carneros / $$$**
Wild-yeast fermentation in oak and stainless steel barrels and no malolactic fermentation make for a wine that's full-bodied and potent, yet perfectly balanced and flat-out delicious.

● **Shafer One Point Five Cabernet Sauvignon / 2013 / Stags Leap District / $$$$** Named for the "generation and a half" of Shafer father-son winemaking, this polished Cab has exuberant black and blue fruit, floral aromatics and velvety tannins.

SIGNORELLO ESTATE

The late Ray Signorello, Sr., planted grapevines at his Napa Valley retreat in the 1970s, planning to simply sell the fruit. But a bumper crop in 1985 left the former oil and gas executive with unsold grapes, and a family brand was born. Today, Ray Signorello, Jr., and winemaker Pierre Birebent make very fine red and white Bordeaux blends and Chardonnays, all estate-grown from their vineyards on the Silverado trail south of Oakville, and all premium- to super-premium-priced. The showpieces are the two wines dedicated to the younger Signorello's parents and selected each vintage from the top barrels in the cellar, the Padrone red and Hope's Cuvée Chardonnay.

○ **Signorello Hope's Cuvée Chardonnay / 2014 / Napa Valley / $$$$**
Named for Ray Signorello, Jr.'s mother, Hope, this is a full-throttle wine with notes of butter, toast, poached pear and caramel; it's best paired with cream-sauce dishes.

● **Signorello Padrone / 2012 / Napa Valley / $$$$**
This mostly Cabernet Sauvignon red honors Ray Signorello, Sr. It's seamless and richly layered, with dense black fruit, silky tannins, oak spice and ample structure for extended cellaring.

SILVERADO VINEYARDS

The late Diane Disney Miller and her husband, Ron (onetime CEO of what became the Walt Disney Company), bought into Napa Valley in the mid-1970s, purchasing a hilltop Stags Leap District site with a spectacular view. The Millers acquired top vineyards around the area as the years went by—Vineburg in Carneros for Chardonnay, for example, and Soda Creek Ranch for Sangiovese and Zinfandel. The winery has also benefited from continuity: Many of its current managers, including winemaker Jon Emmerich, worked with their predecessors and came up through the ranks. Silverado's line of estate-grown wines is consistently well made and deserving of more attention.

○ **Silverado Vineyards Miller Ranch Sauvignon Blanc / 2015 / Napa Valley / $$** From the winery's estate vineyard comes this refreshing, juicy wine, with mouthwatering citrus and tangerine flavors and steely structure.

● **Silverado Vineyards GEO Cabernet Sauvignon / 2012 / Coombsville / $$$$** Named for the winery's Mount George Vineyard in the newish Coombsville AVA, this big, ripe red delivers blackberry fruit, vanillin oak and spice, and an earthy, tannic finish.

SILVER OAK CELLARS

Silver Oaks leapt to fame in the 1980s and '90s—when buyers would line up at the winery for their cases on release day (a tradition that continues)—and has retained a hold on wine lovers' affections ever since. Despite the retirement of founding vintner and guiding light Justin Meyer over a decade ago, and a substantial increase in case production, winemaker Daniel Baron (formerly of Dominus; see p. 37) continues Silver Oak's ways with some of California's most palate-flattering Cabernets. The more forward Alexander Valley bottling is released six months earlier than the Napa Valley Cabernet, but both share a refined smoothness derived partly from extended cellaring.

● **Silver Oak Cabernet Sauvignon / 2011 / Alexander Valley / $$$$** Production costs, not quality, drive the price difference between this Sonoma Cab and the costlier Napa version. It has similarly soft tannins, savory herbaceousness and a riper fruit profile.

● **Silver Oak Cabernet Sauvignon / 2011 / Napa Valley / $$$$** The winery's use of American oak for aging gives its Cabs a savory, herbal note. The Napa bottling is medium-bodied and very drinkable now, with ripe red fruit and supple tannins.

SMITH-MADRONE

The bushy-bearded Smith brothers, Stuart and Charles, were among the first in the valley's modern era to succumb to Spring Mountain's charms. They built their winery themselves in the 1970s from concrete blocks and timber. Dry-farmed and planted on steep grades at between 1,400 and 2,000 feet, this is one of the area's most scenically spectacular and wild vineyards. The brothers' beards are white now, but the Smiths have stuck to their guns, producing 4,000 cases of distinctive, all-estate wine their way, which typically means eschewing big extraction and massive alcohol levels in the reds, and crafting minerally Rieslings and Chardonnays for the long haul.

○ **Smith-Madrone Riesling / 2013 / Spring Mountain District / $$** One of the few hallmark California Rieslings, this is structured and sleek, with only a hint of sweetness to balance racy acidity. Appley and floral, it's a great match for spice-laced pork chops.

● **Smith-Madrone Cabernet Sauvignon / 2012 / Spring Mountain District / $$$** This is a sturdily built, great-value Cab that will only improve with age. Tannic and tight now, it has blackberry, black currant and dried-herb components and excellent acidity.

SOMERSTON ESTATE

Real estate developer Allan Chapman began acquiring a huge swath of the eastern Vaca Mountains in 2004, eventually accumulating over 1,600 acres in two stunning, hidden valleys. Some of the grapes grown on the property are sold to prestigious clients; partner and winemaker Craig Becker puts the rest to use under three labels. The high-end, single-vineyard-block Somerston Estate line is headlined by a massively structured Cabernet Sauvignon. The Priest Ranch label is notable for its value for quality. Priced for everyday drinking, the Highflyer line (Becker is a pilot) draws grapes from all over California.

○ **Priest Ranch Grenache Blanc / 2014 / Napa Valley / $$** A rich wine boasting juicy peach and apple notes with hints of baking spice, it's sweet on the palate, but with enough acidity to balance the mouthfeel. Minerality runs right through it.

● **Somerston Celestial Cabernet Sauvignon / 2013 / Napa Valley / $$$$** Borderline jammy, this is loaded with luscious dark berry and cherry flavor, accented by mocha and dark chocolate notes.

SPOTTSWOODE ESTATE VINEYARD & WINERY

Spottswoode has been making classically structured Napa Valley Cabernet since 1982. Although this in itself puts the estate among the old guard of Napa's modern wine scene, its lovely Victorian house and grounds in St. Helena date to more than 100 years earlier. The wines come chiefly from the family-run property (presided over by Beth Novak Milliken), which has been farmed organically for over 30 years. Spottswoode produces four wines: the triple-digit-priced, all-estate Cabernet Sauvignon; the Lyndenhurst Cabernet, made partly from purchased grapes; the acclaimed Napa-Sonoma Sauvignon Blanc; and a Syrah for club members only—all notable for their balance and elegance, though none is a shrinking violet.

○ **Spottswoode Sauvignon Blanc / 2015 / Sonoma and Napa Counties / $$$** Made largely with Sonoma Mountain grapes, this wine is nervy and focused, with lime, Meyer lemon, kiwi fruit, white peach and dried-herb complexity. An ideal match for oysters.

● **Spottswoode Cabernet Sauvignon / 2013 / St. Helena / $$$$** Bold yet beautiful, this offers pretty floral and dried cranberry aromas, concentrated black and blue fruit and silky tannins. Generous and deeply flavored now, it will remain a great drink for two decades or more.

SPRING MOUNTAIN VINEYARD

A stunningly picturesque estate high above Napa Valley, Spring Mountain comprises three 19th-century vineyard and winery properties, including the late-Victorian Miravalle mansion, made famous as TV's *Falcon Crest* and now used for sit-down tastings. Spring Mountain also has a reputation for experimental sustainable viticulture. The winery farms 226 acres out of nearly 850 on an estate that rises to elevations of 1,450 feet and produces wines as diverse as Pinot Noir, Syrah and Chardonnay. The flagship Elivette red blend is sourced from low-yielding mountain soils that infuse the wine with a notable depth of flavor.

○ **Spring Mountain Vineyard Chardonnay / 2013 / Napa Valley / $$$**
This limited-production wine is worth a search for its purity of peach, tangerine and mineral character.

● **Spring Mountain Vineyard Elivette / 2012 / Napa Valley / $$$$**
An elegant, finely balanced expression of mountain Cabernet Sauvignon (blended with Cabernet Franc, Petit Verdot and Merlot), this displays New World richness and deep fruit, plus Old World tobacco and herb notes. It should age beautifully.

STAGLIN FAMILY VINEYARD

Since its establishment in 1985, this estate has become a cornerstone of Napa's Rutherford District, and its founders, Shari and Garen Staglin, are pillars of the community. Managed by the talented team of Fredrik Johansson (winemaker), David Abreu (vineyard manager; see p. 17) and Michel Rolland (consultant), Staglin's 51 acres of organically farmed vineyards produce some of Napa's most sought-after Cabs. Offerings range from pricey (the entry-level Salus Chardonnay) to extremely pricey (the INEO Cabernet blend), and availability can be limited. All profits from the sales of the three Salus wines—the Chardonnay and two Cabs, named for the Roman goddess of well-being—are donated to mental health research.

○ **Staglin Family Vineyard Salus Chardonnay / 2014 / Napa Valley / $$$**
This medium-bodied Chardonnay shows less oak influence than the Staglin Estate bottling, delivering crisp lemon, melon, pineapple and spice aromas and flavors.

● **Staglin Family Vineyard 30th Anniversary Selection Cabernet Sauvignon / 2012 / Rutherford / $$$$** The 2012 vintage of Staglin's flagship offers intense blackberry and mulberry fruit tinged with pipe tobacco and bittersweet chocolate notes.

STAG'S LEAP WINE CELLARS

In 2007 Warren Winiarski sold this landmark Napa Valley winery to Ste. Michelle Wine Estates and Tuscan giant Antinori, which brought in star consultant Renzo Cotarella. Quality, which had begun to plateau, is on the rise: It's easy to imagine current vintages competing with marquee Bordeaux, as a Stag's Leap Cabernet famously did in winning the Judgment of Paris tasting in 1976. Competition is far stronger now in the valley, but the opportunity—and the superbly situated vineyards—are there for the winery to reclaim the iconic status it once held via its lineup of Bordeaux-style estate reds: Cask 23, S.L.V. and Fay. The less pricey Artemis and Karia bottlings can be terrific, too.

○ **Stag's Leap Wine Cellars Karia Chardonnay / 2014 / Napa Valley / $$$** Sourced from Napa Valley's cool southern end, this crisp, minerally, graceful wine (*karia* is derived from the Greek for "graceful") glows when paired with grilled swordfish.

● **Stag's Leap Wine Cellars S.L.V. Cabernet Sauvignon / 2012 / Napa Valley / $$$$** From 45-year-old vines in the winery's first vineyard, this elegant Cab delivers cassis, dark cherry and dark plum fruit with forest-floor, cedar and Christmas-spice notes.

STAGS' LEAP WINERY

This winery was once famous for two things: some of California's top bottlings of old-vine Petite Sirah, and the feud between its owner, Carl Doumani, and his neighbor, Warren Winiarski, of Stag's Leap Wine Cellars (see above), who couldn't agree on anything (note the apostrophe in the wineries' names). In 1997 Doumani sold out to Beringer (now part of Treasury Wine Estates), and the new owners invested significantly in the 1890s property. Stags' Leap Winery produces a sterling group of wines (especially reds). The Petite Sirah and decades-old field-blend grapes in its vineyards shape the two top offerings: the Ne Cede Malis Petite Sirah and the Cabernet–Petite Sirah blend, Audentia.

○ **Stags' Leap Viognier / 2014 / Napa Valley / $$$**
This firm and focused Viognier has the grape's signature pear, peach and honeysuckle perfume, and a crisp, juicy palate. Delicious with prawns, scallops and spice-rubbed chicken.

● **Stags' Leap The Leap Cabernet Sauvignon / 2012 / Napa Valley / $$$$** While it will benefit from cellaring, this Cab is wonderfully drinkable now, with vivid blackberry and cherry fruit, fine tannins and complex notes of spice and cedar.

STELTZNER VINEYARDS

Richard Steltzner is a true roots and vines man. While still engaged in vineyards management, Steltzner bought into the Stags Leap District way back in 1965—his was only the second Cabernet Sauvignon vineyard in the area—and farmed grapes there for over a decade before his first release in 1977. The Steltzner family, who helped establish the Stags Leap appellation, sold their home vineyard and winery to PlumpJack (see p. 69) in 2012 and now operate out of their facility in the town of Napa. With a capacity of around 9,000 cases, the family-run winery is small, but the Stelzners did retain a Stags Leap District vineyard, and they have clearly not lost their touch with velvety Cabernets.

● **Steltzner Cabernet Sauvignon / 2012 / Stags Leap District / $$$$**
With soft tannins, vivid red and black cherry fruit and hints of vanilla and black pepper, this wine is a delight. What it lacks in intensity and bombast, it makes up for in elegance and drinkability.

STONY HILL VINEYARD

Fred and Eleanor McCrea came upon this rocky patch of land—it had been a goat ranch—high on Spring Mountain in the early 1940s. They were determined to plant Chardonnay, the grape that made the wine they loved in Burgundy, despite the fact that it was unknown to the American drinking public. With the second and third generations of McCreas now running Stony Hill Vineyard, its devoted fans can rest easy: Longtime winemaker Mike Chelini isn't about to change the winery's Chablis-style flagship. Standing firm against fashion for decades, he still vinifies Chardonnay to keep the original fruit, vibrancy and acidity at the fore.

○ **Stony Hill Chardonnay / 2013 / Napa Valley / $$$**
Without malolactic fermentation to soften its minerality, this white is fresh and crisp, with apple, pear and citrus notes. Five years or more in bottle will unveil layers of spice and oak texture complexity.

● **Stony Hill Cabernet Sauvignon / 2012 / Napa Valley / $$$**
Suave tannins and lush dark cherry and plum fruit are countered by bracing acidity and a streak of minerality from nose to finish. Forest-floor, cigar-box and leafy herbal notes add a savory component to this complex, ageworthy wine.

STORYBOOK MOUNTAIN VINEYARDS

Jerry and Sigrid Seps make extraordinary Zinfandels from their old, high-elevation, certified organic vineyards in the Mayacamas Mountains in northern Napa Valley. Zin vines were first planted in these red clay soils in the 1880s, and it is obviously a fine match of grape to *terroir*. Storybook's Zins are not jammy, super-ripe versions of the grape. They are muscular wines with a pleasingly austere edge, built to develop with age. The prize here is the often sold-out Estate Reserve Zinfandel, but the excellent estate Cabernets and Viognier deserve consideration, too. In combination, the winery's Zinfandel and Bordeaux reds produce a synergy in the lovely proprietary wine Antaeus.

○ **Storybook Mountain Viognier / 2014 / Napa Valley / $$$** Red-wine makers see the need for a white on their roster, and for Storybook, it's Viognier. The wine is dry and structured, yet gushes with ripe pear, peach and honeysuckle personality.

● **Storybook Mountain Vineyards Estate Reserve Zinfandel / 2012 / Napa Valley / $$$$** Uncommonly elegant for a Zin, this is lean and focused, with wildflower and savory herb aromas and a palate of moderately ripe yet zesty red and black fruit.

SWITCHBACK RIDGE

The Peterson family makes only three wines, all from a single estate, and all three are potential home runs in most vintages. They certainly know the soil: Though Switchback Ridge began bottling its own wine only in 1999, the Petersons have farmed their 100 acres—21 of them under vine—at the mouth of Dutch Henry Canyon since 1914. The vinifying of the estate's Cabernet Sauvignon, Merlot and Petite Sirah has been under the direction of Robert Foley (formerly of Pride Mountain and Hourglass; see pp. 70 and 49) since the start. His big, ripe, opulent way with these reds has gained the winery an avid following.

● **Switchback Ridge Petite Sirah / 2013 / Napa Valley / $$$** Buckle up for this 16.5 percent alcohol wine, with port-like richness and power, plus jammy boysenberry pie and spicy oak. Its lush texture and ripeness make it ideal for cherry-sauced duck breast.

● **Switchback Ridge Cabernet Sauvignon / 2013 / Napa Valley / $$$$** At 15.5 percent alcohol, this is a big wine, super-ripe, full-bodied and decadent. Chocolate-covered cherries come to mind, with soft tannins and a mouth-coating finish.

TAKEN WINE COMPANY

Here's something new for Napa Valley: a project to produce "millennial driven wines." Taken Wine Company is the creation of Josh Phelps and Carlo Trinchero, two Napa boyhood friends whose fathers—Chris Phelps (see Ad Vivum, p. 19) and Roger Trinchero (see Trinchero Napa Valley, p. 88)—also happen to be in the business. With their emphasis on reasonable pricing and marketing via social media, the young partners seem to be making a splash. Their top-of-the-line bottling is the Taken Cabernet-Merlot blend, priced at under $40. The Complicated wines, from outside Napa, are considerably cheaper, and the Available wines, from Italy, are terrific bargains.

○ **Complicated Chardonnay / 2014 / Sonoma Coast / $$**
With pear, peach and citrus fruit, gentle oak and a fresh finish, this ticks all the boxes for consumer-friendly Chardonnay.

● **Taken / 2013 / Napa Valley / $$$**
This 60/40 Cabernet Sauvignon–Merlot blend is a drink-now wine with smooth tannins and juicy black cherry, blackberry, chocolate and coffee personality.

TERLATO VINEYARDS

This is a sprawling endeavor, as the Terlato family, highly regarded Chicago-area wine importers, have purchased wine properties in Napa (Stags Leap, Rutherford), Sonoma (Russian River Valley, Dry Creek Valley) and in Italy, too. In California, three winemakers produce the Terlato Family Vineyards line under the supervision of Napa-based Doug Fletcher. Its dozen wines include two ultra-premium-priced Napa Valley proprietary red blends: the Cab-dominated Episode, and the newer Galaxy, which blends Syrah with Cabernet and Merlot. Dear to founder Tony Terlato's heart (he imported Italy's Santa Margherita Pinot Grigio for 36 years) is the Pinot Gris, sourced from the Russian River Valley.

○ **Terlato Family Vineyards Pinot Gris / 2014 / Russian River Valley / $$**
Richer and fruiter than an Italian-style Pinot Grigio, Terlato's Pinot Gris delivers juicy citrus and tropical yellow stone-fruit flavors, with a finish that's rich yet refreshing.

● **Episode / 2012 / Napa Valley / $$$$**
This Bordeaux-style blend is redolent of wild blackberry and dark cherry fruit, with polished tannins and spicy oak notes. Luxurious now, it has the structure to improve in the cellar.

TOR KENWARD FAMILY WINES

A familiar figure in the wine industry during the nearly 30 years he represented Beringer, Tor Kenward took the leap into making his own wine after retiring in 2001. His time in the business gave him strong opinions on Napa's and Sonoma's best vineyards, and definite ideas about how to make great wine, including keeping a sharp focus on farming and concentrating on small batches in the cellar. He and winemaker Jeff Ames turn out a range of tiny-production bottlings, many from single vineyards, that can be extraordinary for their layered complexity. The TOR label is for Cabernet Sauvignon and Chardonnay, while the ROCK label goes on his Syrahs and Grenaches.

○ **TOR Hyde Vineyard Chardonnay / 2014 / Napa Valley / $$$** Larry Hyde's illustrious Carneros vineyard supplied the small-berry, small-cluster Wente clone grapes for this intense yet graceful wine marked by palate-cleansing acidity and verve.

● **TOR Cimarossa Vineyard Cabernet Sauvignon / 2013 / Howell Mountain / $$$$** Of the winery's many Cabs, this is the most intriguing, for its concentrated black fruit seasoned with mint, rosemary and *herbes de Provence*. Cellar for five or more years.

TREFETHEN FAMILY VINEYARDS

The third generation of Trefethens is now putting its stamp on the family property, the largest contiguous single-owner vineyard in Napa Valley: a sprawling 600 acres centered on the 19th-century Eschol estate in the Oak Knoll District. The Trefethens have never bought an outside grape, meaning that microclimates on the property—in a relatively cool spot for the valley floor—have had to be matched to grapes with demands as various as thick-skinned, late-ripening Cabernet Sauvignon and aromatic whites like Riesling (with which they have had great success). Though its food-complementing, medium-rich Chardonnays put it on the map, the winery also produces fine Merlot and Cabernet Sauvignon with its trademark elegance.

○ **Trefethen Dry Riesling / 2015 / Oak Knoll District / $$** This scintillating Riesling delivers orange blossom, apricot, tropical fruit and ginger notes, all well preserved by fermentation in stainless steel.

● **Trefethen Cabernet Sauvignon / 2013 / Oak Knoll District / $$$** Blackberry and black currant fruit, dried herbs, subtle oak spice and supple tannins are beautifully balanced here.

TRICYCLE WINE PARTNERS

Founded by Arpad and Peter Molnar and their friend Michael Terrien in 2003, this is a two-label, two-vineyard small-batch wine company. The Molnar brothers grew up on their father's sea-level Poseidon Vineyard in Napa's Carneros region, south of the Mayacamas Mountains. The cool-climate Chardonnay and Pinot Noir bottled under the Poseidon Vineyard label are made with an emphasis on pure fruit rather than jamminess or oak. In the northern Mayacamas, up in Lake County, is Tricycle's 2,640-foot-high Obsidian Ridge Vineyard, which yields Cabernet Sauvignon and Syrah with classic mountain-grape density. The Molnars' Hungarian roots show up in the barrels, imported from Hungary's Kádár cooperage, which the family co-owns.

○ **Poseidon Vineyard Chardonnay / 2014 / Carneros / $$**
A slight (and pleasant) charry note in the aroma leads to a palate that's crisp and clean, reminiscent of lemon oil, Granny Smith apple and white peach, with firm acidity and focus.

● **Obsidian Ridge Cabernet Sauvignon / 2013 / Red Hills Lake County / $$** From a vineyard strewn with heat-retaining obsidian shards, this is one of Lake County's finest wines year after year. It has lush dark-berry flavors, Hungarian oak spice and significant yet ripe tannins. Serve it with New York strip steak.

TRINCHERO NAPA VALLEY

In response to market demand for white wines in the 1970s and '80s, a time when California's vineyards were planted mostly to red varieties, Bob Trinchero invented White Zinfandel at Sutter Home. With those blush-wine profits, the Trinchero family went on to create an ambitious, high-end estate. Over the better part of two decades, they amassed an impressive array of vineyards across Napa's subregions and bought the old Folie à Deux winery in 2004. Winemaker Mario Monticelli (a Philippe Melka protégé) uses the varied vineyards to create over a dozen well-regarded reds (and one white) from Bordeaux grapes.

○ **Trinchero Napa Valley Mary's Sauvignon Blanc / 2015 / Calistoga / $$**
This offers ripe tropical fruit—pineapple, mango and green melon—over citrus, with a snap of lemon acidity on the finish.

● **Trinchero Napa Valley Cloud's Nest Vineyard Cabernet Sauvignon / 2012 / Mount Veeder / $$$$** Give this Cab a few years in bottle before tucking into its opaque black fruit, forest-floor, sandalwood and dried-herb qualities.

TRUCHARD VINEYARDS

In 1973, Texas-born physician Tony Truchard and his wife, Jo Ann, fell in love with Napa Valley, specifically the Carneros region, then considered iffy for wine grapes. They bought an abandoned 20-acre prune orchard and gradually expanded their holdings to some 400 acres. Though Carneros is better known now for Burgundian varieties such as Chardonnay and Pinot Noir, Truchard Vineyards has proved that Cabernet Sauvignon and Syrah can succeed here, too. Now run by Anthony Truchard II (his big brother has his own John Anthony Vineyards brand), the operation still sells grapes to top wineries while bottling its own fine wines at reasonable (for Napa) prices. The Chardonnay is a particular standout.

○ **Truchard Chardonnay / 2014 / Carneros / $$**
Bright and crisp, this Chardonnay has a gentle oak impact, allowing the pear, green apple, citrus and tropical fruit to star.

● **Truchard Cabernet Sauvignon / 2012 / Carneros / $$$**
A Carneros Cabernet? Yes, and it's a good one, thanks to a warm vintage. Fine tannins, medium body, black cherry fruit and underlying toastiness make for a flavorful yet elegant wine.

TURLEY WINE CELLARS

Larry Turley's once-small Napa Valley Zinfandel project got a strong liftoff in the 1990s from its first winemaker, superstar Helen Turley (his sister). With the winemaking reins handed over to the estimable Ehren Jordan and now to Tegan Passalacqua, Turley Wine Cellars continues to soar. Alas, even at their stiff prices, there's a long wait to get on the list to buy these explosively flavorful—and at their best, remarkably complex—Zins and Petite Sirahs. Larry Turley is an old-vineyard enthusiast, and many of his wines, including the sought-after Bedrock and Hayne bottlings, are sourced from decades- or century-old vines. Your best bet: Look for them at wine-oriented restaurants.

● **Turley Juvenile Zinfandel / 2014 / California / $$$**
This young-vine Zin from a multiplicity of top vineyards offers flamboyant red and black fruit and brambly character, flooding the palate with flavor.

● **Turley Hayne Vineyard Petite Syrah / 2013 / Napa Valley / $$$$**
From vines planted in 1953, this jammy, potent wine is a volcano of voluptuous black- and blueberry, with melted dark chocolate and impressive tannins to support the fruit's weight.

TURNBULL WINE CELLARS

This lovely winery prominently situated on Highway 29 is chiefly associated with three things: art, architecture and, most of all, first-rate Cabernet Sauvignon. The late founder, William Turnbull, was a noted architect (he collaborated on Sonoma's Sea Ranch) and an aficionado of fine art photography, as visitors to the winery's gallery can attest. Still family owned, Turnbull produces modest quantities of all-estate-grown wines from four vineyards around the valley, with notable successes as well with Sauvignon Blanc and Viognier. While Turnbull followers most eagerly await the triple-digit-priced top-of-the-line Cabs like the Pierra and Black Label bottlings, more budget-conscious drinkers know just how good the Napa Valley Cabernet Sauvignon bottling can be.

○ **Turnbull Sauvignon Blanc / 2015 / Oakville / $$**
Solving the problem of what to pair with asparagus and artichokes, this wine delivers grapefruit, Rangpur lime notes, crisp texture and just 12.7 percent alcohol.

● **Turnbull Cabernet Sauvignon / 2013 / Napa Valley / $$$**
This Cab offers a lot of bang for the buck. With muscular tannins, concentrated red and black fruit and a savory black-olive edge, it pairs beautifully with rare prime rib.

VENGE VINEYARDS

There was no doubt in Kirk Venge's mind that he would follow his winemaker father, Nils (of Saddleback Cellars fame), into the family business. After graduating from UC Davis in 1998, paying his dues in various cellars and amassing a roster of consulting clients, the younger Venge joined his father in resurrecting the old Rossini Ranch, a ghost winery in Oakville, as Venge Vineyards, with Kirk as winemaker. In 2008, the property was sold to Bill Foley (see Foley Estates, p. 166), but Kirk acquired ownership of the brand and bought a vineyard in Calistoga. Today Venge Vineyards is scoring big with its massive Scout's Honor Zin blend, muscular Oakville Cabernets and unique bottlings like the lively Spettro white.

● **Venge Vineyards Scout's Honor / 2013 / Napa Valley / $$$**
This blend of old-vine Zinfandel, Petite Sirah, Charbono and Syrah tastes balanced and not at all hot (despite its 15.4 percent alcohol), with generous ripe cherry and berry flavors and herbal spice from partial aging in new American oak.

VIADER

Argentinean-born Delia Viader came to Napa Valley in the 1980s with an intimidating résumé of academic degrees and a maverick sense of determination that led her to plant a then-unconventionally spaced and oriented vineyard on a steep Howell Mountain slope. With her son Alan in charge of operations, Viader today is known for spicy, seductive reds, including the original proprietary blend of Cabernet Sauvignon and Cabernet Franc (the winery's signature bottling, nicknamed "Liquid Cashmere") and other outside-the-box offerings like the V Petit Verdot blend (a Napa benchmark for the varietal) and the DARE line, featuring Tempranillo and Cabernet Franc.

● **DARE Cabernet Franc / 2013 / Napa Valley / $$$**
Tobacco, dark chocolate, pencil lead and sage enhance the rich red and black fruit of this bold, plush-tannin, savory red.

● **Viader / 2013 / Napa Valley / $$$$**
This vintage of Viader's flagship "Liquid Cashmere" red relies on near-equal parts Cabernets Sauvignon and Franc for its red-fruit profile and aromas of spice and forest floor. Vanillin oak frames the fruit and supple tannins of this ageworthy wine.

VINEYARD 7 & 8

This winery's history began in 1999, when Manhattan money manager Launny Steffens bought a 40-acre parcel 2,000 feet up on Spring Mountain in Napa Valley. But the real takeoff came in the mid-2000s, when former Peter Michael winemaker Luc Morlet came on board, joining Launny's son Wesley, who had apprenticed at Harlan Estate (see p. 47). In 2014 the reins were handed to the estimable Martha McClellan (Sloan Estate), who has continued the winery's winning ways with small quantities of much-praised, super-premium-priced estate bottlings of Cabernet Sauvignon and Chardonnay. The earlier-drinking Correlation Cabernet is made partly from purchased grapes.

○ **Vineyard 7 & 8 Estate Chardonnay / 2013 / Spring Mountain District / $$$$** Full-bodied and beautifully layered in pear, green apple, white peach and creamy vanillin, it shows generous oak character and a lingering citrus finish.

● **Vineyard 7 & 8 Estate Cabernet Sauvignon / 2012 / Spring Mountain District / $$$$** With its tight tannins, this Cab requires aeration (or cellaring) to reveal its briary wild blackberry and plum fruit and crushed anise seed, graphite and tobacco complexity.

VINEYARD 29

A spare-no-expense venture, Chuck and Anne McMinn's operation is the very successful result of bringing together two fine estate vineyards and two of the most sought-after talents in California winemaking, vineyard manager David Abreu (see p. 17) and winemaker Philippe Melka (see p. 61). Cabernet is the image-maker here: The flagships are the single-vineyard 29 Estate and Aida Estate Cabs. But the winery also produces one of California's best Sauvignon Blancs, the vibrant, structured, Bordeaux-style 29 Estate bottling, as well as the sensational old-vine, dry-farmed Aida Estate Zinfandel. Though most of the 29 and Aida Estate Series wines are luxury priced, Vineyard 29's Cru line, made from purchased grapes, can offer great values.

○ **Cru Sauvignon Blanc / 2014 / Napa Valley / $$$**
The winery's introductory label white is crisp, tart and focused, with hints of lemongrass, grapefruit, white peach and lime zest.

● **29 Estate Cabernet Sauvignon / 2013 / St. Helena / $$$$**
Despite its power and intensity, there is outstanding freshness to this Cab, with palate-tingling black currant and blackberry fruit. Richly oaked and redolent of violets and purple sage blossoms, this beauty will last 20 years in the cellar.

THE VINEYARDIST

An oasis of cultivated civility, this winery is perched on a hidden shoulder of rugged Diamond Mountain. Bay Area lawyer Dirk Fulton and his wife, Becky Kukkola, acquired the estate in 2000 and restored its volcanic-soil vineyards. Star winemaker Mark Herold (see p. 58) talked them into selling off the first five vintages to other wineries before the sensational 2009 hit the heights he expected from the estate and was bottled under the Vineyardist label. The operation turns out a few hundred handcrafted cases a year each of two all–Cabernet Sauvignon wines: the highly pleasurable, super-refined The Vineyardist bottling and the Lazy Susan Ranch Cabernet.

● **Lazy Susan Ranch Cabernet Sauvignon / 2012 / Diamond Mountain District / $$$$** Crafted from younger estate vines, this knockout "second" wine has deep purple color and powerful yet velvety black fruit. New French oak adds mocha and spice notes.

● **The Vineyardist Cabernet Sauvignon / 2012 / Napa Valley / $$$$**
This collectors' magnet offers wildflower, blackberry and fresh earth aromas and a palate that is exotically fruity and velvety.

VOLKER EISELE FAMILY ESTATE

The year 2015 marked a watershed for this family winery in Chiles Valley. Its force-of-nature patriarch, Volker Eisele, passed away, leaving a legacy of pro-agriculture, anti-development activism that helped shaped modern Napa Valley. Reflecting the values of sustainability that Eisele championed, the 400-acre estate's 60 vineyard acres have been organically farmed for four decades. Under Volker's son, Alexander, the winery continues to thrive as a producer of estate-grown Bordeaux-style wines that combine flavor intensity with notable finesse. Among the best-known successes are the two blends: the Graves-style Gemini Sémillon–Sauvignon Blanc and the right bank–style Terzetto red.

○ **Volker Eisele Gemini / 2013 / Napa Valley / $$**
Sémillon takes the lead in this 80/20 Sémillon–Sauvignon Blanc blend. Aging in mostly old barrels added dimension to its lemon curd, guava, fig and citrus aromas and flavors.

● **Volker Eisele Terzetto / 2012 / Napa Valley / $$$$**
This concentrated blend of equal parts Cabernets Sauvignon and Franc and Merlot delivers tangy wild berry, cassis and plum fruit with vanilla, chocolate and savory notes.

VON STRASSER WINERY

Fans of Rudy von Strasser's wines will have to wait a few vintages to assess the effects of the sale of his Diamond Mountain winery and estate vineyard in 2015 and his subsequent purchase of the Lava Vine winery in Calistoga. Von Strasser retained ownership of his brand and inventory—meaning that his long-cellared, top-end Diamond Mountain Estate Cabernets and Reserve wines will continue to be released for a number of years and he'll go on making wines sourced from five Diamond Mountain vineyards. Von Strasser also has a deft hand with wines you won't see everywhere else in the valley, such as his Grüner Veltliner, Petit Verdot and Malbec Port bottlings.

○ **Von Strasser Grüner Veltliner / 2014 / Diamond Mountain District / $$$** Fuller and richer than Austrian versions, this Grüner is a mouthful of ripe peach, Asian pear and mango flavor, closing briskly with tangerine and green apple acidity.

● **Von Strasser Cabernet Sauvignon / 2012 / Diamond Mountain District / $$$** The winery's basic Cab is ripe and rewarding, with red and black cherry fruit enhanced by gentle herbs, espresso and black spice. Firm tannins are matched by plentiful acidity.

WHITEHALL LANE WINERY & VINEYARDS

Visitors to the Whitehall Lane tasting room off Highway 29 south of St. Helena have a pleasant surprise in store. The Leonardini family's winery produces a portfolio of high-quality bottlings—particularly Cabernet Sauvignons and Merlots—many at under $50. (While not bargain-basement, these are yesteryear prices for fine Napa wine.) The family bought the operation in 1993 and embarked on a program of upgrading facilities, purchasing vineyards (they now own seven, totaling 150 mostly valley-floor acres) and dramatically boosting case production, from 15,000 to 50,000. At the top of the line are the much-praised single-vineyard Cabs like the Leonardini Vineyard from St. Helena.

○ **Whitehall Lane Sauvignon Blanc / 2015 / Napa Valley / $$**
This white's floral aromas, tangy citrus and pineapple fruit and pleasantly pungent fresh herbs lead to a dry, lengthy finish.

● **Whitehall Lane Leonardini Estate Cabernet Sauvignon / 2013 / Napa Valley / $$$$** Almost all Cabernet Sauvignon with a splash of Petit Verdot, this shows fine polish and smooth texture. Full-bodied and fruity, with anise, cocoa and tarragon accents, it's ready to drink now and for another eight years.

WHITE ROCK VINEYARDS

The Vandendriessche family acquired this property in 1977, and has farmed the 35 planted acres without pesticides or herbicides for decades. Now in the hands of the second generation (Christopher makes the wine; his brother Michael tends the vines), White Rock goes on making high-quality wine the hard way: The white volcanic ash soils and 20-year-old vines yield a trickle of wine from tiny berries, and the naturally made wines are given an extended two to four years in bottle before release. Despite the expense involved in all this, the balanced, polished wines are very moderately priced for their excellent quality.

○ **White Rock Vineyards Chardonnay / 2013 / Napa Valley / $$$**
Steely, à la Chablis, this Chardonnay has white blossoms and lime cordial aromas and a medium-bodied palate of Meyer lemon, tart apple and yellow peach juiciness.

● **White Rock Vineyards Claret / 2012 / Napa Valley / $$$**
A blend of near-equal parts Merlot, Cabernets Sauvignon and Franc plus a bit of Petit Verdot, this is amazingly well priced for a Napa wine of this quality. Restrained oaking let its plump plum and black cherry aromas and flavors shine.

Sonoma County

CLAIM TO FAME

Sonoma County is almost a world unto itself. Its sprawling landscape is half again as large as the state of Rhode Island, stretching from sea cliffs on the Pacific Ocean to deep redwood groves, broad, khaki-colored rangeland and densely forested mountaintops. There are few places in the world that combine such jaw-dropping scenery with first-rate wine and a vast larder of superb local food to enjoy it with. The numbers say Chardonnay is king here, but Sonoma's 17 AVAs and 450 wineries produce a wealth of wines, including some of America's most sought-after Pinot Noirs, from places like the Russian River Valley and Sonoma Coast; many of the country's greatest Zinfandels, from Dry Creek Valley and elsewhere; and an unmatched array of Cabernet Sauvignon styles. Sonomans like to think of themselves as more down-to-earth than their Napa neighbors, and while there is some truth to this, there is also plenty of wealth and cosmopolitan sophistication on this side of the Mayacamas Mountains, especially in picture-perfect towns like Sonoma and Healdsburg, which make ideal bases for a wine country visit.

REGIONS TO KNOW

ALEXANDER VALLEY The warm, 22-mile-long Alexander Valley, home to 42 wineries, is known for high-quality versions of the kind of big-flavored, juicy, easy-to-love wines that put California on the map. The hillside and gravelly floor are prime Cabernet Sauvignon, Merlot and Zinfandel land; the loamier soils near the Russian River produce Chardonnay and Sauvignon Blanc.

DRY CREEK VALLEY California's Zinfandel heartland has a wealth of old-vine plantings and family winemakers with rare (for California) generations of expertise in the grape. The warm, gently rolling vineyards here also produce very fine Cabernets and rich Syrahs.

LOS CARNEROS The first AVA to be based on climate rather than political borders, this southern area of rolling hills straddling the Napa-Sonoma county line at the foggy upper reaches of San Francisco Bay came into vogue in the 1980s with the realization that Burgundian grapes like Pinot Noir and Chardonnay flourished in cooler climes. Somewhat overshadowed by newer, even cooler coastal areas elsewhere, Carneros still produces many notable still and sparkling wines.

RUSSIAN RIVER VALLEY Here, in Sonoma County's most famous subregion, warm days lead to sharply cooler nights, thanks to the evening fog that travels up the valley from the nearby Pacific. These are ideal conditions for Pinot Noir and Chardonnay—wines that at their best display great natural vibrancy, but with a distinctively Californian fruity ripeness.

SONOMA COAST This sprawling AVA's far western subsection is one of America's most promising Pinot Noir regions. The foggy Pacific fringe is a borderline place for ripening grapes, but one that yields intensely vibrant wines in top vintages.

SONOMA VALLEY Cooled by winds from north and south, the "Valley of the Moon" yields a range of well-balanced wines. This region—30 miles from San Francisco, with the town of Sonoma as its gateway—is a center of the county's wine tourism.

KEY GRAPES: WHITE

CHARDONNAY Sonoma may be famous for reds, but Chardonnay is actually the county's most-planted variety, with a justifiable following of its own, particularly when grown in the cooler portions of Russian River, Carneros and Sonoma Coast.

SAUVIGNON BLANC Dry Creek Valley and Russian River Valley produce sought-after dry Sauvignon Blancs in both oaked and unoaked styles, and a few high-end dessert-wine bottlings.

KEY GRAPES: RED

CABERNET SAUVIGNON Sonoma's Cabernets come in an assortment of styles, from supple, rich and accessible grown on the warm valley floors to more tannic, dense and muscular from higher in the Mayacamas and on Sonoma Mountain.

MERLOT Sonoma produces many notably luscious Merlots from locales like Sonoma Valley and Alexander Valley.

PINOT NOIR Sonoma is one of America's top sources for fine Pinot, including relatively richer wines from the Russian River Valley, racier, leaner styles from the Sonoma Coast and graceful, medium-bodied wines from Carneros.

ZINFANDEL Sonoma's Zinfandel is the deep red, chewy stuff, as opposed to the pink, sweet version. The grape originated in Croatia, but vintners in California, and in Sonoma County in particular, have taken it to new heights. This is the Zin heartland, with the state's largest concentration of old-vine vineyards.

Producers/ Sonoma County

ANTHILL FARMS WINERY

This artisan brand was started as a labor of love by three young Pinot Noir aficionados, Webster Marquez, Anthony Filiberti and David Low, who met while toting hoses around the cellars of esteemed Williams Selyem (see p. 147). All have other winery day jobs but devote considerable time and attention to their far-flung vineyard sources, ranging up into Mendocino County. Since its founding in 2004, Anthill Farms has gained a following for the three winemakers' neo-California way with Pinot and Syrah, which they craft with grace and complexity, rather than high-alcohol richness, from cool-climate sites. Production is extremely limited; join their mailing list to get release notices.

○ **Peugh Vineyard Chardonnay / 2014 / Russian River Valley / $$$**
This wine comes from a vineyard thought to have been planted in the 1940s, making it one of Sonoma's oldest Chardonnay sites. Low yields of intense grapes produced a mouth-coating wine with rich tropical aromas and flavors.

● **Anthill Farms Pinot Noir / 2014 / Sonoma Coast / $$$**
Refreshing acidity frames the juicy cherry and raspberry fruit, with violets, fresh herbs and savory truffle reflecting the wine's cool-climate provenance.

A. RAFANELLI WINERY

A. Rafanelli is one of Sonoma's undersung treasures, partly because it sells its wines only directly from the winery (by phone or in person; no email or online shop), with one release date a year—and there is a waiting list. This small (11,000-case), family-run operation may be tradition bound—Rafanellis have been growing grapes in Sonoma since the early 1900s—but that makes its wines all the more prized by Zin lovers. Winemaker Rashell Rafanelli-Fehlman carries on the family style, which runs to bright, ebulliently juicy reds (Cab and Merlot, as well as Zin). The well-priced, fan-favorite Dry Creek Valley Zinfandel, which makes up more than half of the production, is mostly from the family's own sometimes vertiginous 85 acres.

● **A. Rafanelli Zinfandel / 2014 / Dry Creek Valley / $$$**
Briary berry and cherry fruit melds with creamy oak and sturdy tannins in a wine that, as is usual for this producer, favors subtlety and refinement over ripeness and bombast.

● **A. Rafanelli Cabernet Sauvignon / 2013 / Dry Creek Valley / $$$$**
Rafanelli's Cabernet spends 22 months in French oak and shows an earthy edge to its nicely ripened, black cherry fruit and suave tannins. It will age for 15 years or more.

ARGOT WINES

"Never forget to indulge in the pure extravagance Pinot Noir is capable of," urges Argot's co-owner/winemaker, Justin Harmon. A small, artisan label produced in a custom crush facility, Argot turns out tiny quantities of luscious, full-pleasure wines in a range of generally gentle prices. Harmon's insight in planting Argot's estate vineyard on Sonoma Mountain was that heritage clones of Pinot Noir—those time-tested in California vineyards—might just fare better than fancy newcomers, and fans obviously feel the results bear him out. The flagship wines are the estate Pinots, Chardonnays and Syrahs, but Argot also offers a plethora of small-batch offerings from other vineyards.

○ **Argot Simpatico Ranch Chardonnay / 2013 / Bennett Valley / $$$**
Aged in new French oak barrels, this has a butterscotch/caramel streak from start to finish.

● **Slang Pinot Noir / 2014 / Sonoma County / $$**
Slang is Argot's offshoot label, with grapes sourced from throughout Sonoma. This wine is warm, rich and spicy (think cinnamon-topped berry cobbler), with a fresh finish.

ARNOT-ROBERTS

Childhood pals Duncan Arnot Meyers and Nathan Lee Roberts grew up around wine in Napa Valley but moved to Healdsburg to start their own winery in 2001. They produce 5,000 cases of a dozen or more mostly single-vineyard bottlings: old-vine field blends and overlooked varieties like Ribolla, as well as Cabernet Sauvignon, Chardonnay and Syrah. The wines are fermented with native yeasts, and often bottled unfined and unfiltered. Whites are steel-fermented and aged in neutral barrels to let the fruit shine through. (A second-generation cooper, Roberts uses French oak from Allier to make his own Cabernet barrels.)

○ **Arnot-Roberts Heinstein Vineyard Old Vine White Wine / 2014 / Sonoma Valley / $$$** Sixty-year-old Riesling, Sylvaner and other ancient vines produced this exotic, bracing wine with pineapple, citrus and quince character.

● **Arnot-Roberts Que Syrah Vineyard Syrah / 2014 / Sonoma Coast / $$$$** The winery farms this vineyard located two miles from the Pacific, near Occidental. The chilly climate created a very distinctive wine marked by layers of smoked meat, fresh earth, black pepper and blackberry fruit, and a bright finish.

AUBERT WINES

A rare California cult vintner specializing in Chardonnay, Napa native Mark Aubert was already famous among cognoscenti when he founded his own label in the 1990s, after stints at Peter Michael and Colgin (see pp. 134 and 32). Star vineyard manager Ulises Valdez enables Aubert's fanaticism for low yields of explosively intense fruit (and supplies the grapes for three vineyard-designated wines himself). Aubert's style with both Chardonnay and Pinot is opulent, flavor-packed and artfully balanced despite their high alcohol levels and new oak aging. There is, alas, a waiting list to buy these luxury-priced wines.

○ **Aubert Larry Hyde & Sons Vineyard Chardonnay / 2014 / Carneros Napa Valley / $$$$** Larry Hyde, one of California's most respected grapegrowers, custom-farms grapes for Aubert. The result is this personality-packed wine with vivid floral aromas and viscously rich peach and green apple fruit.

● **Aubert Pinot Noir / 2013 / Sonoma Coast / $$$$** Aubert's "starter" Pinot is a beauty, its velvety tannins wrapping around the bright cherry and dark-berry fruit, with violets and Christmas spice for complexity.

BACIGALUPI VINEYARDS

The Bacigalupi family's story in Sonoma County begins back in 1956, when patriarch Charles, a dentist, purchased a plot of land outside Healdsburg that happened to have an existing vineyard on a portion of it. The Bacigalupi vineyards have been a major factor in the success of the Russian River Valley over the succeeding 60 years: Charles planted what may have been the region's first Pinot Noirs and the vineyards have supplied grapes to many notable wineries. In 2011, the second generation founded the family's namesake label, based on grapes from their current 125 acres of vineyards. Winemaker Ashley Hertzberg has quickly put the brand on the map with full-throttle Zinfandels and juicy Chardonnays and Pinot Noirs.

○ **Bacigalupi Chardonnay / 2014 / Russian River Valley / $$$**
Wild-yeast-fermented in a mix of new and used French oak, this is a lively, minerally wine with essences of lemon oil, white peach, honeydew and hazelnut.

● **Bacigalupi Pinot Noir / 2014 / Russian River Valley / $$$$**
The family's Goddard Ranch and Frost Ranch vineyards provided the grapes for this unfined, unfiltered, utterly refreshing red with cherry, strawberry, spice and vanilla tones.

BALLETTO VINEYARDS

The Balletto family was once the largest produce grower north of the Golden Gate—but market changes in the 1990s turned their minds to wine. Today, they oversee 600 acres of vineyard in the Russian River Valley, selling off 90 percent of the fruit to other wineries and keeping 10 percent for their own label. Distributed by the sprawling Bronco Wine Company empire, Balletto wines are fairly priced and generally solid quality, with Pinot Noirs and Chardonnays as the image makers. But the family's extensive acreage provides opportunities for producing a range of other wines, including Zinfandel and Pinot Gris.

● **Balletto Rosé of Pinot Noir / 2015 / Russian River Valley / $$**
This dry pink wine has generous watermelon, strawberry and citrus fruit and palate-pleasing bright acidity. It's a seriously made wine for casual drinking.

● **Balletto Pinot Noir / 2013 / Russian River Valley / $$**
In the high-price world of Russian River Valley Pinot Noir, this version is an outstanding value, with satiny tannins, juicy dark-red fruit, savory spice and a crisp finish.

BEDROCK WINE CO.

Morgan Twain-Peterson crushed his first wine at age five, with some help from his famous winemaker dad, Ravenswood founder Joel Peterson. Now in his late 30s, Twain-Peterson has an expert hand with Zinfandel, Syrah, Cabernet Sauvignon and Pinot Noir, and particular passions for heirloom grapevines like old-vine Zin, as well as Graves-style whites (Sauvignon Blanc and Sémillon) and fine rosé. Twain-Peterson believes that picking grapes relatively early gives wine the most transparent sense of a site—contrary to the California orthodoxy of letting grapes hang until super-ripe. Look for both of his labels: the boutique Bedrock Wine Co. and the value-driven Sherman & Hooker Shebang.

- **Bedrock Wine Co. Old Vine Zinfandel / 2014 / California / $$** Jammy and generous, with loads of peppery spice and a moderate (for Zinfandel) 14.4 percent alcohol level, this is a well-crafted wine from grapes grown throughout California.
- **Bedrock Wine Co. The Bedrock Heritage / 2014 / Sonoma Valley / $$$** This old-school field blend of Zinfandel and 21 other varieties from Twain-Peterson's own vineyard is a melting pot of brambly red fruit, savory herbs, tobacco and a hint of oak.

BELLA VINEYARDS AND WINE CAVES

Scott and Lynn Adams's small winery in Dry Creek Valley, Sonoma's Zinfandel heartland, is dedicated to that grape in some of its finest, old-vine manifestations. A case in point is the family's own Lily Hill Estate, whose 100-year-old vines provide the grapes for the winery's silky, super-concentrated signature bottling. These are not shy, retiring wines (the small-lot Block 10 Zin from a 110-year-old patch of the Big River Ranch Vineyard, for example, may tip the scales at 15.7 percent alcohol), but consultant Michael Dashe (see Dashe Cellars, p. 107) and winemaker Joe Healy do a notable job of keeping the alcoholic heat out of these blockbusters.

- **Bella Big River Ranch Zinfandel / 2013 / Alexander Valley / $$$** Enticing aromas of dark cherry, licorice and cedar are followed by a mouthful of jazzy blackberry fruit. Bracing acidity keeps the wine lively and refreshing.
- **Bella Hills & Benches Zinfandel / 2013 / Dry Creek Valley / $$$** At 15.4 percent alcohol, this is a Zinfanatic's dream of an intense, immense wine, with briary black raspberry fruit and a chocolate-covered-cherry character.

BENOVIA WINERY

Joe Anderson and Mary Dewane purchased an established vineyard along Sonoma's Westside Road (the Park Avenue of Pinot Noir addresses) and created this ambitious Russian River winery. The couple subsequently acquired two other sites in Sonoma, broadening the estate's range of vineyard microclimates. They also contracted with top growers like Martinelli and partnered with talented winemaker Mike Sullivan. In addition to crafting its wines, co-owner Sullivan is Benovia's general manager, and his family's Four Brothers Vineyard also supplies some of its fruit. Since crushing its first vintage in 2006, the winery has had an impressive run with its nuanced, cool-climate Burgundy-style wines and a fine mountain Zinfandel.

○ **Benovia Chardonnay / 2014 / Russian River Valley / $$$** Fermentation and one year of aging in oak barrels added baking spice and a soft vanillin character to the brisk citrus, white peach and pear aromas and flavors.

● **Benovia Cohn Vineyard Pinot Noir / 2013 / Sonoma County / $$$$** Intense, concentrated grapes yielded a wine with rich red-fruit flavors balanced by minerally acidity and a supple texture.

BEVAN CELLARS

While living far away in Minneapolis, fourth-generation Sonoman Russell Bevan and his partner, Victoria De Crescenzo, were bitten by the wine bug and spent more and more time traveling to California to meet their winemaking heroes. Around the turn of the millennium they headed west for good, settling in Bennett Valley. They were hooked on winemaking from their first hobby-size crush, and Bevan turned out to be singularly gifted at it. His small-lot bottlings of massively sized but elegantly balanced reds have rocketed into triple-digit-priced cult status. As he hones his vineyard sources—Tench and Showket in Napa have been stalwarts—his already remarkable wines will only get better.

○ **Bevan Cellars Dry Stack Vineyard Sauvignon Blanc / 2015 / Bennett Valley / $$$** Aged in a 50/50 mix of stainless steel and French oak, this gets its fresh-fruit character from the former and rich, caramelized notes from the latter.

● **Bevan Cellars Tench Vineyard / 2013 / Oakville Napa Valley / $$$$** A blend of Cabernet Sauvignon and Cabernet Franc, this hefty red is kept balanced by its inviting floral aromas, spicy tobacco and anise notes, and refreshing acidity.

BUCKLIN OLD HILL RANCH

Sonoma boasts some of the oldest vineyards in Northern California, and Bucklin, a tiny, 2,000-case operation, claims one of the oldest in the county, dating to 1885. Otto and Anne Teller bought the place in 1981, when it was in an overgrown, all but commercially unviable state, and nursed the old vines back to health with the aid of Ravenswood's Joel Peterson (Ravenswood bottles a highly regarded Old Hill Zin to this day). Though Zinfandel is the winery's image-maker, Bucklin's vineyard, planted way back when to a classic California field blend, also yields two Ancient field-blend bottlings and a Grenache from 130-year-old vines.

● **Bucklin Old Hill Ranch Ancient Field Blend / 2012 / Sonoma Valley / $$$** Zinfandel, Grenache, Alicante Bouschet and who knows how many other grapes went into this field blend with burly tannins, blackberry, pepper, earth and bramble character. Give it five years to coalesce.

● **Bucklin Old Hill Ranch Grenache / 2014 / Sonoma Valley / $$$** Old- and young-vine Grenache grapes are joined by Carignane, Alicante Bouschet, Syrah and Mourvèdre for an intense wine with layers of interest.

BUENA VISTA WINERY

Hungarian-born Agoston Haraszthy, a California fine-wine pioneer, founded Buena Vista in 1857. A new era for the state's oldest operating commercial winery began in 2011 with Buena Vista's acquisition by the Boisset family of France (see DeLoach, p. 108, and Raymond, p. 71), which funded such improvements as the renovation of the winery's historic cellars. On the wine side, Jean-Charles Boisset, a Burgundian at heart, has recommitted Buena Vista to Chardonnays and Pinot Noirs from the cool Carneros region, and restored the luster of the Private Reserve tier of Chardonnay, Pinot Noir, Cabernet and Zin bottlings.

○ **Buena Vista Private Reserve Chardonnay / 2014 / Sonoma County / $$$** Sourced from a cool, windy site near Sonoma Mountain, the wine has firm acidity to support the rich apple, pear and citrus flavors and toasty oak component.

● **Buena Vista Private Reserve Pinot Noir / 2013 / Sonoma County / $$$$** A strong licorice note runs through this succulent, full-bodied Pinot Noir with cherry pie and mocha character. It's a fine foil for duck breast, squab and herbed lamb.

CARLISLE WINERY & VINEYARDS

Mike Officer operates according to a philosophy that most wine lovers can whole-heartedly support. The onetime software developer is committed to husbanding old-vine vineyards (he is a motive force behind the preservationist Historic Vineyard Society), retaining their distinctions in his wine, and selling it all at reasonable prices. His approach has worked out well: Production rose from five gallons of Zinfandel made in Officer's kitchen to about 7,000 cases today. He was able to quit his day job in 2004, and with college pal Jay Maddox as winemaker, got on with making some of California's most compelling Zins and Rhône-style reds, including benchmark Syrahs, all in a bold, full-flavored style.

○ **Carlisle The Derivative / 2013 / Sonoma County / $$**
Leave it to Mike Officer to find the old-vine Sémillon, Muscadelle, French Colombard and Palomino grapes for this zesty wine with white grapefruit and lemon personality.

● **Carlisle Carlisle Vineyard Zinfandel / 2013 / Russian River Valley / $$$**
From Carlisle's own vineyard, planted in 1927, this complex and powerful red offers dark berry, licorice, loam, tobacco and blood orange character, with soft tannins and a juicy finish.

CERITAS

An up-and-coming star on the *auteur* wine scene, John Raytek, former sommelier at Aspen's The Little Nell and current LIOCO winemaker (see p. 126), started this ambitious label with his wife, Phoebe Bass, a vineyardist who grew up amid the vine rows of her family's esteemed Porter-Bass Vineyard. The pair have scouted out remarkable sites, like the old Peter Martin Ray Vineyards high up in the Santa Cruz Mountains above Silicon Valley for Chardonnay and Cabernet and plots way out on the extreme Sonoma Coast for Pinot Noir. Raytek crafts their small-lot, premium-priced wines in as natural a way possible to emphasize the site and vintage over the hand of the winemaker.

○ **Ceritas Porter-Bass Vineyard Chardonnay / 2013 / Sonoma Coast / $$$$** The biodynamically farmed Porter-Bass vineyard produced this pure, intensely lemony Chardonnay marked by crispness, minerality and gentle oak spice.

● **Ceritas Hacienda Secoya Vineyard Pinot Noir / 2014 / Anderson Valley / $$$** Light in color and graceful on the palate, this is a pretty red, with dark cherry, spice and a pleasant earthy note.

CHALK HILL ESTATE VINEYARDS & WINERY

This vast 1,500-acre estate is the most prominent label of Sonoma County's Chalk Hill subregion. Its four-decade history added another chapter in 2010 when the property was acquired by William Foley for his Foley Family Wines (Sebastiani, Lincourt, Merus). Steve Nelson, formerly of Sebastiani (see p. 140) and Lewis, came on board as winemaker in the spring of 2015, with invaluable continuity provided by the estate's longtime viticulturist, Mark Lingenfelder. As before, Chardonnay—including the tiny-production old-vine Founder's Block bottling—is the star, but Chalk Hill's Bordeaux-style reds have a justifiable following of their own.

○ **Chalk Hill Clone 15 Chardonnay / 2013 / Chalk Hill / $$$$**
This clone-specific wine is full-bodied, rich and yeasty, with a creamy texture, lemony fruit and a caramel/hazelnut finish.

● **Chalk Hill Estate Red / 2012 / Chalk Hill / $$$$**
An unusual blend of Cabernet Sauvignon, Malbec, Petit Verdot, Merlot, Syrah and Carmenère, this exemplifies the winery's focus on weighty, bold wines. At 15.7 percent alcohol, it's super-rich, soft and sumptuous.

CHATEAU ST. JEAN

The Sonoma Valley winery that helped kick-start the county's wine renaissance in the 1970s is today part of the expansive portfolio of Australia-based Treasury Wine Estates. St. Jean is famous to generations of wine tourists for its impressive Goff mansion and gardens in Kenwood and its steady lineup of fine wines. Behind the consistency is skilled winemaker Margo Van Staaveren, who has been with St. Jean for nearly 40 years (almost 30 as a winemaker) and still crafts some of California's pioneering single-vineyard Chardonnays from the likes of Robert Young and Durell, plus such wines as the lovely (and well-priced) La Petite Etoile Fumé Blanc and St. Jean's top red, Cinq Cépages.

○ **Chateau St. Jean Robert Young Vineyard Chardonnay / 2014 / Alexander Valley / $$** This wine offers tight lemon oil, apple and toffee notes now, and the promise of generosity and layered complexity with time in bottle.

● **Chateau St. Jean Cinq Cépages / 2013 / Sonoma County / $$$$**
Cinq Cépages—"five [Bordeaux] varieties" led by Cabernet Sauvignon—is a finely tuned, ageworthy red, with warm boysenberry, black currant, chocolate and black-tea notes.

CLINE CELLARS

Jacuzzi-pump heir Fred Cline was both a founding member of the Rhône Rangers, instrumental in introducing Americans to Rhône-heritage wines like Syrah and Viognier, and an early proponent of sustainable farming. Cline's estate vineyards include his family's ranch in Oakley, east of San Francisco, with its century-old plantings of Zinfandel, Carignane and Mourvèdre; the 350-acre home vineyard in the Carneros region; and a newer acquisition in the Sonoma Coast's cool-climate Petaluma Gap. Cline Cellars has made its name with exuberantly styled, gently priced Zinfandel and Rhône varieties. Sales of the also affordable Cashmere Red and White blends help support charities.

○ **Cline Marsanne Roussanne / 2013 / Sonoma Coast / $$**
Estate vines in Carneros (for the Marsanne) and Sonoma Coast (for the Roussanne) produced this juicy wine with tropical, citrus and honey notes and frisky acidity.

● **Cline Heritage Zinfandel / 2013 / Contra Costa County / $$$**
From Cline's Big Break, Live Oak and Bridgehead vineyards in Oakley, this is a plush wine with big flavors of wild berry, black cherry, espresso and mocha.

COBB WINES

Ross Cobb may not be a household name to wine drinkers, but he's a guru to a considerable number of American Pinot Noir insiders. Trailing an impressive résumé (including Flowers, Williams-Selyem and Hirsch), he began bottling hands-on, small-production wines from his family's Coastlands Vineyard in 2001 and has seen the Cobb wines' reputation expand from there. A denizen of the "true" (i.e., foggy, cold and challenging to farm) Sonoma Coast, Cobb isn't able to make some of his most sought-after wines in difficult vintages, so the winery's already tiny production gets even smaller. Lovers of nuanced, anti-jammy Pinot Noir should put their names on this list.

● **Cobb Diane Cobb: Coastlands Vineyard Pinot Noir / 2013 / Sonoma Coast / $$$$** When Diane and David Cobb planted Coastlands Vineyard, Diane established a nursery block with 20-plus Pinot varieties. The wine made by their son in her honor is elegant, complex and aromatic, with brisk and supple tannins.

● **Cobb Emmaline Ann Vineyard Pinot Noir / 2013 / Sonoma Coast / $$$$** Delicate and focused, this Pinot delivers vivid rose petal aromas, energetic red fruit and spice notes.

COPAIN WINES

Esteemed Francophile winemaker Wells Guthrie turns out exceptionally graceful and subtle Pinot Noirs, Chardonnays and Syrahs—and his fans can rest assured that he'll continue to do so even though he sold Copain to Jackson Family Wines in 2016. Though the winery is located in Sonoma County's Russian River Valley, Guthrie sources most of its grapes up north, in cool, coastal-influenced Mendocino. The glories of the winery are the single-vineyard wines, including the flagship Pinot bottlings from the Kiser vineyard. But Copain's blended Tous Ensemble Chardonnay and Syrah wines are notable bargains, as is the food-friendly Tous Ensemble Pinot.

○ **Laureles Grade Chardonnay / 2014 / Monterey / $$$**
Pinpoint minerality reigns in this bracing wine with lemon, blood orange and white peach fruit. A good match for raw oysters, even better with grilled halibut with caper sauce.

● **Copain Les Voisins Pinot Noir / Anderson Valley / 2013 / $$$**
Refreshing strawberry and black cherry flavors, a hint of spice and mouthwatering acidity mark this supple, balanced Pinot.

DASHE CELLARS

Dashe is the work of the husband-and-wife team of Anne Dashe, who trained at Château La Dominique in St-Émilion, and Michael Dashe, who honed his craft working with the great Paul Draper at Ridge (see p. 184). From their base in downtown Oakland, the Dashes seek out old vines, rocky hillsides and special locales for their *terroir*-based, small-production wines. Though Dashe produces wines from a number of grapes, including Grenache and Riesling, it is best known for its single-vineyard Zinfandels, in styles ranging from the chewy, dark Todd Brothers Ranch bottling to a sweet, late-harvest Zin. Les Enfants Terribles is a line of limited-production wines made in the Dashes' trademark natural style from cool-climate vineyards.

○ **Dashe McFadden Farms Dry Riesling / 2014 / Potter Valley / $$**
Dry yet brimming with juicy peach, apple and apricot fruit, this Riesling has exotic ginger and honey aromas that also shine through on the finish.

● **Dashe Les Enfants Terribles Grenache / Dry Creek Valley / 2014 / $$**
Recalling a Beaujolais *grand cru*, this wild-yeast-fermented Grenache is medium-bodied, lively and exuberant in dark-red fruitiness. An excellent warm-weather red.

DEHLINGER WINERY

Tom Dehlinger helped put the spotlight on Russian River Valley Chardonnay and Pinot Noir starting in 1975 (his were among the first cult Pinots). Now working with his daughters Eva and Carmen, he continues to produce wines that are very much in high demand. They're sold largely through the winery's mailing list, and while they're not inexpensive, Dehlinger has made a commitment to keep prices within reason. Most of the winery's 7,000 cases—including some very fine Syrahs and a highly regarded Cabernet Sauvignon—come from estate vineyards. The second Cab, called Claret, can be a remarkable bargain.

○ **Dehlinger Chardonnay / 2013 / Russian River Valley / $$$**
Despite undergoing full malolactic fermentation in French oak, this wine remains elegant and crisp, with flint, pear, green apple and white peach notes and a citrus tang on the finish.

● **Dehlinger Altamont Pinot Noir / 2014 / Russian River Valley / $$$$**
This smooth-as-silk Pinot delivers intense black cherry and black currant fruit, a round and juicy mid-palate and seamless texture, with a dash of baking spice.

DELOACH VINEYARDS

The 2003 purchase of DeLoach by French wine entrepreneur Jean-Charles Boisset (see Buena Vista, p. 103, and Raymond, p. 71) gradually shifted the venerable brand's focus from Zinfandel and Chardonnay to Pinot Noir, while retaining strong footholds in both of those varietals. Boisset's passion for biodynamic viticulture and Burgundian winemaking techniques (low intervention, limited new oak) has brought a new attention to detail to the top bottlings, including the Estate, O.F.S. and Vineyard Designate lines. There's also a new emphasis on vineyard sourcing, with fruit coming from a number of top growers. DeLoach wines are generally a sure thing, but you need to know what you're buying, as the array of choices can be bewildering.

○ **DeLoach Heintz Vineyard Chardonnay / 2013 / Green Valley of Russian River Valley / $$$** Creamy and mouth-filling, this rich, sumptuous Chardonnay displays peach, Asian pear and hazelnut character and a long, slightly viscous finish.

● **DeLoach Pinot Noir / 2014 / Russian River Valley / $$**
This outstanding-value Pinot has it all: a silky palate, pretty berry and cherry fruit, savory truffle and spice notes and mouthwatering acidity.

DONELAN FAMILY WINES

Hard-driving paper company executive Joe Donelan has seen his high-quality boutique winery rise up the charts twice, once when it was known as Pax Wine Cellars, when Pax Mahle (see Wind Gap, p. 148) was winemaker, and again after Mahle and Donelan's much-publicized 2008 split, when it was renamed. Winemaker Joe Nielsen, the second successor to Mahle, has kept Donelan Family Wines on an upswing, with a stellar lineup of Syrahs, mostly sourced from cool-climate sites that account for the acidity and structure that underlie the wines' fleshiness. Though Syrahs are the winery's calling card, its whites, particularly the sumptuous Chardonnays and Viognier, are not to be overlooked.

○ **Donelan Venus Roussanne-Viognier / 2014 / Sonoma County / $$$**
Roussanne leads here, with Viognier adding honeysuckle and pear notes to the base Meyer lemon, cantaloupe and nectarine character. This is a richly textured wine with juicy acidity.

● **Donelan Obsidian Vineyard Syrah / 2013 / Knights Valley / $$$$**
Similar to a northern Rhône Syrah, this wine is meaty and earthy, rich and spicy. Perfect for slow-roasted pork shoulder.

THE DONUM ESTATE

This high-end, much-praised Pinot Noir project is familiar ground for German-born viticulturist Anne Moller-Racke, who planted Donum's two estate vineyards in the late 1980s and '90s. The vineyards, brand and sister label Robert Stemmler were sold to a Danish partnership in 2011, but the partners have kept Moller-Racke on in an unusual combined role of president and winegrower. With a third vineyard, in Mendocino, on long-term lease, Donum farms all the fruit for its small production itself, in the manner of the great Burgundian estates Moller-Racke admires. All of the Donum Pinot Noirs (and one Chardonnay), including the bottlings with broader appellation labels, are estate-grown and sourced from single vineyards.

○ **Donum Chardonnay / 2013 / Carneros / $$$**
Caramel oak frames this white's rich mélange of Granny Smith apple, citrus and tropical fruit aromas and flavors.

● **Donum Reserve Pinot Noir / 2013 / Russian River Valley / $$$$**
This red has mouth-coating dark cherry and brambly berry fruit, satiny tannins and enough acidity to support the grapes' ripeness. Pair with hearty lamb, beef and duck dishes.

DRY CREEK VINEYARD

David Stare set up shop in Sonoma's Dry Creek Valley in 1972, determined to make Loire-inspired wines. And succeed he did: Two of Dry Creek's most popular bottlings are of the Loire varieties Chenin Blanc and Sauvignon Blanc. But the winery, now under the direction of Stare's daughter, Kim Wallace, has long since come to be identified with hearty reds as well. Its specialties include very fine single-vineyard and old-vine Zinfandels—the Heritage Vines bottling is one of the best Zin deals around. Fans also look to Dry Creek for high-quality, reasonably priced Cabernet Sauvignon–based wines in the soft, juicy Sonoma style, including the elegant, top-tier Mariner Bordeaux-style blend.

○ **Dry Creek Vineyard Sauvignon Blanc / 2015 / Dry Creek Valley / $$** Refreshing acidity firms up this wine's layers of white grapefruit, quince, green melon and pear aromas and flavors.

● **Dry Creek Vineyard Heritage Vines Zinfandel / 2014 / Sonoma County / $$** Year after year, this Zin overdelivers for the price, with brambly raspberry and ripe cherry fruit, background leafy herbs and black pepper, and a succulent finish.

DUMOL

The good news is that this modest-sized (15,000-case) operation produces some of California's most compelling Chardonnays and Pinot Noirs (some notable Syrah and Viognier, too). The bad news is that the winery's dedicated following buys most of the production through the mailing list, so your best bet for tasting these gems is to join up or order them in a restaurant. The winery is named after the children (Duncan and Molly) of the late founding winemaker Max Gasiewicz. Today talented partner and winemaker Andy Smith sources his wines from DuMOL's home vineyard in cool Green Valley, from other Sonoma cool-climate sites and, more recently, from Napa growers as well.

○ **DuMOL Lia Viognier / 2013 / Russian River Valley / $$$** This two-vineyard blend is both ripe and vibrant, with pear, apple, honey and stone-fruit character supported by toasty oak and vanillin. Serve it with roast chicken or mildly spicy curry.

● **DuMOL Pinot Noir / 2013 / Russian River Valley / $$$$** Floral aromas and plump red fruit ride a wave of brisk acidity in this polished, easygoing wine that will develop more complexity with time in bottle.

DUTTON-GOLDFIELD WINERY

Steve Dutton is the son of the legendary wine grower Warren Dutton, who assembled the 1,300 acres (encompassing over 80 separate small vineyards) of Dutton Ranch, centered in the Russian River Valley. Under Steve's management, Dutton Ranch still supplies fruit to many of the region's most esteemed wineries, but he and winemaker/partner Dan Goldfield (formerly of Hartford Family Winery and La Crema; see pp. 117 and 124) cherry-pick some of the top Chardonnay and Pinot Noir lots—plus vineyard designates from elsewhere on the Northern California coast—for their joint venture. Among their specialties are old-vine, dry-farmed Chardonnays first planted by Warren in the cool Green Valley.

○ **Dutton-Goldfield Rued Vineyard Chardonnay / 2013 / Green Valley of Russian River Valley / $$$** At once opulent and focused, this Chardonnay has fleshy tropical and green apple fruit, crème brulée richness and bracing acidity.

● **Dutton-Goldfield Freestone Hill Vineyard Pinot Noir / 2013 / Russian River Valley / $$$$** This bracing Pinot delivers concentrated blackberry and cherry fruit and savory brush and spice notes.

ERIC KENT WINE CELLARS

You may not have caught the name, but if you've seen the wines, you'll remember the labels. Husband and wife owners Kent Humphrey and Colleen Teitgen feature often bold and splashy contemporary art on their bottles. Humphrey pursued a wayward path to winemaking, via academia and advertising, finally chucking it all to learn about wine from the cellar up at age 33. He crafts tiny lots of wines, including Pinot Noir, Syrah and Chardonnay, from carefully selected cool-climate sites, and revels in letting the wines express themselves, whether it's an over 15 percent alcohol Syrah or an under 13 percent Pinot.

○ **Eric Kent Cuvée Renee Sauvignon Blanc / 2014 / Sonoma County / $$** Favoring bright, juicy tropical fruit over green herbs and grass, this Sauvignon Blanc offers mouthwatering pineapple, mango and white peach character.

● **Eric Kent Small Town Pinot Noir / 2013 / Sonoma Coast / $$$** Grapes from five vineyards and multiple clonal selections went into this wine, which was aged 14 months in French oak barrels, 50 percent of them new. The oak frames the bright red fruit and velvety mouthfeel.

FERRARI-CARANO VINEYARDS AND WINERY

With more than 1,900 acres of estate vineyards across five appellations, Ferrari-Carano has done nothing in a small way. Reno hotel-and-casino magnate Don Carano and his wife, Rhonda, constructed their Italianate mansion with its famous gardens near Healdsburg in 1981. Today Ferrari-Carano produces an array of wine in several "family" tiers from its estate vineyards. The reliably fine whites are made at the Dry Creek Valley winery, where the tasting room is located. Reds (including the top cuvées, called PreVail) are made at the project's Mountain Winery Estate, in Alexander Valley. A specialty well known to aficionados: the Eldorado Gold dessert wine.

○ **Ferrari-Carano Fumé Blanc / 2014 / Sonoma County / $**
This fruity, non-fussy Sauvignon Blanc is one of the best values from Sonoma. It has a rich texture, thanks to partial aging in oak barrels, plus tropical and pear flavors.

● **Ferrari-Carano Reserve Cabernet Sauvignon / 2012 / Alexander Valley / $$$$** Impressively rich and supple, this Cab offers full-throttle blackberry, dark cherry and blueberry fruit and chocolate and smoke personality. Ready to drink now with medium-rare steak, it should age nicely over 10 years.

FISHER VINEYARDS

Though long a favorite of critics and insiders, Fisher has rarely received the wider recognition its very fine mountaintop wines deserve. Fred and Juelle Fisher bought the project's original Spring Mountain property in Sonoma County in 1973. Now run by their three children, Fisher Vineyards focuses on a group of Cabernet-based reds from both Napa and Sonoma Counties. The Napa estate, south of downtown Calistoga, produces the ageworthy flagship Coach Insignia Cabernet and two other limited-production reds. The Spring Mountain estate is the source of the Chardonnays, as well as such reds as the broodingly dark, expressive Wedding Vineyard Cabernet Sauvignon.

○ **Fisher Vineyards Whitney's Vineyard Chardonnay / 2013 / Sonoma County / $$$$** Whitney is Fred and Juelle Fisher's winemaker daughter. This Chardonnay from her namesake vineyard is exotic and weighty, with dried peach, citrus and honey notes.

● **Fisher Vineyards Coach Insignia Cabernet Sauvignon / 2012 / Napa Valley / $$$$** Plum, black cherry, cassis and oak spice are the signatures of this elegant, restrained wine.

FLOWERS VINEYARDS & WINERY

When Walt and Joan Flowers founded this winery far out on the extreme Sonoma Coast, you couldn't see much besides fog, redwoods and Hirsch Vineyards. Today the panoramic view takes in an array of neighboring vineyards where prestigious winemakers are trying their luck with Pinot Noir and Chardonnay in these dicey growing conditions. Now partly owned by Quintessa's Huneeus family (see p. 71), Flowers is the home of true believers in vibrant, leaner, more European-profile wines. The two biodynamically farmed estate vineyards, Camp Meeting Ridge and Sea View Ridge, are among California's most promising, and the Sonoma Coast bottlings, while not inexpensive, are a well-priced introduction to Flowers's style.

○ **Flowers Camp Meeting Ridge Chardonnay / 2013 / Sonoma Coast / $$$$** Delicate now, with great energy, steely minerality and hints of Meyer lemon, lemon curd and peach, this wine will fully develop with time, displaying more fruit and richness.

● **Flowers Sea View Ridge Pinot Noir / 2013 / Sonoma Coast / $$$$** From the high-altitude, low-yielding Sea View Ridge Vineyard, this Pinot displays layers of savory spice, cranberry and cherry fruit, and brisk acidity. Grace in a glass.

FRANCIS FORD COPPOLA WINERY

The director's non-film business empire now includes international resorts and restaurants, as well as the magnificent Inglenook Winery in Napa (see p. 50). Coppola also bought Sonoma's Chateau Souverain facility (though not the brand) with the notion of creating a kind of wine theme park. The winery, in Geyserville, may be the only one in the world with a swimming pool, a movie museum and a restaurant with an Argentine *asador* to wood-grill your meat selection. And oh yes: wine. The place bottles a slew of showily labeled wine lines, including Sofia (named after Coppola's daughter), the dim sum–friendly Su Yuen and the limited-production Director's Cut.

○ **Francis Coppola Reserve Catie's Corner Viognier / 2014 / Russian River Valley / $$** Aromas and flavors of honeysuckle, ripe pear and peach get a boost of complexity from hints of baking spice.

● **Archimedes Cabernet Sauvignon / 2013 / Alexander Valley / $$$$** The superstar of the Coppola collection, this Bordeaux-style blend is rich yet remarkably balanced, with savory forest-floor and anise notes accenting the juicy blackberry flavors.

FREI BROTHERS RESERVE

This eco-minded, sustainably farmed winery owned by giant E. & J. Gallo produces a range of wines sourced from top Sonoma appellations—for example, Russian River Valley for Chardonnay and Pinot Noir, Dry Creek Valley for Zinfandel and Alexander Valley for Cabernet Sauvignon—and sells them (labeled "Reserve") at prices generally in the $20 to $25 range. The winery's history dates to its founding by a Swiss immigrant, Andrew Frei, in 1890; by then the home ranch in Dry Creek Valley was already a vineyard. After many decades of buying Frei Brothers' grapes, Gallo purchased the brand itself after Frei's descendants retired in the 1970s.

○ **Frei Brothers Reserve Chardonnay / 2014 / Russian River Valley / $$** This Chardonnay has it all: fresh apple, pear and citrus fruit, spicy oak notes and juicy acidity. It's great with grilled tuna.

● **Frei Brothers Reserve Zinfandel / 2014 / Dry Creek Valley / $$** Juicy, brambly black cherry and red raspberry flavors get a kick of black pepper and clove in this supple, easy-to-drink Zin.

GARY FARRELL VINEYARDS & WINERY

A new era began at this foundational Russian River Valley winery with its purchase in 2011 by the well-heeled VinCraft Group and the recruitment in 2012 of Theresa Heredia, formerly of Freestone, as winemaker. A Pinot Noir and Chardonnay specialist, Gary Farrell has been something of a diamond in the rough but is now fulfilling its potential under Heredia, who has instituted such demanding practices as foot-treading the grapes, using natural yeasts for fermentation and giving the red wines extended contact with the grape skins and seeds after fermentation to soften the tannins. And given the superb vineyards at its disposal (including Rochioli and Durell), Gary Farrell is a winery on the rise.

○ **Gary Farrell Rochioli Vineyard Chardonnay / 2014 / Russian River Valley / $$$** This single-vineyard wine sings with succulent citrus, Asian pear and white peach notes, with gentle, nutty oak and textural richness balanced by brisk acidity.

● **Gary Farrell Hallberg Vineyard Dijon Clones Pinot Noir / 2014 / Russian River Valley / $$$** Pinot Noir clones 667 and 777 grown on the Hallberg ranch went into this rich, lush Pinot. It sports intense dark cherry and briary raspberry fruit, balanced by suave tannins and a refreshing finish.

GLORIA FERRER CAVES & VINEYARDS

Despite the abundance of still wine producers in Carneros in the 1980s, there were no sparkling houses in the region until Spanish wine maven José Ferrer (of the Freixenet empire) established this estate in 1982; the winery opened four years later. Ferrer named the operation after his wife, Gloria, and in short order it was turning out well-regarded sparkling whites and rosés. With its 335 estate acres dedicated mainly to Pinot Noir, that grape takes the lead role in most Gloria Ferrer bottlings, from signature sparklers like the Royal Cuvée and the creamy, lively Blanc de Noirs to the estate's varietal still wines.

○ **Gloria Ferrer Royal Cuvée Brut / 2007 / Carneros / $$$**
First served to the king and queen of Spain on their 1987 visit to California, this is a mouth-filling sparkling wine, with toasty brioche and almond character that comes from bottle aging.

○ **Gloria Ferrer Carneros Cuvée / 2004 / Carneros / $$$$**
The winery's top-flight sparkler is full-bodied and super-creamy, yeasty and toasty—a detailed expression of traditional Champagne-making techniques applied to Carneros grapes.

GOLDSCHMIDT VINEYARDS

Veteran winemaker Nick Goldschmidt produces wines from three continents under a dozen or so labels, including Boulder Bank from his native New Zealand and Chacras from Argentina. His US flagship, Goldschmidt Vineyards, is a Cabernet Sauvignon specialist, whose bottlings from two vineyards, Yoeman in Alexander Valley and Game Ranch in Napa, point up the differences between the two esteemed Cab locales. At the high end are the Goldschmidt Vineyard PLUS wines, made from the four top barrels from each vineyard. The Forefathers label and the wines named after each of Goldschmidt's three daughters (Chelsea, Hilary and Katherine) represent fine values from prime vineyard sites.

○ **Goldschmidt Singing Tree Chardonnay / 2014 / Russian River Valley / $$** Caramel and butterscotch aromas lead to a brisk mouthful of apple, pear and tropical fruit, with the oak retreating to the background. This crowd-pleaser finishes fresh and juicy.

● **Goldschmidt Vineyard Yoeman Vineyard Cabernet Sauvignon / 2012 / Alexander Valley / $$$$** This generous, mouth-filling red showcases the slightly dusty tannins and juicy raspberry and red cherry flavors so common in Alexander Valley Cabernet.

GUNDLACH BUNDSCHU

A multipart saga, this winery—still family owned in its sixth generation—was founded in 1858 and rose to great prominence, only to be devastated when its in-town winery and three family homes were destroyed in San Francisco's 1906 earthquake. The Bundschus persevered, however, and in 1997 managed to add a key portion of Jacob Gundlach's original Rhinefarm Vineyard to their own remaining holdings. Four years later the family stopped relying on outside grapes, and the wines today are made mostly from Rhinefarm fruit. The winery's lineup includes the sought-after flagship Bordeaux reds and a wonderful bargain in the Mountain Cuvée. But many know the brand for its dry Gewürztraminer, one of California's most flavorful.

○ **Gundlach Bundschu Gewürztraminer / 2014 / Sonoma Coast / $$**
Fermentation in mostly stainless steel captures the exotic rose petal, lychee, apple and ginger-spice character of the grape in a dry yet juicy wine. Serve it with spicy curry or pork tenderloin.

● **Gundlach Bundschu Cabernet Franc / 2013 / Sonoma Valley / $$$**
By no means classic from a Bordeaux or Loire standpoint, this distinctive Cab Franc has drawn a cult-like following for its richness, coffee and dark chocolate character and muscularity.

HANNA WINERY & VINEYARDS

Many hobby winemakers dream of turning pro, but Dr. Elias Hanna, a cardiac surgeon, made it happen. Starting in 1985, he expanded a 12-acre vineyard in the Russian River Valley into a thriving winery with more than 600 Sonoma acres in four vineyard locations. Directed for nearly 25 years now by his daughter Christine Hanna and longtime winemaker Jeff Hinchliffe, Hanna is probably best known for its Russian River Valley Sauvignon Blanc, still priced under $20. But it also makes a wealth of reasonably priced (for Sonoma) reds, including top-tier Bordeaux blends from Bismark Mountain Ranch, Hanna's estate vineyard in the Mayacamas Range.

○ **Hanna Sauvignon Blanc / 2015 / Russian River Valley / $$**
Crackling with youthful energy, this has tangy white grapefruit and lemon-lime flavors and a kiss of juicy peach.

● **Hanna Reserve Merlot / 2013 / Alexander Valley / $$$**
Merlot is Alexander Valley's best-kept secret. This version's plump plum and blackberry fruit is beautifully framed by spicy vanillin oak, supple tannins and a long, juicy finish.

HANZELL VINEYARDS

Burgundy-loving former US ambassador to Italy James Zellerbach planted some of California's first post-Prohibition Chardonnay and Pinot Noir in Sonoma County in 1953. Hanzell continues its founder's vision today thanks in large part to the four-decade tenure of winemaker emeritus Bob Sessions, who passed away in 2014. The winery has stayed small, producing around 7,000 cases a year from estate vines, some as old as 60 years. Under current winemaker Michael McNeil, the bottlings are still somewhat closer to the European ideal than the California mainstream (i.e., they're not loaded with sweet fruit and oak). Tightly wound when released, Hanzell's long-lived wines typically benefit from extended cellaring.

○ **Hanzell Sebella Chardonnay / 2014 / Sonoma County / $$$**
Made largely from younger estate vines, this is a bracing, lemony, precise wine that will develop generosity and complexity over the next three years.

● **Hanzell Pinot Noir / 2013 / Sonoma Valley / $$$$**
This Pinot is medium-bodied, minerally and restrained now, but its raspberry and black cherry fruit and firm acidity will become more generous with cellaring, allowing the texture to soften and spice notes to emerge.

HARTFORD FAMILY WINERY

This Jackson Family Wines operation—it's run by the late Jess Jackson's son-in-law Don Hartford—puts its hefty resources into the service of small-batch winemaking. Its typically single-vineyard Chardonnay, Pinot Noir and Zinfandel bottlings rarely top 800 cases each. The vineyard sources for the Chardonnays and Pinots can be highly demanding to farm—many are on the fringes of the extreme Sonoma Coast—and the Zins come from century-old blocks that often contain a field mix of ancillary grapes (Alicante, Petite Sirah, etc.). Often bottled unfined and unfiltered, these tend to be big-bodied, highly expressive wines.

○ **Hartford Court Chardonnay / 2014 / Russian River Valley / $$$**
This elegant wine's gentle toast and popped-corn aromas lead to a snappy yet luscious Meyer lemon, lemon meringue and white peach palate and a fresh, lingering finish.

● **Hartford Court Pinot Noir / 2014 / Russian River Valley / $$$**
Earthy, dark cherry scents and flavors, silky texture and bracing acidity mark this deep-fruited, concentrated Pinot.

HIRSCH VINEYARDS

David Hirsch was the pioneering visionary of far-western Sonoma County. His wind-scoured mountaintop vineyards lie at the edge of the continent, less than a mile from the San Andreas Fault, and are subject to every peril, from frost to flood to earthquake. With luck, his very-low-yielding vines set enough fruit for six extraordinary Pinot Noirs and a tiny amount of Chardonnay, all wines whose flavors reflect not only the marginal climate but also the jumble of soils thrown up along the fault zone. He has had a string of talented winemakers willing to brave the conditions, and the mantle has now fallen upon the worthy Anthony Filiberti (see Anthill Farms, p. 97).

- **Hirsch Vineyards The Bohan-Dillon Pinot Noir / 2014 / Sonoma Coast / $$$** Racy cherry, cranberry and pomegranate flavors ride a wave of brisk acidity in this refreshing wine that would pair beautifully with poached salmon.
- **Hirsch Vineyards San Andreas Fault Pinot Noir / 2013 / Sonoma Coast / $$$** Keeping with the house style of floral aromatics, pure fruit and elegance, this wine offers ripe blackberry, red cherry and cranberry fruit supported by minerally acidity and delicate oak that enhances the mouthfeel.

HOLDREDGE WINES

John and Carri Holdredge's small (2,000-case) family winery in Healdsburg is devoted to Russian River Valley and Sonoma Coast Pinot Noir, and they walk the quality walk. Instead of making more wine from the monumental 2012 vintage, the Holdredges bled off and poured 20 percent of their juice down the drain to increase the juice-to-skin contact and hence their wine's concentration. At the top end of their lineup of highly distinctive Pinots is the Judgment Tree bottling, made from grapes that John had lobbied for years to buy from the esteemed Rochioli Vineyard. The winery's second line, called Oscuro, focuses on such "obscure" Italian varieties as Schioppettino.

- **Holdredge Pinot Noir / 2014 / Russian River Valley / $$$** Multiple vineyards, planted to a mix of clones, produced this beautifully balanced Pinot, with juicy raspberry and dark cherry fruit, oak spice and a subtle earthiness.
- **Holdredge Rolling Thunder Pinot Noir / 2014 / Russian River Valley / $$$** This lavish wine's crisp structure and rich black raspberry fruit make it a perfect match for fatty duck and pork belly.

INMAN FAMILY WINES

Founded in 2000 by Kathleen Inman, who does everything from crafting the wine to driving the forklift to answering the phone, this small Russian River winery reflects not just Inman's winemaking skill, but also her personal values. Those values emphatically include environmental sensitivity, which extends beyond the organic farming of the home Olivet Grange Vineyard into her thinking about every aspect of the operation. Inman's Pinot Noirs directly reflect her outlook as well. She picks earlier than her neighbors to preserve brightness and acidity, and makes these graceful wines very naturally, typically with yeasts from the grape skins. One hidden secret is her superb, tiny-production Blanc de Noir sparkling wine.

○ **Inman Family Blanc de Noir / 2012 / Russian River Valley / $$$$** Made in a *brut nature* style (i.e., no added sugar), this all–Pinot Noir sparkler is bone-dry and scintillating, with apple, citrus and baking spice complexity. Not to be missed by foodies.

● **Inman Family OGV Estate Pinot Noir / 2012 / Russian River Valley / $$$$** Olivet Grange Vineyard (OGV) produced this floral red, with plush texture, tangy red fruit and earthy spice. Medium-bodied and graceful, it finishes with refreshing acidity.

IRON HORSE VINEYARDS

Wine pioneers in the cool, foggy Green Valley subregion of the Russian River Valley in the 1970s, the Sterling family has long made some of California's most refined sparkling wines and some notable still wines from its 160-acre estate Chardonnay and Pinot Noir plantings. But from 2005 through 2012, second-generation scion Joy Sterling and her team undertook a meticulous 82-acre replanting program based on farming knowledge gained since the early days. During it all, longtime winemaker David Munksgard continued to turn out sparkling wines of French-style raciness and leaner-bodied charm.

○ **Iron Horse Wedding Cuvée / 2012 / Green Valley of Russian River Valley / $$$** It's difficult not to fall in love with this Blanc de Noirs sparkler, with its peach, raspberry and blood orange character, creamy yet crisp palate and long, bracing finish.

● **Iron Horse Vineyards Thomas Road Pinot Noir / 2013 / Green Valley of Russian River Valley / $$$$** This elegant Pinot delivers suave tannins, vivid dark cherry and raspberry fruit and hints of forest floor and savory herbs.

JORDAN VINEYARD & WINERY

One of the early Sonoma stars, Jordan was founded in the 1970s by oil-and-gas entrepreneur Tom Jordan, whose ivy-clad winery brought a touch of Napa-style glamour and French-style chic to Alexander Valley. Its first wine consultant, the legendary André Tchelistcheff, hired Rob Davis, who has made the wine here for nearly 40 years, a highly unusual continuity in the California wine world. It is not too much to say that the two wines Davis produces each vintage—a Cabernet Sauvignon and a Chardonnay—are traditionally styled, though the tradition is Jordan's own: restrained, never over-the-top rich or extracted, and offering fruit-forward, food-friendly drinking pleasure.

○ **Jordan Chardonnay / 2014 / Russian River Valley / $$$**
This citrus- and green apple–based wine is crisp and mouthwatering now, and has a remarkable track record for aging into a richer, broader wine in five to 10 years.

● **Jordan Cabernet Sauvignon / 2012 / Alexander Valley / $$$**
One of Sonoma's most Bordeaux-like reds, this Cab boasts forest-floor, loam, bright cherry and black currant character. Expect it to become more expansive with cellaring.

JOSEPH SWAN VINEYARDS

Joe Swan, a former airline pilot who became an early 1970s trailblazer in the cool-climate Russian River Valley—and a much-admired figure of his generation—passed away in 1989. His son-in-law, Rod Berglund, took over the operation and continues to follow in Swan's footsteps, making mostly reasonably priced Pinot Noirs and Zinfandels, plus small bottlings of seemingly whatever interests him from a given vintage (an orange Pinot Gris, for example). These are the kind of hands-on, personal-scale and occasionally idiosyncratic wines that make California vineyards worth exploring. To get an idea of the place, read the amusing wine background descriptions on the winery's website.

○ **Joseph Swan Vineyards Kent the Younger Chardonnay / 2013 / Russian River Valley / $$$** Made from younger vines on Kent Ritchie's Old Wente clone–planted vineyard, this is rich in caramel oak, with bracing Meyer lemon and green apple fruit.

● **Joseph Swan Vineyards Trenton Estate Vineyard Pinot Noir / 2013 / Russian River Valley / $$$$** Delicate and focused, this Pinot offers briary red raspberry and cherry fruit, subtle wood spice and a snappy finish. It's a great match for mushroom-sauced pasta.

J VINEYARDS & WINERY

J Vineyards followers are adopting a wait-and-see attitude after this premier sparkling- and still-wine producer was sold to E. & J. Gallo in 2015. The winery was closely identified with its founder, Judy Jordan, who grew up at her family's Jordan Winery (opposite) but was determined to pursue her own path. Jordan built her own brand, with its stylish J logo, and assembled an impressive team. J's sparkling and still wines—including some wonderful Pinot Gris—are largely based on the nine cool-climate Russian River Valley estate vineyards Jordan acquired over the years. With the change in ownership, J's well-regarded winemaker Melissa Stackhouse turned over the reins to up-and-coming Nicole Hitchcock.

○ **J Cuvée 20 Brut / NV / Russian River Valley / $$$**
Judy Jordan created this nonvintage sparkler to celebrate her 20th vintage at J. It offers frothy Meyer lemon and green apple, subtle yeastiness and a kiss of sweetness.

● **J Vineyards Pinot Noir / 2013 / Russian River Valley / $$$**
This wine's nicely ripened red cherry fruit has a pleasantly earthy, mushroomy note that is one of Pinot's greatest charms.

KAMEN ESTATE WINES

Robert Mark Kamen has written over 20 produced screenplays—among them the *Karate Kid* and *Transporter* series—but his most remarkable work may be the script of his own life, which includes a determined ascent from a childhood in a Bronx public housing project and, most recently, a rebound from a 1996 fire that destroyed his home and half his vineyards. It was after the fire that he decided to produce his own wine. With viticulturalist Phil Coturri planting and farming the biodynamic vineyard and Mark Herold (see p. 58) making the wine, Kamen and his all-star team have turned out a string of successes, highlighted by deep, multilayered Cabernets like the ultra-luxury-priced, top-of-the-line Kashmir Cuvée.

○ **Kamen Sauvignon Blanc / 2014 / Sonoma Valley / $$$**
This estate-grown blend of Sauvignon Blanc and Sauvignon Musqué offers a melange of citrus, tropical and honeydew fruit with floral aromas and palate vibrancy.

● **Kamen Cabernet Sauvignon / 2012 / Sonoma Valley / $$$$**
From its inky color to its full body and opulent dark fruit, this is an explosive wine, yet it's beautifully balanced for its size.

KENDALL-JACKSON

This Sonoma-based megabrand—the foundation of the Jackson Family Wines enterprise—has a straightforward formula for maintaining quality despite its huge size: Source grapes from estate-owned vineyards; judiciously use high-end techniques even on inexpensive wines; and rely on winemaster Randy Ullom to mastermind the cellar. Best known for its ubiquitous Vintner's Reserve Chardonnay, the deep K-J portfolio also includes the Grand Reserve tier, which employs the top 3 percent of estate barrels in a given vintage, and single-vineyard offerings. The apex is the limited-production Bordeaux-style blend Stature, whose vineyard sources, potentially including sites in Napa's Mount Veeder and Atlas Peak and Sonoma's Alexander Valley and Bennett Valley, demonstrate K-J's impressive reach.

○ **Kendall-Jackson Jackson Estate Seco Highlands Chardonnay / 2014 / Arroyo Seco / $$$** From gravelly soils in Monterey County, this Chardonnay is lively and spicy, lean and crisp, with a steely constitution that begs for spice-rubbed roast chicken.

● **Kendall-Jackson Grand Reserve Cabernet Sauvignon / 2013 / Sonoma County / $$** This Cab's depth of flavor, layered complexity and polish give many costlier bottlings a run for their money. It's generous, spicy and firm enough for roast beef.

KENWOOD VINEYARDS

In the heart of Sonoma Valley on the Sonoma Highway's main tourist stretch, Kenwood was an early player in Sonoma's renaissance. Founded in 1970 in the old Pagani Brothers Winery, Kenwood entered a new era with its 2014 sale to Pernod Ricard. The current roster features a slew of bottlings in several price tiers. The Sonoma Series wines, sourced from growers around the county, can offer terrific value. Perhaps the wines most familiar to consumers are the rich reds from the lava-terraced Jack London Vineyard—in the black bottles with a wolf head.

○ **Kenwood Six Ridges Chardonnay / 2014 / Russian River Valley / $$** Gentle oak spice and vanillin character enhance the juicy pear, green apple and white peach flavors of this delicious, balanced Chardonnay; the finish is long and palate-cleansing.

● **Kenwood Jack London Vineyard Cabernet Sauvignon / 2013 / Sonoma Mountain / $$$** Descendants of Jack London grow the grapes for this flagship wine, which has a leafy-herb edge to the plump black cherry and dark plum fruit.

KISTLER VINEYARDS

This is one of California's most sought-after producers of Pinot Noir and Chardonnay, partly because of Steve Kistler's famously meticulous ways—even for growers with whom he has long-term relationships, he is known to be an exacting customer. Given partner Bill Price's vinous reach (see Lutum, p. 177, and Three Sticks, p. 145), Kistler has the luxury of being particular about his vineyard sources (including those the winery owns). The results are head-turning wines that at their best combine a Burgundian tight-knit intensity with California richness and exuberance. Most of the wines are sold via the mailing list, at stiff prices. The winery converted the historic Trenton Roadhouse into a hospitality venue/tasting room in 2014.

○ **Kistler Chardonnay / 2014 / Sonoma Mountain / $$$$**
Vibrant acidity frames this Chardonnay's intense citrus, green apple and pineapple palate. Toasty oak and a hint of butter lend complexity.

● **Kistler Cuvée Catherine Pinot Noir / 2013 / Sonoma Coast / $$$$**
Like most Kistler offerings, Catherine is elegant and nuanced. The delicate red cherry and raspberry fruit is vibrant and the palate ethereal, with leafy herb and loam adding nuance.

KOSTA BROWNE WINERY

This onetime shoestring operation was founded in the late 1990s by Dan Kosta and Michael Browne (later joined by Chris Costello), and their wines were an immediate hit. A series of capital infusions starting in 2009 put KB on solid financial footing and allowed it to build a sleek winery complex in Sebastopol, opened in 2013. Though production of Kosta Browne's big, rich, full-flavored but polished Pinots and Chardonnays has expanded, such has been its cult and wine media success that the winery still struggles to meet demand. Be ready to wait two to three years to get on the mailing list.

○ **Kosta Browne One Sixteen Chardonnay / 2014 / Russian River Valley / $$$$** Named for Highway 116, which runs through the heart of the Russian River Valley, this is a vibrantly fresh yet rich Chardonnay, brimming with juicy apple and citrus fruit.

● **Kosta Browne Keefer Ranch Pinot Noir/ 2013 / Russian River Valley / $$$$** This Pinot is supple, spicy and super-rich, with lavish oak absorbing the luscious cherry and raspberry fruit. Decadent now, it will get even better with age.

KUTCH WINES

As a former NASDAQ trader at Merrill Lynch, Jamie Kutch was used to taking risks at work. But by the mid-2000s, he was up for an even more nerve-racking challenge, as he moved west to enter the luxury Pinot Noir sweepstakes. Kutch has made a big impression for such a recent, boutique-scale operation. This is partly because Jamie Kutch has a native talent for producing luscious, transparently pure Pinot Noir, and partly because he has the good sense to source it from tiny-crop vineyards that yield sensational grapes. The most notable of his sources is the McDougall Ranch, farmed by famed vineyardist Ulises Valdez out on the far Sonoma Coast.

● **Kutch Falstaff Pinot Noir / 2014 / Sonoma Coast / $$$**
Falstaff's cool-climate conditions produced a wine that's savory and earthy, yet loaded with dark red fruit and spice.

● **Kutch McDougall Ranch Pinot Noir / 2014 / Sonoma Coast / $$$**
It's amazing how much flavor Kutch delivers in wines that are just 12.5 percent or so alcohol. This one is silky on the palate, with a mix of dark fruit, woodsy spice and refreshing texture.

LA CREMA

Under the Jackson Family Wines umbrella, La Crema has rebuilt its reputation for high-quality Pinot Noir, Chardonnay and Pinot Gris, an impressive feat given the winery's significant output and mostly gentle prices (the Monterey and Sonoma Coast appellation wines in particular make La Crema a go-to label in restaurants for a highly reliable good value). A key to the operation's success is sourcing—from vineyards in some of Northern California's most Burgundy-variety-loving, cool-climate zones, such as the Russian River Valley and Sonoma Coast, as well as from sites in Oregon's Willamette Valley. Canadian-born winemaker Elizabeth Grant-Douglas puts the grapes through exacting paces, barrel-fermenting the Chardonnays, for example, and hand-sorting the Pinot Noir.

○ **La Crema Pinot Gris / 2014 / Monterey / $$**
Floral aromas flood the nose, and the palate is brisk and dry, with tangerine, lemon drop and yellow stone-fruit character.

● **La Crema Pinot Noir / 2013 / Russian River Valley / $$$**
This Pinot has an intense red cherry aroma and firm tannins framing its black cherry and blackberry fruit. Gentle herbs add complexity.

LANDMARK VINEYARDS

Fiji Water billionaire Stewart Resnick's The Wonderful Company bought this 40-plus-year-old winery in 2011 from Damaris Deere Ford, great-great-granddaughter of John Deere. In the past decade, the reliable Sonoma Valley winery has garnered fresh attention with a series of small-lot wines from high-profile vineyards. These wines have joined other well-known bottlings in Landmark's roster, including the Overlook Chardonnay and Pinot Noir, two of Sonoma's best bargains, and the Grand Detour Pinot Noir. Though the winery is known for Burgundian varietals, it also turns out some worthy Rhône-style reds, such as the Grenache from the estate Steel Plow Vineyard.

○ **Landmark Vineyards Overlook Chardonnay / 2014 / Sonoma County / $$** This Chardonnay's tangy, juicy style relies more on pure citrus and apple fruit than on oak. Vibrant acidity makes it a perfect match for Dungeness crab and lemony chicken.

● **Landmark Vineyards Grand Detour Pinot Noir / 2014 / Sonoma Coast / $$$** Rich dark cherry and berry fruit, lush texture and spicy vanillin oak mark this expressive Pinot Noir.

LAUREL GLEN VINEYARD

Starting with the first vintage in 1981, Patrick Campbell's elegant, firmly structured Sonoma Mountain wines helped prove that Napa's neighbor could also produce top-tier Cabs. In 2011, Campbell sold the winery to industry veteran Bettina Sichel. She enlisted star consultant David Ramey and organic-viticulture guru Phil Coturri to put their stamp on the wines, which are made from grapes grown on a single 16-acre estate. In keeping with tradition, the winery focuses on two bottlings—the estate Cabernet and the more affordable Counterpoint Cabernet. There is also the intriguing Crazy Old Vines Rosé, made from old vines planted in the 19th century.

● **Laurel Glen Counterpoint Cabernet Sauvignon / 2013 / Sonoma Mountain / $$$** Laurel Glen's second wine delivers first-rate pleasure with its juicy plum and wild berry fruit enhanced by smoky, spicy oak. Its Merlot component gives it a softer profile than the flagship Cab's.

● **Laurel Glen Vineyard Cabernet Sauvignon / 2012 / Sonoma Mountain / $$$$** Supple and savory, this all-Cabernet estate bottling displays inviting floral aromas, juicy black cherry and black currant flavors, with hints of minerality and fresh earth.

LIMERICK LANE CELLARS

Well known to insiders, if not to the public generally, this superb Russian River Valley producer of Zinfandel and Rhône varietals (and now Pinot Noir) has been on the comeback trail since Jake Bilbro purchased it in 2011. A son of the owners of Marietta Cellars, he promptly installed his brother Scot as winemaker. The 30-acre estate—first planted in 1910—and its Collins Vineyard have gained a reputation for stylish, beautifully delineated reds that take advantage of the region's cool climate to eschew jammy-ness while not stinting on flavor. Look for the Bilbros to make the most of these great grapes and to add a new chapter to the estate's artisan-wine history.

- **Limerick Lane Syrah-Grenache / 2013 / Russian River Valley / $$$**
From the estate vineyard comes this spicy, pleasantly herbal wine rich in ripe strawberry, cherry and raspberry fruit, with a supple mouthfeel and a crisp finish.

- **Limerick Lane Zinfandel / 2013 / Russian River Valley / $$$**
With 14.6 percent alcohol, this wine is on the balanced, claret end of the Zinfandel spectrum, with juicy red berries, peppery spice, solid acidity and nary a hint of heat.

LIOCO

Former Spago sommelier Kevin O'Connor and his buddy Matt Licklider, a onetime wine importer, share a passion for Chardonnay and Pinot Noir with lithe, vibrant flavors—the kinds grown in Burgundy and in California's coolest wine regions. In 2005 they teamed up to found LIOCO, a label focused on naturally made Pinot and Chardonnay—and increasingly on old-vine Carignane—sourced from prestigious vineyards like Hanzell, Demuth and Hirsch. With rising star John Raytek (see Ceritas, p. 104) at the helm, LIOCO's realistically priced and often outstanding wines are natural-yeast-fermented, low- to non-oak-impacted and bottled with minimal intervention.

- **LIOCO Estero Chardonnay / 2014 / Russian River Valley / $$$**
A handful of cool-zone vineyards contributed to this elegant wine with bracing acidity, crisp citrus and green apple fruit, and an affinity for grilled fish and scallops.

- **LIOCO La Selva Pinot Noir / 2014 / Anderson Valley / $$$**
La Selva ("the forest" in Spanish) has a notable woodsy aspect to its pure cherry and berry fruit. Focused and crisp, it's a fine foil for duck breast and pork tenderloin.

LITTORAI WINES

Ted Lemon deserves his reputation as one of America's most thoughtful and talented winemakers, and in the cold, often foggy reaches of Sonoma and Mendocino Counties he has found the perfect place to make genuinely Burgundian-profile Pinot Noirs and Chardonnays: wines that maintain a tension between ripe and unripe with a racy vibrancy. The myriad soils and microclimates of the Sonoma Coast and Anderson Valley also provide him with a *terroir* laboratory worthy of a lifetime of experimentation. Lemon's response—seeking out superb, sustainably or biodynamically farmed small-vineyard sources and crafting wines with minimal handling—makes this one of the New World's most influential small wineries.

○ **Littorai B.A. Thieriot Vineyard Chardonnay / 2014 / Sonoma Coast / $$$$** Minerally and bracing now, this wine's steely structure suggests cellaring for two years to allow the now-shy lemon, green apple and quince character to evolve.

● **Littorai The Haven Vineyard Pinot Noir / 2014 / Sonoma Coast / $$$$** Littorai's first estate vineyard, a chilly site northwest of Occidental, produced this perfumed, elegant wine with ripe cherry, berry and cola notes. It's a beautifully structured Pinot.

LYNMAR ESTATE

Lynn Fritz grew grapes for several esteemed winemakers before bottling his own wine in the 1990s. He now crafts a roster of small-batch Pinot Noirs and Chardonnays, plus a Syrah, many sourced from the 70 acres of estate vineyards he assembled in the hills bordering the Laguna de Santa Rosa. The original estate Fritz bought in 1980 was the old Quail Hill, which now counts vines as old as 40 years. The Lynmar brand seemed to hit its stride in the mid-aughts under winemaker Hugh Chappelle, and has continued its success under Shane Finley, who came on board in 2012 from cult producer Kosta Browne (see p. 123).

● **Lynmar Estate Rosé of Pinot Noir / 2015 / Russian River Valley / $$** Inviting watermelon, strawberry and cherry liqueur aromas lead to a similar palate that's at once rich and refreshingly citrusy on the finish.

● **Lynmar Estate Quail Hill Vineyard Pinot Noir / 2013 / Russian River Valley / $$$** This is a rich Pinot, with red and black cherry fruit and notes of cola and barrel spice. Plush and lingering in the mouth, it's generous, mouth-filling and great with duck.

MACMURRAY ESTATE VINEYARDS

This winery takes its name from MacMurray Ranch, a stunning western swath of the Russian River Valley that was once owned by actor Fred MacMurray (of *My Three Sons* fame). E. & J. Gallo acquired the property after the actor's death in 1996. Bordering such prestigious neighbors as Rochioli and Gary Farrell, the home ranch's 284 acres of Pinot Noir and Pinot Gris vines are supplemented by a wealth of other Gallo/MacMurray vineyards in the Russian River Valley, Central Coast and Santa Lucia Highlands, which help to fill the tanks of this substantial project. Winemaker Boyd Morrison has enhanced MacMurray's reputation for bottling delicious wines at realistic prices.

○ **MacMurray Pinot Gris / 2014 / Russian River Valley / $$**
This bright, luscious wine puts insipid Pinot Grigio to shame. With juicy peach and pear fruit and accents of citrus and spice, it's a crowd-pleaser.

● **MacMurray Winemaker's Block Pinot Noir / 2013 / Russian River Valley / $$$** Vibrant wild berry and cherry liqueur aromas and flavors and a kiss of vanillin oak mark this rich, velvety wine that finishes crisp and long.

MACROSTIE WINERY AND VINEYARDS

Steve MacRostie sold his namesake winery—founded in 1987—to Australia's Lion Nathan in 2011. The conglomerate, which also owns Oregon's Argyle (see p. 202), is continuing the winery's direction while increasing production. MacRostie made its name on fresh, lively Chardonnays that resisted the oaky-buttery-big alcohol trend in California. Its Pinots, too, produced from up and down the sprawling Sonoma Coast appellation, tend to be marked by their liveliness. The top wines come from the estate-owned Wildcat Mountain Vineyard, and they can be very good, indeed. The winery's lineup is well priced and reliably fine, but for some reason, MacRostie has long flown under the radar.

○ **MacRostie Chardonnay / 2014 / Russian River Valley / $$$**
Caramel oak and lemon chiffon aromas lead to a crisp palate of Asian pear, Granny Smith apple and citrus fruit. Nicely balanced and focused, it's a great mate for veal chops.

● **MacRostie Wildcat Mountain Pinot Noir / 2013 / Sonoma Coast / $$$**
Steve MacRostie's own vineyard is the source of this intense, brambly Pinot Noir, with complex notes of baking spice and leather and subtle vanillin oak.

MARIETTA CELLARS

A name to put on your value-for-quality shopping list, Marietta has grown into a 100,000-case brand with a somewhat contrarian strategy, which includes doing without a fancy tasting room and online store, spending money on fine vineyard land and producing wines blended from multiple vintages, designated only by lot numbers. The Bilbro brothers, Jake and Scot (who are also behind the resurgence of Limerick Lane; see p. 126), bought the winery from their father in 2012, and have continued Marietta Cellars's winning ways with crowd-pleasing, opulent red blends from an idiosyncratic range of grapes.

● **Marietta Cellars Old Vine Red Lot Number 63 / NV / California / $**
Zinfandel, Petite Sirah, Syrah and "mixed Italian black" grapes come together in this nonvintage, great-value red that delivers ripe berry, cherry and spice notes in an easy-drinking style.

● **Marietta Cellars Christo Lot Number 3 / NV / North Coast / $$**
The Bilbro brothers honor their father, Chris, with this multiple-vintage, Rhône-style blend. It's robust and rich in blackberry and blueberry fruit, with a gamey note that makes it a great match for grilled meat.

MARIMAR ESTATE VINEYARDS & WINERY

Marimar Torres grew up in the wine business as a member of Catalonia's Torres wine clan (her brother Miguel runs the family's Spanish and Chilean wineries). Intent on making her own mark, she founded Marimar Torres—now Marimar Estate—in the late 1980s. The winery's efforts are focused around two organically farmed vineyards named for Torres's parents: Don Miguel, in the Russian River Valley, and Doña Margarita, in the "true" foggy Sonoma Coast. Marimar Estate is best known for luscious Chardonnays, but its Albariño is also worth a look. In reds, the emphasis is on Pinot Noir, but there are some inventive blends—like a Syrah-Tempranillo—to tempt the adventurous.

○ **Marimar Estate Albariño / 2014 / Russian River Valley / $$$**
Torres brings a taste of her native Spain to Sonoma with this refreshing wine with jasmine aromas and layers of apple, white peach and citrus flavors.

● **Marimar Estate Mas Cavalls Pinot Noir / 2013 / Sonoma Coast / $$$**
Mas Cavalls is the Catalan term for "horse farm," a nod to the property's equestrian center. The wine shows its cool-climate provenance with woodsy spice accenting the crisp red fruit.

MARTINELLI WINERY & VINEYARDS

Martinelli's longtime association with celebrated consultants Helen Turley and John Wetlaufer launched its massively scaled, exuberantly full-flavored wines into the collector's stratosphere. Turley and Wetlaufer have moved on, but their protégés Bryan Kvamme and Erin Green still oversee the lineup of small-production estate Zins, Chardonnays, Pinot Noirs and Syrahs. The Martinelli family has been growing grapes in the Russian River Valley since the 1880s, and they still sell about 90 percent of their fruit to other wineries. What they bottle themselves is sold mainly online and through their mailing list, at prices ranging from very reasonable to very expensive for sought-after wines like those from the famous Jackass Hill vineyard.

○ **Martinelli Bella Vigna Chardonnay / 2013 / Sonoma County / $$$** This Chardonnay has green apple and white grapefruit succulence and crisp acidity to balance the voluptuousness.

● **Martinelli Three Sisters Vineyard Pinot Noir / 2013 / Sonoma Coast / $$$$** Lavender, spice and cola aromas lead to a palate of wild raspberry and cranberry in this highly perfumed, graceful red.

MAURITSON WINES

Northwestern Sonoma's Rockpile AVA, with its poor soils and steep ridgelines above Lake Sonoma, was until fairly recently land coveted mainly for sheep grazing. Among the first to tap its potential for wine grapes was the Mauritson family, whose forebears had been farming in Dry Creek Valley since 1868. But it wasn't until 1998 that Clay Mauritson released the family's inaugural bottling, a Dry Creek Valley Zin. He then set his sights on Rockpile, and today his operation is one of the AVA's largest growers and producers and the Rockpile Zins are its calling card. The winery turns out four well-regarded lines from Sonoma County: Mauritson, Rockpile, the Charlie Clay Pinot Noir (with chef Charlie Palmer) and the LOAM Cabs.

○ **Mauritson Sauvignon Blanc / 2014 / Dry Creek Valley / $$** Fermentation and aging in stainless steel preserved this white's mouthwatering acidity, with its richness coming from ripe grapefruit, guava and white peach fruit.

● **Mauritson Zinfandel / 2014 / Dry Creek Valley / $$$** Classic Dry Creek briary raspberry and cherry fruit character stands out in this richly flavored, spicy wine that elevates any kind of barbecue to greater heights.

MEDLOCK AMES WINERY

This lovely property on Bell Mountain above Alexander Valley is a holistic enterprise. It produces all of its own energy from solar power, collects and stores its own water and farms its grapes, olive oil and other produce organically from just 55 acres, with another 283 acres left wild. It is well off the beaten track, a fact that inspired partners Chris Medlock James and winemaker Ames Morison to open their popular tasting room and bar in Healdsburg. The wines are limited in production, but broad in range: Numerous small bottlings, all from the estate, showcase different aspects of the vineyards' potential.

○ **Medlock Ames Sauvignon Blanc / 2015 / Alexander Valley / $$**
Some neutral-oak aging adds a slightly creamy texture to this wine's pear, apple and white peach flavors. It's a welcome counterpoint to citrus-based Sauvignons.

● **Medlock Ames Snakepit / 2013 / Alexander Valley / $$$**
Mostly Merlot with a balance of Cabernet Sauvignon, this rich, ripe red offers floral and forest-floor aromas and a smooth palate of jammy red cherry and blackberry.

MERRY EDWARDS WINERY

As her business card proclaims, Merry Edwards is the *Reine de Pinot* ("Queen of Pinot"). A pioneer of clone-specific winegrowing, Edwards has been perfecting her sure-handed style of lush, nuanced Pinot Noir, Chardonnay and Sauvignon Blanc for more than 40 years—her résumé includes stints at the esteemed Mt. Eden and Matanzas Creek—and the wines are often astonishingly good given their somewhat below-the-radar status. Her namesake winery settled into its own beautiful facility near Sebastopol in 2008. One secret: a creamy, estate-grown and -vinified sparkling wine that Merry Edwards's fans wish she'd make more often than every seven to 10 years or so.

○ **Merry Edwards Sauvignon Blanc / 2014 / Russian River Valley / $$$**
Barrel fermentation and aging on the spent yeast lends creaminess and a honeyed character to this wine's racy, subtly herbal tangerine, lychee and guava aromas and flavors.

● **Merry Edwards Meredith Estate Pinot Noir / 2013 / Russian River Valley / $$$** From Edwards's own vineyard, the Meredith Pinot is arguably the most fruity (think black cherry, pomegranate and plum) and richest of her reds, with supple tannins and a lingering, luscious finish.

NALLE WINERY

Doug Nalle is a humorous man with a serious intent and a major stubborn streak. At his winery in the Zinfandel heartland of Sonoma's Dry Creek Valley, he refuses to produce the jammy, high-alcohol Zins that have been an industry fashion for many years. Nalle has instead carved out a niche for graceful, claret-like Zins with plenty of stuffing but also a food-loving elegance. The winery also turns out notable Pinot Noirs, a Chardonnay and a Bordeaux-style blend. Doug and Lee Nalle's son Andrew, now the winemaker, is a fifth-generation Dry Creek Valley farmer—Lee's family has worked the estate vineyard land since 1927, and her Saini family cousins run the vineyard today.

- **Nalle Henderlong Vineyard Zinfandel / 2013 / Dry Creek Valley / $$$** This Zin's ever-evolving notes of wild raspberry, blood orange and leafy herbs are framed by smoky oak. On the lean, tart side now, it will develop over the next five years.
- **Nalle Zinfandel / 2014 / Dry Creek Valley / $$$** Splashes of Petite Sirah and Carignane add interest to this medium-bodied Zinfandel, with cherry and raspberry fruit, gentle spice and remarkably low (for Zin) 13.6 percent alcohol.

PAPAPIETRO PERRY WINERY

This is a two-family operation started by a pair of San Francisco friends, Ben Papapietro and Bruce Perry, as a hobby operation in Papapietro's garage—true American *garagistes*. As the wine bug overcame them, they moved into a facility in Sonoma in the 1990s and began producing commercial lots of Pinot Noir and Zinfandel, plus one Chardonnay. The partners put all of their vineyard- and clonal-designate wines though a similar regime—which includes cold presoaking for gentle extraction and use of the same cultured yeast strains and François Frères barrels. The differences you taste in these wines shine through from the vintage, the vineyard and the grapes.

- **Papapietro Perry Leras Family Vineyards Pinot Noir / 2013 / Russian River Valley / $$$** Ripe, fleshy and opulent, this wine is also balanced and elegant, with supple tannins and juicy red and black cherry, spice, fresh earth and mineral character.
- **Papapietro Perry Peters Vineyard Pinot Noir / 2013 / Russian River Valley / $$$** This cherry-lover's delight is loaded with bright red fruit and toasty vanillin, cola and baking spice. Juicy, supple and generous, it has the structure for veal and pork.

PATZ & HALL

This excellent producer—long under many consumers' radar—was acquired in 2016 by Ste. Michelle Wine Estates (see Chateau Ste. Michelle, p. 233). Plans are to keep the crew, including principals Donald Patz and James Hall, intact and emphasize continuity, which is good news for lovers of Burgundy-style wines. Thanks in part to an all-star collection of vineyard sources, ranging from Mendocino County in the north down to the Santa Lucia Highlands—and including Hyde, Pisoni and Hudson—Patz & Hall has become one of the country's most reliable producers of fine Chardonnay and Pinot Noir. The focus on top fruit from single vineyards gives Patz & Hall's lineup a diversity that showcases an array of flavor and aroma profiles.

○ **Patz & Hall Hudson Vineyard Chardonnay / 2014 Carneros Napa Valley / $$$** From Lee Hudson's acclaimed vineyard, this Chardonnay balances richness with refreshment, and juicy pear, peach and apple fruit with smoky, nutty oak.

● **Patz & Hall Jenkins Ranch Pinot Noir / 2014 / Sonoma Coast / $$$** With bold, spicy cherry, raspberry and pomegranate flavors that flood the mouth, a creamy mid-palate and silky texture, this red begs for beef bourguignon.

PAUL HOBBS WINERY

The protean Paul Hobbs, whose winemaking projects range from Argentina to New York's Finger Lakes, maintains his home base in Sebastopol, California. But even here, his reach extends across boundaries, to the stunning, ultra-luxury-priced Cabs he makes from Napa's iconic Beckstoffer To Kalon Vineyard and other Beckstoffer properties. Closer to home, Hobbs is scarcely less notable for the striking, firm-structured and polished Pinot Noirs and Chardonnays he creates from top Russian River and Carneros vineyard sources like Richard Dinner, Ulises Valdez, Hyde and Katherine Lindsay. Try the second-label CrossBarn wines for a taste of Hobbs's style at a more affordable price.

○ **Paul Hobbs Richard Dinner Vineyard Chardonnay / 2013 / Sonoma Mountain / $$$$** This Chardonnay is dense and intense, with crème brûlée and vanilla seasoning stone-fruit and citrus flavors. For all its richness, it finishes fresh.

● **CrossBarn Pinot Noir / 2014 / Sonoma Coast / $$$** Firm yet supple tannins give the wine backbone. Generous and juicy, it's enhanced by cocoa, savory spice and dried-herb notes.

PEAY VINEYARDS

The Peay vineyard is part of a 280-acre estate in Sonoma County's remote northwestern edge, four miles from the ocean. The site's cool, windy conditions make ripening grapes a vintage-by-vintage, nail-biting exercise for winemaker Vanessa Wong (formerly of Peter Michael) and the Peay brothers, Nick and Andy, who planted their vines here in 1998. The payoff comes in riveting Pinot Noirs, Syrahs and Chardonnays—vibrant, expressive wines with an emphatic sense of place. Even the entry-level bottlings, like the Sonoma Coast Pinots and Chardonnays, are worth seeking out for lovers of racier, higher-acid European-style wines. Check Peay's website to access the more gently priced second-label Cep Vineyards wines.

○ **Peay Chardonnay / 2014 / Sonoma Coast / $$$**
Minerally, taut and lemony, this is a wine to serve now with briny shellfish. Give it a few years in the bottle and it will become more generous, fruity and rewarding.

● **Peay Pinot Noir / 2013 / Sonoma Coast / $$$**
Estate and purchased grapes make up this scintillating wine with cherry and forest-floor aromas and a brisk palate of red fruit, spice and minerality.

PETER MICHAEL WINERY

This highly praised—and highly priced—winery was founded by a Briton, Sir Peter Michael, who bought close to a square mile of volcanic mountainside in Sonoma's Knights Valley in 1982. Limited production and an avid following make its French-named wines hard to find, but persistence (or getting on the mailing list) will reward lovers of full-flavored, palate-saturating Chardonnay and Bordeaux-style reds. Most of the acclaimed Pinot Noirs hail from the Seaview Vineyard, on the cool, rainy Sonoma Coast. Winemaker Nicolas Morlet, who took over from his brother Luc in 2005, makes 15 super-premium bottlings.

○ **Peter Michael Mon Plaisir Chardonnay / 2013 / Knights Valley / $$$$**
Super-rich and exotic, this offers intense honeysuckle, fig and stone-fruit character on a luxuriant palate, with crème brûlée and toasty oak accents.

● **Peter Michael Les Pavots / 2013 / Knights Valley / $$$$**
Brooding, dark and muscularly tannic now, this Cab-based blend has lurking cassis, plum, mocha and cedar character that should emerge more fully with five years of bottle age.

PORTER CREEK VINEYARDS

A father-and-son team, George and Alex Davis, run this small Russian River Valley outfit with hands-on, micromanaged determination. Farming is certified organic and biodynamic. French-trained winemaker Alex—he took over from his dad in 1997—has in some years personally pruned all of the estate's 20 vineyard acres. The Davises made their reputation with Pinot Noir and Chardonnay, later adding Rhône reds and Zin to their roster. The home estate features George's Hill, a steep, terraced slope whose existing vines the elder Davis added to when he bought the place in the late 1970s. All of the wines here are moderately priced for their quality.

○ **Porter Creek Chardonnay / 2013 / Russian River Valley / $$$** With the replanting of George's Hill, the Davis family tapped a nearby old-vine site for this wine. Toasty oak and a hint of butter frame its lean pear and green apple fruit.

● **Porter Creek Fiona Hill Vineyard Pinot Noir / 2012 / Russian River Valley / $$$** The winery's flagship Pinot is elegant and velvety, with mouthwatering red berry, cherry and cola character. Oak sits well in the background, allowing the pristine fruit to shine.

QUIVIRA VINEYARDS & WINERY

Pete and Terri Kight, who bought this Dry Creek Valley stalwart in 2006, have committed it wholeheartedly to biodynamic farming. This has not only raised the creature quotient around the place—chickens, cows, bees—as viticulturist Ned Horton and winemaker Hugh Chappelle seek to make it self-sustaining, but they believe it also allows them to harvest mature fruit at lower sugar levels, which in turn produces more balanced wines. Chappelle (formerly of Lynmar Estate; see p. 127) oversees a limited, high-quality portfolio that plays to Dry Creek Valley's viticultural strengths, but may be unique in its focus on Sauvignon Blanc, Zinfandel and Grenache, plus small-lot bottlings of other Rhône-style blends.

○ **Quivira Refuge Sauvignon Blanc / 2014 / Dry Creek Valley / $$** Aged in barrels, in contact with spent yeast cells, this Sauvignon Blanc is marked by smoky aromas, mouth-filling texture and crisp pineapple, quince and lime flavors.

● **Quivira Wine Creek Ranch Grenache / 2014 / Dry Creek Valley / $$$** This juicy, vivacious Grenache offers red cherry, red raspberry and strawberry pie character and silky, Pinot Noir–like texture.

RADIO-COTEAU

Highly regarded artisan winemaker Eric Sussman creates wines from cool-climate coastal-vineyard sources in the Sonoma Coast, Russian River Valley and Mendocino's Anderson Valley, and he has a talent for dialing up complexity and flavor intensity while also achieving balance and vibrancy. Certified biodynamic, Radio-Coteau focuses on small lots of super-distinctive wines that Sussman handles in the old-fashioned way, using natural fermentations with all native yeasts and bottling unfined and unfiltered. Pinot Noirs like the multivineyard La Neblina blend and the single-vineyard Savoy made Sussman's name, but his Chardonnays, Syrahs and even a Riesling and a Zin also showcase the skill and energy he lavishes on every wine.

○ **Radio-Coteau Wingtine Chardonnay / 2013 / Sonoma Coast / $$$$** Named for a tool used to break up soil, this is racy and refined, with lemon, green apple, pear and pineapple scents and flavors.

● **Radio-Coteau La Neblina Pinot Noir / 2013 / Sonoma Coast / $$$** La Neblina (Spanish for "the fog") offers fresh red fruit, woodsy spice, smooth texture and a refreshing finish. A good match for charcuterie and roast pork.

RAMEY WINE CELLARS

David Ramey is one of California's most respected trendsetting winemakers. After working with the legendary Moueix family in Bordeaux and at prestigious producers like Dominus and Rudd (see pp. 37 and 75)—and gaining a reputation along the way for groundbreaking Chardonnays, Cabernets and Syrahs—Ramey and his wife, Carla, created their own label in 1996. He sources grapes from a dazzling collection of top vineyards, including Chardonnay from Sonoma's sea-cooled reaches and Cabernet from the warmer Napa Valley. Two well-received Pinot Noirs have now been added to the strong lineup. Though the top bottlings soar into the triple-digit range, there are still remarkably well-priced wines to be had here.

○ **Ramey Ritchie Vineyard Chardonnay / 2013 / Russian River Valley / $$$$** Intensely flavored grapes from 41-year-old vines went into this white, with tons of Meyer lemon, pear, mango, caramel and cream character. A brisk finish keeps it balanced.

● **Ramey Pinot Noir / 2014 / Russian River Valley / $$$** There's a briary, sarsaparilla character to this gently oaked red's vibrant cherry compote and blackberry flavors.

RAVENSWOOD

When Joel Peterson started making Zinfandel in the 1970s, he was an evangelist for bold, full-throttle, deeply purple Zins that were as far from the prevailing White Zinfandel blush wines as you could get. His "No Wimpy Wines" credo remains operative at Ravenswood to this day, even though the megabrand became part of the portfolio of the wine giant Constellation Brands in 2001. Ravenswood produces wine from as many as 10 varieties (five main ones) and in four pricing tiers, from entry-level wines in the Vintners Blend series to the midprice County series and the somewhat pricier single-vineyard offerings. There are fine values across the roster here for lovers of tooth-purpling reds.

● **Ravenswood Old Hill Zinfandel / 2013 / Sonoma Valley / $$$**
Made with grapes from a field-blend vineyard dating to 1852, this three-quarters Zinfandel bottling offers brambly red fruit, spice, brawny tannins and a promise of improving with age.

● **Ravenswood Icon / 2012 / Sonoma County / $$$$**
Honoring the pre-Prohibition "mixed blacks" wines, this blend combines Carignane, Petite Sirah, Zinfandel, Alicante Bouchet and Garnacha in a black-fruit, juicy, spicy taste of history.

RED CAR WINERY

Part of the post-millennium wave of "do things the right/hard way" wineries, the partners in this boutique producer, led by winemaker Carroll Kemp, positioned themselves out in the chill, foggy reaches of the Sonoma Coast, where, as hands-on farmers, they are practicing biodynamic and organic viticulture and making their wines with native yeasts and natural acidity. Their vibrant, well-regarded Pinot Noirs, Chardonnays and Syrahs have gained a strong insider following, though their marketing techniques may have confused some consumers at first. Red Car's early releases carried fanciful proprietary names, such as The Aphorist and Dreaming Detective, that are now mostly gone. These wines sell themselves on the genuine distinction of their vineyard and appellation names.

○ **Red Car Chardonnay / 2013 / Sonoma Coast / $$$**
Exotic floral and citrus scents lead to a white grapefruit and Granny Smith apple palate, with caramel notes on the finish.

◐ **Red Car Estate Vineyard Pinot Noir / 2013 / Fort Ross-Seaview / $$$$**
This vibrant wine displays racy acidity, minerality, crunchy red cherry, cranberry and raspberry fruit and a hint of forest floor.

RIVERS-MARIE

Thomas Rivers Brown is arguably the most famous California winemaker unknown to the general public—partly because the wines he has crafted for producers like Outpost (see p. 66), Maybach and Schrader tend to be made in small quantities and sold through mailing lists at stiff prices. But when he and longtime partner Genevieve Welsh combined their middle names and launched their own wine label, the insiders who lionize Brown clambered on board. Rivers-Marie now has a lengthy waiting list to buy wines. The offerings are two-fold: the much-sought-after Burgundian-style Pinot Noirs and Chardonnays from the Sonoma Coast, and powerful, dark Cabernets from Napa, like those that first made Brown's reputation.

● **Rivers-Marie Pinot Noir / 2014 / Sonoma Coast / $$$**
Vibrantly fruity and succulent, this Pinot boasts dark cherry, raspberry and plum flavors on a suave, expansive palate.

● **Rivers-Marie Silver Eagle Vineyard Pinot Noir / 2014 / Sonoma Coast / $$$** Viticulturist extraordinaire Ulises Valdez's own vines near Occidental yielded this polished red, with intense cola, black cherry, black currant and licorice character, firm structure and subtle toasty oak. Cranberry and pomegranate mark the crisp, lingering finish.

ROCHIOLI VINEYARDS & WINERY

The Rochiolis were pioneering vintners in Sonoma's now-prized Russian River Valley, and third-generation winemaker Tom has long made this a name to reckon with in American Pinot Noir, both for the estate-based wines the winery bottles itself and for the proud Rochioli Vineyard designation on the labels of the top producers they sell to. Unusual for a Pinot specialist, Rochioli's Sauvignon Blanc has developed its own avid following, but it is the estate's Burgundy-inspired, single-vineyard Pinot Noirs and Chardonnays that cause collectors to salivate. It can take years to get on the winery's mailing list for those wines, but fortunately Rochioli's other offerings are more widely available.

○ **Rochioli Sauvignon Blanc / 2015 / Russian River Valley / $$$**
Rochioli's relatively obtainable foundation white is crisp and racy, with grapefruit leading to more subtle green melon notes.

● **J. Rochioli West Block Pinot Noir / 2013 / Russian River Valley / $$$$**
This ethereal, elegant wine is notable for its pure red and black cherry fruit, succulence, velvety texture and layered complexity.

RODNEY STRONG VINEYARDS

Rodney Strong helped break new ground for Sonoma winemaking when he retired from his Broadway dancing career and founded this winery in 1959. Owned since 1989 by the Klein family, and run by Tom Klein, a former McKinsey management consultant, the brand has benefited from the Kleins' investments. With an assist from star consultant David Ramey (see Ramey Wine Cellars, p. 136), longtime winemaker Rick Sayre presides over a substantial 900,000-plus-case operation that has developed a strong reputation for putting value in the bottle at the entry-level prices, and for crafting top-end single-vineyard wines like the signature Alexander's Crown Cabernet Sauvignon.

○ **Rodney Strong Estate Vineyards Chardonnay / 2014 / Sonoma Coast / $$** Half of the grapes were fermented in new French oak, and the toast, caramel and baking spice character shines through, joining pear, apple and citrus fruit.

● **Rockaway / 2012 / Alexander Valley / $$$$**
This is a plush Cabernet, with loads of ripe red and black fruit and mild tannins. Vanillin oak, toast and tea leaf add interest.

SBRAGIA FAMILY VINEYARDS

Ed Sbragia made his name as Beringer's longtime head winemaker, a job that required him to balance quality and high-volume production. At his own Dry Creek Valley venture, the big-volume demands are off—he makes about 12,000 cases total—and his own winemaking personality comes through in premium-priced, small-lot wines from select vineyards and blocks that are bold and full-flavored but with a polished refinement. A special place in Sbragia's heart is reserved for the Gino's Vineyard Zinfandel: Named for his father, the vineyard is a place where Sbragia played as a child and introduced his son Adam, who now works with him, to viticulture.

○ **Sbragia Home Ranch Chardonnay / 2014 / Dry Creek Valley / $$**
The family's vineyard produced this generous wine filled with ripe tropical, citrus and stone-fruit aromas and flavors. It has oak spice and hazelnut accents and a bright, juicy finish.

● **Sbragia La Promessa Zinfandel / 2013 / Dry Creek Valley / $$$**
Founder Ed Sbragia's promise to his father, Gino, to continue to make Dry Creek Valley wines is fulfilled in this vibrant Zin, with wild raspberry, plum, spice and vanillin oak character.

SCHERRER WINERY

This is the type of winery—one where the winemaker grows up on the soil— that's more common in Europe than in the States. Fred Scherrer spent his youth among the wine rows of the Alexander Valley property purchased by his great-grandfather in 1899 and farmed by his namesake grandfather and, for some 70 years now, by his father, Ed. After a decade as the winemaker at Dehlinger (see p. 108), Fred left in 1997 to get started in earnest on his own label. He made his mark with graceful Zins from the family's 100-year-old vines, and followed up with Cabs, Chardonnays and Rhône varieties, and well-received Russian River Valley and Sonoma Coast Pinot Noirs, whose refined balance underscores his Dehlinger background.

- **Scherrer Dry Rosé of Syrah / 2014 / Sonoma County / $$** Juicy strawberry, cherry and watermelon fruit rides a wave of refreshing acidity. Perfect with salads, fruit tarts and, come late November, Thanksgiving dinner.
- **Scherrer Old and Mature Vines Zinfandel / 2014 / Alexander Valley / $$$** A bright, exuberant Zin, this has aromas of lavender and potpourri and a palate of fresh raspberry and black cherry.

SEBASTIANI VINEYARDS AND WINERY

Part of Bill Foley's ever-expanding winery portfolio (Chalk Hill, Merus, Kuleto) since 2008, this historic brand has been staging a quality revolution: lowering production, rethinking winery and farming practices and reshuffling its vineyard roster. Sebastiani's longtime winemaker, Mark Lyon, a holdover from the previous regime, oversees a big lineup of sub-appellation and single-vineyard image makers designed to showcase Sonoma County's diversity. At the top end of the portfolio is the triple-digit-priced Cherryblock Cabernet, but bottlings like the Dry Creek Zinfandel, the Russian River Valley Chardonnay and the Sonoma Coast Pinot Noir offer fine quality at gentler prices.

- **Sebastiani Sauvignon Gris / 2014 / Russian River Valley / $$** This Sauvignon Gris is a winner for its racy guava and green apple fruit, gentle herbs and bracing finish. It's a match made in oyster heaven.
- **Sebastiani Old Vine Cabernet Sauvignon / 2013 / Sonoma County / $$$** Made from 40- to 50-year-old vines, this Cab offers intense black currant and black cherry fruit, with notes of orange rind, black tea and graphite adding complexity.

SEGHESIO FAMILY VINEYARDS

When the Crimson Wine Group (Pine Ridge, Archery Summit) bought Seghesio in 2011, they acquired one of the first names in Zinfandel: Seghesios were growing Zin in Sonoma County in 1895, and buying prime vineyard land over the decades since. This affords certain luxuries: The vines that produce Seghesio's spicy, briary Old Vine Zinfandel, for example, are on average about 70 years old. The new owners kept on fourth-generation winemaker Ted Seghesio, who produces an extensive lineup that also includes small lots of Italian specialties, like Arneis and the Venom Sangiovese.

○ **Seghesio Arneis / 2015 / Russian River Valley / $$**
Twenty acres at Seghesio are planted to this Italian variety, named the "little rascal" for being difficult to grow. This version is medium-bodied and rich in pear and tropical fruit, with brisk acidity.

● **Seghesio Rockpile Zinfandel / 2013 / Rockpile / $$$**
Grapes from Rockpile, next to Dry Creek Valley, are grown at 800 to 2,100 feet in rocky soils, and develop into muscular, spicy Zins like this one.

SIDURI WINES/NOVY FAMILY WINES

This 20-plus-year-old producer rose to cult heights on founders Adam and Dianna Lee's talent for vineyard scouting. Named for the Babylonian wine goddess, the Siduri label bottles small lots of Pinot Noir from 20 different sites, including such prestige vineyards as Pisoni, Rosella's and Clos Pepe. When the Lees sold their operations to Jackson Family Wines in 2015, Adam signed on to craft wines for at least three more years, now with access to a whole new array of Jackson-owned vineyards. Also included in the sale was the Lees' Novy brand, which focuses on cool-climate Syrah (plus Zinfandel and Chardonnay), also from an exhilarating—or bewildering—variety of sources.

● **Novy Susan's Hill Vineyard Syrah / 2013 / Santa Lucia Highlands / $$$** Chocolaty oak melds with exuberantly ripe blackberry and plum fruit, black pepper and Asian spice in this big, intense wine that finishes long and refreshing.

● **Siduri Keefer Ranch Vineyard Pinot Noir / 2013 / Russian River Valley / $$$** Crackling acidity makes for a lively drink, with juicy red raspberry and Bing cherry fruit. Silky tannins and a hint of vanilla and cocoa lend complexity to this classy effort.

SIMI WINERY

Simi Winery has been operating continuously since 1876—it weathered Prohibition thanks to a legal loophole—and not surprisingly has seen some ups, downs and changes in ownership; it's now part of wine giant Constellation Brands. Simi's recent history has been blessed with some fine winemakers, from Zelma Long, who brought the winery to its zenith of quality in the early 1980s, to Nick Goldschmidt (see p. 115) and Steve Reeder, and now Susan Lueker, who oversees a 500,000-case portfolio that includes both solid values in the Sonoma County Chardonnay and Sauvignon Blanc bottlings and the connoisseur-worthy Landslide and Reserve Cabs.

○ **Simi Sauvignon Blanc / 2014 / Sonoma County / $**
This well-priced white delivers crisp citrus, apple and tropical fruit character and a rounded, lush mouthfeel. It shows best when served with grilled fish and shrimp, and with cheeses.

● **Simi Cabernet Sauvignon / 2013 / Alexander Valley / $$**
This is an excellent value for a well-made Cabernet with bright red cherry and black currant fruit, supple, slightly dusty tannins and a long, juicy finish.

SOJOURN CELLARS

This boutique project began on the tennis court as two playing partners, Craig Haserot and winemaker Erich Bradley, actually followed through on one of those "let's start our own winery" conversations. They have put in a lot of serious work since 2001, notably in gaining access to some stupendous Pinot Noir, Cabernet Sauvignon and Chardonnay grapes. Headliners include the Beckstoffer Georges III Vineyard Cabernet from Napa and Gap's Crown Vineyard Pinot Noir from the Sonoma Coast. The wines do their sites of origin justice; this is a reliable source of fine wine at generally reasonable prices. Given Sojourn's small production, fans may want to get on the mailing list.

○ **Sojourn Chardonnay / 2014 / Sonoma Coast / $$$**
The Gap's Crown, Durell and Sangiacomo vineyards yielded the grapes for this bracing wine with ripe peach, pear and tangerine fruit, hazelnut and a light caramel note.

● **Sojourn Gap's Crown Vineyard Pinot Noir / 2014 / Sonoma Coast / $$$** Firmly structured and intense, this brims with dark cherry and blueberry fruit, spicy oak and a forest-after-a-rainstorm note on the nose and finish. Cellar for up to 10 years.

SONOMA COAST VINEYARDS

Owned by Sonoma-based Vintage Wine Estates (Cartlidge & Browne, Cosentino, Girard), SCV bottles what it calls "wines on the edge"—Pinot Noirs, Syrahs, Chardonnays and a Sauvignon Blanc from the "extreme Sonoma Coast," meaning out near the ocean where fog, cold and rain result in a very different climate and growing season from those of inland vineyards. Veteran winemaker Tony Austin aims to create wines of nervosity, with a Burgundy-style tautness and liveliness—an admirable challenge in this highly changeable vineyard environment where, as the winery notes, the first grapes may ripen and be picked after the last grapes in Napa Valley are safe in the cellar.

○ **Sonoma Coast Vineyards Gold Ridge Hills Chardonnay / 2014 / Sonoma Coast / $$** This two-vineyard blend offers a taut palate of peach, grapefruit and tropical fruit and an underlying oak character that supports, yet doesn't obscure, the brilliant fruit.

● **Sonoma Coast Vineyards Freestone Hills Pinot Noir / 2011 / Sonoma Coast / $$$** Crisp cranberry, pomegranate and red cherry fruit and a savory earth note mark this spicy, elegant Pinot. Pair it with tea-smoked duck and anything with mushrooms.

SONOMA-CUTRER VINEYARDS

Chardonnay has long been the star of this estate, which came to prominence as a rare cult producer of white wine in Sonoma under its founder, former fighter pilot Brice Jones (now of Emeritus). Though the winery was sold to Brown-Forman in 1999, and no longer generates quite as much heat, Sonoma-Cutrer's Australian-born winemaker Mick Schroeter still crafts a range of fine Chardonnays, including the entry-level Russian River Ranches and upper-end Les Pierres and The Cutrer bottlings, as well as Russian River Valley Pinot Noirs. With its array of activities—from croquet to wine and food seminars—Sonoma-Cutrer is also a familiar stop on the wine tourist trail.

○ **Sonoma-Cutrer The Cutrer Chardonnay / 2013 / Russian River Valley / $$$** The aroma recalls an apple pie just out of the oven and the flavors are similar: golden apple, nectarine, butterscotch and spice. Terrific with Thai coconut shrimp curry.

● **Sonoma-Cutrer Pinot Noir / 2013 / Russian River Valley / $$$** This lip-smacking red displays luscious, nearly viscous dark cherry and berry fruit with mouthwatering acidity on the finish and baking spice in the background.

ST. FRANCIS WINERY & VINEYARDS

With its lovely tasting room, sweeping views and mission bell, St. Francis has been a fixture on Sonoma Valley visitors' itineraries for decades. Founded in 1979 by San Francisco businessmen Joe Martin and Lloyd Canton, the winery was sold in 2004 to the Kopf family, owners of the New York–based wine importer and distributor Kobrand. St. Francis established its reputation with soft, full-bodied Sonoma Chardonnays, Merlots and Zinfandels. The entry-level Sonoma Valley Merlot and Old Vines Zin are notable bargains. Katie Madigan and Chris Louton have taken over the duties of founding winemaker Tom Mackey, while vineyard manager Jake Terrell oversees the estate's 400 sustainably farmed vineyard acres in Sonoma Valley and Russian River Valley.

○ **St. Francis Behler Vineyard Chardonnay / 2014 / Sonoma Valley / $$**
Bold and buttery, this was fermented in French oak and boasts crowd-pleasing tropical and citrus fruit, vanillin oak and an affinity for fettuccine Alfredo and lobster Thermidor.

● **St. Francis Old Vines Zinfandel / 2013 / Sonoma County / $$**
This superb-value Zin was sourced from vines ranging in age from 55 to 100 years. Juicy, brambly berries, black pepper and creamy vanillin oak make it a pleasure to drink.

STONESTREET ESTATE VINEYARDS

It would take grand wines indeed to live up to the hype generated by this Jackson Family Wines property. But for deep-pocketed fans of full-throttle, massively built Chardonnays and Cabernets, Stonestreet is a name to reckon with. Winemaker Lisa Valtenbergs's lineup of single-vineyard—really single-block—wines is assembled from some 235 separate blocks and sub-blocks on the estate, with an array of differing sun exposures, soils and elevations. That these vineyards really are remarkable can be seen from the roster of prestigious wineries that have bought the fruit, including Harlan, Marcassin and Peter Michael.

○ **Stonestreet Sauvignon Blanc / 2014 / Alexander Valley / $$$**
This complex, Loire-like white delivers bracing structure, grapefruit and tangerine fruit, and spice and vanillin accents.

● **Stonestreet Rockfall Vineyard Cabernet Sauvignon / 2012 / Alexander Valley / $$$$** With a muscular tannic grip and brisk wild berry and blueberry fruit, this youthful, vanillin-inflected wine will transform to elegant with time.

STUHLMULLER VINEYARDS

Fritz Stuhlmuller followed the European pattern in developing his winery: He grew up working in his parents' 150-acre vineyard, poised where the Alexander Valley, Chalk Hill and Russian River Valley converge. With the dirt of the place under his fingernails, Stuhlmuller built his winery literally from the ground up. In 1996 he decided to keep some of the grapes his parents usually sold and begin bottling wine. His family-run operation, with Danish-born winemaker Leo Hansen in charge of the cellar, now produces some 12,000 cases of generally moderately priced, estate-grown Chardonnays and Cabernet Sauvignons, plus a smattering of well-regarded Zinfandels.

○ **Stuhlmuller Vineyards Estate Chardonnay / 2014 / Alexander Valley / $$** Forward, juicy apple, pear and guava flavors mark this fresh, clean, judiciously oaked white.

● **Stuhlmuller Vineyards Cabernet Sauvignon / 2013 / Alexander Valley / $$$** Herbal, forest-floor notes can be found in Cabernet Sauvignon, and Hansen picked the grapes for this wine early enough to preserve that character. There's plenty of black cherry and berry fruit, too, and polished tannins.

THREE STICKS WINERY

"Billy Three Sticks" was the nickname hung on William S. Price III by his childhood surfing pals in Hawaii. Now several decades on, with a hugely successful private equity career behind him, Price is one of California's most dynamic wine entrepreneurs, owner of the famous Durell and Gap's Crown Vineyards and with ownership interests in several wineries (see Kistler, p. 123, and Lutum, p. 177). Refined and silky, the Three Sticks single-vineyard Chardonnays and Pinots—with several bottlings from Price's own vineyards—were already very good, but the future is brighter still. Star winemaker Bob Cabral, longtime guru at Williams Selyem (see p. 147), joined Three Sticks in 2015.

○ **Three Sticks Origin Chardonnay / 2014 / Sonoma Valley / $$$** Fermented in concrete "eggs" and aged in stainless steel, this Chardonnay from the Durell Vineyard is remarkably rich and creamy, with bright tropical, white peach and citrus flavors.

● **Three Sticks Pinot Noir / 2014 / Russian River Valley / $$$** This is an elegant and finely textured Pinot, with delicate floral aromas, fruit ranging from blood orange to red cherry and dark berry, a silky mouthfeel and a crisp finish.

TROMBETTA FAMILY WINES

This is a new, all-hands-on-deck, small family winery, led by the mother-daughter team of Rickey Trombetta Stancliff (the guiding force) and Erica Stancliff (the winemaker); Rickey's husband, Roger, and son, Michael, pitch in as well. Trombetta produces vineyard-based Pinot Noir and Chardonnay from cool-climate sites around the Petaluma Gap, the 15-mile-wide wind and fog funnel that draws cold air back and forth from the Pacific through the coastal mountains. With Paul Hobbs (see p. 133) as consultant and top-notch fruit from area vineyards like Gap's Crown and Petersen, Trombetta is off to a roaring start.

○ **Trombetta Gap's Crown Vineyard Chardonnay / 2014 / Sonoma Coast / $$$** The vineyard is in the chilly, wind-whipped Petaluma Gap region, and Chardonnays from it have good minerality and laser-like acidity. This version's steely, lemony nature complements grilled sea bass and shrimp.

● **Trombetta Gap's Crown Vineyard Pinot Noir / 2013 / Sonoma Coast / $$$$** Intriguing and utterly pleasant black pepper and Asian spice notes mark this luscious, silky, long-finishing wine with deep black and blue fruit and fine structure.

VÉRITÉ

The late wine mogul Jess Jackson was so impressed by Bordeaux winemaker Pierre Seillan that he brought him to California, gave him the run of the company's hundreds of acres of Sonoma County vineyards and basically told him to knock himself out. Seillan took him at his word, settling on three Bordeaux-style blends that are based not on single *terroirs*, but rather on Seillan's skills in blending the best grapes he can get in a given vintage. La Muse is Merlot-based; La Joie, Cabernet Sauvignon; and Le Désir, Cabernet Franc. All three are stratospherically priced, when you can find them, and built to cellar and age.

● **Vérité La Joie / 2012 / Sonoma County / $$$$**
Mostly Cabernet Sauvignon, with splashes of Merlot, Cabernet Franc and Petit Verdot, the left bank–leaning "joy" blend is smoky and dense now, with gripping tannins. It has a history of gaining softness and generosity by the 10-year mark.

● **Vérité La Muse / 2012 / Sonoma County / $$$$**
In Seillan's version of a Bordeaux right bank Merlot-based blend, toasty oak enhances, without overwhelming, the plump black cherry and plum palate, accented by a salty, licorice note.

WALTER HANSEL WINERY

Stephen Hansel built on his father Walter's modest start: The latter kicked things off by planting 250 vines; the younger Hansel today farms 80 acres in the southern Russian River Valley, and sources all of his 12,000 cases of Pinot Noir, Chardonnay and Sauvignon Blanc from the estate. These are sleeper wines well worth seeking out. Though not exactly inexpensive, Hansel's fragrant, expressive cuvées sell for much less than comparable wines. Their style is inspired by Burgundy, so fans of overblown, sweetly ripe wines should look elsewhere.

○ **Walter Hansel The Meadows Vineyard Chardonnay / 2013 / Russian River Valley / $$$** Enticing aromas of buttery, baked peach pie lead to a firm palate of peach, pineapple, lemon zest and hazelnut, with a hint of honey on the finish.

● **Walter Hansel The South Slope Vineyard Pinot Noir / 2013 / Russian River Valley / $$$** Planted to the Dijon 777 clone, the vineyard produced an exuberant wine with dense black fruit, full body and copious amounts of spice and cherry cola.

WILLIAMS SELYEM

One of California's premier small wineries, Williams Selyem has kept its artisan cred despite immense consumer demand, making Pinot Noir, Zinfandel and Chardonnay with an attention to detail that allows the minimal-interference approach to actually work. The winery understood early on that cool, hard-to-farm places could yield distinctive fruit; its sources range from now-famous vineyards to off-the-grid grape patches. Only the most determined (and deep-pocketed) fans will be able to acquire one of Williams Selyem's single-vineyard wines. Happily, the winery does produce several more-accessible multivineyard bottlings. A new era began here with the 2015 harvest as Jeff Mangahas (formerly of Hartford Family; see p. 117) succeeded longtime winemaker Bob Cabral.

○ **Williams Selyem Heintz Vineyard Chardonnay / 2014 / Russian River Valley / $$$** Warm days and cold nights at the vineyard allowed for the development of this white's ripe tropical fruit flavors and palate-cleansing acidity.

● **Williams Selyem Westside Road Neighbors Pinot Noir / 2014 / Russian River Valley / $$$$** Vines along Healdsburg's Westside Road supplied the fruit for this wine that is loaded with cranberry, cherry and raspberry goodness. Cellaring will only improve it.

WIND GAP

Pax Mahle proves that there are second acts in American lives. He left his highly regarded namesake winery, Pax, after a falling out with his backer (see Donelan Family Wines, p. 109) and founded this hyper-artisan label that pushes the envelope on cool-climate viticulture with a roster of wines both familiar—like Pinot Noir, Chardonnay and Syrah—and esoteric, like Trousseau Gris. Native yeast–fermented for as long as it takes, given little to no aging in new oak that might mask flavors, and bottled unfiltered, these are state-of-the-art, artless wines made by a preeminent talent. Visitors can sample Mahle's style at the tasting room in Sebastopol's buzzing The Barlow complex.

○ **Wind Gap Trousseau Gris / 2015 / Russian River Valley / $$**
Mahle is one of the few Californians to produce this French varietal. The wine is florally aromatic and crisp, full of pear, nectarine, cantaloupe and pineapple flavors, with a racy finish.

● **Wind Gap Armagh Vineyard Syrah / 2013 / Sonoma Coast / $$$**
This Petaluma Gap vineyard yielded a meaty, smoky wine with a distinct bacon fat character, tons of spice and pure blueberry fruit. For all its substance, it's under 13 percent alcohol. Magic.

WOODENHEAD VINTNERS

Thoughtfully made small-production Pinot Noir and Zinfandel are the focus at Nikolai Stez and Zina Bower's Woodenhead Vintners. Stez ranges up and down the coast, through Humboldt, Mendocino and Sonoma Counties and the Santa Cruz Mountains AVA, to tap vineyard sources for his personal-expression wines. His years as assistant winemaker to the great Burt Williams at Williams Selyem (see p. 147) have given him a light-handed touch in the cellar, which employs such artisan techniques as hand-punchdowns and basket pressing. Notable curiosities include the still wines Stez makes from the French Colombard grape and his estimable méthode champenoise sparkler.

○ **Woodenhead Halfshell White French Colombard / 2014 / Russian River Valley / $$** This light-bodied, minerally wine with hints of lime and tropical fruit is fresh-tasting and ideal for raw oysters, as well as delicate white fish and ceviche.

● **Woodenhead Bertoli Vineyard Zinfandel / 2013 / Russian River Valley / $$$** Vines planted some 75 years ago produced this medium-bodied Zin, flush with wild berry, Asian spice, brown sugar and vanilla personality.

Other California

CLAIM TO FAME

There is much more to California winemaking than the stellar output of Napa and Sonoma. Santa Barbara, Mendocino and Central Coast wineries now produce some of the state's most sought-after wines, as well as a vast amount of affordable, very good everyday bottles. But even in these well-established regions, the best is yet to come. As ambitious, young artisan winemakers fan out north, south, east and especially west, and gain an increasingly nuanced understanding of lesser-known regions' affinities for different grapes and winemaking styles, there is a dawning recognition that in the future, seriously fine California wine will be coming from some very unexpected places.

REGIONS TO KNOW

CENTRAL COAST This umbrella AVA includes a diverse swath of Pacific Coast wine lands from the San Francisco Bay Area to **Santa Barbara County** (see p. 150). **Monterey**, on an ocean-cooled peninsula, specializes in Chardonnay and Pinot Noir, with significant bottlings of aromatic whites like Sauvignon Blanc and Riesling. Inland from Monterey but still receiving the benefit of ocean breezes, the **Santa Lucia Highlands** AVA produces boldly flavored Pinot Noirs and Chardonnays. The forested, almost hidden **Santa Cruz Mountains** AVA above Silicon Valley may be one of the most underrated in California, particularly for Pinot Noir and Chardonnay. The warm, inland **Paso Robles** AVA produces rich, flavorful reds, from Cabernet and Zinfandel to an array of Rhône-style Syrah, Grenache and Mourvèdre bottlings.

LAKE COUNTY Tucked away above northern Napa within the North Coast AVA, Lake County has long been known for Sauvignon Blanc. Its **Red Hills** region is gaining acclaim of its own for well-priced Cabernet Sauvignon.

LODI & SIERRA FOOTHILLS The Lodi AVA, in the sprawling Central Valley, is America's bargain-wine destination. Dry, warm weather and vast expanses of vineyard plantings make it the nation's largest producer of Cabernet Sauvignon, Chardonnay, Merlot and Sauvignon Blanc, in addition to its signature juicy, tarry Zinfandels. Old-vine Zins are also the calling card of the emerging Sierra Foothills AVA.

MENDOCINO COUNTY This county in the North Coast AVA, north of Sonoma, is one of California's most charmingly eccentric wine regions, in places a kind of hidden pocket of the '60s. There is sky-high potential, especially in **Anderson Valley**, for vibrant Pinot Noir, Chardonnay and sparkling wines produced from them. The county also turns out some of California's best Gewürztraminer and top-notch old-vine Zinfandels.

SANTA BARBARA COUNTY A world-class wine-producing area with a key geographic quirk: The Pacific Coast mountains here run east–west, not north–south, bringing ocean breezes coursing through the **Santa Ynez** and **Santa Maria Valleys**. Wineries here have often been trendsetters, planting very-cool-climate Pinot Noir and Chardonnay in the **Sta. Rita Hills**, for instance, or concentrating on traditional Rhône Valley varieties.

KEY GRAPES: WHITE

CHARDONNAY California's most widely planted variety is bottled in styles ranging from plump and bland in warm-vineyard, less expensive bottlings to highly processed (plenty of crowd-pleasing oak, alcohol and butter) to taut, racy and minerally from colder locales.

PINOT GRIS/GRIGIO This light-bodied white variety is on the upswing. Though there are still plenty of listless bottlings around, the best have a delicate fruitiness underpinned by a lively, citrusy cut of acidity.

RIESLING Whether this grape, beloved by sommeliers and wine-and-food-pairing fans, will ever have its long-predicted breakthrough in California is questionable. But there are some attractive, affordable bottlings (Monterey is one notable source) and a handful of ambitious efforts by premium winemakers.

SAUVIGNON BLANC Choose your style: Versions of this wine in California recapitulate those found around the globe, from New Zealand–ish tropical fruit and grassiness to Bordeaux-like barrel fermented and aged to crisper, lighter Loire styles.

VIOGNIER, MARSANNE & ROUSSANNE These luscious, often exotically fruited Rhône white grapes can be found bottled separately or in combination. There are some fine bottlings from the North Coast counties, but the Central Coast is the go-to region for these varieties.

KEY GRAPES: RED

CABERNET SAUVIGNON This Bordeaux grape transplants triumphantly well to California, making signature wines for top producers from the warmer areas of Mendocino to the mountain vineyards of the Central Coast and inland to Paso Robles. As in Bordeaux, Cabernet in California is often the basis of blends that include traditional complementary grapes like Merlot and Cabernet Franc (and sometimes untraditional ones like Syrah), but for many vintners here, Cabernet Sauvignon stands alone.

MERLOT In California, Merlot is produced in accessible, soft, mouth-filling versions in the same regions as Cabernet, often at more welcoming prices.

PINOT NOIR The grand, gloriously perfumed, notoriously elusive grape of Burgundy grows best in the cooler-climate regions of Mendocino's Anderson Valley, the Santa Lucia Highlands and Santa Barbara County.

SYRAH The noble red of the northern Rhône Valley has shown a Malbec-like willingness to make many fruity, attractive, good to very good wines in California. But only a few top producers, particularly in the Central Coast, have unlocked the grape's native complexity and balance of subtlety and power.

ZINFANDEL California's gift to the wine world—so transformed from its European origins as to be virtually unrecognizable—Zinfandel thrives in top bottlings, many from old vines, from Mendocino and Paso Robles, and in affordable and pleasing tongue-purplers from Lodi.

Producers/ Other California

ADELAIDA CELLARS

Perched high in the Santa Lucia Mountains in Paso Robles's recently created Adelaida District AVA, the Van Steenwyk family's onetime weekend retreat has become an ambitious, 15,000-case winery operation. Winemaker Jeremy Weintraub (formerly of Seavey; see p. 77) works 168 acres of breeze-swept, chalk-and-limestone-soil vineyards planted to an astonishing 23 grape varieties. As their qualities have revealed themselves over time, the various parcels have come to be dedicated to particular plantings: the Viking vineyards, for example, to Bordeaux grapes, Bobcat Crossing to Portuguese grapes.

○ **Adelaida Version White / 2013 / Adelaida District / $$$**
This Roussanne-Viognier-Grenache Blanc blend has a scent of hothouse flowers and white peach and honeycomb flavors.

● **Adelaida Version Red Reserve / 2013 / Adelaida District / $$$**
A dark-fruit scent and blueberry compote flavors mark this mostly Syrah-Mourvèdre blend (with 8 percent Grenache).

ALBAN VINEYARDS

In the cool southern end of Edna Valley on the Central Coast, contrarian John Alban is one of the most influential California winemakers of the past quarter-century. On the cutting edge of planting Rhône grapes—including Viognier, Roussanne, Syrah, Grenache and Mourvèdre—Alban crafts wines that are paradigm shifts for Cabernet- and Chardonnay-centric California. Though relatively few will get to taste his dense, complex single-vineyard Syrahs, the influence they and other top Alban bottlings have had on his peers has been profound.

○ **Alban Vineyards Viognier / 2014 / Edna Valley / $$$**
With exuberant aromatics, large structure, great intensity of flavor and a gorgeous richness, this is benchmark Viognier.

● **Alban Vineyards Reva Syrah / 2011 / Edna Valley / $$$$**
This wildly exotic Syrah opens with scents of bacon, black cherry, olive and violets. It teeters on excess but stays balanced, tethered to supple tannins and buoyed by lacy acidity.

AU BON CLIMAT WINERY

Both Jim Clendenen and his wines are instantly recognizable: Gregarious and a fan of loud shirts, Clendenen is as idiosyncratic as he is famous. His wines, meanwhile, are sleek and coolly elegant, with a structure that bears the stamp of Clendenen's formative stint in Burgundy in 1981, the year before he and then-partner Adam Tolmach (see The Ojai Vineyard, p. 180) founded Au Bon Climat in Santa Barbara County. Today this trailblazing winery turns out some of California's most flavorful but refined Chardonnays and Pinot Noirs. Clendenen sources grapes from acclaimed Central Coast vineyards, including the iconic Bien Nacido in the Santa Maria Valley subregion. The Santa Barbara County bottlings are striking bargains.

○ **Au Bon Climat Nuits-Blanches au Bouge Chardonnay / 2012 / Santa Maria Valley / $$$** This Chardonnay offers a caramel scent from lees, oak-adorned apple flavors and a sumptuous texture.

● **Au Bon Climat La Bauge Au-dessus Pinot Noir / 2012 / Santa Maria Valley / $$$** There's a fine-boned Burgundian quality to this elegant Pinot, with tart plum flavors, a nori scent and a grainy, peppery feel to the tannins.

BECKMEN VINEYARDS

Well known to aficionados, Beckmen deserves a much wider audience for some of Santa Barbara County's most intriguing Rhône-style wines (at still-reasonable prices). The Beckmen family's wines—made by Tom and Judy Beckman's son Steve—are sourced mostly from the estate's 150 acres planted to grapevines across two Santa Ynez Valley vineyards: the Winery Estate vineyard near Los Olivos and the biodynamically farmed Purisima Mountain Vineyard on Ballard Canyon. The winery produces some of California's most nuanced Syrahs and finest Grenaches—luscious, tongue-purpling wines with great energy and lift. But don't overlook the popular, entry-level Cuvee Le Bec, a blend of Grenache, Syrah, Mourvèdre and Counoise.

● **Beckmen Vineyards Cuvee Le Bec / 2013 / Santa Ynez Valley / $$** Mostly Syrah and Grenache, the 2013 bottling is forward and sappy, redolent of macerating cherries and raspberry, with irresistibly forward fruit.

● **Beckmen Vineyards Block Six Syrah / 2013 / Ballard Canyon / $$$** The winery's top Syrah, this concentrated red is all black fruits, figs and blackberries, with a mildly smoky, spicy top note.

BERNARDUS WINERY

Former Olympic skeet shooter and racecar driver Ben Pon, a cosmopolitan Dutchman, founded a small luxury-lifestyle empire in and around Carmel but reserved his greatest efforts for this ambitious winery project. Longtime winemaker Dean DeKorth's top price tier operates on two tracks. One features the estate-produced Bordeaux-style wines, including the showpiece Bordeaux-blend Marinus, from the Carmel Valley. On the other track are the Burgundy-style wines sourced from cooler vineyards in the Santa Lucia Highlands, including highly regarded bottlings from such elite sites as Pisoni, Sierra Mar and Rosella's Vineyards. The entry-level Monterey County Pinot Noir, Chardonnay and Sauvignon Blanc are typically great values.

○ **Bernardus Sierra Mar Vineyard Chardonnay / 2013 / Santa Lucia Highlands / $$$** Oak-driven and ripe, with a toffee-scented aroma and pineapple and golden apple flavors, this is a big-shouldered Chardonnay with plenty of richness.

● **Bernardus Pinot Noir / 2012 / Santa Lucia Highlands / $$$** Dark as Syrah and with a similar level of extract, this inky red smells like blue fruits complemented by caramelly oak.

BIG BASIN VINEYARDS

Wild and scenic, all but enveloped in aerial views by Big Basin Redwood State Park, this Santa Cruz Mountains artisan project bears the strong imprint of owner Bradley Brown's personal principles. He acquired the overgrown property in the late 1990s, leaving 90 percent of it wild and cultivating the rest organically. Early advice from consultant John Alban (see Alban Vineyards, p. 152) influenced, among other things, the clonal selections planted in these challengingly steep vineyards. Brown's estate Rhône plantings yield radically small harvests of intense grapes, which he ferments naturally, with up to 39 months in barrel.

● **Big Basin Vineyards Gabilan Mountains GSM / 2012 / Monterey County / $$$** Grenache leads in this high-toned, raspberry-scented blend with Syrah and Mourvèdre. The flavors are dark, more Syrah focused, with tar and black pepper accents.

● **Big Basin Vineyards Rattlesnake Rock Syrah / 2012 / Santa Cruz Mountains / $$$** This cool-climate Syrah from Big Basin's home vineyard opens with subtly spicy notes and aromas of carob and mace. Anise highlights adorn plum and cassis flavors, and there's a smoky overlay to the finish.

BIRICHINO

The name (pronounced bee-ri-KEE-no) means "mischievous" in Italian, and it's one to remember, even if you may have to access the small production via the internet. Winemakers Alex Krause and John Locke founded their Santa Cruz winery on Italian Malvasia, of all grapes, but have branched out to Grenache, Cinsault, and Chenin Blanc—their only concession to anything remotely popular is Pinot Noir. They focus on old-vine fruit, including grapes from vineyards dating to the 19th century (the Bechthold Cinsault, from 1886) and early 20th century (the Besson Grenache, from 1910), plus "some from the late Disco Era." Prices are refreshing, with most wines under $25.

- **Birichino Bechthold Vineyard Cinsault / 2014 / Mokelumne River / $$** Light and charming, this strawberry-scented red has a peppery top note. The flavors are more given to cherry and red plum, but the acidity is pleasingly brisk and vibrant.
- **Birichino Besson Vineyard Grenache / 2013 / Central Coast / $$** An earthy salvo of tar and turf leads to strawberry/raspberry fruit flavors that are at once macerated and bright, with a fresh, nimble texture that ripples with acidity.

BLACK KITE CELLARS

Black Kite is a true family affair: Donald and Maureen Green acquired their remote acreage above Mendocino's Anderson Valley in 1995; their daughter and son-in-law, Rebecca and Tom Birdsall, cofounded the winery in 2003. From the estate's Kite's Rest Vineyard come three elegant block-designated Pinot Noirs (including the acclaimed Redwoods' Edge Pinot) and two bottlings (Kite's Rest and the Angel Hawk reserve, made only in top years) blended from the vineyard's three blocks. The winery stepped outside its estate starting in 2010 to source Pinot Noir and Chardonnay from star vineyards like Gap's Crown in Sonoma Coast and Soberanes in Santa Lucia Highlands.

- **Black Kite Gap's Crown Vineyard Pinot Noir / 2013 / Sonoma Coast / $$$** Dark as Syrah and almost as intense, this is a cool-climate Pinot Noir that behaves like a warm-climate wine, with carob scents and plum flavors framed by generous oak.
- **Black Kite Angel Hawk / 2013 / Anderson Valley / $$$$** The 2013 Angel Hawk reserve is almost profligate in its intensity and ripeness. This lavish Pinot gains depth and extravagance from its oak treatment.

BOGLE VINEYARDS & WINERY

The Bogle family has been farming in California's Clarksburg region since the late 1800s—the siblings who manage the estate now are the sixth generation. The family ventured into grape growing relatively late (in 1968), but they now farm 1,600 acres of vineyards in Lodi and in the prime but overlooked Sacramento Delta region. The winery also sources grapes from sites in numerous other subregions, from Mendocino down to Monterey, to produce its expansive portfolio of value-price wines, typically blends from several regions with a California appellation. Especially notable are the Petite Sirah and Old Vine Zinfandel, the latter produced from 60- to 80-year-old vines.

● **Bogle Vineyards Old Vine Zinfandel / 2013 / California / $**
Lean and vinous, with a purple plum scent marked by peppery tannins, this straight-ahead red has the structure and forward fruit for barbecue.

● **Bogle Vineyards Petite Sirah / 2013 / California / $**
Sourced from Clarksburg and Lodi vineyards, this great-value Petite Sirah shows a dramatic concentration of purple power, with a black raspberry burst of flavor on the finish.

BONNY DOON VINEYARD

Talented, iconoclastic Central Coast vintner Randall Grahm sold his successful Cardinal Zin and Big House brands in 2006 and the Pacific Rim label in 2010 to focus on matters closer to his heart—his eclectic range of biodynamically farmed, *terroir*-driven wines, made mostly from Rhône varieties and lesser-known Italian and Spanish grapes. Grahm is capable of hitting the heights and of disappointing, too, but Bonny Doon has been one of the most dynamic wineries in California for many years. The exuberant Rhône-style Le Cigare Volant is the flagship here, but the white and rosé Cigare bottlings and the Clos de Gilroy Grenache-Syrah-Mourvèdre can be outstanding values.

○ **Bonny Doon Vineyard Le Cigare Blanc / 2013 / Arroyo Seco / $$**
The emollient richness of this single-vineyard Roussanne, Grenache Blanc and Picpoul Blanc blend is undercut by a zippy beam of lemony acidity from the Grenache Blanc.

● **Bonny Doon Vineyard Le Cigare Volant / 2011 / Central Coast / $$$**
Mourvèdre and Grenache lead in this Rhône-style red, marked by a vinous scent of tar and tanbark. The flavors are quiet and gentle, wild berries in a thicket, buoyed by lively acids.

BONTERRA ORGANIC VINEYARDS

This Mendocino winery was organic before organic was cool—starting back in 1993—and it has not only stayed the course, but upped the ante, with several hundred acres of its McNab Ranch, Butler Ranch and Blue Heron vineyards, plus the winery itself, now certified biodynamic. Under the ownership of Chilean giant Concha y Toro since 2011, Bonterra has maintained a holistic approach that incorporates wildlife, gardens and food (including cooking webcasts). It doesn't hurt that the wines, especially the notable Zinfandel and Viognier bottlings, tend to overdeliver for the price. Except for winemakers Bob Blue and Jeff Cichocki's very fine higher-priced flagships—the Rhône-style The Butler; The McNab, a Bordeaux blend; and The Roost, a Chardonnay—Bonterra wines generally sell for under $20.

○ **Bonterra Viognier / 2014 / Mendocino County / $$**
Aromas and flavors of peaches and pear, along with a creamy middle palate and rich mouthfeel, mark this classic Viognier.

● **The Butler / Mendocino County / 2012 / $$$**
This Syrah-based Rhône-style blend from Butler Ranch is dark and brooding, with a jammy middle palate and firm tannins.

BREWER-CLIFTON

This much-praised label entered a new era in 2015 when founders Steve Clifton and Greg Brewer sold a majority share to industry insider Ken Fredrickson. Brewer, formerly of Melville (see p. 178), remains as winemaker, while Clifton pursues his other wine projects: the Italian varietal label Palmina and the French grape–focused La Voix. Now using all-estate-grown fruit, Brewer-Clifton continues to celebrate the Cal-Burgundian possibilities of Pinot Noir and Chardonnay from Santa Barbara County's cool-climate Sta. Rita Hills AVA. The winery's track record in producing sophisticated, intense, full-bodied wines has placed it at the forefront of this intriguing region.

○ **Brewer-Clifton 3D Chardonnay / 2013 / Sta. Rita Hills / $$$$**
A broad, complex Chardonnay, this displays scents of loam, ripe apple and citrus and rich flavors nicely framed by classic Sta. Rita Hills acidity.

● **Brewer-Clifton 3D Pinot Noir / 2013 / Sta. Rita Hills / $$$$**
Impressively earthy, with tart cherry and wild-berry aromas, this Pinot offers focused, long-lasting flavors, as savory as rye.

CALERA WINE COMPANY

Josh Jensen spent years in the early 1970s scouring the West Coast for the limestone soils he associated with the great vineyards of Burgundy. He found what he was looking for in this remote place in the Gavilan Mountains, 40 miles southeast of Santa Cruz, as suited to a bandit's hideout as to Pinot Noir—Calera's are still the only vineyards in the Mt. Harlan AVA. The winery specializes in Viognier and boldly flavored wines from Burgundian grapes. The not-inexpensive single-vineyard estate offerings, like the Selleck, Reed and Jensen bottlings, have made Josh Jensen one of California's most respected vintners. The Central Coast line, made with purchased fruit, offers great value.

○ **Calera Viognier / 2013 / Mt. Harlan / $$$**
The chalk soils of Mt. Harlan give this redolent Viognier a firm mineral foundation. The wine leads with pear and lees accents, its flavors flecked by chalky grip.

● **Calera Reed Vineyard Pinot Noir / 2013 / Mt. Harlan / $$$$**
This Pinot has a sunny, red plum core of fruit and depth of flavor, without being overripe. Plum and dark cherry flavors are leavened by cluster spice, with a mineral grip on the finish.

CAMBRIA ESTATE WINERY

Barbara Banke (Jess Jackson's widow) acquired a major portion of the Tepusquet Vineyard in 1986 and has since worked to expand the family's holdings there. Now a vast 1,600-acre estate, Cambria is located in Santa Barbara County's Santa Maria Valley, whose east-west orientation funnels cool ocean breezes inland. This climate is ideal for growing Pinot Noir and the high-acid Chardonnay that accounts for about 60 percent of Cambria's production. Longtime winemaker Denise Shurtleff excels with other varieties, too, turning out smaller-production Syrah and Pinot Gris. The juicy, accessible Benchbreak Chardonnay and Pinot Noir bottlings can be wonderful bargains.

○ **Cambria Benchbreak Chardonnay / 2014 / Santa Maria Valley / $$**
This offers generous scents of pineapple and sweet corn with nutty oak. A lively acidity runs through the rich, juicy fruit.

● **Cambria Benchbreak Pinot Noir / 2013 / Santa Maria Valley / $$**
An expression of cool Santa Maria Valley character, this Pinot's aromas are an herbaceous cross between nori and pine. Its currant and plum fruit flavors are dark and a little muted, ideal for grilled chicken.

CAMERON HUGHES WINE

A man with a plan since he began selling wine out of his station wagon in 2002, Cameron Hughes is a *négociant* who buys wine from others, bottles it and sells it, often for far less than the wine's price under its original name. Consumers have responded to his eye—and palate—for a bargain, evident in his globe-spanning five labels, from the anonymous Lot Series (each of whose wines is assigned a unique lot number) and the everyday-drinking CAM Collection to the grapes-to-glass Hughes Wellman Napa Valley Cabernet Sauvignon. It's a family venture, as his cofounder and wife, Jessica Kogan, oversees marketing and sales, including direct-to-consumer sales from their website.

○ **Cameron Hughes CAM Collection Chardonnay / 2014 / Monterey County / $** This zippy, lemony Chard is crisp and clean, with the acid structure for sipping in the afternoon.

● **Cameron Hughes Lot 469 Cabernet Sauvignon / 2013 / Napa Valley / $$$** Full-on Cabernet from the master collaborator and blender, this wine is powerful and bold, with blackberry flavors and ripe, suave tannins. A lot of wine for the price.

CHANIN WINE CO.

Precocious Gavin Chanin founded his wine company in 2007—two years before he graduated from UCLA with an art degree (those are his paintings on the labels). Chanin is a Santa Barbara true believer, bottling only unblended, single-vineyard Chardonnay and Pinot Noir from some of the area's most respected growers, including Bien Nacido and Sanford & Benedict. He is also an ideologue in the best sense of the word, determined to let those vineyards' flavors shine transparently through without winemaking additives or filtering, and at alcohol levels that emphasize balance and finesse over super-richness. Chanin also insists that his vineyard sources be organic or sustainably farmed.

○ **Chanin Bien Nacido Vineyard Chardonnay / 2014 / Santa Maria Valley / $$$** Luminous and lean, this brisk white offers scents of lime and lees, followed by flavors that recall Thai pineapple dishes, with just enough oak to frame the proceedings.

● **Chanin Bien Nacido Vineyard Pinot Noir / 2013 / Santa Maria Valley / $$$** This red exhibits brilliant color and bright transparency in the glass, but it's richer than it looks, with a lactic breadth to the red cherry fruit that enriches the texture.

CLOS LACHANCE WINERY

Co-owners Bill and Brenda Murphy—he's a former Hewlett-Packard executive who saw his home winemaking hobby "run amok"—sited Clos LaChance in the Lion's Gate Valley (next door to the Santa Cruz Mountains appellation) at the turn of the millennium, thanks to a timely land deal with the nearby CordeValle luxury resort. The family-run operation (the couple's daughters are heavily involved) has become a go-to label for good values, producing an array of wines in three tiers: the single-vineyard Designate Series; the Reserve Series varietal bottlings; and the Estate Series wines (five varietals and a Meritage blend), with extremely attractive price tags, typically under $20.

● **Clos LaChance Reserve Merlot / Central Coast / 2012 / $$** Merlot's red-fruited side comes to the fore in this wine, a red cherry and strawberry mélange grounded by caramelly oak.

● **Clos LaChance Reserve Pinot Noir / Santa Cruz Mountains / 2012 / $$$** Dark and velvety, with a scent of macerating plums and a hint of pine frond, the reserve Pinot has a foresty feel to its tannins that suggests pouring for duck.

COVENANT

Jeff Morgan, a former bandleader and wine writer, joined with wine and food magnate Leslie Rudd (former owner of Dean & DeLuca) to fill a need for fine kosher wine. Their critically acclaimed offerings—particularly the luscious Solomon Lot 70 Cab and the Covenant Napa Cabernet—have made this small project a name to be reckoned with. Sourced from top Napa vineyards and produced under rabbinic supervision, the more steeply priced Covenant-label wines are kosher for Passover; the newer Tribe and Mensch wines are also *mevushal* (i.e., the grapes are specially heat treated so that the wine remains kosher even if handled by non-Jews). The more affordable Red C label includes a red blend, a Sauvignon Blanc and a rosé.

○ **"Red C" Sauvignon Blanc / 2014 / Dry Creek Valley / $$** Classic warm-region Sauvignon Blanc, full of grapefruit and fresh melon flavors with an herbal edge, this appealing white also happens to be kosher.

● **Covenant Solomon Lot 70 Cabernet Sauvignon / 2014 / Napa Valley / $$$$** While not inexpensive, Covenant's lush, layered top bottling is the best kosher Cab made in the US; it's also, all religious considerations aside, a world-class bottle of wine.

DAOU VINEYARDS & WINERY

Located 2,200 feet up on the west side of Paso Robles, this is the inspired project of two Lebanese-French brothers, Daniel and Georges Daou. The brothers have poured their passion (and funds from their tech IPO) into the old Hoffman Mountain Ranch property, which they acquired in 2007 and began restoring in 2012. Their stated aim is to produce a Cabernet that rivals the world's best, and the top wine, the triple-digit-priced Soul of a Lion, is by many estimations well on the way. But vintner Daniel has much else on offer, including estimable Bordeaux-style wines and a luscious Cabernet-Syrah.

○ **Daou Reserve Chardonnay / 2014 / Paso Robles / $$$**
Rich, ripe, wildly over the top, this classic California Chardonnay delivers scents of caramel and butter, flavors like a pineapple dessert and a long, satisfying finish.

● **Daou Cabernet Sauvignon / 2013 / Adelaida District / $$$$**
Easier on the wallet than the Soul of a Lion bottling, the estate Cab is luxurious to the point of sweet when first poured, with plush black plum scents and flavors that lean darker, toward fig, all framed by sumptuous oak.

DENNER VINEYARDS

Denner has become a player to be reckoned with in the Central Coast Rhône varietal scene in a relatively short time. Located on the western side of Paso Robles, the estate is inland, but still marine-influenced thanks to the east–west corridor of the Templeton Gap. Its 130 planted acres yield 20 mostly Rhône-style grape varieties, though Cabernet Sauvignon makes up about one-third of the plantings (with Syrah accounting for almost another quarter). Owner Ron Denner's former career as a Ditch Witch construction equipment dealer is reflected in the names of some of these sought-after Rhône blends, like the Ditch Digger and the Dirt Worshipper.

○ **Denner Vineyards Theresa / 2014 / Paso Robles / $$$**
With Roussanne leading its parade of varieties, this white blend opens with whey and preserved lemon scents, followed by rich, quince compote–like flavors and a zippy, appley finish.

● **Denner Vineyards The Ditch Digger / 2013 / Paso Robles / $$$$**
About half Grenache, with Mourvèdre, Syrah, Counoise and Cinsault components, this high-toned red has red cherry and tar aromas, a dark plum and cherry core, and suave tannins.

DIERBERG VINEYARD/STAR LANE VINEYARD

Jim and Mary Dierberg, longtime owners of the well-regarded Hermannhof Winery in Missouri, had a yen to produce the kind of traditional European grapes that weren't well suited to conditions back home. In 1996 they bought an old Santa Barbara County cattle ranch and transformed it into Star Lane Vineyard, dedicated to Bordeaux varietals. The next year they purchased the property that would become the Pinot Noir– and Chardonnay-centric Dierberg, and in 2003 acquired their third vineyard, Drum Canyon, in the Sta. Rita Hills. The Dierbergs tracked down and experimented with numerous cuttings to create the "spice box" for blending their expressive wines.

● **Dierberg Pinot Noir / Santa Maria Valley / 2013 / $$$**
Hints of smoke and seaweed lead off this Pinot's aromas. It's more forward and juicy on the palate, with a demonstrative oak frame and dark blue berry flavors.

● **Star Lane Vineyard Astral Cabernet Sauvignon / 2010 / Happy Canyon of Santa Barbara / $$$$** A reserve made in a cool year, this wine has a tobacco-like scent framing dark currant and fig flavors. A pleasing savoriness is developing as the wine ages.

DOMAINE ANDERSON

The Rouzaud family that controls Champagne Louis Roederer and its pioneering Mendocino project, Roederer Estate (see p. 185), is extending its reach to the cool, foggy Anderson Valley. The family began this new still wine venture in 2011 with the purchase of the Dach winery and vineyard, and they haven't stinted on investment. Among other things, the hillside Pinot Noir acreage was replanted with clones from such elite sources as Domaine de la Romanée-Conti and Calera (see p. 158). Winemaker Jerry Murray was brought in from Oregon's Van Duzer to craft Anderson's estate Chardonnay and Pinot, as well as two single-vineyard wines, from the Dach and Walraven vineyards.

○ **Domaine Anderson Chardonnay / 2014 / Anderson Valley / $$$**
This savory white shows a mostly lactic character, with a scent of kefir and lees and golden apple and pear fruit off in the distance. It's a rich wine worth cellaring.

● **Domaine Anderson Pinot Noir / 2013 / Anderson Valley / $$$**
Tobacco and tar aromas adorn a pure red cherry core of fruit, textbook for the Anderson Valley. The flavors are simple but marvelously detailed, with a lacy delicacy to the acids.

DOMAINE DE LA CÔTE

Rajat Parr and Sashi Moorman, the hands-on partners behind Sandhi (see p. 186), produced their first Pinot Noirs from this new venture with the 2011 vintage. Located in the far western Sta. Rita Hills, the estate's 65 organically farmed acres, spread among five dramatically differing vineyard plots, were part of the Evening Land Vineyards project, which Moorman had originally helped develop. Parr and Moorman's controversial approach—including low alcohol levels, taut acidity and non-interference winemaking—has garnered them a close following. The tiny production is sold through their mailing list and at the winery.

● **Domaine de la Côte Sta. Rita Hills / 2013 / Sta. Rita Hills / $$$**
This Pinot sees only 50 percent whole cluster fermentation, in neutral barrels. It's dark and mildly plummy, with savory scents and olive, tanbark and kelp-like flavors at the forefront for now. A year's cellaring should bring more balance.

● **Domaine de la Côte Bloom's Field / 2013 / Sta. Rita Hills / $$$$**
This wild and herbal Pinot offers aromas of violet, pepper, flower petals and smoke, dark currant flavor laced with cluster spice and a surprisingly tender texture.

DONKEY & GOAT WINERY

Berkeley-based Donkey & Goat is owned and run with evangelical fervor by Jared Brandt and his wife, Tracey (their website includes a Manifesto). Rhône-style wines, particularly the Syrahs sourced from cool-climate vineyards, are the mainstays here, but the winery also turns out some well-regarded Pinot Noir and versions of Chardonnay. The owners go far beyond the usual natural winemaking (no adding lab yeast or enzymes, fining or filtering, or over-oaking) to ban, for example, the use of plastic bins and containers in the winemaking process. The whole point is to allow the fruit and *terroir* to come to the fore.

○ **Donkey and Goat Sluice Box / 2013 / El Dorado / $$**
Hewing to their non-interventionist approach, the Brandts use minimal sulfites in their wines. For this ripe and incredibly aromatic white blend from California's emerging El Dorado region, they added only one-sixteenth the legal limit.

● **Donkey & Goat Fenaughty Vineyard Syrah / 2013 / El Dorado / $$$**
Lean in the extreme, this savory, smoky Syrah offers scents of a dirty martini, a whiff of black currant and a palate that's more about texture.

DREW

Jason Drew served apprenticeships under some of the wine industry's most notable names, including John Kongsgaard and Bryan Babcock. His dream of working for himself came true when he discovered a 26-acre orchard in Mendocino Ridge for sale. Planted to Pinot Noir in 2011, and producing its first commercial crop in 2014, it is the farthest west—i.e., closest to the ocean—vineyard in Mendocino County. Meanwhile, mailing-list members have the best chance of tasting his estate wines and graceful translations of Pinot, Syrah and Albariño from some of Mendocino's top small-grower vineyards. These aren't the easiest places in California to ripen grapes, but the best wines that emerge have a taut, lively distinctiveness.

- **Drew Fog-Eater Pinot Noir / 2013 / Anderson Valley / $$$** From the foggy "deep end" of the Anderson Valley, this quiet, leafy red is delicate and transparent in its flavors and texture.
- **Drew Perli Vineyard Syrah / 2013 / Mendocino Ridge / $$$** This is consistently one of California's greatest Syrahs. Its scents of peppercorn and rose petal lead to delicate flavors resembling blackberry tea.

EDMUNDS ST. JOHN

Steve Edmunds is a true California maverick, making Rhône-style wine—in Berkeley—long before Rhône was fashionable. His 1,200 to 1,500 cases a year are personal, *terroir*-driven wines sourced from four carefully curated vineyards and defiantly out of the high-alcohol, heavy-extraction mainstream. These wines, he says, "favor energy over power, freshness over richness." They are often built for the long haul—particularly the Syrahs from sources like Fenaughty and Barsotti—and are less immediately palate-flattering when young, but the best offer up astonishments as they mature.

- **Edmunds St. John Bone-Jolly Gamay Noir / 2014 / El Dorado County / $$** The exuberant, happy-making fruitiness of mountain Gamay is leavened here by a granitic dusting of minerals. It's cheery and bright, rippling with acidity and ready for a chill.
- **Edmunds St. John Fenaughty Vineyard Syrah / 2012 / El Dorado County / $$$** The 2012 Fenaughty, like its predecessors, displays a nice tension between fresh spice—peppercorn and bay laurel—and a warmer baked spice component, like mace, all in the service of black granite-tinged fruit.

EPOCH ESTATE WINES

Geologists and self-proclaimed wine nuts Bill and Liz Armstrong have thrown themselves wholeheartedly into this acclaimed Paso Robles brand. In a little over a decade they bought and reinvigorated the warm-by-day Paderewski Vineyard; bought and planted the cooler Catapult vineyard (in the Pacific wind tunnel of the Templeton Gap); bought and transformed the almost 200-acre, 1882 York Mountain Winery property, which they replanted in 2015; and built a gleaming new winery. Along the way, winemaker Jordan Fiorentini has put the project on the map for lovers of Paso Robles Rhône-style wines with a roster of flavorful, all-estate-grown blends that carry names like Ingenuity, Authenticity and Veracity.

○ **Epoch Estate Wines White / 2014 / Paso Robles / $$$**
This peachy blend of Viognier and Grenache Blanc offers lemon curd sweetness and crisp, zippy acidity.

● **Epoch Estate Wines Ingenuity / 2012 / Paso Robles / $$$$**
Suave, dark and plummy, this plush red, a blend of mostly Syrah, with Mourvèdre, Grenache and Petite Sirah, displays the cocoa and dark plum flavors of the Syrah, a modicum of juiciness from the Grenache and fine ripe tannins.

FEL WINES

Spring 2014 marked the official transition of Anderson Valley's Breggo, much admired by Pinot Noir lovers, to FEL under the new ownership of deep-pocketed Canadian Cliff Lede (see Cliff Lede Vineyards, p. 31). FEL (the letters are Lede's mother's initials) began its new era with several advantages, not the least of which is that Breggo's longtime winemaker, Ryan Hodgins, is still in the cellar, and the project retains its pipeline to the top-notch Mendocino and Sonoma Coast vineyard sources—like Savoy, Hirsch and Ferrington—that were a key factor in Breggo's success. FEL also makes notable Chardonnay and a Pinot Gris.

○ **FEL Pinot Gris / 2014 / Anderson Valley / $$**
This composed Pinot Gris is pretty at first pass, with a biscuity lees scent complementing quince and yuzu flavors. But with a sweet core of apple fruit, it's far richer than it smells.

● **FEL Pinot Noir / 2014 / Anderson Valley / $$$**
The Anderson Valley courses through this forward Pinot, from the herbed red cherry scent to the pure, piercing directness of its red fruit flavor.

FESS PARKER WINERY & VINEYARD

Baby boomers recognize the late Fess Parker as the man who portrayed Davy Crockett and Daniel Boone (note the coonskin cap on most of the labels), but for a new generation of wine drinkers the name conjures up top-notch Santa Barbara County wine. The winery in Los Olivos is part of a mini lifestyle empire that includes Fess Parker Wine Country Inn and the Bubble Shack (selling sparkling wine called Fesstivity). Parker's son, daughter and son-in-law run the enterprise and oversee the winery's extensive vineyard acreage. Winemaker Blair Fox's single-vineyard Pinot Noir, Syrah and Chardonnay are well made, reliably delicious and moderately priced for their quality.

○ **Fess Parker Ashley's Chardonnay / 2014 / Sta. Rita Hills / $$$**
Full-bodied and rich, with a peachy scent and a luxurious texture, this white (named for Parker's daughter) seems ready to overwhelm, but cool-climate briskness gives it poise.

● **Fess Parker Ashley's Pinot Noir / 2013 / Sta. Rita Hills / $$$**
Ashley's Pinot combines well-oaked dark cherry sweetness and a tarry, mineral-inflected density of flavor. It's a big wine that manages to hang on to its balance.

FOLEY ESTATES

The chairman of a Fortune 500 title insurance company, Bill Foley hit the ground running in the wine business: He bought Santa Barbara's Lincourt in 1996 and has since added Chalk Hill, Sebastiani, Kuleto, Merus and Firestone. But Foley Estates is one of his gems. The winery farms about 520 acres of micro-mapped vineyards (each small plot is farmed, harvested and fermented separately) in the Sta. Rita Hills. Among its holdings are the home Rancho Santa Rosa and Rancho Las Hermanas vineyards. Winemaker Lorna Kreutz crafts Foley's richly flavored Chardonnays, Pinots and a Syrah, a portfolio that includes a number of single-vineyard wines from the estate.

○ **Two Sisters Chardonnay / 2013 / Sta. Rita Hills / $$$**
Intensely floral, redolent of citrus blossom and lemon curd with a hint of oak, this wine has a saline briskness to its texture and a cool-weather freshness that calls for Dover sole.

● **Foley Barrel Select Pinot Noir / 2012 / Sta. Rita Hills / $$$**
Dark and spiced when first poured, with a scent of ink and tea and plum skin, the wine has a focused, gentle texture, with the depth of flavor for squab.

FOXEN VINEYARD & WINERY

Bill Wathen and Dick Doré founded Foxen Winery in 1985 in Santa Maria Valley on land once owned by Doré's great-great-grandfather William Benjamin Foxen. They were quality pioneers here, favored early on by insiders for their full-flavored yet European-weight Chardonnays, Pinots and Syrahs. All these years later, their vineyard-focused small lots of character-filled wines are still superb. Wathen and Doré showcase their Bordeaux and Cal-Ital wines at their historic "tasting shack" (most of the Foxen 7200 range is available only there), while the core Burgundy and Rhône wines can be sampled at their solar-powered winery down the road. The entry-level bottlings aren't cheap, but they can be terrific bargains for their quality.

● **Foxen Pinot Noir / 2013 / Santa Maria Valley / $$$**
Foxen brings out the depth of Pinot Noir, especially in its bottlings from the cool, foggy Santa Maria Valley. This version has dark berry aromas and broad, gripping tannins.

● **Foxen Tinaquaic Vineyard Syrah / 2012 / Santa Maria Valley / $$$**
This intense, complex Syrah delivers anise, rose and pepper scents and a dark purple haze of fruit.

GALLO SIGNATURE SERIES/GALLO ESTATE WINES

Winemaker Gina Gallo produces these two distinct, upper-price tiers that provide the local-*terroir* face of the global megabrand. The Signature Series, priced between $30 and $40, utilizes some of Gallo's own top vineyards to produce AVA-specific wines—the Cabernet is produced from a Napa Valley vineyard acquired from William Hill, for instance. There is also a Russian River Valley Chardonnay and a Santa Lucia Pinot Noir. The extremely limited-production Gallo Estate wines—a Cabernet, a Pinot Noir and a Chardonnay—are culled from the best of the best of the company's Sonoma vineyard holdings.

○ **Gallo Signature Series Chardonnay / 2013 / Sonoma Coast / $$$**
Full-bodied and savory when first poured, with scents of vanilla, toasty oak and butter, the wine opens with air to reveal ripe pear fruit framed nicely by caramel.

● **Gallo Signature Series Cabernet Sauvignon / 2012 / Napa Valley / $$$** This Cab is dark and concentrated in the glass, but with air, its purple plum scent takes on a brambly spice note. The flavors are forward and supple: plums and black cherries supported by smooth, polished tannins.

GOLDENEYE

It is hard to recall now, with Anderson Valley producing so many great Pinot Noirs, just how hit-or-miss Pinots were when Napa's Duckhorn Vineyards (see p. 38) set up shop here with Goldeneye in 1996. The Merlot-oriented Duckhorns shortened their Pinot learning curve by planting 20 different clones of the variety on 13 different rootstocks spread over three vineyards. By 2012, when Michael Fay succeeded longtime winemaker Zach Rasmuson (Duckhorn itself had passed into the hands of a private equity firm in 2007), Goldeneye had a reputation for consistently fine Pinots that are dark and filled in, but with the lively lift of natural acidity that is an Anderson Valley hallmark.

- **Goldeneye Pinot Noir / 2013 / Anderson Valley / $$$**
  Soft, red-fruit brightness peaks through the dark pomegranate compote in this classic Anderson Valley Pinot. Sumptuously oaked, it requires air for the fruit and wood to come together.
- **Goldeneye Confluence Vineyard Pinot Noir / 2012 / Anderson Valley / $$$$** A warm wine from a cool climate, this is a rich and powerful Pinot, marked by tarry plum flavors, coffee-tinged wood tones and lavish oak. Cellar it to let the oak integrate.

GRASSINI FAMILY VINEYARDS

The Grassini family had owned their property in Happy Canyon for decades before Larry and Sharon Grassini decided to plant wine grapes there in 2002. Fortunately for the couple's Bordeaux-centric ambitions, Happy Canyon benefits from the warmest microclimate in the Santa Ynez Valley, but nighttime temperature drops help lock in the grapes' acidity. This is a lovely winery—the building is constructed from 100-plus-year-old reclaimed fir timbers—in a fairy tale setting. The family sells nearly half of the grapes from their 35-acre vineyard, but winemaker Bradley Long turns the rest into rich red Bordeaux blends, along with a Sauvignon Blanc.

- **Grassini Articondo / 2013 / Happy Canyon of Santa Barbara / $$$**
  Named for Larry Grassini's Italian immigrant grandfather, this impressive Cab-based blend is sleek and dark, with purple plum and fig flavors and ripe, extracted tannins.
- **Grassini Equipo / 2013 / Happy Canyon of Santa Barbara / $$$**
  In this warm Cabernet–Petit Verdot blend, the latter variety delivers a firm grip and a silky purple plushness of texture, leavening the powerful Cabernet tannins.

HALTER RANCH VINEYARD

Swiss billionaire Hansjörg Wyss began acquiring this tucked-away, now 2,000-acre property in Paso Robles's Adelaida District in 2000. By then, Halter Ranch had already served as the backdrop for Ronald Reagan's 1967 announcement that he would seek reelection as California's governor, and its 1885 Victorian farmhouse had starred in the spider-attack flick *Arachnophobia*. The property also boasts the world's largest coast live oak tree. Under winemaker Kevin Sass, the estate's diverse 281 acres of vineyard are planted to some 14 grape varieties. While Halter Ranch has made its name with Syrah and the Bordeaux-style red blend Ancestor, it is emerging as a source of delicious Tempranillo and Grenache Blanc as well.

○ **Halter Ranch Grenache Blanc / 2014 / Adelaida District / $$**
Plush and fruity, with a modest lees accent in the background, this generous white is marked by quince and melon aromas and an exuberant freshness of acidity on the finish.

● **Halter Ranch Ancestor / 2013 / Adelaida District / $$$**
Named for the estate's record-breaking Ancestor oak tree, this flagship Cab–Malbec–Petit Verdot blend displays scents of tar and cassis, forward purple fruit flavors and gripping tannins.

HANDLEY CELLARS

After stints with Richard Arrowood at Chateau St. Jean (see p. 105), and Jed Steele at Edmeades, groundbreaking winemaker Milla Handley moved to the Anderson Valley in the late 1970s. At the time, the idea of making world-class Chardonnay and Pinot Noir in Mendocino County was a distant glimmer, but that glimmer caught Handley's eye. In 1982 she established her own winery, now a robust but modest-sized 10,000-case operation, where she helped pioneer the cultivation of Burgundian and Alsatian grapes in the region. Her much-visited, folk-art-bedecked tasting room is a fine place to sample Handley's refined, racy Chardonnays, rose petal–scented Gewürztraminer and small-lot sparkling wines.

○ **Handley Gewürztraminer / 2014 / Anderson Valley / $$**
Soft and sensuous, this dry white has a scent of rose petals and white cherries, quince-like flavors and a spicy finish.

◑ **Handley Reserve Pinot Noir / 2012 / Anderson Valley / $$$**
This Pinot is always a bit circumspect. Its aromas of cranberry and strawberry lead to flavors that are deeper and spicier.

HARTLEY OSTINI HITCHING POST

For visitors to the Hitching Post Restaurants in Casmalia and Buellton over the years, these wines conjure up grilling steaks, wood smoke and the sight of luxuriously mustachioed Frank Ostini, whose family has owned the business since 1952. In 1979 Ostini and pal Gray Hartley made a batch of wine in an old whiskey barrel. Their efforts caught on with the restaurants' regulars as production grew. By the time the movie *Sideways* featured the wine and the restaurant, Hartley and Ostini's Pinot Noir hobby had become a commercial operation that, with a boost from the movie, now produces about 15,000 cases a year of juicy, seamless, well-filled-out reds—just right for your rib eye.

- **Hartley Ostini Hitching Post Cork Dancer Pinot Noir / 2013 / Santa Barbara County / $$** Bright and fresh when first poured, with air, this Pinot delivers a tart cranberry scent framed by tarry, fleshy oak notes. Its red cherry flavors are marked by the graham-cracker sweetness of oak.
- **Hartley Ostini Hitching Post Highliner Pinot Noir / 2013 / Santa Barbara County / $$$** The Pinot Noir made famous by *Sideways* is fresh and mildly herbal in 2013, with a scent of kelp-like sea air and a strawberry core of flavor.

JAFFURS WINE CELLARS

Although he owns no vineyards, Rhône-wine specialist Craig Jaffurs has propelled his Rhône-oriented label to the forefront of California Syrah in particular, thanks to his skill in scouting top Santa Barbara County vineyards, like Stolpman, Bien Nacido and Larner, and in making the most of their fruit. These skills are most evident in his reserve Upslope Syrah bottlings that blend his top lots every year, but also in highly regarded versions of Grenache, Petite Sirah and Rhône whites. His winery, located in downtown Santa Barbara, remains a small operation (5,000 cases); many of its very-limited-production wines either are available only to club members or sell out all too quickly.

- **Jaffurs Grenache / 2012 / Santa Barbara County / $$$**
This red displays the exuberance of warm-climate Grenache, its strawberry flavors given complexity by whole-cluster spice.
- **Upslope Syrah / 2013 / Santa Barbara County / $$$$**
A reserve Syrah from multiple vineyard sources, this wine is inky black and brooding, with an herbal scent overlaying blackberry fruit of remarkable concentration and depth.

JEFF COHN CELLARS

Jeff Cohn is one of those winemakers who can't resist making a lot of different wines. While he was winemaker at Rosenblum, he made more than 70 wines a year; at his own small operation in Oakland, he may turn out 21 labels annually, combining grape varietals (seven each in The Impostor and Smoke & Mirrors wines), or giving a number of single vineyards their due. A key to his success is his skill as a vineyard scout, sourcing grapes from down the coast at Fess Parker in Santa Barbara to Rockpile in Sonoma and Stagecoach in Napa.

- **Jeff Cohn Rockpile Vineyard Syrah / 2013 / Rockpile / $$$** Dark and intense, with scents of asphalt, fruit skin and blueberry jam, this red offers a dense core of black fruits, kissed by milk chocolate oak, and firm minerality at the finish.
- **Jeff Cohn St. Peter's Church Vineyard Zinfandel / 2013 / Alexander Valley / $$$** This is a tooth-staining Zin of a singular intensity, with brambly, port-like scents of blackberries and toasty, mocha-tinged oak. The flavors are at once burly and vinous.

J. LOHR VINEYARDS & WINES

Jerry Lohr, a sometime real estate developer and son of South Dakota farmers, has an obvious passion for land. Starting with his first vineyard purchase in Monterey County in 1971, his sprawling wine venture now encompasses 1,178 vineyard acres there devoted to cooler-climate grapes; 3,249 acres in Paso Robles planted to Bordeaux and Rhône red varieties; and 35 acres in Napa Valley. (Lohr also manages hundreds of acres more in Monterey County and Paso Robles.) The output is similarly diverse: four price tiers under the J. Lohr label, topped by the Bordeaux-style Cuvée Series wines; value-priced bottlings under the Cypress Vineyards label; and the Ariel nonalcoholic wines.

- **J. Lohr Cuvée PAU / 2012 / Paso Robles / $$$** PAU (short for "Pauillac") is the Cuvée Series' Cabernet Sauvignon–based blend. With anise and rosemary aromas adorning a rich, purple texture, it's quite a bit more forward than Bordeaux versions, but suits a steak.
- **J. Lohr Cuvée POM / 2012 / Paso Robles / $$$** "POM" here stands for Pomerol. This Merlot-driven blend has a plush red and black plum scent accented by cedar and cherry. The flavors are brighter and more focused than PAU's, making it a good match for smoked chicken.

JONATA

Despite a somewhat challenging beginning—one French consultant advised planting asparagus rather than wine grapes on the property—this venture has rocketed, for some collectors, to the height of cult-worthiness, with prices at the high end of the Santa Barbara spectrum. Now owned by Screaming Eagle mogul (and St. Louis Rams owner) Stan Kroenke and his wife, Ann, Jonata has brought a whiff of Napa-like glamour to the Central Coast. Winemaker Matt Dees turns out cellar-worthy Bordeaux blends, Syrahs and a Sangiovese, all from the Ballard Canyon estate's 84 planted acres, and the venture has been scrupulous about not bottling wines from sub-par vintages.

● **Jonata Todos / 2012 / Ballard Canyon / $$$**
Syrah dominates this dark, powerful, multivariety blend. The wine's Cabernet Sauvignon, Merlot, Sangiovese and Cab Franc components loosen its limbs and lend it a red-fruited lift.

● **Jonata La Sangre de Jonata / 2012 / Ballard Canyon / $$$$**
Full-bodied and powerful in 2012, this mostly Syrah bottling has unearthly richness. Its peppery aromas of iron, black currant and fig lead to flavors that are just shy of over the top.

JUSTIN VINEYARDS & WINERY

With its sleek Just Inn boutique hotel and restaurant and handsome tasting room, Paso Robles's JUSTIN is an upscale center of Central Coast wine tourism. Founded by former investment banker Justin Baldwin (and sold to the owners of Fiji Water in 2010), this winery operation is worth a visit on its own merits. Though it produces a range of bottlings, JUSTIN is mainly a Cabernet Sauvignon specialist, with the Bordeaux-style Isosceles as its image-maker. The Cab Franc–Merlot blend Justification is also worth seeking out, as is the varietal bottling of Cabernet Sauvignon. The winery's numerous other offerings include the allocated Focus Syrah, a Viognier and dessert wines.

○ **JUSTIN Viognier / 2014 / Paso Robles / $$**
Made in an unabashed Central Coast style, this is a big wine, with big fruit, big alcohol and big body. It delivers hefty flavors of peach with a hint of apricot and a creamy finish.

● **JUSTIN Isosceles / 2013 / Paso Robles / $$$$**
Plush and dark, this Cab-dominant blend seems to revel in the Paso Robles heat, with brambly dark fruits moving to fig and cassis, a lavish oak complement and furry, ripe tannins.

KALIN CELLARS

Terry and Frances Leighton's Kalin Cellars is not only a California original, it's a world original. Berkeley microbiologist Terry's grounding in winemaking theory and practice gave him the confidence to pioneer almost every aspect of today's artisan-wine doctrine, from scouting distinctive vineyard sources to minimal-interference winemaking to bottling wines unfiltered. Few winemakers, if any, have taken the financial hit Leighton takes in cellaring bottles under perfect conditions for extra years until release. Among his multilayered offerings are Meursault-like Chardonnays, gorgeously textured Sauvignon Blancs and a trickle of sparklers that should be the envy of big-label producers.

○ **Kalin Cellars Cuvee LV Chardonnay / 1995 / Sonoma County / $$$**
Still a baby after 20-plus years in bottle, this Chardonnay offers a honeyed mélange of peach and tropical fruits. The flavors are long and exotic; the textures are enriched by age.

○ **Kalin Cellars Semillon / 2000 / Livermore Valley / $$$**
With its scents of golden raisin and nutty lees, tropical flavors and textures driven by oak and age, this Sémillon from pre-Prohibition plantings achieves a rare longevity.

KEPLINGER

This hands-on boutique project is a cult-label in the making. Helen Keplinger, who co-owns the winery with her husband, DJ Warner, has put together an impressive California résumé, including a post as winemaker at Napa superstar Bryant Family. But it is her stint in Spain's Priorat region that she credits with sealing her love of Rhône-style wines. Sourcing grapes from the hillsides of El Dorado County, Russian River Valley, Amador County and elsewhere, Keplinger produces tiny quantities—about 1,800 cases in all—of ultra-naturally produced wines under proprietary names (Basilisk, Caldera, Lithic, Sumo) that sell out through its mailing list.

● **Keplinger Lithic / 2013 / Sierra Foothills / $$$$**
In an impressive balancing act, the generous dark fruits of this Grenache-Mourvèdre-Syrah blend are held in line by its overall minerality and the granitic feel of tannin.

● **Keplinger Sumo / 2013 / Sierra Foothills / $$$$**
A Petite Sirah–heavy blend with Syrah and Viognier, this is a weighty red, but the fruit is irresistibly forward and the flavors almost puzzlingly nimble for such a massive wine.

L'AVENTURE WINERY

French-born Stephan Asseo took his wine degree and experience in owning Bordeaux châteaux to the limestone soils of western Paso Robles and the Santa Lucia Mountains. After remarkably few vintages, Asseo's dense but silky, full-throttle reds have become among the most renowned in the appellation. The wines' concentration is achieved at the cost of volume—Asseo says that his yields work out to about one bottle per vine. Well-heeled drinkers who are fortunate enough to secure a bottle of, say, the Estate Cuvée or Côte à Côte can taste the added dimension. The Syrah-Cabernet-Petit Verdot Optimus blend offers a more accessible entry point.

● **L'Aventure Côte à Côte / 2013 / Willow Creek / $$$$**
An MGS—Mourvèdre, Grenache, Syrah—blend, this wine isn't shy, though the Mourvèdre makes it more of a red-fruited experience, with strawberries and maraschino cherries grounded by plenty of heat and tannin.

● **L'Aventure Estate Cuvée / 2013 / Willow Creek / $$$$**
This estate bottling traditionally marries Syrah, Cabernet and Petit Verdot. It's an explosive dark bomb of a red, with plump fruit and massive tannins.

LAYER CAKE WINES

Layer Cake's goal, "Luxury everyone can afford," is met in palate-flattering wines that at their best are remarkable values, all under $20. To produce them, the winemaking team travels to what must seem like an endless succession of seasonal harvests—the wines come from four continents, five countries and both hemispheres. The flamboyant owner and winemaker Jayson Woodbridge, who also owns Napa Valley's luxury-priced Hundred Acre (see p. 49), shows some ingenuity in putting the layers in the Layer Cake: The California appellation Cabernet Sauvignon, for example, is blended from one vineyard in Sonoma County's Alexander Valley and another in Paso Robles.

○ **Layer Cake Chardonnay / 2014 / Central Coast / $**
A scent of oak and juicy pear and apple fruit mark this inviting white, with flavors of vanilla and pineapple on the finish.

● **Layer Cake Cabernet Sauvignon / 2014 / California / $**
This dark and simple Cab opens with a pretty red-fruit scent. Its flavors lean toward purple jam, juicy and clean, with surprising balance for the price.

LIEU DIT WINERY

This Lompoc operation is one of the rare US wineries focusing on Loire-inspired Sauvignon Blanc and Chenin Blanc, with Cabernet Franc, Malbec and a rosé of Pinot Noir on the roster as well. The boutique (4,000–4,500-case) project of longtime pals Justin Willett, also the founder/owner/winemaker at Tyler (see p. 193), and Eric Railsback, a sommelier who comes out of the ferment of wine talent at Michael Mina's RN74, Lieu Dit is firmly in the vibrant-wine, higher acidity, no-fruit-bomb camp of winemaking. Sourcing grapes from top vineyards like Grassini Family (see p. 168) and Sanford & Benedict, the partners are showcasing the Loire Valley–Santa Barbara County affinity.

○ **Lieu Dit Chenin Blanc / 2014 / Santa Ynez Valley / $$**
Celery leaf and parsley aromas support a melon fruit profile. The wine has good ripeness but finishes dry and crisp.

● **Lieu Dit Cabernet Franc / 2013 / Santa Ynez Valley / $$**
In this charming Cab Franc, modestly spiced, pure red fruit takes over the palate with a tart firm presence. It's balanced and clean, with a nice ripple of fresh acidity.

LIQUID FARM

For years, "anything but Chardonnay" has been a mantra for certain wine drinkers, but now a backlash is on. Influential winemakers like Chris Gorman (see Ashan, p. 228) and Charles Smith (see Sixto, p. 253) in Washington and this already-cult-status project in Santa Barbara County are exalting the grape. Liquid Farm's founders, Nikki and Jeff Nelson, are self-professed "white Burgundy freaks," who strive for energy, minerality and balance in their takes on the French Chardonnays they love. Starting with four barrels in 2009, they have gained critical acclaim, producing a range of Chardonnays including the Chablis-style White Hill and the Meursault-style Golden Slope. Also on the roster are a fine Bandol-style Mourvèdre rosé and, as of the 2014 vintage, a red, the Radian Vineyard Pinot Noir.

○ **Liquid Farm White Hill Chardonnay / 2014 / Sta. Rita Hills / $$$**
This generous white's tropical scents—leaning toward peach, with a leesy accent—give way to a full-flavored palate and a texture marked by lean salinity.

● **Liquid Farm Rosé / Happy Canyon of Santa Barbara / 2015 / $$**
This cheery Mourvèdre-based rosé is all strawberry and salinity in the glass, with a mouthwatering freshness.

LONGORIA WINES

Long a fixture on the Santa Barbara wine scene, Rick Longoria moved into a new winery and tasting room facility in August 2014 after many years of making wine in what is now known as the Lompoc Wine Ghetto. His production—about 2,500 to 3,000 cases—has inched up only modestly over the years. And despite an expanded portfolio, his first loves, Chardonnay and Pinot Noir, remain the winery's forte. Longoria's pride and joy are the bottlings from his Fe Ciega ("blind faith") Vineyard, about nine acres of mesa land in the western Sta. Rita Hills. His bevy of other small-lot wines includes two red blends: the art-label Blues Cuvée and Evidence, a Bordeaux-style blend.

○ **Longoria Rita's Crown Vineyard Chardonnay / 2013 / Sta. Rita Hills / $$$** A well-structured Chardonnay from a warm site in a cool place, this wine leads with scents of peach and sweet corn, its mineral component lending structure as well as a salty savor.

● **Longoria Fe Ciega Vineyard Pinot Noir / 2013 / Sta. Rita Hills / $$$** Tightly wound, this firmly structured Pinot takes its time to relax before the graceful purple plum and currant fruit reveals itself. Decant it, or cellar it for a few years.

LORING WINE COMPANY

The labels of Loring's vineyard-designated bottlings feature a purple or green spray-paint-stenciled logo and a photo of the source vineyard (the winery's all-star team of growers includes Garys', Rosella's, Clos Pepe and Kessler-Haak vineyards). Brother and sister owners Brian and Kimberly Loring, who produce "Chardonnay, Pinot Noir and whatever else strikes our fancy," have a nose for great California vineyards and seemingly want to bottle a wine from each one. They also produce a less expensive line of AVA blends. The wines are purposely varied—the Lorings want them to reflect the vineyards and growers—but they are typically at the rich, fruity and boisterous end of both the Chardonnay and Pinot Noir spectrums.

● **Loring Wine Company Clos Pepe Vineyard Pinot Noir / 2014 / Sta. Rita Hills / $$$** Blue indigo in a glass, this dark Pinot has a scent of purple flowers and crushed blueberries. On the palate it's plush and extracted, with ripe, dark fruit.

● **Loring Wine Company Garys' Vineyard Pinot Noir / 2014 / Santa Lucia Highlands / $$$** All purple plum and black cherry, this Pinot packs a wallop in its extract and violet-tinged dark-fruit finish.

LUTUM WINES

Wine magnate Bill Price (see Three Sticks, p. 145) met the then 27-year-old winemaker Gavin Chanin at an "In Pursuit of Balance" meeting, a group dedicated to dialing back alcohol and fruit-bomb richness levels in California wine. Chanin, Price realized, had a rare talent for crafting Chardonnays and Pinot Noirs with a leaner, low-oak profile that let their natural aromas and flavors shine. Price and Chanin set up shop in Lompoc and assembled a lineup of top vineyards to realize their vision of making pure, vibrant translations of Pinot and Chardonnay, including designated bottlings from Bien Nacido, La Riconada, Sanford & Benedict and Price's own Gap's Crown and Durell.

○ **Lutum Gap's Crown Vineyard Chardonnay / 2014 / Sonoma Coast / $$$** Gavin Chanin's gift for making streamlined, nuanced Chardonnay is evident in this ginger-scented white. Despite the above-14 percent alcohol, it's poised and light on its feet.

● **Lutum Durell Vineyard Pinot Noir / 2014 / Sonoma Coast / $$$** This is a graceful, brightly juicy Pinot from Bill Price's acclaimed Durell Vineyard in Sonoma County.

MARGERUM WINE COMPANY

Doug Margerum has been a foundational figure in the Santa Barbara wine scene as a restaurateur, promoter and finally winemaker. At his own winery, he presides over as idiosyncratic a roster as you're likely to find, including Syrah and Pinot Noir rooted to the spot in Santa Barbara County's Sta. Rita Hills, lightly sweet Pinot Gris from Washington State, Sauvignon Blancs and so on. Add in the fact that Margerum is the winemaker and a partner at Italian grape specialist Cent'Anni (whose wines are produced at his Buellton facility), and you get the idea of a vinous Renaissance man. Margerum is also a partner in the well-known Wine Cask restaurant in Santa Barbara and operates two downtown tasting rooms.

○ **Margerum Sybarite Sauvignon Blanc / 2014 / Happy Canyon of Santa Barbara / $$** There's warmth to this Sauvignon Blanc in its melon and golden apple scents, but it remains balanced and fresh, its mid-palate roundness shored up by bright acidity.

● **Margerum Colson Canyon Vineyard Syrah / 2013 / Santa Barbara County / $$$** This ripe Syrah leads with plum and cocoa notes. On the palate it's balanced and fine, its black plum flavors leavened by dusty tannins.

MCPRICE MYERS

McPrice "Mac" Myers has made his name as a producer of flavorful, high-quality wines that offer great value for the price—all fall within a $25 to $60 price band. Myers has proven to have a shrewd eye for purchasing grapes. From his Paso Robles winery, he reaches into Santa Barbara and San Luis Obispo Counties to source his three collections of Rhône-style blends and single-grape wines. Most familiar are the crowd-pleasing Blue Collar Series wines (formerly labeled Barrel 27), with humorous names like High on the Hog and Head Honcho. Also on the winery's roster are Proprietary and Single-Vineyard Series bottlings.

● **High on the Hog Grenache / 2013 / Santa Barbara County / $$$**
Not shy, this hefty red has generous, jammy cherry scents and deep red-plum flavors, with plenty of body. It would be ideal for barbecue.

● **McPrice Myers L'Ange Rouge / 2013 / Santa Barbara County / $$$**
This heady, Grenache-driven red has a scent of plum compote with a little bit of earth, possibly from the Mourvèdre in the blend. It's ripe and satisfying.

MELVILLE VINEYARDS AND WINERY

This is one of Santa Barbara County's premier wine producers, with a reputation based on a New World–Old World balancing act of silkiness and layered finesse rather than on blockbuster power. The patriarch of the family operation, Ron Melville, purchased two Sta. Rita Hills vineyards in the 1990s, now comprising 120 planted acres, and all of Melville's wines—Pinot Noir, Chardonnay and Syrah—are sourced from these estate vines. The Melville operation began a new era in 2015, as star winemaker Greg Brewer (see Brewer-Clifton, p. 157) handed over the reins to Ron's son Chad, who worked beside Brewer for years (and makes his own Samsara label; see p. 185).

○ **Melville Chardonnay / 2014 / Sta. Rita Hills / $$**
A tropical-fruity Chardonnay with a distinct citrus aspect, Melville's flagship white smells of lime, guava and melon with a chalky mineral note.

● **Melville Pinot Noir / 2014 / Sta. Rita Hills / $$$**
A value for Central Coast Pinot Noir, this bottling is cool but concentrated, with an inky hue. Despite the suggestions of power, the wine carries itself with remarkable finesse.

MORGAN WINERY

One of the leading wineries in the cool, coastal Monterey County region, Dan Morgan Lee and his wife Donna's operation is best known for its Pinot Noir and Chardonnay. Though they produce an array of wines from various sources—including from the region's illustrious Rosella's and Garys' vineyards—the centerpiece of their efforts is their own Double L Estate in the Santa Lucia Highlands. The site is so influenced by the cooling proximity of the ocean that summertime high temperatures average in the mid-70s. With this organically farmed vineyard, planted in 1997, now fully mature, and winemaker Gianni Abate in place since 2005, Morgan is reaching for new heights.

○ **Morgan Double L Vineyard Chardonnay / 2014 / Santa Lucia Highlands / $$$** Fairly toasty at the outset, this generous white has a golden core of fruit flavor surrounded by oak notes and lifted by acidity.

● **Morgan Double L Vineyard Pinot Noir / 2014 / Santa Lucia Highlands / $$$** Rushing winds in the Santa Lucia Highlands make for exceptionally thick grape skins, which accounts for this Pinot's great concentration. In 2014 it's forward and ripe.

MOUNT EDEN VINEYARDS

Gifted winemaker Jeffrey Patterson runs the cellar at his Santa Cruz Mountain estate, which was founded in the 1940s in the hills overlooking what is now Silicon Valley. Mount Eden's long-respected wines are gaining new cachet as sophisticated buyers come to appreciate the more restrained styles that result from the purposeful combination of Patterson's Old World wine-making techniques and the cool climate of Mount Eden's vineyards, some at 2,000 feet up. Patterson crafts top-notch Cabernet Sauvignons, but his record with the winery's legacy grapes—Pinot Noir and Chardonnay—often overshadows them. The Domaine Eden label offers the estate's style at a lower price.

● **Mount Eden Vineyards Cabernet Sauvignon / 2011 / Santa Cruz Mountains / $$$$** This is a stunningly complex wine—no jam, no flash, just the essence of Cab savoriness, with a haunting tension between its cedar accents and succulent plum fruit.

● **Mount Eden Vineyards Pinot Noir / 2012 / Santa Cruz Mountains / $$$$** This estate Pinot Noir displays the spiciness of the Mount Eden clone, with rose and cedar accents adorning the wine's delicate but persistent red fruit flavor.

NAVARRO VINEYARDS

Laid-back Navarro is a familiar stop for Mendocino County tourists on Anderson Valley's Route 128 wine road. Most of its production is sold directly, either from the tasting room or via its website. Founders/owners Ted Bennett and Deborah Cahn run the winery with their children, Sarah and Aaron Cahn-Bennett, and they are perhaps best known among aficionados of dry Gewürztraminer—often among California's best—and Méthode à l'Ancienne Pinot Noir. But Navarro also offers a broad slate of other options, from Edelzwicker and Riesling to a Roussanne-Marsanne blend and various nonalcoholic grape juices. The gently priced wines are typically made in a lighter, elegant style that suits the table well.

○ **Navarro Vineyards Riesling / 2013 / Anderson Valley / $$**
There's a high-toned, almost floral quality to this Riesling's peachy aroma. On the palate, though, the wine is more demonstrative and succulent.

● **Navarro Vineyards Méthode à l'Ancienne Pinot Noir / 2013 / Anderson Valley / $$$** Navarro's "traditional method" Pinot is a quiet wine, leafy and autumnal, with dark strawberry accents.

THE OJAI VINEYARD

A winemaker's winemaker, Adam Tolmach is a pioneer in combining *terroir*-driven vineyard scouting, low-intervention cellar work and minimal artifice (including little new oak) to allow distinctive grapes and vineyards to shine through. Jim Clendenen's original partner in Au Bon Climat (see p. 153), Tolmach has gone his own way, but retains the restless curiosity that marked their joint efforts. Ojai produces only about 8,000 cases a year, but they are divided among some 24 different wines. Though its roster includes Roussanne, Riesling and Riesling dessert wines, most fans identify Ojai with stylish, not overly rich Pinot Noir, Syrah and Chardonnay sourced from top vineyards like Fe Ciega, Bien Nacido and White Hawk.

● **The Ojai Vineyard Pinot Noir / 2014 / Santa Barbara County / $$$**
Dark berry aromas, a deep core of flavor and a spicy note on the finish mark this savory Pinot Noir.

● **The Ojai Vineyard Syrah / 2014 / Santa Barbara County / $$$**
This dialed-back Syrah leads more with spice than fruit, and aromas suggesting cloves, pepper and a hint of dried beef. Persistent acidity lifts its plum and black cherry flavors.

PALI WINE COMPANY

Pali is a labor of love from two Pinot Noir connoisseurs, Tim Perr and Scott Knight, whose onetime garage-style operation has now grown to 23,000 cases a year. The duo produce their wines in Lompoc but roam from Oregon's Willamette Valley to the Sta. Rita Hills of Santa Barbara County successfully searching out worthy vineyards. Among other things, Pali's fans love its remarkable price-to-value ratio. The affordable line of Pinots offers regional blends named for neighborhoods in the proprietors' hometown of Pacific Palisades ("Pali") at prices typically under $30. The pricier but still reasonable vineyard-designated line includes bottlings from esteemed growers like Durell, Shea and Fiddlestix.

● **Pali Summit Pinot Noir / 2013 / Sta. Rita Hills / $$**
A ripe expression of the Sta. Rita Hills, with dark, extracted, blackberry flavors and an exotic, clove-like finish.

● **Pali Wine Co. Fiddlestix Vineyard Pinot Noir / 2013 / Sta. Rita Hills / $$$$** An iconic vineyard in the Sta. Rita Hills yielded this Pinot Noir, whose spice notes leap out when first poured: cinnamon and clove atop inky purple fruit.

PAUL LATO WINES

Polish-born Paul Lato, a onetime Toronto sommelier, is a great American success story—a man who has worked very hard through many lean years to get to where he is, which is in the upper echelon of Central Coast Pinot Noir and Syrah producers. Self-taught, with a little help from his friends, like Au Bon Climat's Jim Clendenen (see p. 153), Lato produces tiny quantities of wine in numerous bottlings. Though fancifully named (Seabiscuit, Atticus, Belle de Jour, Duende), these are often single-vineyard-sourced. Lato's personal credibility has won him access to grapes from some of the region's most coveted vineyards, including Larner, Pisoni and Hilliard Bruce.

○ **Paul Lato Belle de Jour Chardonnay / 2013 / Sta. Rita Hills / $$$**
A poised tension between warm citrus notes (think lemon curd) and nutty lees accents is this wine's hallmark.

● **Paul Lato Duende Pinot Noir / 2014 / Santa Maria Valley / $$$$**
Light and mildly savory, this Gold Coast Vineyard bottling has a nori scent and red fruit reminiscent of Santa Maria Valley's strawberry fields. On the palate it's slightly darker, more cherry and raspberry, with a savory dried-kelp finish.

PIEDRASASSI

Winemaker Sashi Moorman (see Domaine de la Côte, p. 163, and Sandhi, p. 186) sometimes seems to be on a mission to demonstrate the diversity of what is possible in California wine. Lompoc-based Piedrasassi is his own boutique label, which sells out instantly. Here Moorman focuses on producing limited quantities of Syrah by his own lights, which in the case of this variety means generally early harvesting to retain vibrant acidity, plus natural fermentations with native yeasts in large, neutral barrels that don't impose oaky flavors on the wine. Also on the roster are an idiosyncratic Sauvignon Blanc, which is given extended skin contact for a richer mouthfeel, à la Napa Chardonnay in the 1980s; and a light, fruit-forward Sangiovese.

○ **Piedrasassi Sauvignon Blanc / 2013 / Santa Barbara County / $$$**
An orange wine—fermentation on the grape skins gives it a darker hue—this Sauvignon shows wild herb notes against a salty citrus background, with a texture as gripping as a red's.

● **Piedrasassi Syrah / 2013 / Santa Barbara County / $$$**
This subtle Syrah offers appealing currant and plum fruit, but it's the wine's texture that impresses the most: finessed and silky, with fine-as-silt tannins.

PISONI VINEYARDS & WINERY/LUCIA WINES

Did Burgundy fanatic Gary Pisoni really hop over the wall at Domaine de la Romanée-Conti to snare the cuttings that became the "Pisoni clone"? We may never know, but he is a determined man, planting grapevines on his father's water-free Santa Lucia Highlands cattle ranch back in 1982 (the sixth well attempt finally came in) and creating the vineyard that has become one of California's most famous sources of Pinot Noir grapes. With his sons—winemaker Jeff and business manager/grape grower Mark—he later founded the Pisoni label, which turns out one coveted estate Pinot Noir each vintage. Pisoni also bottles highly regarded Pinot, Chardonnay and Syrah under the Lucia label and the limited-production Lucy rosé.

● **Lucia Pinot Noir / 2013 / Santa Lucia Highlands / $$$**
Deep purple in color, this Pinot has plenty of fruit on the juicy palate, with softly herbal accents of sage and bay laurel.

● **Pisoni Estate Pinot Noir / 2013 / Santa Lucia Highlands / $$$$**
The clove-blackberry flavors of this benchmark Santa Lucia Highlands Pinot are intense and juicy, spicy, almost explosive.

QUPÉ WINE CELLARS

This pioneering Central Coast Rhône Ranger winery was sold to wine entrepreneur Charles Banks in 2013, but founder Bob Lindquist has stayed on and is keeping on—fashioning delicious Syrah, for starters. The talented Lindquist makes small-lot, single-vineyard bottlings from vineyards he has worked with for years (including his own). Qupé's affordable Central Coast Syrah offers a fine sampling of his spicy, vibrant style. Sometimes overshadowed by his reds, Lindquist's whites also deliver incredible quality for the price. Lindquist and his wife, Louisa Sawyer Lindquist, farm their own Edna Valley vineyard biodynamically; among other offerings, Louisa's Spanish-varietal Verdad wines are sourced from there.

● **Qupé Syrah / 2012 / Central Coast / $$**
Qupé's baseline Syrah melds cool-climate spiciness and warm-climate fruit with a clean snap of acidity.

● **Qupé Bien Nacido Hillside Estate Syrah / 2011 / Santa Maria Valley / $$$** One of the winery's flagships, this Syrah is cool and dark, with scents of pepper, rosemary and dried beef.

RHYS VINEYARDS

Silicon Valley venture capitalist Kevin Harvey's silky Pinots, Syrahs and Chardonnays have been enthusiastically received by America's wine press, and by consumers who buy out these pricey wines via the mailing list. With Javier Tapia as winegrower and Jeff Brinkman in charge of the cellar, the winery farms its six Santa Cruz Mountains estates and one in Anderson Valley organically and biodynamically, and goes a step further with costly low-tech initiatives, such as investing in scores of small, one-ton fermenters to separate tiny lots of wine and providing the cave space for natural fermentations of Chardonnay to work themselves out over a year if need be. Another example of going the extra mile is the labor-intensive practice of foot punchdowns.

○ **Rhys Horseshoe Vineyard Chardonnay / 2013 / Santa Cruz Mountains / $$$$** This is a quiet wine that takes nearly a day to open up; once it does unfurl, it offers nutty, leesy notes and pineapple-tropical fruit yet stays savory and mineral-driven.

● **Rhys Horseshoe Vineyard Pinot Noir / 2013 / Santa Cruz Mountains / $$$$** From the first pour, this wine exudes elegance. Its wild strawberry flavors are impressive, but what will seduce you ultimately is its lissome, silky texture.

RIDGE VINEYARDS

A few things have changed around Cupertino and what is now Silicon Valley since Ridge began production high up on Monte Bello in 1962. But Ridge Vineyards—one of California's most celebrated and reliable fine-wine labels—has only gained in reputation. Its iconic stature rests both on Monte Bello, the profound, world-class Cabernet-based blend sourced from the winery's home hilltop vineyard in the Santa Cruz Mountains AVA; and on some of California's premier old-vine Zinfandels, notably the Sonoma Geyserville and Lytton Springs bottlings. But presiding guru Paul Draper turns out a plethora of exciting wines at a range of prices. Much underappreciated: his remarkable hand with silky Chardonnays.

- **Ridge Lytton Springs / 2013 / Dry Creek Valley / $$$**
  Ridge's flagship Zinfandel blend is like a black cherry cobbler framed by modest oak—an unlikely combination, but it works.
- **Ridge Monte Bello / 2013 / Santa Cruz Mountains / $$$$**
  A warm vintage for Monte Bello yielded a more approachable, Cab-heavy blend in 2013. But it remains true to form with its mint-cassis aroma, black plum fruit and gravelly minerality.

ROAR WINES

This producer's sought-after wines are crafted by the "other" Santa Lucia Highlands Gary, Gary Franscioni, who partners with Gary Pisoni (see p. 182) in Garys' Vineyard and Soberanes Vineyard, two of ROAR's prime sources. Franscioni, whose family farming roots here go back three generations, is himself the owner of the esteemed Rosella's Vineyard, named for his wife, and the high-altitude Sierra Mar. No surprise, then, that ROAR's small production of voluptuous, complexly flavored Pinots, Chardonnays, Syrahs and Viogniers are single-vineyard-based wines from this collection of famous Santa Lucia sites, plus some fruit from the neighbors over at Pisoni. These wines sell quickly; fans are advised to jump on the mailing list.

- **ROAR Garys' Vineyard Pinot Noir / 2014 / Santa Lucia Highlands / $$$** There's a bit more savoriness in this vineyard designate Pinot, a character probably derived from the cool wind that constantly blows over the Highlands' sloping vineyards.
- **ROAR Pinot Noir / 2014 / Santa Lucia Highlands / $$$**
  Not the shy type, this creamy red's black cherry fruit and licorice accents roll along, carried by the rich, smooth texture.

ROEDERER ESTATE

When famed Champagne house Louis Roederer came to the US in 1982, it chose not to follow Mumm and Domaine Chandon to Napa Valley. Instead, then-president Jean-Claude Rouzaud followed his own instincts about where to grow the best Pinot Noir and Chardonnay for sparkling wines. Today the Roederer winery in Mendocino's Anderson Valley crafts some of America's finest sparklers. Adhering to Champagne tradition, Roederer adds reserve wines, aged in French oak casks, to its cuvées. The older wines lend depth and nuance beyond their price to the nonvintage brut and brut rosé. The vintage white and rosé L'Ermitage wines easily rival French Champagnes in quality.

○ **Roederer Estate Brut / NV / Anderson Valley / $$**
A blend of Chardonnay and Pinot Noir, this domestic sparkler is always among the country's most graceful and affordable, with a fine mousse, lean apple flavors and invigorating acidity.

○ **Roederer Estate L'Ermitage Brut / 2005 / Anderson Valley / $$$**
While the nonvintage Brut is typically more generous (and simpler), L'Ermitage is thrillingly dry, taut and racy, with layers of flavor.

SAMSARA WINE COMPANY

This is a boutique project by Melville Vineyards scion Chad Melville (see p. 178) and his wife, Mary, who have cherry-picked Pinot Noir, Syrah and Grenache from what they call "micro-sites" in some of the Sta. Rita Hills' top vineyards, including Larner, Turner and, of course, Melville itself. In what may be a preview of Melville wines to come now that Chad has taken the helm at the family property, Samsara uses a high percentage of whole clusters in its fermentations, with the idea that the stems absorb some of the simple fruitiness of the wine and contribute more complexity. Though the wines aren't inexpensive, prices are very reasonable given their acclaim.

● **Samsara Larner Vineyard Grenache / 2012 / Ballard Canyon / $$$**
Grenache grown in a cool, sandy vineyard gives this wine a cherry-red exuberance; winemaker Chad Melville uses whole-cluster fermentation to add some structure and focus.

● **Samsara Melville Vineyard Syrah / 2012 / Sta. Rita Hills / $$$**
The savory aromatics in this stylish Syrah are thrilling: bergamot, pepper and smoke. The flavors then head toward ripe blueberry but never lose that savory edge.

SANDHI

Sandhi has exerted an influence on new-wave California winemakers far beyond its tiny size. A Pinot and Chardonnay specialist in the cool-climate Sta. Rita Hills, Sandhi was founded in 2010 by wine entrepreneur Charles Banks (see Mayacamas, p. 60) and two notable partners: sommelier Rajat Parr and winemaker Sashi Moorman (see Piedrasassi, p. 182). Its wines are defined both by what they are not (not over-rich, over-alcoholic or over-oaked) and by what they hope to be: naturally made, with a transparency that showcases their vineyard and vintage. Both reds and whites are fermented naturally, in neutral vessels (the reds in concrete; the whites in older barrels) to preserve and enhance their distinctiveness.

○ **Sandhi Sanford & Benedict Chardonnay / 2013 / Sta. Rita Hills / $$$**
The old vines at Sta. Rita Hills' oldest vineyard yielded a savory, earthy Chardonnay in 2013, with the kind of lean, granular mouthfeel that Raj Parr describes as "crunchy."

● **Sandhi Pinot Noir / 2013 / Sta. Rita Hills / $$$**
A dark, windswept wine, it nevertheless has both a lightly floral aroma and a sneaky delicacy; it's like a pomegranate tart, and just as invigorating.

SANFORD WINERY

In the early 1970s, Richard Sanford and Michael Benedict planted the first Pinot Noir vines in the Sta. Rita Hills, then a low-profile area in Santa Barbara County. Their home vineyard, Sanford & Benedict (later joined by the adjacent La Rinconada), became one of Santa Barbara's first breakout stars, and put both the Sta. Rita Hills and Sanford Winery on connoisseurs' radar. If Sanford, now majority-owned by the wine-importing Terlato family of Chicago, no longer enjoys the same cultish reputation, the Terlatos have continued to up the ante here, producing flowery, full-bodied small-lot Pinot and Chardonnay.

● **Sanford Pinot Noir / 2013 / Sta. Rita Hills / $$$**
Typically blended from the two estate vineyards, this Pinot is more forward than its single-vineyard counterparts: Think warm strawberry compote with a spritz of lemon acidity.

● **Sanford Sanford & Benedict Vineyard Pinot Noir / 2013 / Sta. Rita Hills / $$$$** From this historic vineyard, winemaker Steve Fennell crafts a wine that's supple and floral at once, a savory mélange of cranberry and red cherry framed by subtle oak.

SAXUM VINEYARDS

Few if any wineries have been more instrumental in the rise of western Paso Robles's vinous prestige than this small (5,500-case) operation from local-boy-made-good Justin Smith and his wife, Heather. Justin was 10 when his father, James, bought Saxum's headliner vineyard, James Berry. These days, Justin is turning out dense, closely knit Rhône-style wines that have quickly shot up in quality, price and renown. Unfortunately for most drinkers, Saxum's luxury-priced Grenache, Syrah and Mourvèdre bottlings sell out mostly through the mailing list. On the roster are eight vineyard-oriented wines, including the Bone Rock and Broken Stones blends, and the relatively new offering from the vineyard of former football great Terry Hoage.

● **Bone Rock / 2013 / Paso Robles / $$$$**
Structured and powerful, this blackberry-scented, mostly Syrah blend (the balance being Mourvèdre, Grenache and Roussanne) comes from old vines of the James Berry Vineyard.

● **Saxum James Berry Vineyard / 2013 / Paso Robles / $$$$**
This Rhône-style blend walks a line between the dark, heady richness of Grenache and Syrah and the more red-fruited notes of Mourvèdre and Counoise.

SCHARFFENBERGER CELLARS

This now-resurrected label was one of Anderson Valley's seminal sparkling wine producers. Founded by John Scharffenberger in 1981, the brand went through many changes in both ownership and name—it was called Pacific Echo for several years—before being bought by Maisons Marques & Domaines, the parent company of a nearby former rival, now stablemate, Roederer Estate. MMD has retained Tex Sawyer, the winemaker here since 1989, and is working to restore the luster of the Scharffenberger name with MMD's resources and vineyard access. Certainly a success from a quality standpoint, the winery currently makes two lovely sparklers with an emphasis on fruit and creaminess of texture at very attractive prices.

○ **Scharffenberger Brut Excellence / NV / Mendocino County / $$**
This sparkling wine's plush mousse and bright grapefruit scents give way to pleasantly broad fruit flavors.

● **Scharffenberger Brut Rosé Excellence / NV / Mendocino County / $$**
Festive and appealing, this is a well-priced salmon-colored sparkler with sweet, almost candied strawberry pastille flavors.

THE SCHOLIUM PROJECT

A former professor of philosophy, Abe Schoener defies the conventional wisdom of never letting the public taste your experiments. Seemingly every one of the quirkily named wines he makes in small quantities has an envelope-pushing intent. Schoener himself describes his project as a "modest" one, "undertaken for the sake of learning." The wines, like the forced-carbonation Blowout sparkler, for example, can be polarizing, but both they and Schoener himself have garnered an avid following. Ideal for the wine-curious with a sophisticated palate, Scholium is the cutting edge in action. Check the website for all manner of tiny bottlings ("particular prizes for the initiates").

○ **Naucratis / 2013 / California / $$**

Verdelho from the Sacramento River Delta area yields pungent scents of pear, lemon and orange oil, all held in a literally cloudy suspension; like many of Abe Schoener's wines, it's odd but captivating.

● **Gardens of Babylon / 2013 / Suisun Valley / $$$**

A regularly changing blend, in 2013 this wine is mostly Petite Sirah and Cabernet Sauvignon, with a burly, heady scent, accented by high-toned floral notes.

SEA SMOKE

Sea Smoke derives all of its wines from its biodynamically farmed home vineyards, planted in 1999 in what can be seen almost as a game of chicken: How far out toward the cold Pacific Ocean in the Sta. Rita Hills are you brave enough to plant? The sea smoke—that is, the fog—comes right up the Santa Ynez River to blanket these vineyards and, ideally, give their Pinot Noirs extended weeks of hang time to ripen slowly without shooting off the alcohol-level charts. What may strike the drinker as remarkable is the richness typical of these wines; they are not lean, angular and Burgundian, but rather silky, rounded and mouth-filling, particularly the Ten bottling.

○ **Sea Smoke Chardonnay / 2013 / Sta. Rita Hills / $$$**

This posh white delivers plenty of oak-driven flavor and a peachy scent that opens into more golden apple on the palate.

● **Sea Smoke Southing Pinot Noir / 2013 / Sta. Rita Hills / $$$**

Opulent and forceful, this dark Pinot offers intense purple fruit with oak-caramel flavors. It's a powerhouse wine—impressive, though admittedly not to every Pinot fan's taste.

STOLPMAN VINEYARDS

Tom Stolpman sought a cool-climate, limestone-soil vineyard and bought this 220-acre property in Santa Barbara's Ballard Canyon in 1990. After successfully selling its dry-farmed, organic grapes to elite labels like Sine Qua Non and Ojai (see p. 180), the Stolpman family began bottling its own Rhône varietals in 1997. In 2001 winemaker Sashi Moorman came on board—it was here that he made the reputation that led to his work at Domaine de la Côte and Sandhi (see pp. 163 and 186). The wines are generally impressive, especially the Syrahs and Roussannes, and reasonably priced for the quality. Some of the very-limited-production estate wines are available only through Stolpman's wine club.

○ **L'Avion / 2012 / Ballard Canyon / $$$**
Heady and rich, with a plushness that pushes into tropical territory, this all-Roussanne wine has great body and length.

● **Stolpman Vineyards Originals Syrah / 2013 / Ballard Canyon / $$$**
From Ballard Canyon's oldest Syrah planting, the fruit for this exotic red is mostly whole-cluster-fermented, which gives it an exotic, heady spice character.

TABLAS CREEK VINEYARD

Launched in Paso Robles in 1987, this joint venture between importer Robert Haas and the Perrin family of Châteauneuf-du-Pape is among California's most influential producers of Rhône-style wines, not least because its nursery sells vine cuttings imported from the Perrins' iconic Château de Beaucastel, contributing to the explosion of Rhône-style wines on the Central Coast and beyond. Paso Robles is known for reds, and Tablas Creek makes them in spades, including Panoplie, a spicy, broodingly dark Mourvèdre-based wine. The whites, such as the Esprit de Tablas (formerly Esprit de Beaucastel) Blanc blend, and rosés are worth looking for, too. The wallet-friendly Patelin de Tablas wines can also be wonderful.

○ **Tablas Creek Vineyard Esprit Blanc de Tablas / 2013 / Paso Robles / $$$** This white relies heavily on Roussanne, which gives it richness; the Picpoul and Grenache Blanc in the blend provide lift as well as the peaches-and-cream core of flavor.

● **Tablas Creek Vineyard Esprit de Tablas / 2013 / Paso Robles / $$$**
The winery's flagship red is primarily Mourvèdre (the balance being Syrah, Grenache and Counoise). Think strawberries and currants with a little fresh black pepper ground on top.

TALLEY VINEYARDS

The Arroyo Grande wine scene's leading light, Brian Talley, comes from a family that has been farming in the Central Coast since 1948. Today (in addition to other crops) the Talleys oversee 195 vineyard acres spread among six sites in the Arroyo Grande and Edna Valleys, none better known than Rosemary's Vineyard, which grows like a garden plot around the home of matriarch Rosemary Talley. It yields a world-class yard crop of lively, floral, blossom-accented Pinot Noir and Chardonnay that have become a Talley hallmark. The roughly 30,000-case operation reserves its Talley Vineyards label for estate-produced Pinot and Chardonnay; several of the under $30 Bishop's Peak wines are sourced partly or entirely from outside growers.

○ **Talley Vineyards Rosemary's Vineyard Chardonnay / 2014 / Arroyo Grande Valley / $$$** This nutty white offers aromas of pear and lemon curd, with modest oak imparting a caramelized, tarte-Tatin impression. Its breadth and length are admirable.

● **Talley Vineyards Rincon Vineyard Pinot Noir / 2013 / Arroyo Grande Valley / $$$$** The Talley Pinots have entered a fresh new era, framed by oak but not driven by it. What's revealed in the 2013 Rincon is leafy, red pomegranate fruit and hints of tobacco, with a mineral finish.

TENSLEY

Joey and Jennifer Tensley's family operation has been a hit since its first releases in 1999. Their wines ring the chimes of both critics and lovers of big-scaled but nuanced Rhône-style wines sold at very fair prices. At the core of Tensley's 5,000-case offerings are a handful of vineyard-designated Syrahs sourced from top sites around Santa Barbara County, led by the meaty, intense Colson Canyon Vineyard bottling. The sought-after Noir bottling comes partly from Colson Canyon Vineyard, which Tensley now owns, and partly from the winery's new home estate vineyard, which was first harvested in 2013.

● **Tensley Colson Canyon Vineyard Syrah / 2014 / Santa Barbara County / $$$** Still a baby, Joey Tensley's Syrah from Colson Canyon is rich and generous right now, the olive and bacon scents supporting plum and currant flavors.

● **Tensley Turner Vineyard Syrah / 2014 / Santa Barbara County / $$$** The scent of violets, bergamot and pepper all complement this wine's dark, vibrant fruit component.

TERRA D'ORO WINERY

This Trinchero-owned (see p. 88) property is a 70,000-plus-case brand formerly known as Montevina (a label still used for the lower-priced offerings, typically $10 to $12). Farming 500 estate acres, the "Land of Gold" is among the best-known wineries in Amador County, not least for its signature Zinfandels, which include the very-old-vine Deaver Vineyard bottling and the inky Home Vineyard Zin. But Terra d'Oro is also notworthy for its wide range of Cal-Ital wines, such as Barbera, Pinot Grigio and Sangiovese. Prices remain very affordable, with the spicy entry-level Terra d'Oro Zinfandel marketed at around $18.

● **Terra d'Oro Barbera / 2013 / Amador County / $$**
A standby of Sierra Foothills vineyards, Barbera gets quite ripe in Amador yet retains its acidity in this bright-berried, sappy red.

● **Terra d'Oro Home Vineyard Zinfandel / 2013 / Amador County / $$**
From vines that will turn 40 next year, this warm Zin has a spiced blackberry scent and dark, mocha-tinged fruit supported by smooth, clove-scented tannins.

TERRE ROUGE WINES/EASTON WINES

Operating on the Sierra Nevada slopes of Amador County, well outside the Napa-Sonoma orbit, Bill Easton bottles under two labels: Terre Rouge for Rhône-style wines, and Easton for more traditional wines like Zinfandel. Between the two, he may produce 28 different, mostly small-lot wines a year, but it's the Syrahs and old-vine Zins that are his calling cards. Though the winery's star, the eight-top-barrels-in-the-cellar Terre Rouge Ascent Syrah, is expensive, the heart of the portfolio is very well priced, including gems like the Sentinel Oak and DTR Ranch Syrahs and the surprising white Enigma, a creamy blend of Marsanne, Viognier and Roussanne.

○ **Terre Rouge Enigma / 2014 / Sierra Foothills / $$**
Marsanne, Viognier and Roussanne blend perfectly here: not too fruity, not too heavy, nor structured. Instead it's a vibrant, tropical white, ideal for a summer afternoon.

● **Terre Rouge Les Côtes de l'Ouest Syrah / 2013 / California / $$**
As well priced a Syrah as any in California, this warm red leads with scents of raspberry and game, with a lightness of fruit that invites afternoon sipping.

THACKREY & COMPANY WINE-MAKERS

Bolinas, California, is gorgeous, Bohemian to its roots and a bit hard to find. This is also not a bad description of Bolinas-based Sean Thackrey's often superb wines, produced in small quantities for three decades and still flying below the radar of all but his devoted followers, though this may change as production has climbed to 10,000 cases a year. Thackrey was a California Syrah pioneer, and his monumental Orion, now sourced from Napa's Rossi Vineyard, should be a reference point for the more recent generation of Rhône Rangers, except that Thackrey goes his own way. Who else would let their grapes ferment outside under the stars for the first 24 hours, a technique said to go back to the ancient Greek poet Hesiod?

● **Thackrey & Co Pleiades XXIV / NV / California / $$**
This irresistibly exuberant kitchen-sink blend comes in editions, not vintages. In the 24th version, Zinfandel provides dark berry flavors; other varieties add cinnamon-like spice.

● **Orion / 2013 / St. Helena / $$$$**
From a century-old Napa Valley vineyard in St. Helena, this red is frequently wild and intense, its gamey scent competing with inky black fruit. The tannins are at once fine and fierce.

THOMAS FOGARTY WINERY

One of the stalwarts of the Santa Cruz Mountains AVA, this highly regarded winery was established in 1981—the same year as the AVA itself—by heart surgeon and inventor Dr. Thomas Fogarty, and is now run by his son, Thomas Fogarty, Jr. Winemaker Nathan Kandler works alongside founding winemaker Michael Martella, sourcing fruit for these small-lot wines from Santa Cruz and Monterey. But the core of Fogarty's offerings are the Pinot Noirs and Chardonnays from estate-owned micro-plot vineyards like Rapley Trail, Langley Hill and Portola Springs, and the more southerly Gist Ranch, which produces the winery's Bordeaux varieties, bottled under the Lexington label.

○ **Thomas Fogarty Chardonnay / 2011 / Santa Cruz Mountains / $$$**
Drawn from mostly estate vineyards, this white displays the salty immediacy of the Pacific's influence and the citrusy delicacy of Santa Cruz's cool climate.

● **Thomas Fogarty Rapley Trail Vineyard Pinot Noir / 2012 / Santa Cruz Mountains / $$$$** The Rapley Trail Pinot is reticent at first, but with air, its leafy cherry flavor emerges with quiet elegance.

A TRIBUTE TO GRACE WINE COMPANY

Grenache may be the most underappreciated of fine-wine grapes, but in California it has an accomplished missionary in Angela Osborne. A New Zealander who came to the US in 2006, Osborne has in short order turned up obscure but stellar plantings of the grape all over the state for her lineup of all-Grenache, mostly single-vineyard wines. Her sleuthing has led to nearly-80-year-old vines at Hofer Ranch in the Cucamonga Valley, to the 3,200-foot-high Santa Barbara Highlands Vineyard and to Shake Ridge Vineyards in the Sierra Foothills owned by mentor Ann Kraemer (see Yorba Wines, p. 195) and her family. The winery's name is a tribute not only to Osborne's grandmother Grace, but to the gracefulness of these elegant wines.

- **A Tribute to Grace Santa Barbara Highlands Grenache / 2013 / Santa Barbara County / $$$** This expressive red is pale and delicate at first, then becomes more forceful and fruit-driven; there's far more flavor than color here, no small feat.
- **A Tribute to Grace Shake Ridge Ranch Grenache / 2013 / Amador County / $$$$** Density and dark cherry flavors mark this eminently ageworthy Grenache.

TYLER WINERY

The winery's mission statement paints the picture: "Tyler is dedicated to producing wines of delicacy and balance, where structure and nuance are favored above all else." Owner-winemaker Justin Willett, also of Lieu Dit (see p. 175) and Vallin, is part of a next-wave movement of California vintners aiming to dial back overripeness and high-alcohol levels in order to let the subtle flavors and aromas of the grapes express themselves. At Tyler, Willett produces Pinot Noir and Chardonnay from the cool Sta. Rita Hills and Santa Maria Valley AVAs, with an emphasis on old-vine vineyards. The overall output may be small (some 6,500 cases), but within that he crafts 15 different bottlings, each showcasing a particular *terroir*.

- **Tyler Chardonnay / 2013 / Santa Barbara County / $$$**
This lean, lemony white has a brisk acidic structure and a leesy, salty, mineral tang.
- **Tyler Pinot Noir / 2013 / Sta. Rita Hills / $$$**
Dark and deep when first poured, this Pinot feels over-concentrated. But with air the wine gains clarity, its tart berry flavors propelled by vibrant acidity.

VARNER

Twin brothers Bob and Jim Varner have raised the profile of their tiny Santa Cruz Mountains winery by becoming, of all things, Chardonnay specialists. They haven't turned their backs on the pure gratification that ripe California fruit brings to Chardonnay—and that sometimes gets their offerings dismissed by wine snobs. But the Varner brothers' deft hand with the variety lends it a structured, delineated European finesse that puts their wines into a different league. Fans also appreciate their touch with Pinot Noir (under both the Varner and Neely labels) and the often remarkable value of their Foxglove second label, typically sourced from the Central Coast and offering far more pleasure and complexity than you'd expect for under $20.

○ **Varner Bee Block Chardonnay / 2014 / Santa Cruz Mountains / $$$**
There's an old-fashioned golden-apple richness to this Chardonnay at first, plus a generous amount of oak, but with air, the wine comes into focus, ending up elegant, even posh.

● **Varner Hidden Block Pinot Noir / 2013 / Santa Cruz Mountains / $$$**
This Pinot's poise is the first thing you notice, the play of its foresty scent with its perfumed cherry core; with air, the fruit comes forward, with just enough leafy savor to balance it out.

VILLA CREEK CELLARS

Another star from western Paso Robles, one of California wine's most dynamic sub-regions, Villa Creek is the wine label of Cris and JoAnn Cherry, who also own the winemaker hangout Villa Creek Restaurant in downtown Paso Robles. Not surprisingly for someone so woven into the local wine scene, Cris is able to access fruit from some of Paso's top vineyards, including Denner and James Berry (see Saxum Vineyards, p. 187). He produces 3,000 cases of red, white and rosé Rhône-style wines in a vibrant, luscious style that has attracted a following—the mailing list is the way to go here. Fortunately, the prices remain very attractive.

● **Villa Creek Avenger / 2013 / Paso Robles / $$$**
Syrah is the lead variety here, making the wine considerably darker and spicier than the Cuvée bottling. Coffee, tar, meaty black-fruit flavors, full-bodied tannins—grill a steak for it.

● **Villa Creek Willow Creek Cuvée / 2013 / Paso Robles / $$$**
This is one of Villa Creek's crowd-pleasers, a Grenache-heavy Rhône blend with the exuberance of that variety on full display, and ripe tannins bringing up the rear.

WENTE VINEYARDS

Located an hour's drive east of San Francisco, Wente is the Livermore Valley's most important wine operation, and California's oldest continuously operating family-run winery. C.H. Wente founded the estate in 1883, and his fifth-generation descendant Karl Wente now oversees wine production. It's no small operation, with nearly 3,000 estate acres of vineyard and visitor facilities that include a tasting room, a restaurant and a golf course. Though the label may be best known for providing reliable values, ambitious cuvées such as the Nth Degree and Small Lot tiers, made in micro-batches in a winery within the winery, are gaining Wente a new generation of admirers.

○ **Wente The Nth Degree Chardonnay / 2013 / Livermore Valley / $$$$** This sumptuous bottling uses Wente Chardonnay clonal selections, giving the wine a broad palate with scents of baked apple, pineapple and caramel.

● **Wente Charles Wetmore Cabernet Sauvignon / 2013 / Livermore Valley / $$** Wente's estate Cab from legacy vines reflects the allure of this historic property. A generous complement of oak bolsters the wine's black fig and black raspberry flavors.

YORBA WINES

Much-admired Napa Valley vineyard manager Ann Kraemer scouted the North Coast for a spot to put down her own roots and settled on underappreciated Amador County, in the Sierra Foothills. In the 46 planted acres of her high-altitude Shake Ridge Vineyards, she grows an eclectic mix of grapes—Zinfandel, Barbera and Tempranillo among them—for a long client list. But winemaker Ken Bernards (Ancien Wines) reserves some of the best for the property's own-label Yorba wines, including the Shake Ridge Red, an "expression of the ranch" that must be one of the very few blends in the world to have combined among its constituent varieties Mourvèdre, Malbec and Graciano.

● **Yorba Barbera / 2011 / Amador County / $$** A little bottle age brings a lot of composure to this concentrated red, with its dark plum core; lasting, peppery tannins are the final impression, together with the bright acidity.

● **Yorba Tempranillo / 2010 / Amador County / $$$** Quite forward for a six-year-old wine, this stylish Tempranillo is dense and concentrated, with a mocha-like depth and tannins that feel firm and refined at once.

Oregon

Anyone who loves Oregon Pinot Noir–and more people do every year–should thank Eyrie Vineyards' founder David Lett. In the mid-1960s, Lett trekked north from California in search of something quite elusive. What he was looking for, and found, was a growing climate that could yield Burgundian Pinot Noir: intense and complexly aromatic, yet graceful above all. Five decades later there are 676 bonded wineries in Oregon and over 27,000 acres of vinifera grapes. In addition to Pinot Noir (the state's most planted variety), Pinot Gris, Chardonnay and Riesling thrive here. Plus, a recent string of terrific vintages–2014 and 2015 especially–means that now is a great time to start exploring Oregon's ever-more-impressive wines.

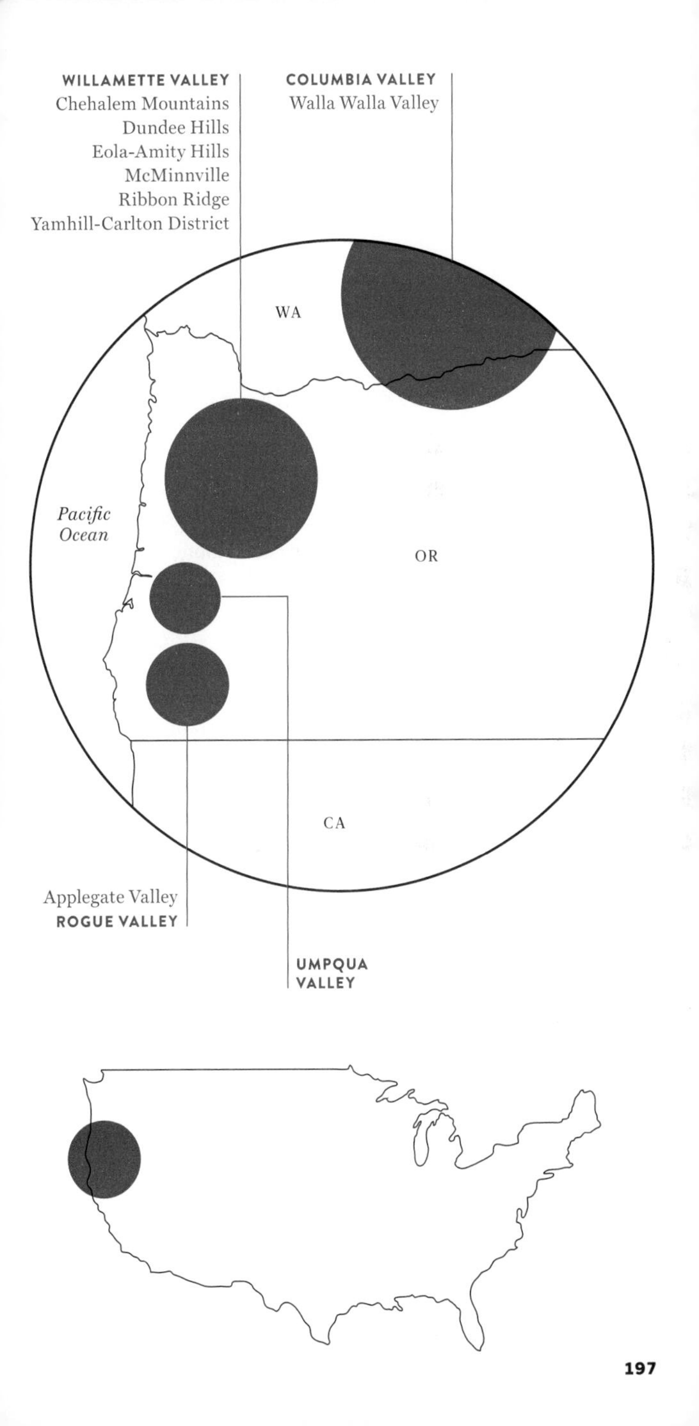
WILLAMETTE VALLEY
Chehalem Mountains
Dundee Hills
Eola-Amity Hills
McMinnville
Ribbon Ridge
Yamhill-Carlton District
COLUMBIA VALLEY
Walla Walla Valley
WA
Pacific Ocean
OR
CA
Applegate Valley
ROGUE VALLEY
UMPQUA VALLEY

REGIONS TO KNOW

ROGUE VALLEY Southern Oregon's Rogue Valley is actually three distinct river valleys: **Bear Creek** and **Applegate** (which claims its own AVA) are known for Bordeaux and Rhône varieties; the cooler **Illinois Valley** in the west produces Pinot Noir and Alsace whites.

UMPQUA VALLEY The exceedingly diverse range of landscapes and microclimates in the "Hundred Valleys of the Umpqua" allows for production of just about every desirable wine grape.

WILLAMETTE VALLEY Stretching from Portland in the north to Eugene in the south, this broad valley is home to most of the state's population as well as three-fourths of its wine production. Oregon's Pinot Noir heartland, Willamette Valley encompasses six subregions: the cool hills of **Chehalem Mountains**, practically in suburban Portland; the highly esteemed, densely planted **Dundee Hills**; the ocean-cooled **Eola-Amity Hills**; **McMinnville**, site of the annual International Pinot Noir Celebration; the compact, typically dry-farmed **Ribbon Ridge**; and the **Yamhill-Carlton District**, home to some of the state's top wineries.

KEY GRAPES: WHITE

CHARDONNAY Oregon has long produced more Pinot Gris than Chardonnay, but the Chardonnay that does get made here can be very good, with subtle fruit flavors and lively acidity. Along with Pinot Noir, Chardonnay is also the foundation of some excellent Oregon sparkling wines.

PINOT GRIS Oregon sets the American standard for this Alsace-style white. Although Pinot Gris varies in profile, its typical expression here is generous and full-bodied, with pear, citrus and stone-fruit flavors and a refreshing acidity.

RIESLING & PINOT BLANC These aromatic whites are making headway, with a handful of small vintners achieving notable success, particularly in the Willamette Valley.

KEY GRAPES: RED

PINOT NOIR Representing more than half of the state's wine production, Oregon Pinot Noir comes in a range of profiles, but the classic version is silky smooth, with delicate berry flavors and firm acidity. The best bottlings are worthy of comparison with any Pinot Noirs in the world.

Producers/ Oregon

ABERRANT CELLARS

Winemaker Eric Eide gave up selling fine wine and began crafting it himself at the Willamette Valley winery he founded in 2009. Conscientious farming, plus hands-on, low-tech and low-oak-influence winemaking, have made his flavorful, nuanced Pinot Noirs (including an intriguing Pinot Noir Blanc) the darlings of critics. Aberrant's darkest, richest offering is the aptly named Carpe Noctem ("Seize the Night"). The Latin names Eide gives his wines express the qualities he achieves through blending vineyards and lots that he follows throughout the growing season with a true believer's devotion.

- ○ **Aberrant Cellars Philtrum Pinot Noir Blanc / 2014 / Willamette Valley / $$$** Neutral, quiet and elegant like many white Pinots, this one leads with a hint of nutmeg adorning white cherry and apple flavors. Its texture is sleek, balanced and suave.
- ● **Aberrant Cellars Confero Pinot Noir / 2014 / Willamette Valley / $$** Exuberant in its youth, this elegant strawberry-scented red has a mild foresty top note. Its flavors are saturated and mouth-filling, with the substance to age.

ADELSHEIM VINEYARD

One of the foundational names in Oregon wine, Adelsheim has been a leader and talent-incubator for the industry ever since David and Ginny Adelsheim bought their small Chehalem Mountains estate in 1971. Starting with 15 acres in their Quarter Mile Lane Vineyard, the Adelsheims and their partners have expanded to farm more than 200 acres. The winery is known for small-lot and single-vineyard Pinot Noirs—winemaker David Paige may have 180 separate fermenters going during a typical harvest—but Adelsheim's reputation for vibrant, graceful wines extends to its Chardonnays and Pinot Gris as well, which are typically far more affordable than the ever-pricier reds.

○ **Adelsheim Pinot Gris / 2014 / Willamette Valley / $$**
There's a pleasing tension between the bright apple flavor and broad, savory character of this estate Pinot Gris. With its zippy texture and mineral edge, it's made for white meat.

● **Elizabeth's Reserve Pinot Noir / 2013 / Willamette Valley / $$$**
From several of Adelsheim's top vineyard sources, "the Lizzie" is typically fresh and graceful, with subtle floral scents and a delicate, vibrant red-cherry flavor.

ANAM CARA CELLARS

Nick and Sheila Nicholas, the owners of Anam Cara ("friend of my soul" in Celtic), came to wine through pizza—they owned a pizza chain with an outlet in Napa Valley that opened new horizons for them. In 2001 they broke ground on the hillside plot in the Chehalem Mountains that would become the Nicholas Estate, the vineyard source for their supple, restrained and elegant wines. Many of the original trees remain on the site of this now sustainably farmed former orchard. The newest vineyard block was planted according to the biodynamic calendar (moon, planets and stars), and it includes more acres of the Pinot Noir that has been most responsible for the operation's growing reputation.

○ **Anam Cara Nicholas Estate Dry Riesling / 2012 / Chehalem Mountains / $$** Scented with apple, Meyer lemon and a whiff of petrol, this Riesling is crisp and very dry, with a delicate touch of minerality.

● **Anam Cara Nicholas Estate Pinot Noir / 2012 / Chehalem Mountains / $$$** Pretty and floral with a hint of smoke, this light-toned red has good acidity and a pleasingly grainy texture.

ANDREW RICH WINES

Andrew Rich may have studied winemaking in Dijon, the Burgundian West Point of Pinot Noir, but the Rhône was his first love; he went on to pursue it at California's Rhône-centric Bonny Doon. Later, operating out of the Carlton Winemakers Studio, Rich founded his own label in 1995. He makes three very fine Oregon Pinot Noirs, each a blended cuvée from grapes grown around the Willamette Valley, but his portfolio also includes an array of generally delicious Rhône-style wines—Roussanne, Syrah and the Tabula Rasa red and Grenache-Mourvèdre rosé blends—typically produced in small lots and often sourced from Washington.

● **Andrew Rich Coup d'Etat / 2012 / Columbia Valley / $$**
A Grenache-Mourvèdre-Syrah blend from the iconic Ciel du Cheval Vineyard in Washington's Red Mountain AVA, this sappy red leads with heady raspberry scents from Grenache; firm tannins gird its juicy flavors.

● **Andrew Rich The Knife Edge Pinot Noir / 2012 / Willamette Valley / $$$** Brooding and tense when first poured, this dark-edged Pinot presents an initially smoky and savory profile. With air, a mélange of plum and cinnamon flavors comes into focus.

ANTICA TERRA

It has not taken long for Antica Terra's remarkable wines to disappear into the pricing stratosphere, but it is hard to argue that they don't merit their prices. Winemaker Maggie Harrison cut her teeth under the exacting Manfred Krankl at Sine Qua Non in Southern California. His super-ripe style doesn't translate to Oregon's more marginal climate, but Harrison has clearly internalized Krankl's ability to make wines that are immediately palate-appealing yet reveal distinctive layer after layer as you sip. Her calling-card Pinots—adorned with some of the world's most beautiful wine labels—are notable for their depth of character and fine-tuned tension between richness and acidity.

● **Angelicall Rosé / 2014 / Willamette Valley / $$$$**
This unique, very red rosé offers a heady scent of earth, anise and tanbark over spiced cherry. Its flavors are exotic and assertive, a mostarda mélange of strawberry and spice.

● **Botanica Pinot Noir / 2014 / Willamette Valley / $$$$**
Evocative rosy spice notes adorn the heady plum fruit of this seductive and boundlessly concentrated Pinot.

ARCHERY SUMMIT

This well-funded, highly regarded winery is the Oregon outpost of California-based Crimson Wine Group (Pine Ridge, Seghesio). Winemaker Christopher Mazepink, who took the reins here in 2013, benefits from 120 estate acres in the Dundee Hills and Ribbon Ridge AVAs, including the celebrated Arcus Estate. The acreage is divided into many small blocks, all densely planted and low-yielding, with rootstocks and oak regimes adapted to each, and farmed with various versions of organic and biodynamic viticulture. Known for its richly expressive Pinot Noirs, which have fetched high prices from collectors for many years, Archery Summit also makes a delicious and affordable Pinot Gris and a rosé called Vireton.

● **Archery Summit Premier Cuvée Pinot Noir / 2013 / Willamette Valley / $$$** The dark-fruit character—plums, blueberry—of Archery Summit's entry level Pinot Noir is framed, but not overpowered, by dark oak flavors.

● **Archery Summit Arcus Estate Pinot Noir / 2013 / Dundee Hills / $$$$** Dark, with scents of molasses and black plum, this rich red has flavors of fresh black fig and a firm texture with plenty of oak tannin. It's a wine built for the cellar.

ARGYLE WINERY

One of Oregon's more individualistic wineries, Argyle is actually part of the corporate hierarchy of parent company Kirin. But fans of Argyle's outstanding sparkling wines—among America's very best—and still Pinot Noirs and Chardonnays know that winemaker Nate Klostermann has a way with elegant, vibrant wines that are typically more sophisticated than showy. The Extended Tirage bottlings, made in top years, are sparkling wine benchmarks. The whimsically named Spirithouse and Nuthouse wines are among Oregon's finest Pinot Noirs; the entry-level Pinot and the barely oaked basic Chardonnay are solid values.

○ **Argyle Knudsen Vineyard Brut / 2011 / Dundee Hills / $$$** Focused and crisp, with a lemony sharp edge, this sparkler offers a suite of flavors that start out broad and mouth-filling and finish citrusy and clean.

● **Argyle Nuthouse Pinot Noir / 2013 / Eola-Amity Hills / $$$** This Pinot is from a single vineyard in the Eola-Amity Hills AVA. It's clean and light, with a red raspberry scent, lean cherry flavors and plenty of acidity on the finish.

ARTERBERRY MARESH

Third-generation Oregon winemaker Jim Maresh was raised on the Dundee Hills farm his grandparents bought in 1959 and first planted to grapes in 1970. The Pinot Noir and Chardonnay he produces from Maresh Vineyard's non-irrigated old vines are the flagships of his highly esteemed label, which also includes limited-quantity bottlings from neighboring vineyards. All of the wines are, as the winery says, "transparent and unadorned," with no added sugar or acid, neutral oak aging and no fining or filtering. They are also difficult to obtain unless you sign up for the mailing list.

○ **Arterberry Maresh Chardonnay / 2013 / Dundee Hills / $$$$**
This golden Chardonnay melds a Maconnais purity of apple flavor with a modest touch of caramelly oak and a focused, fresh acidity.

● **Arterberry Maresh Maresh Vineyard Pinot Noir / 2013 / Dundee Hills / $$$** The shy red fruits of this Pinot Noir seem held in check by some classic Dundee Hills red-dirt minerality. The flavors lean toward a slightly tart red cherry that's assertive in its acid structure.

A TO Z WINEWORKS

Before its purchase of Rex Hill (see p. 216) in 2006, A to Z Wineworks owned neither vineyards nor a winery. Rather, the posse of talents behind this sizeable label—including Michael Davies and Cheryl Francis (both Chehalem alums) and Sam Tannahill (formerly of Archery Summit)—made A to Z's name by buying finished wines, then using their skills to create juicy, balanced blends from Oregon's major varietals. This now-familiar restaurant brand is many wine drinkers' introduction to fine Oregon Pinot Noir, and a strong track record has also made A to Z a reliable label for often superior Chardonnay and Pinot Gris at hard-to-beat prices.

○ **A to Z Pinot Gris / 2014 / Oregon / $**
In this crisp, light and refreshing Pinot Gris, A to Z's statewide sourcing guarantees an especially generous core of fruit—juicy quince and apple—framed by a mineral tang.

● **A to Z Pinot Noir / 2014 / Oregon / $$**
A warm, saturated core of flavor gives this dark-cherried Pinot Noir depth and richness. It's a structured, well-rounded and affordable red to uncap for Wednesday-night meals.

BEAUX FRÈRES

Wine critic Robert Parker and his brother-in-law Michael Etzel (the *beaux frères*) bought an 88-acre former pig farm on Ribbon Ridge near Newberg in the late 1980s and set about practicing what Parker had been preaching. Vines are cropped to very low yields to gain flavor intensity, and a meticulous regimen of minimalist winemaking is followed, including natural fermentations with indigenous yeasts, long aging on the lees and no fining or filtration. The original home property, which produces the rich, polished flagship Beaux Frères Vineyard Pinot Noir, is now farmed biodynamically. Crafted to showcase their fruit, soil and vintage without winemaking cover-ups, these are connoisseurs' wines with prices to match.

- **Beaux Frères Pinot Noir / 2013 / Willamette Valley / $$$**
  Lush at the outset, with a scent of autumn leaves and juicy cherry, this Pinot Noir has a firmness and a fine, dusty texture grounding its generous fruit.
- **Beaux Frères The Beaux Frères Vineyard Pinot Noir / 2013 / Ribbon Ridge / $$$$** Older vines from the estate vineyard, and most likely the loving care of biodynamic farming, give this ethereal wine a purity and a precision that is thrilling and rare.

BELLE PENTE VINEYARD & WINERY

This is a well-regarded, personal-scale, artisan operation. Owners Brian and Jill O'Donnell left careers in Silicon Valley to pursue their winemaking dreams at the 70-acre hillside (*belle pente* means "beautiful slope") estate they established near Carlton in 1994. Pinot Noir, much of it grown on the couple's non-irrigated, organically and biodynamically farmed property, put Belle Pente on the map, but the winery is also known for opulent whites, including a full-flavored Pinot Gris, an all-estate Chardonnay and an Alsace Edelzwicker-style blend called Belle Oiseau. Realistic prices are another Belle Pente hallmark.

- **Belle Pente Pinot Noir / 2013 / Willamette Valley / $$**
  An absurdly well-priced red that features almost two-thirds estate-grown grapes, this wine is nimble and lifted, with leafy berry scents giving way to a warm cherry core of flavor.
- **Belle Pente Estate Reserve Pinot Noir / 2012 / Yamhill-Carlton / $$$**
  This offers a cool, expressive mélange of bright red cherry fruit with notes of bark, spice, cinnamon, sassafras and dried leaves. Its elegant red fruit flavors yield to a more floral finish.

BERGSTRÖM WINES

Founded by Portland surgeon John Bergström and his wife, Karen, in 1999, the winery is now run by their son Josh, who studied winemaking (and met his future wife) in Burgundy. The five estate vineyards—now encompassing 84 acres around the Willamette Valley—are biodynamically farmed and yield Pinot Noirs and Chardonnays of great poise, energy and depth. Among the 10,000 cases produced here are a number of sought-after single-vineyard bottlings , including those from the steep Gregory Ranch in the Pacific Coast Range and from Bergström's Temperance Hill block, so high and cool that it's sometimes not harvested until November.

○ **Bergström Sigrid Chardonnay / 2013 / Willamette Valley / $$$$** Sigrid is typically unremittingly plush, and the 2013 vintage is no exception, with its scents of golden apple and generous flavors of pear and smoky lees.

● **Bergström Bergström Vineyard Pinot Noir / 2013 / Dundee Hills / $$$$** With its red-fruited hues and fine, grainy grip of tannin, Bergström's flagship single-vineyard Pinot beautifully shows off the volcanic, red-dirt Dundee Hills *terroir.* Whole-cluster fermentation lends a tea-like spice.

BIG TABLE FARM

Former Napa Valley winemaker Brian Marcy and artist-farmer Clare Carver moved to Oregon in 2006 to pursue a vision of natural land cultivation and stewardship that encompasses vegetables, pigs, hens, cows and winemaking. Their small-production lots of native-yeast-fermented, unfined, unfiltered wines are headlined by Marcy's vineyard- and vintage-driven Pinot Noirs and Chardonnays. Big Table Farm's bottlings of Alsace varieties, particularly those from the old-vine Wirtz Vineyard, which Marcy farms, have a cult following. Check the website for release dates, since all these wines sell out quickly.

● **Big Table Farm Pelos Sandberg Vineyard Pinot Noir / 2013 / Eola-Amity Hills / $$$** This Pinot is delicious, accessible and complex all at once, with firm tannins framing the supple, juicy freshness of red cherry fruit.

● **Big Table Farm Pinot Noir / 2013 / Willamette Valley / $$$** Light and pretty in 2013, with scents of raspberry and bramble, this high-acid red has a juicy red cherry core of flavor. It merits a chill.

BRICK HOUSE VINEYARDS

One of Oregon's pioneering practitioners of organic and biodynamic viticulture, this Ribbon Ridge estate is the dream of former globe-trotting CBS foreign correspondent Doug Tunnell. The wines from Brick House's 40-acre estate (surrounding the Tunnells' actual brick house) are treated with the same care and natural approach as the vineyards. The Chardonnay, for example, is fermented with native yeasts, aged in seasoned French barrels rather than new ones to let the fruit shine through, and bottled unfiltered. The Pinots—headed by the velvety Evelyn's, are the stars here, but Brick House has also gained a reputation for its Gamay.

● **Brick House Gamay Noir / 2014 / Ribbon Ridge / $$** Exuberant, vibrant Gamay from outside Beaujolais? Yes, indeed. This cranberry-scented red has a core of juicy red fruits, made thrilling by its lift and mouthwatering acidity.

● **Brick House Cuvée du Tonnelier Pinot Noir / 2014 / Ribbon Ridge / $$$** The 2014 vintage of the barrelmaker's cuvée has a wild cherry aroma framed by caramelly oak. Its flavors are plush and supple, the oak receding nicely with air.

BRITTAN VINEYARDS

When Robert Brittan, the longtime winemaker at Stags' Leap Winery, left Napa Valley to pursue his Pinot dreams, he wasn't looking to make things easy. The 128-acre hillside site he found in 2004 in the foothills of the Coast Range near McMinnville provides plenty of challenges: It is cool, windy and above all rocky, as the name of Brittan's calling card Pinot Noir bottling, Basalt Block, implies. But in the expert hands of the scholarly, thoughtful Brittan, the site yields superb, vibrant wines, including small amounts of Chardonnay and Syrah that have attracted the attention of collectors. Given the quality of Brittan's wines, the prices remain quite reasonable—for now.

○ **Brittan Vineyards Chardonnay / 2013 / Willamette Valley / $$$** Rich at first, abetted by a sumptuous oak impression, this wine settles into a clean array of lemon curd and golden apple flavors, leading to a nutty finish.

● **Brittan Vineyards Basalt Block Pinot Noir / 2013 / Willamette Valley / $$$** True to its name, there's a mineral savor to this wine's red-fruit aromas of black cherry and pomegranate. Precise tannins guide its firm texture.

BROOKS

While still an assistant winemaker at WillaKenzie (see p. 220), Jimi Brooks founded his Eola-Amity Hills winery in 1998, only to pass away suddenly in 2004, leaving behind an eight-year-old son, Pascal, and a winery to run. As chronicled in the film *American Wine Story,* Brooks's sister, Janie, with the help of vintner friends and volunteers, stepped in to save the winery for Pascal. Today, Janie Brooks Heuck follows in her brother's footsteps, farming the estate vineyard organically and biodynamically. Winemaker Chris Williams continues to emphasize nuance and delicacy in a roster that ranges from the flagship Janus Pinot Noir to much-appreciated whites, including superb Rieslings and the Alsace-varietal blend Amycas.

○ **Brooks Riesling / 2013 / Willamette Valley / $$**
Bone-dry, savory and exotic, this Riesling offers a whiff of petrol and tropical fruits on the nose and a racy, mouth-watering texture. A lemon-lime terseness marks the finish.

● **Brooks Janus Pinot Noir / 2013 / Willamette Valley / $$$**
Always a blend of the winery's most focused and intense lots, Janus in 2013 has a heady plum-like depth to its flavors, marked by a clingy grip of tannin. A fantastic match for duck.

CAMERON WINERY

Cats, geese, goats, chickens and bees all play a role in Cameron's sustainable home vineyard—read all about them on the winery's website—and in the idiosyncratic spirit of this throwback, artisan winery. Owner-winemaker John Paul has his own ideas about viticulture, but they are grounded in science (he has a doctorate in marine biochemistry) and years of close-to-the-soil work. A leading light in the Deep Roots Coalition, which eschews irrigation, Paul crafts superb Chardonnays and Pinot Noirs from the home Clos Electrique vineyard. Often compared to Burgundies, his wines capture the full essence of the *terroir.*

○ **Cameron Clos Electrique / 2013 / Dundee Hills / $$$$**
This year's Clos Electrique Chardonnay is broad and savory, with its wet-stone scent and golden-pear flavor enhanced by a hint of caramel and stony minerals.

● **Cameron Winery Ramato Pinot Grigio / 2014 / Dundee Hills / $$**
Extended skin contact gives this Pinot Gris a brilliant salmon hue, but on the palate, it delivers mostly richness, like cherries macerating in Chardonnay. A one-of-a-kind wine.

CHEHALEM

Harry Peterson-Nedry was a pioneering planter on Ribbon Ridge back in 1980. With his partners, Bill and Cathy Stoller, Peterson-Nedry expanded the estate's vineyard holdings in the 1990s with the addition of Corral Creek Vineyards in the Chehalem Mountains and Stoller Vineyards in the Dundee Hills. From the unoaked INOX Chardonnay to the Pinot Noirs and wildly aromatic Pinot Gris and Rieslings, Chehalem's wines typically reflect Peterson-Nedry's obsession with purity, freshness and crisp acidity, sometimes at the expense of palate-flattering fleshiness and fruit. These are not so much market-driven wines as they are distinctive products of a consistent style. Harry is now assisted by daughter Wynne, as Chehalem enters its second generation.

○ **Chehalem Corral Creek Vineyards Riesling / 2013 / Chehalem Mountains / $$** This Riesling offers impressive herbal aromatics (tarragon, lemon thyme), tense green apple and apple blossom flavors and a mouthwatering finish.

● **Chehalem Ridgecrest Vineyards Pinot Noir / 2013 / Ribbon Ridge / $$$** A hint of smoke and stem spice lend complex aromatics to this cherried red. The texture is at once firm and nimble.

CRISTOM VINEYARDS

Cristom has a remarkable story of continuity: Winemaker Steve Doerner and vineyard manager Mark Feltz have been in place since Paul Gerrie bought the property in 1992. Why mess with success? Cristom's Pinot Noirs—whole-cluster-fermented with native yeasts and bottled unfiltered—have long been some of the state's most acclaimed wines; the Viogniers are also regularly among Oregon's best. The four estate-sourced, single-vineyard Pinot bottlings named for family matriarchs are relatively rare (in top vintages there is also a luxury Signature Cuvée), but the three more accessible multivineyard blends, including the relatively affordable Mt. Jefferson Cuvée, can also be outstanding.

● **Cristom Mt. Jefferson Cuvée Pinot Noir / 2013 / Willamette Valley / $$** A blend of grapes from all of the estate vineyards goes into Cristom's most accessible Pinot Noir. A basalt-like minerality grounds its dark red-fruit flavors and broad sweep of spice.

● **Cristom Jessie Vineyard Pinot Noir / 2013 / Eola-Amity Hills / $$$** In this aromatic Pinot, tea-like scents lead to haunting cherry and plum flavors, with whole-cluster spice filling out the finish.

DOMAINE DROUHIN OREGON

Established in the late 1980s, this outpost of Burgundy's Maison Joseph Drouhin winery has deftly blended things French (including head winemaker Véronique Drouhin-Boss and her brother, vineyard manager Philippe) with things Oregonian—"French soul, Oregon soil," as their slogan goes. The results are wines of place, with a French refinement and polish but also a richness and warmth that is pure New World. Pinot Noir is the focus in Drouhin's Dundee Hills vineyard (only 11 of the 124 acres are planted to Chardonnay). The entry-level Willamette Valley Pinot remains realistically priced for excellent quality, while the Laurène and Louise cuvées are among America's Pinot benchmarks.

○ **Domaine Drouhin Edition Limitée Chardonnay / 2013 / Dundee Hills / $$$$** Harmonious and seductive, this gorgeous Chardonnay melds generous golden-pear fruit and a toasty, savory lees character, all leading to an elegant hazelnut-parfait finish.

● **Domaine Drouhin Laurène Pinot Noir / 2013 / Dundee Hills / $$$$** This is a casually elegant, savory and forward Pinot, with a leafy, almost Burgundian feel to its texture. Fine, lacy acidity gives a boost to the wine's strawberry flavors.

ELK COVE VINEYARDS

Elk Cove has been a sturdy source for Oregon Pinot Noir ever since Pat and Joe Campbell took charge of their first vineyard in 1974. They pulled up to the small plot towing the trailer that would be home for them and their five children for a year. Today Elk Cove is arguably at the top of its game under the youngest son, Adam, who sources his single-vineyard and limited-release Pinot Noir offerings from six estate vineyards covering 350 acres (plus some judiciously purchased fruit). But the winery also places great emphasis on its whites—Pinot Blanc, Pinot Gris, Riesling and the luscious dessert-wine blend Ultima.

○ **Elk Cove Vineyards Pinot Gris / 2014 / Willamette Valley / $$** A juicy, brisk white with ripe quince and lemon scents and apple flavors, it has enough flesh to remind you that you're nowhere near Italy.

● **Elk Cove Vineyards Roosevelt Pinot Noir / 2013 / Yamhill-Carlton / $$$$** This generously oaked red has an equally generous candied black-cherry flavor, fulsome and round without being over the edge.

ERATH

Longtime winemaker Gary Horner continues the work that Dick Erath began back in 1969 at this venerable Dundee Hills winery. After acquiring the property in 2006, Washington's Ste. Michelle Wine Estates made considerable investments (and boosted production), and the wines have rewarded the outlays. Horner has a broad palette to work with, including 13 single-vineyard sites, but across the board his Pinot Noirs tend to be made in an aromatic, medium-rich style that falls between Oregon and typically riper California Pinots. The exceptions to the rule are the two amped-up, top-end Magique collection wines: a red Pinot Noir, La Nuit Magique ("The Magic Night"), and a white Pinot Noir, Le Jour Magique ("The Magic Day").

○ **Erath Pinot Gris / 2014 / Oregon / $**

With lime zest scents and flavors that are zingy and a bit savory with a saline tang, this has the freshness for salt prawns.

● **Erath Pinot Noir / 2013 / Oregon / $$**

This is a balanced and lean Pinot Noir, displaying cranberry and red cherry aromas, plus a whiff of smoke and a dollop of sumptuous oak for flavor and structure.

EVESHAM WOOD

This is a name to seek out, not only for the bright, refined, Burgundian-profile Pinot Noirs that have earned this boutique-size producer a following since 1986, but also because the wines offer remarkable value in today's market—from the entry-level Willamette Valley Pinot Noir to the top-of-the-line Cuvée J bottling. Haden Fig owner Erin Nuccio bought Evesham from founders Russ and Mary Raney in 2010. It has been a relief to Evesham's fans that Nuccio clearly shares Russ's winegrowing and winemaking values, including his taste for picking balanced—as opposed to super-ripe—fruit and intervening as little as possible once it's in the winery.

● **Evesham Wood Pinot Noir / 2014 / Willamette Valley / $$**

More fruit-forward than the winery's Le Puits Sec bottling, this Pinot Noir features a plush center of plum and black cherry with a pleasant earthiness at the gentle finish.

● **Evesham Wood Le Puits Sec Pinot Noir / 2013 / Eola-Amity Hills / $$$**

Clean and brisk, this red leads with scents of cranberry and a floral top note—think rose petals and cherry blossoms. Its flavors lean toward forest floor, with a pretty earthiness.

THE EYRIE VINEYARDS

This is the winery that began it all in modern Oregon wine history. Its late founder, the visionary winemaker David Lett, came up from California in 1965 with 3,000 vine cuttings to plant Pinot Noir in the supposedly "too rainy" Willamette Valley. Lett proved the doubters wrong, and along the way also bottled America's first Pinot Gris. Now run by his son Jason, Eyrie sources grapes from five venerable estate vineyards, all unirrigated and essentially organically farmed (the Reserve Pinot Noir and Chardonnay come from 50-year-old vines). Jason continues his father's emphasis on small-lot fermentation and wines of grace and balance rather than power and high alcohol.

○ **The Eyrie Vineyards Pinot Blanc / 2014 / Dundee Hills / $$**
Bright and limpid, with a crisp apple scent and a hint of salinity and leesiness on the palate, this feels tense and a bit austere at first but broadens dramatically with aeration.

● **The Eyrie Vineyards Pinot Noir / 2013 / Willamette Valley / $$$**
This is a light-bodied, pretty Pinot Noir with a brickish color and strawberry-tobacco scents. Its flavors are lean and wonderfully delicate yet remain firm through the finish.

J. CHRISTOPHER WINES

One of Oregon's most intriguing small wineries, J. Christopher is the brainchild of Old World wine enthusiast (and rock guitarist) Jay Somers and his friend and business partner, the estimable Mosel Valley producer Ernst Loosen. Somers had been producing his wine for years at others' facilities, but Loosen's backing allowed him to break ground on his own winery in 2010. Perhaps surprisingly, the new venture doesn't produce Riesling, relying instead on an impressive Sancerre-style Sauvignon Blanc as its signature white wine. But Pinot Noir is the focus here, with fruit sourced from Olenik, Abbey Ridge and an array of other top vineyards in addition to the organically farmed 21-acre home vineyard, Appassionata.

● **J. Christopher Pinot Noir / 2013 / Willamette Valley / $$**
Fresh and delicate, with scents of raspberry and forest-floor accents, this vibrant red gets more ample with air and has the ripe tannins to pair with lamb.

● **J. Christopher Lumière Pinot Noir / 2013 / Eola-Amity Hills / $$$**
The dark, well-structured Lumière Pinot Noir has the grippy mineral tang that's an Eola-Amity Hills signature.

KELLEY FOX WINES

This is the very small (about 2,000 cases) label of the much-lauded former Scott Paul winemaker and David Lett acolyte, Kelley Fox (her winery's first vintage was in 2007). Fox produces a handful of Pinot Noir bottlings from two of Oregon's top vineyards, Momtazi and Maresh. Seriously hands-on, she farms her designated patch of Maresh mostly by herself and serves as the winery's one-woman staff—her tasks include foot-treading the grapes to macerate the skins. Fox says that she has no desire to make "safe" wines, and these are very much individualized, artisan efforts, resembling one another mostly in achieving great intensity of flavor and aroma without sacrificing gracefulness.

● **Kelley Fox Wines Maresh Vineyard Pinot Noir / 2013 / Dundee Hills / $$$** All red fruits and prettiness, this lean Pinot Noir has a scent of red cherries and blossoms, a hint of stem spice and the sort of vibrant acidity that merits a slight chill.

● **Kelley Fox Wines Momtazi Vineyard Pinot Noir / 2013 / McMinnville / $$$** A flowery nose gives way to a lean raspberry scent and flavors that are dark in character but light in expression. The nimble tannins and vibrant acidity bring Burgundy to mind.

KEN WRIGHT CELLARS

Ken Wright has been one of Oregon Pinot Noir's leading lights since 1986, not only as a producer (he also founded Panther Creek), but also as a leader in helping to establish northern Willamette Valley's six sub-AVAs and in refashioning the little town of Carlton—his much-visited tasting room occupies the former train station. The single-vineyard, place-based philosophy Wright evolved early in his career remains essential to his efforts, as evidenced in the complex, stylish, top-of-the-line Pinots from vineyards like the McCrone, Savoya and Guadalupe, and even in the selection of fruit for companion label Tyrus Evan. Still, the more affordable Willamette Valley Pinot blend can be a wonderful wine in its own right.

○ **Ken Wright Cellars Pinot Blanc / 2013 / Willamette Valley / $$** Mineral and light with a melony scent and broad quince flavors, this white is aged in neutral wood on its lees, which adds a seductive richness to its texture.

● **Ken Wright Cellars Pinot Noir / 2013 / Willamette Valley / $$** This well-priced, cherry-scented red is elegant and fine-boned, framed by but not dominated by oak.

KING ESTATE WINERY

Founded by the King family in 1991, this estate is best known for three things: terrific Pinot Noir and Pinot Gris—in various bottlings in different styles and at different prices—and a 1,000-plus-acre property, located southwest of Eugene, which includes gardens, orchards, a restaurant and wetlands. The brand's top wines are the estate-grown King Estate Domaine offerings, as well as a number of vineyard designates. The Acrobat tier offers super value; the King Estate wines are a step up. The King family also produces the North by Northwest wines, with grapes sourced from throughout the Columbia River Basin, reaching up to Walla Walla, Washington, for instance, for Cabernet Sauvignons and Syrahs.

○ **King Estate Domaine Pinot Gris / 2014 / Oregon / $$**
Always a bit more tropical and stone-fruited than the King Estate Pinot Gris, this attractive Domaine bottling leads with a scent of white peach that gives way to a finish informed by a wheaty lees note.

○ **King Estate Pinot Gris / 2014 / Oregon / $$**
Crisp apple accents, hints of lemon curd and a tangy, citrusy freshness mark this well-made, well-priced Pinot Gris from the variety's leading producer in Oregon.

LANGE ESTATE WINERY

This is a small family winery, operated by a father-son team, with mom handling the day-to-day business and doubling as greeter in the winery's panoramic tasting room. Don and Wendy Lange moved up to the Dundee Hills from California some 30 years ago with Pinot Noir in mind, and they were mentored by Dick Erath and David Lett. Along the way they pioneered the neutral barrel fermentation of Pinot Gris. The Langes' son, Jesse, is the winemaker now, producing highly regarded Pinot Noir, Pinot Gris and Chardonnay with hands-on care, including fermenting the Pinot Noirs Old World–style in small, open-top fermenters.

○ **Lange Three Hills Cuvee Chardonnay / 2013 / Willamette Valley / $$$**
This Chardonnay is opulent, even a bit leesy, at first pass, but with air, its golden apple fruit comes roaring to the center, followed by a nutty savor at the finish.

● **Lange Pinot Noir / 2013 / Willamette Valley / $$**
An earthy soy scent gives way to a red cherry core of flavor in this impressive Pinot Noir. Its finish is all turf and red earth.

LEMELSON VINEYARDS

Environmental lawyer Eric Lemelson combines modern tech (in his sophisticated, gravity-flow winery) and low tech (all certified organic farming; natural winemaking, including native- yeast fermentations) to make his sought-after Pinot Noir and some very well-priced Chardonnay, Pinot Gris and Riesling. Most of Lemelson's 13,000 cases are sourced from seven estate vineyards, a notable diversity of sites that greatly enhances the complexity of the wines. The 164 planted acres are scattered across three Willamette Valley AVAs, at elevations ranging from 220 feet to nearly 1,000 feet. Matt Wengel, formerly of Napa's Clos Pegase, took over the winemaking reins at Lemelson in the spring of 2015.

○ **Lemelson Dry Riesling / 2014 / Willamette Valley / $$**

Scents of passion fruit and lemon race from the glass but give way to a salty, limey mineral texture that's bone-dry and racy.

● **Lemelson Thea's Selection Pinot Noir / 2013 / Willamette Valley / $$**

Sourced from organic estate vineyards, this Pinot leads with a whiff of blue flowers and dried leaves. Its flavors are dark and satisfying, the black plum fruit given contour by a savory vinous spice.

MONTINORE ESTATE

Nestled in the foothills of the Coast Range in the northern Willamette Valley, Montinore cast a spell over New York winemaker Rudy Marchesi on a visit in 1992. He began working with the winery in various capacities and one thing led to another: By 2005, his family had moved to Oregon and he owned the place. Marchesi and his team oversee 212 acres, all certified biodynamic and organic. About half the acreage is devoted to Pinot Noir and another substantial portion given to Pinot Gris, but much of the remaining acreage is planted to grapes such as Teroldego, Lagrein and Müller-Thurgau that make Montinore seem like an outpost of Alto Adige.

○ **Montinore Estate Pinot Gris / 2015 / Willamette Valley / $$**

This racy Pinot Gris displays lime zest accents and a brilliant, saline mineral spine that supports and seems to drive it.

● **Montinore Estate Reserve Pinot Noir / 2014 / Willamette Valley / $$**

Whole-cluster stem spice and brilliant acidity deftly counterbalance this Pinot Noir's crystalline cherry and ripe raspberry flavors.

PHELPS CREEK VINEYARDS

International airline pilot Bob Morus enjoys altitude even when on the ground: He planted his vineyards at a vertiginous (for Oregon) 900 to 1,200 feet in the Columbia Gorge AVA, which makes for dramatic shifts between day and night temperatures and helps to preserve acidity. The small 5,000-case winery has attracted a following for its silky, complex Pinots and Chardonnays. Morus's success is due in no small measure to the talented Alexandrine Roy of Burgundy's Domaine Marc Roy, whom he persuaded to become his director of winemaking. These wines aren't inexpensive, but they offer sophisticated proof that Oregon Pinot Noir isn't all about the Willamette Valley.

○ **Phelps Creek Chardonnay / 2014 / Columbia Gorge / $$$**
Luminous when first poured, this vibrant wine carries a scent of white cherry and caramel. Its succulent golden apple flavors and lees notes are tempered by just enough acidity.

● **Phelps Creek Cuvée Alexandrine Pinot Noir / 2013 / Columbia Gorge / $$$** This is a suave, savory red with pronounced tobacco and turf notes adorning soft, delicate cherry flavors.

PONZI VINEYARDS

Dick Ponzi and his wife, Nancy, established Ponzi Vineyards in 1970 and went on to become iconic figures of modern Oregon winemaking. Ponzi's reputation for producing top-flight Pinot Noir, Chardonnay and Pinot Gris in particular has only been burnished over time. Several family members are now involved here, but what goes into the bottle rests with vintner daughter Luisa, who brought her years of study and training in Burgundy back to the family's 130 acres of sustainably farmed vineyards, most of them in the Chehalem Mountains AVA. Ponzi's broad range of offerings includes the pricey single-vineyard Aurora and Madrona bottlings and bargains, too, especially in fresh, vivid whites such as Pinot Gris and Pinot Blanc.

● **Ponzi Tavola Pinot Noir / 2014 / Willamette Valley / $$**
Lipsmacking and brimming with youthful energy, this is a well-priced Pinot marked by lively cherry scents, a red-earth feel to its tannins and a vibrant acid-driven finish.

● **Ponzi Pinot Noir Reserve / 2012 / Willamette Valley / $$$**
Dark and spicy, lavish with charry oak flavors, this well-structured Pinot needs plenty of air before a pure shot of cherry flavor bursts through.

RAPTOR RIDGE WINERY

In the midst of tech careers, Scott and Annie Shull followed an urge to embrace a simpler (or at least more rural) life, with Scott making the original Raptor Ridge wines in a converted horse barn in 1995. The success of the brand—though it remains small at 10,000 cases—allows the Shulls more leeway these days; improvements include a handsome winery built in 2010. They named their 18-acre estate vineyard Tuscowallame, said to be an indigenous word meaning "where the owls dwell," a reference to the resident raptors that help control grape-loving migratory birds. The Shulls supplement their own grapes with fruit from top vineyard sources, such as Gran Moraine, Shea and Olenik.

- **Raptor Ridge Barrel Select Pinot Noir / 2013 / Willamette Valley / $$** Light and floral in such a warm vintage, this delicate red leads with scents of violet that give way to tart red cherry flavors.
- **Raptor Ridge Shea Vineyard Pinot Noir / 2013 / Yamhill-Carlton / $$$** Focused, concentrated, a touch savory, this is a dark, plummy red with a soil-like mineral edge to its dark-fruited tannins.

REX HILL

Founded in 1982, Rex Hill was one of Oregon's early-wave wineries; it caught a second wind in 2007 when the partners behind A to Z Wineworks (whose sometimes overlapping labels also include William Hatcher and Francis Tannahill) purchased the property. Among other things, the new owners are adamant about sustainable agriculture and beyond: Rex Hill's own vineyards are now farmed biodynamically. A to Z winemaker Michael Davies has also bumped up the quality of the wines, which can be among Oregon's best. In addition to the often superb fruit from its estate and rock-strewn Jacob-Hart vineyards (both in the Chehalem Mountains), the winery has long-term relationships with prestige growers like Shea.

- **Rex Hill Pinot Noir / 2013 / Willamette Valley / $$$** Lifted and light, with a bright cherry pomegranate scent, Rex Hill's 2013 regional Pinot bottling has a juicy ease of entry and delicious briskness.
- **Rex Hill Jacob-Hart Estate Vineyard Pinot Noir / 2013 / Willamette Valley / $$$$** This wine is a touch dusty when first poured, but with air, a fresh strawberry scent emerges. It's plush and fresh at once, with hints of red earth and humus, and an attractive caramel note on the finish.

ROCO WINERY

Rollin Soles left Argyle—the winery he had cofounded and led to national prominence (see p. 202)—in 2013 to devote himself full-time to this artisan venture. Soles and his wife, Corby (the "co" of "ROCO"), bought the Chehalem Mountains property that would become the winery's Wits' End home vineyard in the mid-1980s, but they didn't begin commercial production until 2003. Wits' End today has expanded to 17 acres and is the source of ROCO's top Pinot Noirs, Private Stash and Wits' End. Soles sources other single-vineyard Pinots and Chardonnays, such as the Marsh and Knudsen bottlings, from longtime contacts. Though a still-young venture in wine terms, Soles's deft touch has already put ROCO among Oregon's stars.

○ **ROCO Chardonnay / 2014 / Willamette Valley / $$$**
A crisp cut-apple scent and broader, pear-like flavors mark this bright Chardonnay. A touch of oak lends palate weight, but it's the pure fruit flavor that gives the lasting impression.

● **ROCO Gravel Road Pinot Noir / 2013 / Willamette Valley / $$**
Light cranberry and dried raspberry scents give way to a palate that's light, clean, tart and refreshing, with more lift and acidity than its 14 percent alcohol would suggest in Oregon.

SINEANN

Sineann's owner-winemaker Peter Rosback describes his full-flavored wines as "not for the faint of palate." He started his Willamette Valley winery—its name derives from the Gaelic for Ireland's River Shannon—in 1994, in partnership with David O'Reilly, who left to found Owen Roe later in the decade. Rosback has since gone very much his own way. In fact, he's gone all over, producing wines sourced from carefully selected sites in Oregon and Washington and making springtime winemaking forays to New Zealand. Rosback is a rare vintner who manages to produce consistently fine wines from a range of grapes, traditions (Bordeaux and Burgundy, for example) and places.

○ **Sineann Pinot Gris / 2014 / Columbia Gorge / $$**
There's remarkable breadth and depth in this juicy Pinot Gris, with scents of melon and biscuity lees, round quince-like flavor, good acidity and impressive body.

● **Sineann Pinot Noir / 2014 / Oregon / $$**
This Pinot leads with cherry and plum flavors, adorned by a hint of turf. It's plush and forward, with a generous texture.

SOKOL BLOSSER WINERY

In the 1970s, Bill Blosser and his wife, Susan Sokol Blosser, bought an abandoned prune orchard in the Dundee Hills to plant grapevines. Guided today by the second generation—son Alex is the winemaker and daughter Alison is the CEO—the winery has been rejuvenated, thanks in part to the addition of an architecturally striking, cedar-lined second tasting room that signals the operation's ongoing vitality. Alex oversees a diverse, roughly 92,000-case portfolio that includes, among much else, the image-making Pinot Noirs and the affordable Evolution line, consisting of the popular Evolution white, a surprisingly seamless blend of up to nine varieties; a Sangiovese-based red; a new Pinot Noir; and a dry méthode champenoise sparkler.

○ **Evolution Lucky No. 9 / NV / America / $**
One of the first and most successful of Oregon's kitchen-sink whites, this is a simple, enjoyably zippy wine with a hint of melony lusciousness and a crisp finish.

● **Sokol Blosser Pinot Noir / 2013 / Dundee Hills / $$$**
This Pinot is polished and suave when first poured, but as it opens, an appealing, dusty red-soil tannin seems to frame the fresh cherry flavors, lending structure and complexity.

SOTER VINEYARDS

It was a vote of confidence in Oregon at the highest level when Tony Soter, a pioneering California winemaker and consultant (Spottswoode, Araujo and Etude), moved to the Willamette Valley in 1997. Among other things, Soter produces one of the New World's most impressive sparkling wines, a brut rosé made from painfully low-yielding vines and bottled drier than many French Champagnes. His still Pinot Noirs under the Soter label from his home Mineral Springs Vineyard are among Oregon's most refined and accomplished wines. The North Valley label, from purchased fruit, and the early-drinking Planet Oregon wines offer more affordable versions of Soter's deft style.

● **Soter Mineral Springs Brut Rosé / 2011 / Yamhill-Carlton / $$$$**
A wine of gorgeous, coppery salmon color and assertive flavors, this rosé is very Pinot-like in its white cherry scent and creamy, red-fruited depth.

● **Soter Mineral Springs Ranch Pinot Noir / 2013 / Yamhill-Carlton / $$$** This composed, graceful Pinot Noir is a study in spiced black plum and dark-paneled oak.

ST. INNOCENT WINERY

Although this highly regarded Eola-Amity Hills winery produces a small amount of white wine, its hallmark is Pinot Noir—specifically, the small-lot Pinots made by owner-winemaker Mark Vlossak from an all-star roster of Willamette Valley sites, including his own Zenith Vineyard and standout plots of other vineyards, like Momtazi and Shea. Vlossak's thoughtful, calculated winemaking, which emphasizes vintage and vineyard differences rather than covering them up, has earned him a strong following. The wines' small production and relatively reasonable prices can make the vineyard designates, in particular, hard to find. Fortunately, Vlossak's delicious Villages Cuvée, which blends fruit from several vineyards, is more readily available.

○ **St. Innocent Freedom Hill Vineyard Pinot Blanc / 2014 / Willamette Valley / $$** Racy, bright and focused, this light white leads with an apple scent and slightly broader pear flavors but is brought to a close by a dusty, chalky mineral tang.

● **St. Innocent Zenith Vineyard Pinot Noir / 2013 / Eola-Amity Hills / $$$** St. Innocent's home-vineyard Pinot bottling is savory and concentrated in 2013, with scents of tea and cinnamon, dark plum flavors and a firm minerality.

TRISAETUM

It is a testimony both to the skills of Trisaetum's winemaker-owner James Frey and to his winery's sophisticated facility that it was chosen as the interim site for Burgundy's Maison Louis Jadot to launch its first American venture. Trisaetum itself produces an extensive array of highly praised Pinot Noir and Riesling bottlings, and recently added a Chardonnay to its portfolio. The core of its offerings come from three sustainably farmed, non-irrigated estate vineyards: its home plantings in the Ribbon Ridge AVA, a small plot in Dundee Hills AVA and a rocky slope in the foothills of the Coast Range.

○ **Trisaetum Coast Range Estate Riesling / 2014 / Yamhill-Carlton / $$** This off-dry Riesling is plush and juicy, with an appealing apple scent and flavors that hint at white peach.

● **Trisaetum Ribbon Ridge Estate Pinot Noir / 2014 / Ribbon Ridge / $$$** Light and mineral, with a red cranberry scent and deeper, strawberry flavors, this wine gains gravitas with a day's aeration. Its satisfying grip works well with roast chicken.

WILLAKENZIE ESTATE

Named for a sedimentary soil unique to the Willamette Valley, this boutique estate is known for its tiny lots of clone- and site-specific Pinot Noirs. Cofounder Bernard Lacroute planted the estate's first vineyards in the early 1990s, but the place really hit its stride at the turn of the millennium when talented winemaker Thibaud Mandet came on board. The two Frenchmen combine an Old World sensibility with a technological bent—punch-downs, for example, are done by a Lacroute-designed "Big Foot" robot. Budget-minded drinkers should look out for WillaKenzie's more affordable Pinot Blanc, Pinot Gris and Gisèle Pinot Noir, which offer plenty of drinking pleasure.

○ **WillaKenzie Estate Pinot Blanc / 2014 / Yamhill-Carlton / $$** Richer than many Pinot Blancs from the valley, this forward white is succulent, plump as a honeydew, and yet finishes with a mouthwatering acidity that's thoroughly refreshing.

● **WillaKenzie Estate Pierre Léon Pinot Noir / 2013 / Yamhill-Carlton / $$$** Expressive of the sedimentary soils the winery is named for, Pierre Léon is dark, plummy and rich, with a satisfying graham cracker sweetness from oak.

WILLAMETTE VALLEY VINEYARDS

From the run-down plum orchard cleared and replanted by founder Jim Bernau in 1983, Willamette Valley Vineyards has grown into one of Oregon's largest producers, and one of the few to be traded on NASDAQ. The winery's ongoing, self-underwritten public offering means that it is owned by some 9,000 shareholders. Head winemaker Joe Ibrahim farms 500 acres and produces almost all of the winery's Pinot Noir from estate grapes. The single-vineyard Pinot Noirs tend to be pricey, but the sweet spot for reds is in the midrange. Willamette Valley Vineyards is also a prime source for well-priced Chardonnay, Pinot Gris and Riesling bottlings that overdeliver.

○ **Willamette Valley Vineyards Pinot Gris / 2014 / Willamette Valley / $$** This wine smells ripe but reads dry and fresh when tasted. It's willowy and graceful, with lime and lychee scents and broad quince flavors.

● **Willamette Valley Vineyards Estate Pinot Noir / 2014 / Willamette Valley / $$** Fresh, juicy and fruit-forward, this crowd-pleasing Pinot offers red cherry flavors, balanced with enough acidity to bring contour and detail to that forward fruit.

WINDERLEA VINEYARD AND WINERY

Few "second career" wineries in the United States have been planned as meticulously as Winderlea, the next chapter in the lives of former financial executives Bill Sweat and Donna Morris, who took up residence in the Dundee Hills in 2006. To realize their vision of perfumed, silky, never-over-extracted Pinot Noir, they turned to talented winemaker Robert Brittan (see p. 206); to guide the conversion of their vineyards to biodynamic farming, they enlisted eminent French consultant Philippe Armenier. The home Winderlea Vineyard (formerly Goldschmidt), renowned neighboring vineyards like Maresh and Murto, and the Winderlea-farmed Meredith Mitchell Vineyard in McMinnville supply the grapes for a roster of wines that quickly put this estate on the map.

○ **Winderlea Chardonnay / 2014 / Willamette Valley / $$$** Toasty lees and ripe fruit abound in this generous Chardonnay from multiple valley sources. Its flavors are more golden than green, with a nutty warmth to the finish.

● **Winderlea Crawford Beck Vineyard Pinot Noir / 2014 / Eola-Amity Hills / $$$** Despite its youthful forward cherry fruit, there's an inherent savory quality to this Pinot, with humus-like earth and rocky mineral notes adorning its firm, dark flavors. It has all the structure needed to pair with duck breast.

Washington State

People tend to think of Washington as they do of Seattle: coastal, rainy and full of coffee bars. But it's the state's vast, dry eastern section over the Cascade Range that's the heartland of America's second-largest wine industry. The region has produced world-class wines since the 1970s, particularly Bordeaux- and Rhône-style reds. Now the state is at its peak of production, with a record wine-grape harvest in 2014. Washington remains a fine source for affordable Rieslings and Chardonnays, but its top wines are silky, aromatic versions of Cabernet Sauvignon, Merlot and Syrah. With them, Washington's winemakers have combined the best of the Old and New Worlds to create a style that's distinctively their own.

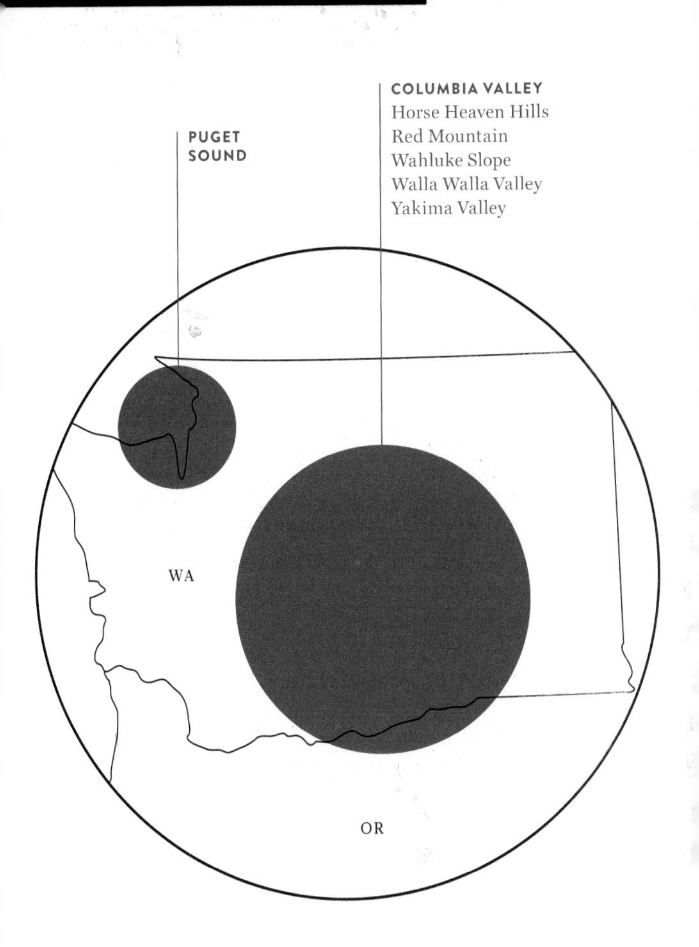
COLUMBIA VALLEY
Horse Heaven Hills
Red Mountain
Wahluke Slope
Walla Walla Valley
Yakima Valley
PUGET
SOUND
WA
OR

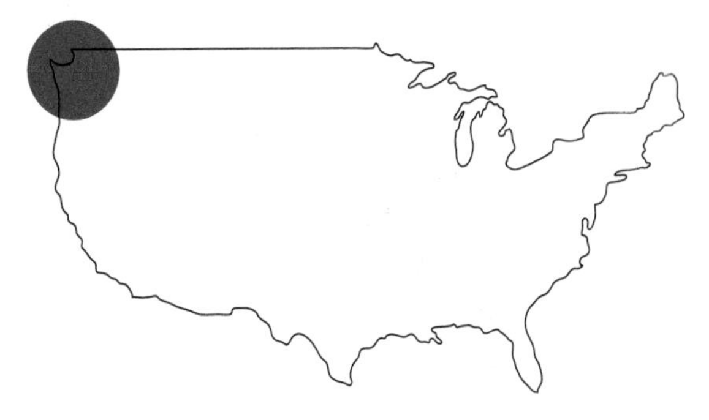

REGIONS TO KNOW

COLUMBIA VALLEY Lying mostly in Washington's dry central and southern regions (with a small section in Oregon), this catch-all AVA covers one-third of the state, grows 99 percent of its wine grapes and encompasses 10 smaller, more site-specific AVAs.

HORSE HEAVEN HILLS These well-drained slopes with cooling winds off the Columbia River are planted with some 37 grape varieties, but it's the Bordeaux-style reds and earthy, elegant Syrahs that make this one of the state's premier wine regions.

RED MOUNTAIN A small AVA within Yakima Valley (see below), Red Mountain has an outsized reputation for producing some of the state's most prized Cabernet Sauvignon, Merlot and Syrah.

WAHLUKE SLOPE This south-central district, one of Washington's warmest and driest, is planted chiefly to heat-loving red grapes like Merlot, Cabernet and Syrah.

WALLA WALLA VALLEY Located in southeastern Washington and straddling the Oregon border, this AVA is one of America's premier Cabernet Sauvignon and Merlot growing regions, with exciting Syrahs also in the mix.

YAKIMA VALLEY The first AVA created north of California back in 1983, this district accounts for over a third of the state's vineyard land. While its warm Red Mountain subregion yields some of America's top Cabernet Sauvignons, Yakima Valley's more moderate zones are a major source of Chardonnay and Riesling.

KEY GRAPES: WHITE

CHARDONNAY Washington produces not only benchmark Chardonnays in the more affordable price brackets but also some world-class wines from top producers and cooler vineyards.

PINOT GRIS Not as well known here as in neighboring Oregon (though Washington's production is actually greater), this white variety, often made in a fresh, fruit-driven style, is on the rise—more than tripling in volume over the past few years.

RIESLING Washington is the country's largest producer of Riesling. Cool nights and temperate growing conditions allow the grapes to be crafted into a range of styles from dry to sweet.

SAUVIGNON BLANC, VIOGNIER & GEWÜRZTRAMINER These white varieties, which do well in Washington's northern climate, represent just over 10 percent of the state's white grape production. Gewürztraminer tends to yield ripe and floral wines, usually in an off-dry style.

SÉMILLON Though production is relatively small, Washington sets an American benchmark for this luscious grape, in both dry and dessert-style bottlings.

KEY GRAPES: RED

CABERNET SAUVIGNON Despite years of acclaim, Washington Cabs still fly a bit under consumers' radars. They offer many terrific values, from under-$20 bottlings to high-end cuvées that compete with the world's best. Smooth-textured and bold, they're typically more restrained than California's riper offerings.

MERLOT Washington is arguably the country's best source of delicious Merlot; its top bottlings have a distinctive, spicy complexity and seductive depth.

SYRAH Walla Walla Valley, Wahluke Slope and Yakima Valley and its Red Mountain subregion are among the Washington locales that provide ideal conditions for Syrah. At its best, this grape yields wines in a riper version of the classic Rhône style, with a mix of peppery, earthy flavors and firm structure.

Producers/ Washington State

ABEJA

Of the five main grape varieties Abeja bottles, Cabernet Sauvignon is its core mission and the one whose success has propelled the winery into the ranks of the state's top producers. Dan Wampfler, formerly of Dunham Cellars (see p. 237), now crafts the Abeja portfolio, using grapes from two estate vineyards in the Walla Walla Valley—Heather Hill and Mill Creek—supplemented with fruit from a few top growers. The Beekeeper's Blend, a Cab-based multigrape mix, offers a sense of Abeja's full-flavored style at a relatively affordable price.

○ **Abeja Chardonnay / 2014 / Washington / $$$**
This sumptuous Chardonnay's golden apple core of flavor is offset by caramelly oak and a toasty, leesy finish.

● **Abeja Cabernet Sauvignon / 2012 / Columbia Valley / $$$**
Scents of cedar frond and sweet cherry play off one another in this firm Cabernet. Its texture is juicy but not loose, with tannins and acid leading to a precise and satisfying finish.

AIRFIELD ESTATES WINERY

When Airfield Estates released its first wines in 2005, it was starting with a big advantage: Four generations of the Miller family have farmed this Yakima Valley property, once the site of a World War II flight-training airbase and now encompassing some 900 vineyard acres planted to 27 varieties. Current owner Mike Miller, grandson of founder H. Lloyd Miller, made the decision to bottle some of the family's grapes instead of selling off the entire production. Mike's vintner son, Marcus, oversees an extensive lineup of wines notable for their generally fine quality, reasonable prices and World War II–era aircraft names.

○ **Airfield Lightning / 2013 / Yakima Valley / $$**
A Rhône-style blend of mostly Viognier and Roussanne, this creamy white has tropical peach flavors and a pillowy texture.

● **Airfield Aviator / 2012 / Yakima Valley / $$$**
Round, dark, juicy and rich, this Bordeaux-style blend has a vinous scent and flavors that resemble plum compote.

ÀMAURICE CELLARS

Fifth-generation Washingtonians with timber-industry roots, the Schafer family founded this winery in 2004 with a commitment to sustainable farming. Winemaker Anna Schafer, a protégé of international star Paul Hobbs—she worked harvests for him in Argentina—now crafts one of Washington's finest Malbecs, Amparo, as well as top-notch Cabernets and Bordeaux-style blends. She also has a sure hand with whites, including elegant Viogniers. Though grapes from premier growers play a major role here, the winery's own 13-acre vineyard, planted in 2006 at 1,500 feet up in the Mill Creek Valley area of Walla Walla, is now yielding its own intriguing fruit for wines like the deep red Owl and Crown.

○ **àMaurice Cellars Viognier / Marsanne / 2014 / Columbia Valley / $$$**
Viognier prettiness combines with Marsanne structure and weight in this strong and graceful white.

● **àMaurice "Owl and Crown" / 2013 / Walla Walla Valley / $$$$**
Dry-farmed estate fruit gives this Cabernet Sauvignon a cool blue aspect. The tannins are youthful, the texture effortlessly fluid and elegant. It's an ageworthy wine you can drink young.

ANDREW WILL WINERY

Chris Camarda's artisan winery turns out some of Washington's—and the USA's—most coveted Bordeaux-style reds (plus a little Sangiovese). Though located on Vashon Island near Seattle, the winery owes its fame and fortune to eastern Washington vineyards. Camarda is renowned for his silky, refined and site-specific Bordeaux-style blends, sourced from some of the state's top sites, like Ciel du Cheval (Red Mountain) and Champoux (Horse Heaven Hills). Tiny quantities and high prices make these wines inaccessible to most. Luckily, Camarda also makes a series of excellent wines that give a more affordable taste of his talent (look for the black-labeled bottles).

● **Andrew Will Two Blondes Vineyard / 2012 / Yakima Valley / $$$$**
Camarda's own vineyard bottling always has a blue hue. Half Merlot in 2012, the red blend is mildly herbal, with blueberry scents limned with pine fronds, and a cool acidity to close.

● **Sorella / 2012 / Horse Heaven Hills / $$$$**
Cabernet leads here, and it's at its most refined. This sinewy, textural marvel is packed with dark red plum fruit and its acid-tannin structure feels invigorating and lithe.

ASHAN CELLARS

The motto at this Woodinville operation, established in 2012, is "Artisan Chardonnay of Washington State." It is the alternate-side brainchild of restless auteur Chris Gorman (see Gorman Winery, p. 240), best known as the creator of tongue-purpling Red Mountain reds like The Evil Twin. Here, Gorman has put vineyard scouting at the center of the exercise, turning up, for example, some of the state's oldest Chardonnay vines at Kestrel View Estate Vineyard and 40-plus-year-old plantings at Celilo. The single-vineyard wines are typically barrel-fermented, often in 100 percent new French oak, using native yeasts for both primary and secondary fermentations. The Stainless Steel bottling eschews oak entirely, relying on the purity of the fruit.

○ **Ashan Celilo Vineyard Chardonnay / 2013 / Columbia Gorge / $$$**

From one of the Gorge's most famous Chardonnay sources, this feels cool and limpid, with golden apple and pine scents. The fruit is delicate and fresh, marked by savory lees accents.

○ **Ashan Kestrel Vineyard Chardonnay / 2013 / Yakima Valley / $$$**

There's much warmth in this buttery white, with scents of baked apple and lees alongside a caramel center. The flavors are focused and wood-framed, ideal for chicken breast.

AVENNIA

Run by Microsoft alumnus Marty Taucher and winemaker Chris Peterson, who helped put DeLille Cellars (see p. 236) on the connoisseur's map, this is a pan-French-influenced winery that aims to make graceful Washington wines with roots in both Bordeaux (Cabernet Sauvignon and Sauvignon Blanc) and the Rhône Valley (*Avennia* is inspired by the Roman name for Avignon). From its first releases in 2010, Avennia has scored notable successes with both types. This Woodinville-based winery gives its offerings poetic names—Oliane (Sauvignon Blanc), Arnaut (Syrah), Sestina (a Bordeaux blend)—and the best of them are already becoming well known in wine circles.

● **Avennia Arnaut Syrah / 2013 / Yakima Valley / $$$**

Boushey Vineyard's more feral quality lurks beneath the dark purple fruit and peppery tannin grip of this balanced red.

● **Avennia Sestina / 2013 / Columbia Valley / $$$$**

About three-quarters Cabernet Sauvignon, this cool red emits a pleasing herbal note of evergreen mint. The flavors of cassis fruit adorned with violet are forceful and persistent.

BAER WINERY

Renowned for its supple, mostly Merlot–Cabernet Franc flagship blend called Ursa, Baer is a small (3,400-case) family-owned winery that persevered after the death of its founder, Lance Baer, in 2007. Following Baer's vision, his father and sister run the operation today from its headquarters in Woodinville's winery-rich Warehouse District. All of the wines are sourced from Stillwater Creek, Novelty Hill's acclaimed estate vineyard located on the Royal Slope of the Frenchman Hills in eastern Washington. Though the Baer portfolio includes an unoaked Chardonnay called Shard, winemaker Erica Orr's primary focus is on Ursa and three other Bordeaux-style blends, Arctos, Callisto and Star, all notable for their generous fruit.

● **Baer Winery Star / 2012 / Columbia Valley / $$$**
This Bordeaux right bank–style Merlot–Cabernet Franc blend has plush plum and cherry flavors and a mildly grainy texture that keeps the wine focused and persistent.

● **Baer Winery Ursa / 2012 / Columbia Valley / $$$**
The addition of Cabernet Sauvignon and Malbec gives this red a darker feel and a denser structure than Star's. Its cedary scent leads to black plum flavors framed by sturdy tannins.

BARNARD GRIFFIN WINERY

When Rob Griffin arrived in the Columbia Valley to work at Preston Wines in 1977, the conventional wisdom held that Washington was too cold to sustain wine grapes. Since 1983, when he and his wife, Deborah Barnard, established their winery in Richland, Griffin has refuted those assumptions, as well as the notion that terrific wine has to be costly. His top-tier Reserve Cabernet Sauvignons reach up to $40—still a fine deal in today's market. His familiar Columbia Valley label wines demonstrate Griffin's deft touch at putting juicy, supple, lively wines into the bottle at even more affordable prices.

● **Barnard Griffin Cabernet Sauvignon / 2013 / Columbia Valley / $$**
This is a lush and juicy Cabernet Sauvignon from a leader in the value category. Fruit-forward black plum scents give way to dark, mocha-inflected berry fruit and soft, plush tannins.

● **Barnard Griffin Merlot / 2013 / Columbia Valley / $$**
A bit more red-fruited than its Cab counterpart, Barnard Griffin's Merlot is no less lush and juicy, tending more toward cherries and red plums, with slightly more acid, too.

BETZ FAMILY WINERY

A legendary figure in Washington wine circles, Master of Wine Bob Betz headed up winemaking research for Chateau Ste. Michelle (see p. 233) before starting this microwinery in 1997. The project has met with universal acclaim—at least among as much of the universe as such a small, super-premium-priced winery could reach. Betz's deep, luscious reds are among Washington's finest—you have the sense that each one is an intelligently, passionately plotted-out project. The Betz family sold the winery to a South African couple in 2011, but Bob Betz remains in the cellar and out walking the top-notch vineyards that are the sources for these wines.

● **Betz La Côte Rousse Syrah / 2013 / Red Mountain / $$$**
The warmth of Red Mountain's fabled Ciel du Cheval Vineyard translates here to a concentration that will leave your teeth stained. It begs to be served with barbecue.

● **Betz Père de Famille Cabernet Sauvignon / 2012 / Columbia Valley / $$$$** This mostly Cabernet, mostly Red Mountain wine offers unparalleled concentration and depth in 2012. Its notes of tar and roses, black plum and fig flavors and dusty tannins will make you think of Bordeaux.

BRIAN CARTER CELLARS

The accolades directed at the one-of-a-kind wines created by Brian Carter reflect not just his skills as a master blender and grape scout, but also a consumer thirst for new taste experiences. Carter knows the Washington wine scene and its vineyards like the back of his hand. He arrived in the state in 1980, was a longtime winemaker at Paul Thomas and co-owned Apex before formally launching this project in 2006. Today, Brian Carter Cellars bottles an ambitious range of intriguing, at times outside-the-box blends with fanciful names, such as the Rhône-style white Oriana or the Super Tuscan–style red Tuttorosso.

○ **Brian Carter Cellars Oriana / 2013 / Yakima Valley / $$**
With its sweet peach and apricot aromas, Viognier is the core variety in this sumptuous Viognier-Roussanne-Riesling blend; the 13 percent of Riesling provides the mouthwatering acidity.

● **Brian Carter Cellars Tuttorosso / 2012 / Yakima Valley / $$$**
Sangiovese's dusty, red-fruited grip is what gives the Tuttorosso (Italian for "all red") Sangiovese-Cabernet-Syrah blend its inimitable Tuscan character.

BUTY WINERY

Nina Buty (pronounced "beauty") cofounded this Walla Walla boutique winery in 2000, and she soon brought on board highly regarded California-based consultant Zelma Long. The headliner among Buty's multivariety reds is the Rediviva of the Stones, an unusual (outside of Australia) combination of Syrah and Cabernet Sauvignon that emphasizes perfume over power; the more Cabernet-heavy Columbia Rediviva is a more muscular version. The whites include an appealing Sémillon–Sauvignon Blanc–Muscadelle blend. Winemaker Chris Dowsett's preference for supple tannins, moderate alcohol levels and judicious use of new oak lends the wines particular finesse. A second label called Beast, with many one-time bottlings, allows Dowsett to follow his curiosity and push his talent.

● **Buty Columbia Rediviva / 2012 / Horse Heaven Hills / $$$**
Cabernet-heavy in 2012, with a modest Syrah kicker, this wine offers deep plum and black cherry flavors and dusty tannins.

● **Buty Rediviva of the Stones / 2013 / Walla Walla Valley / $$$**
This is a remarkable expression of Syrah from Buty's organic Rockgarden Estate vineyard. Syrah's meaty, smoky wildness is tamed, in part, by Cabernet Sauvignon's firm mineral tannin.

CADARETTA

The Middleton family founded their small, high-quality Cadaretta label in Walla Walla in 2005, but they have been in business in Washington since the 19th century (*Cadaretta* was the name of a family-owned timber freighter). The three wines in general release—the SBS Sauvignon Blanc–Sémillon, a Cabernet Sauvignon and a Syrah—have been widely praised in their early vintages, and the Cabernet in particular can be hard to find. Joining Cadaretta's Vine Society mailing list is the way to go here; the winery also bottles smaller-lot wines for members only. Buried Cane is the Middletons' affordably priced line.

○ **Cadaretta SBS Sauvignon Blanc–Semillon / 2014 / Columbia Valley / $$** Made to resemble the brisk, saline Sauvignon-Sémillon blends of Australia, this one fits the bill with its lemon-tinged melon scents and clean, salty mineral tang.

● **Cadaretta Cabernet Sauvignon / 2012 / Columbia Valley / $$$**
Plush and smoky, with an uncanny depth of dark plum flavor, this big red flirts with savory notes in its meaty scent and has a dark, brown-herb medley of flavor on the finish.

CADENCE

This small-scale enterprise run out of Seattle was founded by a wine-loving couple, Benjamin Smith and Gaye McNutt, who ditched engineering and legal careers respectively and followed their Bordeaux-loving hearts into the vineyards. They discovered the grapevines they dreamed of in the Red Mountain area, specifically at Tapteil and Ciel du Cheval Vineyards—some of Washington's most celebrated sites. Their own tenderly planted Cara Mia vines, source of the fine Camerata blend, may very well join that list. Intensely flavored Bordeaux-style reds are the calling cards here, with the powerful concentration of Red Mountain's small-berried grapes carrying through in each.

- **Cadence Bel Canto / 2012 / Red Mountain / $$$**
  Cabernet Franc–based, with small amounts of Merlot and Petit Verdot, this wine is a study in blue, offering blueberry fruit with a hint of pine frond. Its tannins are firm and gripping, with enough acidity to delineate them.
- **Cadence Camerata / 2012 / Red Mountain / $$$**
  Cadence's Cabernet Sauvignon blend is powerful and brooding, with black fig flavors that take a day to emerge, framed by massive black tannins.

CAYUSE VINEYARDS

Frenchman Christophe Baron, whose family has tended vines in the Marne Valley of Champagne, father to son, since 1677, was visiting a friend in Walla Walla in 1996 when he was struck by a *coup de foudre*—love at first sight—for a pile of stones. The Châteauneuf-like sight rooted Baron to the spot (it's now his Cailloux Vineyard), and he stayed on to produce sensational Rhône-style wine (Bionic Frog Syrah, anyone?), plus much more, from his biodynamically farmed vineyards. Charismatic and confident, Baron has developed quite a following, and many of his pricey wines sell out through his mailing list as futures.

- **Bionic Frog / 2013 / Walla Walla Valley / $$$$**
  Wildly exotic, with an umami barrage of smoke, leather, mushroom, olive and smoked meat, this luxury-priced Syrah has a plush texture that belies its wild, feral complexity.
- **Cayuse Cailloux Vineyard Syrah / 2013 / Walla Walla Valley / $$$$**
  Co-fermented with small amounts of Viognier, this heady, plummy red has a sanguine depth of flavor and a crushed-stone minerality that is intense and lasting.

CHARLES SMITH WINES/K VINTNERS

These two labels (and several others) share an owner and winemaker, Charles Smith—a shaggy-haired former sommelier who moved to Walla Walla after a stint overseas as a rock band manager. For all his flamboyance, Smith is a meticulous winemaker who insists on low yields and intense fruit that he doesn't bury under planks of oak or winemaking processes. As a result, his top wines, like the K Vintners The Beautiful Syrah, are typically exotic, full-throttle, ultra-complex and very rich; they're made in tiny lots and often sold at fairly high prices. His namesake brand includes affordable wines with names like Kung Fu Girl Riesling and The Velvet Devil Merlot.

○ **Kung Fu Girl Riesling / 2014 / Washington / $**
Kung Fu Girl is svelte and leesy in 2014, with a scent of apples marked by a biscuity savor. Flavors are dry, but not too dry, clean and pure; a good match for pad Thai.

● **K The Beautiful Syrah / 2013 / Walla Walla Valley / $$$**
This heady Syrah is brambly and sweet, with a scent of crushed blueberries and a good mineral grip to the finish.

CHATEAU STE. MICHELLE

Chateau Ste. Michelle, one of the many Ste. Michelle Wine Estates brands, is the state's largest and most famous wine producer—the legendary André Tchelistcheff, a great booster of then-unknown Washington wine, made the first wines here in 1967. Its Woodinville visitors' facilities have also made Ste. Michelle the most familiar name to Washington wine tourists. Chateau Ste. Michelle has for years been an innovator, a talent incubator and a highly reliable source for delicious wine at fair prices. (It's hard to beat the Indian Wells Red Blend for value, but even the reserve-tier Ethos wines are realistically priced.) One important project: the partnership with the Mosel's Ernst Loosen that created the Eroica Rieslings.

○ **Eroica Riesling / 2014 / Columbia Valley / $$**
Pure, driven and precise, this offers brilliant golden apple scents, balanced flavors of pear and a hint of peach and a mineral tension that draws the wine to a luminous close.

● **Chateau Ste. Michelle Ethos Reserve Merlot / 2012 / Columbia Valley / $$$** This red's sumptuous dark scents of mocha and black cherry give way to flavors that are plump, round and lavish, with dark oak contributing to ripe, plush tannins.

COL SOLARE

Another Chateau Ste. Michelle international joint venture, this collaboration with Tuscany's iconic Marchesi Antinori is based in a design magazine–worthy winery dramatically situated on Red Mountain. Despite its Italian heritage, Col Solare produces two Bordeaux-style blends: the luxury-priced Col Solare flagship, with a touch of Syrah added to the Cabernet Sauvignon–based mix; and Shining Hill, the winery's second offering, made from the best of the remaining lots. To create these majestically scaled, supple but powerful reds, winemaker Darel Allwine has had his pick of some of the region's top fruit while waiting for Col Solare's own vineyard to come into full production (it now supplies more than two-thirds of the blends).

● **Shining Hill / 2012 / Red Mountain / $$$**
A bit less powerful than the flagship, this is a blend of mostly Cabernet Sauvignon with Cab Franc, Merlot and Malbec; the latter two account for the red fruits that come through.

● **Col Solare / 2012 / Red Mountain / $$$$**
In the winery's Cab-based flagship red, a scent of cedar in an oak-tinged frame gives way to the full depth of Red Mountain blackberry and black fig flavors, and a mass of tannin.

COLUMBIA CREST

If this label seems to be ubiquitous on store shelves, there's a good reason: Very few large-production wineries anywhere make better wine consistently at such reasonable prices. Winemaker Juan Muñoz-Oca can draw on the winery's 30-plus years of experience—not common in Washington—to produce its extensive, three-tiered lineup. Made in the Columbia Crest Petit Chai ("little barrel room"), described as "a winery within the winery," the beautifully crafted, small-lot Reserve wines can be revelations. The H3 line bottlings, sourced from the winery's home Horse Heaven Hills AVA, are remarkable in their own right as serious bargains worth tracking down.

○ **Columbia Crest Reserve Chardonnay / 2013 / Horse Heaven Hills / $$** This ripe white leads with golden apple and white fig scents and is generously kissed by rich, buttery oak flavors.

● **Columbia Crest H3 Les Chevaux / 2012 / Horse Heaven Hills / $**
An expression of Horse Heaven Hills, this lush red blend has scents of mocha and red cherry and bright, forward flavors, with just enough tannins to give the wine a light frame.

COLUMBIA WINERY

This winery—one of the cornerstones of the modern Washington wine industry—marks its 55th anniversary this year. Still often identified with its pioneering longtime winemaker, the late David Lake, Columbia went through a series of ownership changes that saw it (and sister winery Covey Run) pass into the extensive portfolio of E. & J. Gallo Winery in 2012. Winemaker Sean Hails works throughout the Columbia Valley to source his grapes. Though he crafts lovely wines in the premium-price range, many drinkers will be happy to come across Columbia's bargain-priced entry-level bottlings, including a graceful Merlot and Cabernet Sauvignon and the Composition red blend.

- **Columbia Merlot / 2013 / Columbia Valley / $$**
  This Merlot opens with a scent of red fruits—plum, cranberry and dried cherry. Its flavors have a lean and focused texture, with brisk acidity guiding a firm finish.
- **Columbia Element / 2012 / Wahluke Slope / $$$**
  Aromas of herbs and pine sap are thrown into high relief against purple fruit flavors, dry and firm, with a touch of astringency that calls for braised lamb.

CORLISS ESTATES

This ambitious, spare-no-expense project is the brainchild of Seattle real estate developer and wine collector Michael Corliss. (A sister winery, Tranche Cellars, focuses on Rhône- and other Mediterranean-style wines.) Corliss releases limited quantities of only three wines—a Cabernet Sauvignon, a Bordeaux-style blend and a Syrah—drawn from Corliss's own extensive and diverse acreage in Red Mountain, Yakima Valley and Walla Walla Valley. Full-time winemaker Andrew Trio is assisted by stellar California consultant Philippe Melka. The resulting wines have gained instant fame for their elegance and polish and for the exciting nuances revealed by Corliss's insistence on keeping them in the cellar for years longer than the norm.

- **Corliss / 2011 / Columbia Valley / $$$$**
  Remarkably fresh and suave for a Bordeaux blend with bottle age, this leads with scents of cedar and black tea, in support of black cherry and plum. The texture is seductive and seamless, with a gentle tension between savory and fruit, and the finish is firm and satisfying.

CÔTE BONNEVILLE

Orthopedist Hugh Shiels and his wife, Kathy, planted the DuBrul Vineyard above the Yakima River in the Rattlesnake Hills in 1992. Since then, the steeply sloping site has steadily gained a place among Washington's most sought-after wine-grape sources. Among its current clients are Woodward Canyon, Pursued by Bear and Betz Family. But client No. 1 is the Shiels family itself, for their Côte Bonneville winery. The winemaker here is the Shiels's UC Davis–trained daughter, Kerry, who turns out small-lot wines noted for their finesse, elegance and ageability. Côte Bonneville was one of the first Washington wineries to cross the triple-digit price line, and its wines—reds especially—are generally aimed at deep-pocketed drinkers.

○ **Côte Bonneville Riesling / 2014 / Yakima Valley / $$**
Off-dry and pretty, this Riesling offers focused peach and caramel apple flavors and a pleasingly intense texture.

● **Carriage House / 2009 / Yakima Valley / $$$**
Softly expressing its age, this Bordeaux-style red offers aromas of cured meat and dried plums, flavors that reflect cedar and tobacco, and a suave texture. It's ready for drinking right now.

DELILLE CELLARS

One of Washington's top wineries since the 1990s, this stylish Woodinville-based operation turns out a succession of refined, multilayered, ageworthy Bordeaux-style wines under the DeLille label—including the Chaleur Estate, D2 and Four Flags bottlings—and an equally stunning group of Rhône-inspired wines (the Signature Syrah, especially) under the Doyenne label. Longtime winemaker Chris Upchurch deftly produces seamless wines from a variety of top vineyards, including Harrison Hill's Cabernet blocks, among the oldest in the state. The single-vineyard Grand Ciel line features a Cab and a Syrah, both sourced entirely from DeLille's first estate vineyard.

○ **DeLille Cellars Chaleur Estate / 2014 / Columbia Valley / $$$**
Aged in oak on its lees, this blend of Sauvignon Blanc and Sémillon has an aroma of melon and quince and rich, nutty flavors accented with caramelly oak.

● **DeLille Cellars Four Flags Cabernet Sauvignon / 2012 / Red Mountain / $$$$** This powerful Cab offers mildly savory sage and cedar scents, but its lasting impression is of intensity and concentration, with impressive acidity driving all that mass.

DENHOED WINE ESTATES

Since planting their first grapevines in Washington in 1956, the Den Hoed family steadily built up their vineyard holdings, acquiring in 1997 the prime Wallula Vineyard site, terraced above the Columbia River in the Horse Heaven Hills. In 2008, brothers Andy and Bill Den Hoed sold most of Wallula to an investment group headed by Allen Shoup, founder of Long Shadows Vintners (see p. 245). In partnership with Shoup and Rob Newsom of Boudreaux Cellars, the brothers produce two acclaimed red wines sourced from their old Walulla property, which they still manage: the all-Cabernet Andreas, named for their father, and Marie's View, named for their mother.

- **Den Hoed Andreas Cabernet Sauvignon / 2012 / Horse Heaven Hills / $$$$** Backward and a bit spicy when first poured, with air this wine becomes brooding and powerful, with a plummy core and long, cocoa-like tannins.
- **Den Hoed Marie's View / 2012 / Horse Heaven Hills / $$$$** This leafy, refreshing red delivers scents of cedar and fresh cherry and tannins that are dark and focused but fine and relatively delicate. It begs to be served with steak.

DUNHAM CELLARS

Dunham Cellars cofounder and guiding light Eric Dunham passed away in 2014, but his winery continues on the course he set. Dunham's fledgling wine company took up residence in a World War II hangar at the Walla Walla airport in the late 1990s, where it remains today. Appellation Management Group, the winery's affiliated vineyard management company, has been instrumental in securing grapes and in planting the Kenny Hill estate vineyard acquired in 2008. Meanwhile, Dunham Cellars continues to rack up successes, both with single-vineyard Cabs and Syrahs—especially those from a long-term source, Lewis Vineyards—and with whimsically named (e.g., Three Legged Red), value-priced wines that can be excellent bargains.

- **Dunham XVIII Cabernet Sauvignon / 2012 / Columbia Valley / $$$** Generous dark fruit and sumptuous oak are the hallmarks of this posh Cabernet, with flavors scored by fine dusty tannins.
- **Dunham Syrah / 2012 / Columbia Valley / $$$** The plummy varietal flavors of this dark and very oak-driven Syrah are given a capacious oak frame, with caramel and chocolate adding length to the finish.

DUSTED VALLEY

Northern Wisconsin may seem a long way from wine country, but brothers-in-law Corey Braunel and Chad Johnson, and Cindy and Janet, the sisters they married, all followed their winemaking dreams to Walla Walla back in 2003. They have made some complex and delicious wines here; the Rhône-style Syrahs and blends have met with particular success, as has the Chardonnay. The main Dusted Valley line is produced in limited quantities and generally priced accordingly; the Boomtown label offers great value. True to their heritage, Braunel and Johnson age some of their wines in Wisconsin oak barrels.

● **Dusted Valley Squirrel Tooth Alice / 2014 / Red Mountain / $$$** Generous and plush, this Mourvèdre-Grenache-Syrah blend has loads of red cherry and plum flavor; the Mourvèdre provides uplifting acid.

● **Dusted Valley Stained Tooth Syrah / 2013 / Columbia Valley / $$$** Made in a warm style with enough balance to keep it poised and a bit earthy, this Syrah has plum flavors and dusty tannins that recall the Valley's fine, wind-blown loess.

EFESTĒ

A group of family members and friends founded EFESTĒ in Woodinville in 2005. (The name is pronounced as the letters F-S-T, the initials of the founders' last names.) Winemaker Peter Devison sources grapes from vineyards around the Columbia Valley (including three estate vineyards planted, but not owned, by EFESTĒ), but his cellar treatment—native yeasts, limited or no fining and filtering—emphasizes each lot's individuality. The stated aim here is that "great wines should have personality," and EFESTĒ has succeeded admirably. Best known for pricey Cabernet and Syrah, the winery also puts out the well-regarded, well-priced Evergreen Riesling and the distinctive Sauvage Sauvignon Blanc that are well worth a look amid the big reds.

○ **EFESTĒ Evergreen Riesling / 2014 / Ancient Lakes of Columbia Valley / $$** Riesling from this cool new AVA is always nervy; this one leads with a mildly tropical note, but the flavors are tart and brisk, with a lemony tang that calls for white fish.

● **EFESTĒ Jolie Bouche Syrah / 2012 / Yakima Valley / $$$** Dark and brooding, this is a cool-climate Syrah pushed to maximum ripeness, with scents of black fig and cherry giving way to a smoky, mocha-inflected texture.

FIDELITAS WINES

This is one of Washington's most carefully focused wineries, and one of its most consistently high-quality producers. Owner and winemaker Charlie Hoppes was a longtime protégé of Mike Januik (see p. 242) and a mainstay of numerous Chateau Ste. Michelle projects before striking out on his own to produce Bordeaux red and white blends from Red Mountain. His powerful, voluptuous wines are sourced from an all-star roster of vineyards, including Ciel du Cheval, Champoux, Quintessence and Klipsun; the first bottling from Hoppes's own Red Mountain estate vineyards was released in 2015. These are all sought-after wines, made in tiny quantities, so your best bet for acquiring them may be through the mailing list.

○ **Fidelitas Klipsun Vineyard Optu White / 2014 / Red Mountain / $$$**

This Bordeaux-inspired Sauvignon Blanc–Sémillon blend has caramelly oak flavors and a huge core of pear and melon fruit.

● **Fidelitas Optu / 2012 / Red Mountain / $$$**

Mostly Cabernet Sauvignon, with Merlot, Cabernet Franc and Petit Verdot, this wine is plummy and opulent, its exuberant fruit tamed by classic Red Mountain tannic oomph.

FIGGINS

The son of Leonetti Cellar founder Gary Figgins (see p. 245), Chris Figgins now leads the family enterprises, which also include the Toil Oregon winery and the Lostine Cattle Company. At FIGGINS, he has lavished his considerable skill and focus on a 32-acre vineyard nestled in the foothills of Walla Walla's Blue Mountains. The estate makes just two wines, a luxury-priced Bordeaux-blend Estate Red Wine and a trickle of Riesling. Not surprisingly, given Figgins's reputation, the first release of the Estate Red, from the 2008 vintage, was a notable event for Washington wine collectors, and the five much-praised vintages released since have been quickly snapped up.

○ **FIGGINS Riesling / 2014 / Walla Walla Valley / $$**

This is bright and citrusy, with a wheaty lees note, when first poured, but with air, crisp pear and apple flavors emerge.

● **FIGGINS Estate Red Wine / 2012 / Walla Walla Valley / $$$$**

Dense and powerfully built, this blend of Cabernet, Merlot and Petit Verdot leads with scents of graphite, mocha and plum. Its texture is massive and the extract tooth-staining, with tannins providing an uncanny length.

FORCE MAJEURE VINEYARDS

One of Washington's most avidly sought-after artisan producers, Force Majeure has undergone a dramatic evolution. Gone are the buzzy Collaboration Series wines made by various vintners from Ciel du Cheval Vineyard grapes (2013 was the last vintage). Instead, the project now focuses on wines created by its own all-star team: winemaker Todd Alexander, who decamped from Napa Valley cult star Bryant Family Vineyard; lauded consultant Helen Keplinger; and foundational Yakima Valley viticulturist Dick Boushey. With the 2014 vintage, Force Majeure enters a new phase, fielding a full lineup of Bordeaux- and Rhône-style wines from its own Red Mountain estate vineyard.

- **Force Majeure Force Majeure Vineyard Cabernet Sauvignon / 2013 / Red Mountain / $$$$** A wine with an intense, monolithic power in its ferrous Red Mountain tannins and inky, black fruit, it needed two days uncorked to reveal itself, when a fig and cassis expression came forth. This is one for the cellar.
- **Force Majeure Force Majeure Vineyard Syrah / 2013 / Red Mountain / $$$$** In this big, posh and stylish red, bramble and cassis aromas give way to a mocha flavor that expands with aeration. Its compelling minerality makes it a great foil for barbecue.

GORMAN WINERY

Chris Gorman is one of the most familiar figures in Washington's new wave of ambitious, small-scale producers. A one-man band for most of the years since his first vintage in 2002 (he now has an assistant winemaker), Gorman first focused on full-throttle Bordeaux- and Rhône-style red blends from Red Mountain with the provocative names that are his signature (e.g., The Evil Twin, The Bully, The Devil You Know). Though he still turns out fewer than 8,000 cases a year, the restless Gorman has branched out into projects like the Ashan Chardonnays (see p. 228), and may bottle small lots of whatever strikes his interest.

- **Gorman Winery The Devil You Know / 2013 / Columbia Valley / $$** Slightly brighter though no less formidable than The Bully, this blend of mostly Cabernet, Merlot and Malbec is juicy and red-fruited, with a dark cherry core of extracted flavor.
- **Gorman Winery The Bully Cabernet Sauvignon / 2012 / Red Mountain / $$$** With its dark fruit and leathery tannins, this wine is forceful, but no bully. The flavors are supple and forward; the texture is formidable, but also full of vibrancy.

GRAMERCY CELLARS

This Walla Walla winery has developed a devoted following since its first releases from the 2007 vintage. The wines are notable for their quality, but also for the philosophy behind them. Gramercy's founder-vintner Master Sommelier Greg Harrington, his wife, Pam, and their partner, assistant winemaker Brandon Moss, seek to make complex, refined red wines that boast modest alcohol, bright acidity and subtle oak. Harrington's careful choice of vineyard sites—firmer grapes for the Lagniappe Syrah from Red Willow; softer ones for the Walla Walla Syrah from Les Collines—results in wines that are well worth following for fans of top Rhône- and Bordeaux-style reds.

- **Gramercy Cellars Lagniappe Syrah / 2013 / Columbia Valley / $$$**
  There's a tension in this Syrah between black pepper and more feral, meaty scents. Its purple fruit core makes it a fine match for lamb shoulder.
- **Gramercy Cellars John Lewis Syrah / 2013 / Walla Walla Valley / $$$$**
  With complex scents of lavender, bergamot and other cluster spices, dark currant flavors and supple tannins, this succulent red has a quiet energy coursing through it.

HEDGES FAMILY ESTATE

Red Mountain AVA pioneers, Tom and Anne-Marie Hedges (he's a Washington native; she's from Champagne, France) broke ground on their estate in 1989. Over the years, they have been among the appellation's great promoters and emblematic producers. The winery today is a true family affair: Daughter Sarah is the winemaker and son Christophe is the general manager. From their biodynamically farmed estate vineyards come the top-of-the-line, all-Cabernet La Haute Cuvée bottling; the intensely flavored Bordeaux-style Red Mountain red blend; and the superb DLD Syrah. Look also for the more affordable CMS blends and the House of Independent Producers (HIP) line, which showcases prime Columbia Valley vineyards.

- **CMS / 2013 / Columbia Valley / $**
  This blue-fruited, grippy blend of Cabernet, Merlot and Syrah gets buoyancy from the Syrah and structure from the Cab.
- **Hedges Family Estate / 2012 / Red Mountain / $$**
  Capturing the heft of Red Mountain, this mostly Cab-Merlot flagship blend is a powerfully tannic expression of the place, with blue fruits supported by the savory, rye-inflected tannins.

THE HOGUE CELLARS

Starting with six acres of Riesling vines planted in 1974 on the Hogue family's Columbia Valley farm, this project had grown into one of the state's largest producers by the time brothers Mike and Gary Hogue sold it to the Canadian company Vincor in 2001. (Wine giant Constellation acquired Vincor in 2006.) Winemaker Greg Winter, formerly of Sonoma's Valley of the Moon, oversees a portfolio that specializes in affordable, aromatic whites (with Riesling still the winery's calling card), plus well-made Cabernet, Merlot and Syrah in four collections. The Genesis line maintains notable quality at under $20, while the top-end Reserve wines offer considerable pleasure for not much more.

- **Genesis Meritage / 2012 / Columbia Valley / $$**
  Of the Bordeaux varieties in this Meritage blend, it's Malbec that seems to guide the wine's aromas of licorice and anise. The fruit here is pure red and refreshing, ideal for a steak.
- **Genesis Syrah / 2012 / Columbia Valley / $$**
  Fresh and red-fruited with a cedary accent, the Genesis Syrah delivers smoky, dark plum flavors with a fine tannic grip.

JANUIK WINERY

Mike Januik made his reputation as head winemaker at Chateau Ste. Michelle for most of the 1990s. He is still in Woodinville, and he still oversees a multibrand operation, but with a major difference: Now he heads two modest-sized labels, Novelty Hill and his own Januik, taking both in his own direction. Januik's years at Chateau Ste. Michelle gave him a unique insight into the state's best vineyards, especially those that have matured now into world-class sites. His highly regarded reds benefit from this perspective and from his relationships with top vineyard sources like Champoux, Bacchus, Klipsun and Ciel du Cheval.

- **Januik Klipsun Vineyard Merlot / 2013 / Red Mountain / $$**
  A red-fruited, comely Merlot from a vineyard known for its power and intensity, the 2013 vintage has a split personality: It's frisky at first, but powerful in the finish.
- **Januik Champoux Vineyard Cabernet Sauvignon / 2013 / Horse Heaven Hills / $$$** Champoux Cabs are typically firm, concentrated and wildly intense, but in Mike Januik's confident hands there's also a savory leafiness to the cedar and plum flavors of this beautiful, vinous red.

KERLOO CELLARS

Ryan Crane has kept things small in order to do them his way, which means following his palate to the Wahluke Slope for one of Washington's top Tempranillos and foot-treading his Syrah and Grenache. Crane ("kerloo," by the way, is apparently the call a crane makes) started his winery in 2007 on a shoestring budget. It has flourished thanks to word-of-mouth among fans of his elegant but full-flavored reds (and a fine rosé) from choice vineyards like Les Collines and StoneTree. The Walla Walla operation now has a new facility (and tasting room) in Seattle's SoDo district, the namesake of its SoDo Cellars second label.

- **Sodo Cellars Wingman / 2014 / Washington State / $**
  This (mostly Grenache) Grenache-Syrah-Mourvèdre blend was sourced mainly from cooler Yakima sites, which may account for the prettiness and high tone of its red-fruit flavors: cherries and red plum, with a smoky core.
- **Kerloo Les Collines Syrah / 2013 / Walla Walla Valley / $$$**
  Generous and ripe when first poured, this wine takes a jammy direction, but with air, its savory, licorice and dried-beef flavors gather, all in a mineral frame.

KIONA VINEYARDS AND WINERY

This is a vineyard-based operation that draws from some of the most sought-after grapes in Washington. Patriarch John Williams (with his friend Jim Holmes of Ciel du Cheval) came out to then-desolate Red Mountain and put down roots in 1975, an eternity ago on the Washington wine timeline. Now operated by the second and third generations of the family, Kiona's vineyard holdings have grown to 250 acres, and its wine portfolio may include almost a dozen varietals including offerings like Lemberger and Zinfandel. The highest praise here is generally reserved for the Old Block Cabernet Sauvignon and the very fine ice wines and late-harvest Rieslings.

- **Kiona Lemberger / 2013 / Red Mountain / $**
  Kiona was one of the state's first Lemberger producers, and its version is pleasingly sappy and fruit-driven, with boysenberry and bramble flavors and a mineral tang to its tannins.
- **Old Block Cabernet Sauvignon / 2012 / Red Mountain / $$$$**
  From 1975 plantings, this dark-fruited colossus of tannin and flavor leads with ferrous, blackberry scents. Its grip is iron-fisted, but an elegance persists throughout.

LAUREN ASHTON CELLARS

Dentist-turned-vintner Kit Singh launched this impressive, Woodinville winery (named for his children, Ashley Lauren and Ashton Troy) in 2009, and his early offerings have been praised for their polish, purity and craftsmanship. Singh makes wine with what he terms a French sensibility, including a restrained hand with oak. The top-tier bottlings here are the Proprietor's Cuvée and Cuvée Arlette—a Bordeaux-style left bank–right bank pair of spicy, robust reds sourced from Red Mountain—and the Rhône-style Cuvée Mirabelle. But Singh has a deft touch with dry whites as well, including the ripe, often mineral-driven, Sauvignon Blanc–based Cuvée Méline.

- **Lauren Ashton Cuvée Mirabelle / 2012 / Columbia Valley / $$$**
  One-third each Grenache, Syrah and Mourvèdre, this has a compelling Grenache-like scent of red maraschino cherry, and a fleshy, juicy middle shored up by rustic Mourvèdre tannins.
- **Lauren Ashton Proprietor's Cuvée / 2012 / Columbia Valley / $$$$**
  This Cab-Merlot blend has plenty of charry oak and tar aroma. Its flavors are weighty and plush, driven by a dark chocolate and mocha oak character framing muted black fruits.

L'ECOLE NO. 41

Marty and Megan Clubb left corporate jobs in San Francisco in 1989 to take over a tiny winery started by Megan's parents near Walla Walla. The Clubbs focused L'Ecole No. 41 on Bordeaux varietals, including a top-notch Sémillon, and later added Syrah and Chardonnay to the roster. The original children's drawing of the former schoolhouse that is their home base has given way to a more "grown-up" version on the label—a better reflection, perhaps, of their elegant wines. L'Ecole draws much of the fruit for its top wines from decades-old partnerships with Seven Hills (which the Clubbs co-own) and Pepper Bridge. Its very promising Ferguson estate vineyard was first harvested in 2010.

- **L'Ecole No. 41 Perigee / 2013 / Walla Walla Valley / $$$**
  From the Seven Hills Vineyard, the Perigee Bordeaux-style blend has a savory, dusty note that feels grippy, but the vineyard's warm red-fruit character shines through.
- **L'Ecole No. 41 Ferguson / 2013 / Walla Walla Valley / $$$$**
  A mostly Cabernet Bordeaux-style red, this has dark plum flavors and a powerful structure derived from the thin, rocky basalt soils of the young Ferguson Vineyard.

LEONETTI CELLAR

Arguably Washington's most sought-after collectors' label (along with Quilceda Creek; see p. 250), Leonetti was Walla Walla's first commercial winery and has been a reference point for the US (and arguably the world) for nearly 40 years. The talented visionary founder, Gary Figgins, has handed off the reins to his son Chris (see FIGGINS, p. 239), who has proven to be more than a worthy successor, taking Leonetti's Bordeaux-style wines (and Sangiovese) even farther into the quality stratosphere. Deep-pocketed wine lovers who want to taste some of the most extraordinarily layered red wines produced in the New World should sign up immediately.

● **Leonetti Cellar Merlot / 2013 / Walla Walla Valley / $$$$**
Leonetti has some of the oldest Merlot plantings in the Walla Walla Valley, which may account for the grippy power in this savory, cedary red, with lavish oak and generous cherry flavor.

● **Leonetti Cellar Reserve / 2012 / Walla Walla Valley / $$$$**
All about structure when first poured, this mostly Cabernet red is aged nearly two years in oak. Cellar it for a decade or more—if you can resist its dark plum, cedary sumptuousness.

LONG SHADOWS VINTNERS

One of Washington's most high-profile wine projects, this is the second act of longtime Chateau Ste. Michelle CEO Allen Shoup. Long Shadows bottles seven distinctive luxury wines made by global winemaking stars like Bordeaux's Michel Rolland (Pedestal), Napa Valley's Philippe Melka (Pirouette) and Armin Diel (Poet's Leap) of Germany's Nahe region. These often extraordinary bottlings are made at Shoup's state-of-the-art Walla Walla facility from an impressive roster of vineyards—Boushey, Sagemoor, Conner Lee. Long Shadows' own vineyard, the stunning The Benches (formerly part of DenHoed's Wallula; see p. 237), a series of geologically formed terraces above the Columbia River, is now supplying more grapes to the project.

○ **Poet's Leap Riesling / 2014 / Columbia Valley / $$**
Long Shadows' joint effort with Armin Diel, this Riesling is luminous and pure in its 2014 edition, with peach and golden apple scents and a leesy accent to its generous but taut flavors.

● **Chester-Kidder / 2012 / Columbia Valley / $$$**
Mostly Cabernet and Syrah, this plush dark red displays a scent of smoke and graphite and juicy black plum flavors.

MAISON BLEUE FAMILY WINERY

Jon Meuret's upmarket, Francophile Walla Walla project focuses on single vineyard–sourced Rhône varietals to make wines whose restrained, highly polished style still allows, as the winery notes, for "a controlled New World opulence." Since opening his doors in 2007, Meuret has accumulated an outstanding roster of top Columbia Valley vineyard sites, and in a side venture (Domaine J. Meuret), he is now reaching down into Oregon and the Columbia Gorge for Pinot Noir and Chardonnay. His core wines, especially the Syrahs and Grenaches and Marsanne-based Métis Blanc, have taken Washington Rhône-o-philes by storm. Prices remain very moderate considering the acclaim, but this is certainly subject to change.

○ **Maison Bleue Métis Blanc / 2012 / Columbia Valley / $$**
In this dry and wheaty Marsanne-based white, leesy, savory accents overlay a broad quince base of flavor. Pair this with blackened chicken.

● **Maison Bleue Bourgeois Grenache / 2013 / Columbia Valley / $$$**
A heady cross of kirschwasser and cherry tobacco scents leads to a bright, lean, compact red-fruit flavor. A plush and simple red made for barbecue.

MARK RYAN WINERY

The partners in this buzzy venture are clearly talented: Mark Ryan McNeilly and Mike MacMorran have boosted this one-time garage winery to national visibility thanks to their deft management of big-flavored, whopper-size wines (many with more than 15 percent alcohol) that nevertheless emerge from the glass as balanced and multifaceted. Their first successes were wines like the muscular, Red Mountain fruit–based Long Haul Merlot blend and the also Red Mountain–sourced, top-end Lonely Heart Cabernet Sauvignon. Most of these sought-after wines are made in tiny lots. Look to the BTR Cellars line for more affordable (and available) versions of the winery's style.

● **Mark Ryan Winery Long Haul / 2013 / Red Mountain / $$$**
A blend of mostly Merlot and Cabernet Franc, Long Haul is bright and red-fruited, with powerful, dusty tannins.

● **Mark Ryan Winery Lonely Heart Cabernet Sauvignon / 2013 / Red Mountain / $$$$** Mark Ryan reds are among the most powerful on offer at Red Mountain. This Cab's aromatic delicacy, leafy top notes and scents of blue flowers temper all that force.

MERCER WINE ESTATE

When you farm 1,951 acres of vineyard, you are spoiled for choice in selecting your fruit. When your family has been farming that land for five generations (Mercer's farming operation also yields 365 million pounds of produce each year), you know how to grow it. Brothers Rob and Will Mercer oversee this sprawling operation in the Horse Heaven Hills. Providing relief from Washington wines' price creep, winemaker Jessica Munnell, a Ste. Michelle alumna (her husband is Columbia Crest's Juan Muñoz-Oca; see p. 234), produces a slew of highly reliable bottlings in three price tiers: the fruit-forward, bargain-priced Canyons line, the midrange Estates bottlings and the top-tier but still wallet-friendly Reserve wines.

○ **Mercer Canyons Riesling / 2013 / Yakima Valley / $**
Plush and half-dry, with a tropical aroma of peaches and apricot blossoms, this brisk white gives way to apple and pear fruit with enough zippy acidity to close the wine nicely.

● **Mercer Canyons Cabernet Sauvignon / 2013 / Columbia Valley / $$**
The 2013 Mercer Canyons Cab displays sun-warmed flavors of dark plum and black fig, with a kiss of vanilla oak.

MILBRANDT VINEYARDS

Brothers Butch and Jerry Milbrandt sell most of the grapes they grow on their sprawling land holdings—nine vineyards totaling nearly 2,500 Columbia Valley acres. Beginning in 2005, the brothers began keeping some grapes back to bottle under their own names. Winemaker Josh Maloney focuses his efforts on the Milbrandts' Wahluke Slope AVA vineyards for the reds and on the geologically dramatic Ancient Lakes of the Columbia Valley AVA (which the Milbrandts were instrumental in establishing) for the whites. The Milbrandt-Maloney mesh clearly works, as these wines generally succeed at every price level, from the everyday Traditions bottlings to the ambitious Bordeaux-blend Sentinel red.

● **Milbrandt Vineyards The Estates Clifton Hill Vineyard Syrah / 2012 / Wahluke Slope / $$$** This inky black Syrah has plummy flavors, with a pleasing herbal note lending some nice complexity.

● **Milbrandt Vineyards Sentinel / 2012 / Wahluke Slope / $$$**
Dark-fruited and full-bodied, with powerful lashings of new oak, this warm-climate red is a kind of poster child for the brooding power of Wahluke Slope.

NORTHSTAR WINERY

Part of the Ste. Michelle Wine Estates portfolio, this Walla Walla winery was founded in the early 1990s with the talented winemaker Jed Steele in charge. Northstar's focus was on Merlot, which at the time looked to be Washington's up-and-coming grape. Fashion has since mostly moved on to Cabernet and Syrah, but Steele's successor (and protégé), winemaker David "Merf" Merfeld, continues to turn out some of the state's very best Merlots—a reminder of how vibrant, polished and ageworthy that wine can be when given the star treatment usually accorded to Cabernet Sauvignon (which Northstar, no surprise, also handles very well).

- **Northstar Red Blend / 2012 / Walla Walla Valley / $$$**

  Northstar's Cab-Merlot blend tastes dark and succulent, with a plush raspberry ripeness that takes on a brisk, leafy savor with air. This is a wine tailor-made for a leg of lamb.
- **Northstar Premier / 2012 / Columbia Valley / $$$$**

  Powerful and well built, this 100 percent Merlot bottling has the depth of flavor and the sumptuous oak character to age, or to decant and enjoy now with braised beef.

OWEN ROE

David O'Reilly and his partners at this category-defying, bi-state label make Pinot Noirs (and a Pinot Gris) in Oregon, while also earning praise for the wines they produce north of the state line. Owen Roe's new Yakima Valley facility turns out Syrahs, Cabs and Bordeaux- and Rhône-style blends; the unique Abbot's Table blend (Zinfandel, Sangiovese, Lemberger, Malbec, etc.); and whites, including Chardonnay and Riesling from the DuBrul Vineyard. The label produces several high-end bottlings as well as a bevy of affordably priced wines, which may cause some consumer confusion. But it helps that the quality is generally strong across the portfolio, and occasionally outstanding.

- **Abbot's Table / 2013 / Columbia Valley / $$**

  An approachable, crowd-pleasing blend of mostly Zinfandel and Sangiovese, Abbot's Table has a scent of grainy cherry and flavors that darken toward a plum and red cherry mélange.
- **Ex Umbris / 2013 / Yakima Valley / $$**

  This is a full-bore Syrah, inky and concentrated, with scents of white pepper, flavors of blackberry and black cherry and enough savory notes to lend complexity.

PEPPER BRIDGE WINERY

Owned by three families—the McKibbens, the Goffs and the family of Swiss-born winemaker Jean-François Pellet—this vineyard-based winery has been a Walla Walla foundation stone since 1998. The focus here is on ageworthy Merlots, elegant Cabernet Sauvignons and other red blends, sourced from three renowned estate vineyards: Pepper Bridge, Seven Hills and Les Collines. Pepper Bridge has consistently produced very fine wine across multiple price points. In addition to the Cab and Merlot bottlings, Pellet crafts the Pepper Bridge and Seven Hills single-vineyard red blends (sold only to wine club members); Trine, a Bordeaux blend whose name honors the three proprietor families; and small amounts of Sauvignon Blanc.

● **Pepper Bridge Merlot / 2013 / Walla Walla Valley / $$$**
Attractively blending supple sweet oak and juicy red fruit, this well-built Merlot has the substance to age and the red cherry charm to go beautifully with lamb chops.

● **Pepper Bridge Trine / 2012 / Walla Walla Valley / $$$$**
This red delivers dark scents of cinnamon and black berries and a poweful tannic payload. The tightly wound flavors are built to age, with good acidity prying open the structure.

PURSUED BY BEAR

TV and film star Kyle MacLachlan, a Yakima native, returned to his Washington roots with this label, which he launched in 2005 in collaboration with the winemaking team at Dunham Cellars (see p. 237). The label's good-humored name came from the famous Shakespearean stage direction in Act III of *The Winter's Tale*, but the project's high-end Cabernet Sauvignon is more refined and supple than theatrically flamboyant. There is also a Syrah, Baby Bear, first bottled in 2008 to celebrate the birth of MacLachlan's son, and a rosé, Blushing Bear, newly released in 2016. Top vineyards, such as DuBrul, Phinny Hill and Los Oidos, supply the grapes.

● **Baby Bear Syrah / 2012 / Columbia Valley / $$$**
This modern, oak-driven Syrah offers caramel scents, plush black cherry fruit and cocoa-laced dark blackberry flavors.

● **Pursued by Bear Cabernet Sauvignon / 2012 / Columbia Valley / $$$$**
Sumptuous oak leads the charge in this flagship red, with tobacco and caramel notes framing a core of plum compote flavors. Big-shouldered and generous, this is meant for ribeye.

QUILCEDA CREEK

One of the world's great Cabernet winemakers, Paul Golitzin is a scion of both Russian and wine aristocracy. His father, Alex, founded Quilceda Creek in 1979 in the converted garage of their home in Snohomish with the guidance of Alex's uncle, the legendary winemaker André Tchelistcheff. With Paul as winemaker since 1992, this extraordinary small winery produces a densely layered flagship Cabernet Sauvignon, two vineyard-designates and a relatively affordable second label, CVR. All are instantly snatched up, mostly via the winery's mailing list.

- **Quilceda Creek CVR / 2013 / Columbia Valley / $$$**
  Made from declassified lots not used for the flagship bottlings, this heady Cab-based blend has a dark plum scent adorned with caramelly oak and elegantly framed juicy red fruits.
- **Quilceda Creek Cabernet Sauvignon / 2013 / Columbia Valley / $$$$**
  This spectacularly elegant Cabernet shows posh cedar and red cherry scents and a texture of uncanny finesse, but not without power. A classic that will age beautifully.

RASA VINEYARDS

A holder of degrees from MIT, Stanford and, not incidentally, UC Davis (an MS in Viticulture and Enology), Indian-born winemaker Yashodhan "Billo" Naravane worked for 16 years in the computer industry before he and his brother Makrand ("Pinto"), founder of the computer networking company Plexus Technologies, decided to ditch it all and pursue their vinous dreams in the Walla Walla Valley. They bought 28 acres of cobblestone fields in the new Rocks District of Milton-Freewater AVA, and planted their first Syrah vines in 2016. Meanwhile, their early vintages of wines like the Primus Inter Pares Grenache and Bordeaux-blend Fianchetto, sourced from some of Washington's top vineyards, have made Rasa a critics' favorite and these luxury-priced, small-production wines a hot ticket.

- **Primus Inter Pares / 2013 / Walla Walla Valley / $$$**
  This Grenache opens with scents of earthy strawberry, black tar and meat. There's a liqueur-like kirsch note to the lifted flavors and an over-the-top intensity to the finish.
- **Fianchetto / 2012 / Walla Walla Valley / $$$$**
  This rich, ripe red blend—about half Cabernet Sauvignon, plus Cabernet Franc and Merlot—has a lush sweetness to the fruit and shows ample evidence of its 30 months in new oak.

REYNVAAN FAMILY VINEYARDS

The Reynvaan family founded their Walla Walla winery in 2004, put son Matt in charge of the vineyards and cellar, and watched their wines almost immediately rocket up the critics' lists. The magic comes from two red varieties (Cabernet Sauvignon and Syrah) and three whites (Viognier, Marsanne and Grenache Blanc) grown in two distinctive estate vineyards—In the Rocks and Foothills in the Sun—and produced in various combinations. The In the Rocks Syrah, for instance, is co-fermented with a portion of Viognier, Côte-Rôtie-style. Layered, vividly flavored and lingering, these superstar Washington wines sell out quickly via the winery's allocation list.

● **Reynvaan Foothills Reserve Syrah / 2013 / Walla Walla Valley / $$$$**
This Syrah is less demonstrative than the In the Rocks bottling, but more elegant for it. Scents of cassis and smoked meat lead to a refined but savory acid-driven palate.

● **Reynvaan In the Rocks Syrah / 2013 / Walla Walla Valley / $$$$**
More given to peppercorn and smoke than to the feral, meaty elements typically found in Rocks District Syrahs, this wine's relative restraint is still wildly expressive and exotic.

ROTIE CELLARS

Founded in 2007 by Sean Boyd, who was previously in the oil and gas industry, this Walla Walla winery is an homage to Rhône Valley wines. Boyd takes his motto, "Old World wines from New World vines," to heart, making bright, high-natural-acid wines that often need additional cellaring time to show their best. The whites are all stainless steel–fermented to retain crispness; the reds are judiciously oaked to complement the natural flavors. The result is food-loving wines in a more European vein. Reflecting the Rhône's geographic divide, Boyd makes Northern and Southern versions of his reds and whites. Prices remain reasonable given the wines' enthusiastic reception.

○ **Rotie Southern White / 2015 / Washington / $$$**
Viognier, Roussanne and Marsanne combine here to yield a subtly peachy scent, with a fruit blossom background. The flavors are round and a touch leesy.

● **Rotie Northern Blend / 2013 / Walla Walla Valley / $$$**
The 5 percent Viognier added to Syrah imparts a hint of peach to the wine's macerated plum, cardamom and pepper scents. The flavors are dark and spicy, with a basalt grip.

SAVAGE GRACE WINES

This winery's name reflects its owner's sense of what makes a good wine: The grapes must go through a struggle to produce a graceful wine. His name also happens to be Michael Savage, and his wife's name is Grace. When Savage opened up shop in 2011 in Woodinville's Warehouse District, he had a clear direction: to make European-style wines for the table that would be balanced, un-manipulated and lower in alcohol (than typical New World wines). His early wines, including some cooler-climate surprises like Pinot Noir, Riesling and Grüner Veltliner, are moderately priced and generally very well made.

○ **Savage Grace Riesling / 2014 / Columbia Gorge / $$**
This graceful Riesling delivers much more weight than its dry, lifted lime-zest aromas would suggest. A half-dry sweetness on the palate leads to a slatey mineral finish.

● **Savage Grace Pinot Noir / 2013 / Columbia Gorge / $$**
Balanced and pure, this Pinot has an aroma of red cherry and a hint of tar and rye. It's lean and a bit delicate, with an elegant suavity to its red cherry flavors.

SEVEN HILLS WINERY

In early 2016, the McClellan family sold this benchmark Walla Walla winery to the Napa-based Crimson Wine Group, owners of Pine Ridge Vineyards and Archery Summit Winery (see pp. 68 and 202) among many other premium wine properties. Winemaker Casey McClellan continues to produce the Seven Hills portfolio in his trademark refined, restrained style. His presence should also ensure the continuity of the winery's longstanding relationships with top-tier vineyards, such as Klipsun, Ciel du Cheval and Seven Hills. The well-priced Riesling is a big seller here, but the Bordeaux-style reds—including bottlings of less well-represented grapes like Carmenère, Malbec and Petit Verdot—are the image makers.

● **Seven Hills Ciel du Cheval Vintage Red Wine / 2013 / Red Mountain / $$$** Showing both brawn and grace, this "big blue" red blend opens tense, but with air, a whiff of dark cherry comes through. With its firm tannins, this is made for cellaring.

● **Seven Hills Seven Hills Vineyard Cabernet Sauvignon / 2013 / Walla Walla Valley / $$$** This savory red delivers a lovely, leafy mint scent when first poured. It has great structure and plenty of tannin for steak.

SIXTO

Chardonnay rarely figures in discussions of Washington's standout wines, although there have long been fine examples. Projects like Chris Gorman's Ashan (see p. 228) and this instant cult venture from Charles Smith (see p. 233) and Brennon Leighton, who brings his own insider cred from the whites he produced at EFESTĒ (see p. 238), are putting Washington Chardonnay on wine connoisseurs' radar. Named for musician Sixto Rodriguez of *Searching for Sugar Man* fame, SIXTO aims to resurrect the state's overlooked patches of old-vine Chardonnay. It produces tiny quantities of three single-vineyard bottlings, plus Uncovered, a blend of the three vineyards that is a bit easier on the wallet, if you can find it.

○ **Sixto Frenchman Hills Chardonnay / 2013 / Washington / $$$**
This tarte Tatin– and golden apple–scented Chardonnay is ripe, rich and fully lactic, with a lavish oak presence.

○ **Sixto Roza Hills Chardonnay / 2013 / Washington / $$$**
Lighter and more citrus-driven than its Frenchman Hills counterpart, this appley white has an appealing vibrancy, with a more focused pear core of flavor.

SLEIGHT OF HAND CELLARS

This Walla Walla winery's small-production, exuberantly styled wines—also exuberantly named and labeled with stage-magic motifs—have been a hit since their launch in 2007. The brainchild of vintner Trey Busch, the line offers something for everybody, from very affordable fine Riesling to the top-end reds like the right bank Bordeaux–style blend Archimage, the Illusionist Cab and the Levitation Syrah (reasonably priced given the marketplace). The combination of serious winemaking and light-hearted pleasure is clearly working: The winery has added a second barrel room to handle increased production.

● **Sleight of Hand Cellars The Illusionist Cabernet Sauvignon / 2012 / Columbia Valley / $$$** This is a mouthful, with a dark blue fruit character that starts out delicate and floral, violet and lavender. Its flavors are concentrated and supple all at once, with an evergreen filigree informing the finish.

● **Sleight of Hand Cellars The Psychedelic Syrah / 2013 / Walla Walla Valley / $$$** Heady and exotic, this delivers scents of olives, smoked meat and leather when first poured, but with air, a dark plum core falls into place, with balance and elegance.

SPARKMAN CELLARS

Chris Sparkman made extensive contacts in the wine business in his former job as general manager of Seattle's Waterfront Seafood Grill, and they came in very handy when he entered the business in 2004—Charles Smith (see p. 233) drew up the basics on napkins and Mark McNeilly (see Mark Ryan Winery, p. 246) made the first two vintages. Sparkman has since established a reputation for making mouth-filling wines in a big-boned, full-out style. Based in Woodinville's Warehouse District, Sparkman turns out roughly 25 bottlings of well-regarded, small-lot wines across a spectrum of grape varieties.

- **Sparkman Ruckus Syrah / 2012 / Red Mountain / $$$**
  A mass of inky tannin grounds this warm-climate Syrah's flavors of black fig and inky dark plum. It's an exuberant red and a perfect match for a slab of ribs.
- **Sparkman Stella Mae / 2012 / Columbia Valley / $$$**
  A blend of Cabernet, Merlot and Petit Verdot from warm Columbia Valley sites, this wine is at once dark and elegant, with a leafy Bordeaux sentiment and fine, firm tannins.

SPRING VALLEY VINEYARD

In a state that produces an outsize number of stunning Merlots, Spring Valley's silky, sophisticated Uriah, a Merlot-based blend, is a showstopper. But that original wine is now only one entry in a strong lineup of pricey, prestigious reds from Spring Valley, such as the Cabernet Sauvignon–based Uriah counterpart, Frederick, that are typically full-bodied, super-ripe and—being all estate-sourced—distinctively wines of a place. The winery's Corkrum Derby family proprietors partnered with Ste. Michelle Wine Estates in 2005, but they continue to run their winery and vineyard and kept talented winemaker Serge Laville (as well as the labels featuring photographs of Corkrum ancestors).

- **Spring Valley Vineyard Frederick / 2012 / Walla Walla Valley / $$$**
  You can almost taste the windblown soils of its Palouse Hills estate vineyard source in this spicy Cab-based red blend. Its scents of cinnamon and mace frame a black plum fruit core.
- **Spring Valley Vineyard Uriah / 2012 / Walla Walla Valley / $$$**
  Merlot and Cabernet Franc predominate in this supple and savory Bordeaux-style blend. Scents of cedar frond and tobacco leaf give way to fruit that is sunny, elegant and vibrant with acidity.

SYNCLINE WINERY

It is surprising enough that besides luscious Syrahs and Grenache-Syrah-Mourvèdre blends, James and Poppie Mantone's family winery produces Rhône-style varietal wines from Picpoul, Cinsault and Counoise, but Pinot Noir? In Washington? Part of the secret is that Syncline is in the Columbia Gorge AVA, which straddles the Washington-Oregon border and provides a unique growing climate for many grapes. The Mantones gathered 15 vintages of weather data before planting additional acres on their Steep Creek Ranch estate vineyard, which they farm biodynamically. Though their wines are very highly regarded, the Mantones have kept things small (6,000 cases) through a desire to stay close to everything and hands-on.

- **Syncline Subduction Red / 2014 / Columbia Valley / $$**
  Syrah provides the verve in this Grenache-Syrah-Mourvèdre blend; splashes of Cinsault and Counoise add lift and acidity. This is a plush, ample and totally satisfying wine.
- **Syncline Mourvedre / 2013 / Red Mountain / $$$**
  Classic Mourvèdre from an appellation that gets things ripe, this dark red has a meaty scent and a pure core of purple cassis, with a fine strawberry rim of flavor.

TAMARACK CELLARS

In just under 20 years, this first-rate, family-owned winery tucked into a renovated firehouse in a former US Army airfield in Walla Walla has seen sales soar to 25,000 cases. Owners Ron and Jamie Coleman and winemaker Danny Gordon have managed this partly by bottling some extraordinary wines from top vineyard sites like Ciel du Cheval, Tapteil and Sagemoor, and partly by offering a range of well-priced options all the way down to a bargain rosé of Mourvèdre. Though the top wines are much appreciated, Tamarack's highest-profile bottling is the Firehouse Red kitchen-sink blend.

- **Tamarack Cellars Firehouse Red / 2013 / Columbia Valley / $$**
  Eleven varieties went into Tamarack's 2013 kitchen-sink blend. It's a study in red fruits, cherry and plum mainly, with a hint of tobacco that lends complexity.
- **Tamarack Cellars Ciel du Cheval Vineyard Reserve / 2011 / Red Mountain / $$$** The cool vintage gave a savory grounding to the dark, dense fruit and firm tannins of this full-bodied Cabernet Sauvignon–based blend.

TENET WINES

Another of Chateau Ste. Michelle's international collaborations (see Chateau Ste. Michelle and Col Solare, pp. 233 and 234), Tenet focuses on fine Rhône-style wines, taking advantage of the relatively recent availability of mature vines in Washington. Ste. Michelle winemaker Bob Bertheau enlisted the collaboration of Châteauneuf-du-Pape star Philippe Cambie and Costières de Nîmes leading light Michel Gassier to produce the velvety, limited-production Tenet GSM (Grenache-Syrah-Mourvèdre) blend and the intensely flavored The Pundit Syrah. Also on the roster is a companion Syrah, Le Fervent, produced by Gassier in Costières de Nîmes. All three wines have met with critical acclaim; The Pundit and Le Fervent are particular bargains.

● **The Pundit / 2013 / Columbia Valley / $$**
Mostly Syrah, with splashes of Grenache, Mourvèdre and Viognier, this dark, smoky red has a scent of mocha and fig and a depth of flavor that calls to mind Châteauneuf-du-Pape.

● **Tenet GSM / 2013 / Columbia Valley / $$$**
This GSM blend is as luscious and lavish as any from Columbia Valley vineyards. Carob and licorice scents give way to the darkest blackberry fruit framed by supple black tannins.

TENOR WINES

This high-end spin-off brand from the Otis family's Matthews Winery in Woodinville makes big claims—"...we only release a wine when we feel it is world-class"—but it's not bragging if you can do it. Tenor focuses on 100 percent single-variety wines, which winemaker Aryn Morell bottles only in what he feels are the best years. For Malbec, apparently, only the 2009, 2012 and 2013 vintages made the grade; for Chardonnay, 2012, 2013 and 2014. The bottom line is that Tenor walks the walk, bottling rich, luscious and layered collectors'-market wines that have wowed tasters since their first releases.

○ **Tenor Chardonnay / 2014 / Columbia Valley / $$$**
Rich and lactic, with scents of pineapple and clarified butter, this full-bodied white has a big, generous mouthfeel to go along with golden apple and pear flavors.

● **Tenor Cabernet Sauvignon / 2013 / Columbia Valley / $$$$**
This opens with a scent of cinnamon followed by flavors of blue cassis and black cherry, with the acidity to keep the palate lifted. A rich complement of oak provides firm tannins.

VA PIANO VINEYARDS

Justin Wylie is a fourth-generation Walla Wallan who came of age just as the wine boom was transforming this charming, once sleepy agricultural town. He caught the fever, and after many garage experiments and hands-on lessons from local luminaries, released Va Piano's first bottlings in 2005. His small-lot wines, most of them sourced from the well-regarded estate vineyards, have gone from strength to strength, with prices rising in step with demand and production costs. Wylie's touch with fruit from sought-after sources like Les Collines, Klipsun and DuBrul places his wines among the top expressions of those sites.

- **Va Piano DuBrul Vineyard Cabernet Sauvignon / 2013 / Yakima Valley / $$$$** Tightly coiled, with scents of black soil and ink and a violet floral note, this dark Cab is focused and intense. Firm but fine tannins frame cassis and black tea flavors.
- **Va Piano Les Collines Vineyard Syrah / 2013 / Walla Walla Valley / $$$$** Dark and vinous, with a sense of coiled power beneath aromas of olive, tan bark and black fig, this wine is built to age and yet reveals a rippling, feral intensity in its youth. Decant before serving to ease the intensity.

WALLA WALLA VINTNERS

Myles Anderson and Gordy Venneri are the kind of guys everybody wants to succeed. They spent 13 years and countless hours, mostly in Anderson's basement, making wine seemingly by any means that occurred to them. Over time, they found their homemade wines, which they once couldn't give away, suddenly in demand. In 1995 they went pro—their winery in the foothills of the Blue Mountains now produces 6,500 cases a year. But Anderson and Venneri never forgot where they came from, extending help to many fledgling winemakers. The duo's wines, mostly red Bordeaux varietals plus Syrah and Sangiovese, have garnered a following for their sumptuous, crowd-pleasing smoothness and fair pricing.

- **Walla Walla Vintners Syrah / 2013 / Walla Walla Valley / $$$** This estate-sourced wine is dark and blue-fruited, with flavors of black plum and a whiff of wood smoke and sorrel.
- **Walla Walla Vintners Washington State Cuvée / 2013 / Washington / $$$** Cabernet leads the six varieties in this juicy, fruit-forward blend. Black cherry and cocoa aromas are followed by more structured flavors and a leafy, vinous finish.

WATERBROOK WINERY

A trailblazer in the Walla Walla wine business back in 1984 (founder Eric Rindal was only in his 20s at the time), Waterbrook got a second lease on life when it was bought by Precept Wine (owners of Canoe Ridge and Gruet, among many other brands) in 2006. One of Walla Walla's largest wineries, known for its approachable, fruit-forward style, Waterbrook makes frequent appearances on "best buy" lists, and small wonder—winemaker John Freeman offers a slew of wines at modest prices across the portfolio, from the popular Mélange series to the top-tier Reserve wines. All are solid values.

- **Waterbrook Mélange Founder's Red Blend / 2014 / Columbia Valley / $** This kitchen-sink blend is about half Merlot in 2014. Its chewy compote of cherry and plum flavors makes it a go-to Wednesday-night red.
- **Waterbrook Reserve Malbec / 2013 / Columbia Valley / $$** This dark red leads with scents of cassis and black plum, followed by a whiff of violets. The flavors are focused and vinous, with a plummy core of fruit.

WATERS WINERY

Waters was part of the next wave in Washington Syrah when it opened its doors in 2005, an artisan producer dedicated to making Old World–style wines—meaning moderate in alcohol and food-friendly, as opposed to the super-ripe Syrahs then making headlines in the wine press. The brand was purchased in 2013 by TR Wines, which wisely kept the original winemaker, Jamie Brown, in place and the style consistent. Waters's small-quantity, reasonably priced wines, such as the Interlude red blend and Forgotten Hills Syrah, have developed a dedicated following over the years. The Cabernet-based 21 Grams, a luxury, very-limited-production bottling whose labels showcase the art of Makoto Fujimura, is a cult favorite.

- **Waters Interlude / 2012 / Washington / $$** Mostly Merlot and Cabernet, this accessible blend opens with a scent of cedar and pine frond, followed by spiced-plum flavor, with a savory, leafy finish.
- **Waters Syrah / 2013 / Washington / $$$** A multivineyard bottling, this smoky red has an inky dark-fruit character tending toward plum and fig, with fiercely grippy Syrah tannins.

WOODWARD CANYON WINERY

Though its fame has grown since Rick Small and his wife, Darcey Fugman-Small, founded this benchmark New World winery in the Walla Walla Valley in 1981, Woodward Canyon's output is still modest (about 15,000 cases, 7,000 of which are of second-label Nelms Road wines). The winery's approach is old-school, opting for tiny-lot fermentations (for the reserve bottlings), and traditionally styled, balanced wines that are made to age gracefully. Crafted by winemaker Kevin Mott since 2003, Woodward Canyon's signature wines are astonishingly textured Cabernet Sauvignons—the best seem to disappear into collectors' cellars almost as soon as they are bottled—and superlative Chardonnay, but a trove of other pleasures also emerges from this fantastic cellar.

- **Woodward Canyon Artist Series #22 Cabernet Sauvignon / 2013 / Columbia Valley / $$$** Sourced from many of the state's top vineyards, the 2013 Artist Series Cab is rich, dark and concentrated, with blackberry and cacao scents and formidable tannins. It has a decade or two of cellar potential.
- **Woodward Canyon Old Vines Cabernet Sauvignon / 2013 / Washington / $$$$** This powerful red was made from 1970s plantings at Sagemoor and Champoux. Its black fig and cocoa scent has a caramel oak accent. The flavors are old-vine-dense, with a beam of red fruit shining through somber tannins.

Northeast

The new millennium has brought fresh energy to Northeastern winemaking, as ambitious artisan producers take the reins of existing wineries or strike out on their own. Given the challenges of northern winters–and in many places, humid summers and rainy autumns–hardy native and hybrid grapes are still quite evident here. But some areas–notably in New York and individual wineries elsewhere in the region, including Massachusetts, Rhode Island, New Jersey and Pennsylvania–are well established as growers of European vinifera grapes. At their best, Northeastern wines offer a graceful alternative style to the more robust California norm and give locavores more broadly appealing nearby wine choices.

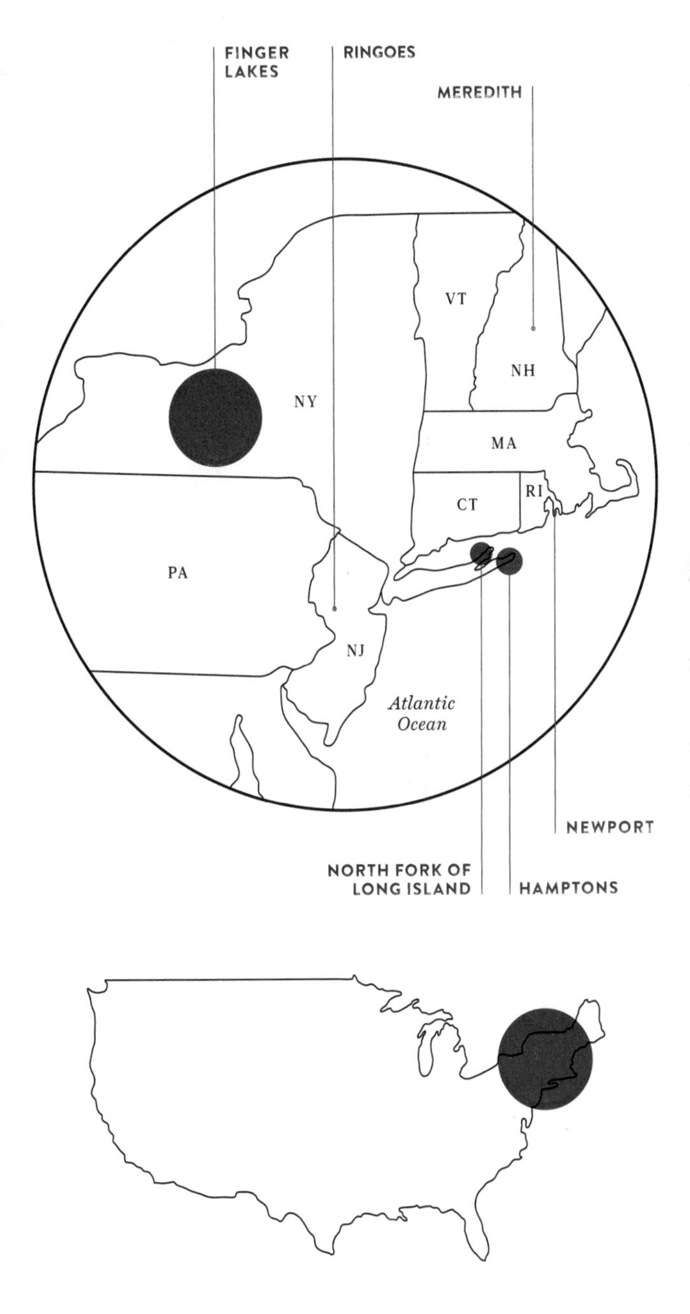
FINGER LAKES
RINGOES
MEREDITH
VT
NH
NY
MA
RI
CT
PA
NJ
Atlantic Ocean
NEWPORT
NORTH FORK OF LONG ISLAND
HAMPTONS

New York

CLAIM TO FAME

America's third-largest wine-producing state is home to more than 400 wineries and some 1,600 vineyards. New York's two premier viticultural regions, Long Island and the Finger Lakes, both produce high-quality wines that deserve to be better known (especially in New York City). The Long Island AVA, which encompasses the North Fork and Hamptons AVAs, has several distinct advantages as a winegrowing region, not the least of which are its built-in audience of Hamptons vacationers and many deep-pocketed winery owners. Classic European vinifera grape varieties, such as Cabernet Sauvignon, Chardonnay, Merlot and Cabernet Franc, thrive in Long Island's moderate, maritime climate, which is sometimes compared to that of Bordeaux's Médoc. Upstate, the Finger Lakes vineyard region continues to impress with its sophisticated dry and ice-wine style Rieslings, and is gaining new recognition for its Gewürztraminers and Pinot Noirs.

KEY GRAPES: WHITE

CHARDONNAY Both Long Island and the Finger Lakes produce graceful, generally medium-bodied Chardonnays with firm acidity and refined aromatics.

GEWÜRZTRAMINER This low-yielding, frost-sensitive grape is not widely planted in New York, but there are a few good bottlings, mostly from the Finger Lakes region.

RIESLING Top Finger Lakes wineries produce some of the country's finest Rieslings, in both dry and dessert styles. New York's preeminent white wine merits a broader audience.

SEYVAL BLANC & VIDAL BLANC These French-American hybrids are widely planted in the Finger Lakes region. Seyval at its best makes juicy, soft wines with Chenin Blanc–like character. Crisp, high-acid Vidal has great potential for late-harvest and ice wines.

KEY GRAPES: RED

CABERNET FRANC An up-and-comer from several New York regions, Cabernet Franc is earlier ripening and better adapted to cool conditions than its relative Cabernet Sauvignon.

CABERNET SAUVIGNON Long Island produces nuanced, medium-bodied Cabernets with great success in riper vintages.

MERLOT This is arguably Long Island's signature grape; some deliciously silky, lively examples are made here.

Producers/ New York

ANTHONY NAPPA WINES

Wanderlust brought world travelers Anthony and Sarah Evans Nappa together: The two Americans met while pursuing their studies (Anthony's in viticulture and enology) at Lincoln University in Christchurch, New Zealand. After further travels, the pair eventually settled down on Long Island, where Anthony's day job is winemaker at Raphael. His passion project, however, is creating this array of well-received, small-lot bottlings from North Fork and Finger Lakes fruit, many with Italian proprietary names (e.g., Ripasso, Tredici, Bordo). Nappa is also the force behind The Winemaker Studio in Peconic, a cooperative tasting room that showcases small producers, experimental lots and library wines.

○ **Anomaly / 2014 / New York / $$**
This white wine made from Pinot Noir is deceptive: Expect ripe cherry aromas and flavors, despite the transparent hue.

○ **Luminous / 2014 / Finger Lakes / $$**
The name of this lightly sweet Riesling seems apropos, given the wine's shimmering minerality and weightless character.

ANTHONY ROAD WINE COMPANY

John and Ann Martini planted their first Finger Lakes vineyard in 1973 to 100 percent hybrids. Since then they have switched over to just about all vinifera, saving only the Vignoles. Their son Peter manages the 25 planted acres of estate vineyard and 55 planted acres nearby that are part of a joint project with the legendary Sonoma vineyardists of the Robert Young family. Whites, notably Riesling, Chardonnay and Pinot Gris, are the stars at Anthony Road, but the winery also turns out rosés, varietal reds and red blends. Longtime cellar assistant Peter Becraft has taken over the head winemaker role from Johannes Reinhardt, who stepped down to concentrate on his Kemmeter Wines project but remains a consultant here.

○ **Anthony Road Devonian / NV / Finger Lakes / $**
With a name that's a nod to the geological history of the Finger Lakes region, this white blend is crisp and appealing.

○ **Anthony Road Riesling Dry / 2015 / Finger Lakes / $$**
Bracing and vivid, this lean Riesling demonstrates the potential of Finger Lakes *terroir*.

BEDELL CELLARS

A Cutchogue winery with world-class ambitions, Bedell was founded by Kip Bedell in the early 1980s during the first wave of the North Fork wine renaissance, and has had attention and capital lavished on it since 2000 by film producer Michael Lynne (*The Lord of the Rings*, *Hairspray*). Winemaker Richard Olsen-Harbich, a 30-plus-year veteran of the Long Island wine scene, has received particular acclaim for his red wines, especially Merlot (the 2009 bottling was served at President Obama's second inaugural lunch); he also makes very fine Malbec and Cabernet Franc. These are expensive wines by New York standards, but Bedell doesn't measure itself by that regional ruler alone.

○ **Bedell Taste White / 2014 / North Fork of Long Island / $$$**
Made primarily of Albariño, with small percentages of Sauvignon Blanc, Viognier, Chardonnay and Riesling, this white blend offers layered, complex flavors—though at a high price for the region.

● **Bedell Cabernet Franc / 2014 / North Fork of Long Island / $$$**
Floral and focused, this savory red points up the potential for Cabernet Franc in Long Island's vineyards.

BLOOMER CREEK VINEYARD

Kim Engle is one of the Finger Lakes' most ambitious vintners, practicing a close-to-the-earth, unmanipulated style of winemaking. His stylistic goals are avowedly Old World—he aims to make wines of elegance and subtlety rather than power—and his path to getting there is a painstaking one, including using no synthetic sprays, fermenting with native yeasts, not adding sugar or acid and generally eschewing fining and filtration. It also means harvesting at various stages of ripeness and taking what the year gives him in terms of botrytis ("noble rot") development. Engle's deft hand has drawn connoisseurs' attention to his small production Rieslings, Cabernet Francs and Pinot Noirs.

○ **Bloomer Creek Vineyard Tanzen Dame Auten Vineyard Dry Riesling / 2013 / Finger Lakes / $$** Fresh apple and lime notes lifted by a floral aroma make this single-vineyard white hard to resist.

● **Bloomer Creek Vineyard White Horse Red / 2012 / Finger Lakes / $$** Its name may be a nod to Bordeaux's famous Cheval Blanc, but this lithe and peppery Cabernet Franc–based wine really recalls a Loire red in its style.

CHANNING DAUGHTERS WINERY

Walter Channing planted some of Long Island's first Chardonnay vines on a former potato farm in Bridgehampton in 1982. Today his boutique winery—with partners Christopher Tracy as winemaker and Long Island viticultural pioneer Larry Perrine as consultant and CEO—is one of the region's benchmark producers. Still sourcing some of its grapes from those original vines, and much of the rest from the even older North Fork Mudd Vineyard, Channing Daughters makes some of the island's most intriguing "other grape" wines, including whites from Tocai Friulano and Malvasia and red blends comprising Blaufränkisch and Dornfelder, as well as top-rated wines from more familiar grapes like Merlot and Chardonnay.

○ **Sylvanus / 2013 / The Hamptons, Long Island / $$** Resinous and a little tannic from skin fermentation (unusual for whites), Sylvanus is a Muscat-dominated field blend that's an acquired taste but rewards those who give it a chance.

● **Over & Over Variation Eight / NV / Long Island / $$$** A testimony to Christopher Tracy's adventurous winemaking, this multiply-*ripasso*'d, multivintage, multivariety red is smoky, peppery and truly unique in the wine world.

DR. KONSTANTIN FRANK VINIFERA WINE CELLARS

With a little pardonable exaggeration, the winery website credits the late Konstantin Frank with "elevating the New York wine industry from a state of happy mediocrity to a level that today commands world attention." He was, in fact, a one-man turning point. Frank arrived from the Ukraine in the early 1950s with the thunderbolt idea that European-style vinifera grapes—not just the hardy hybrids then planted—could prosper in cold areas like the Finger Lakes. His son Willy, and Willy's son Frederick, in turn have proved him right, famously producing some of America's most distinctively vibrant Rieslings, but also lovely sparking wines and, more recently, fine, juicy reds.

○ **Dr. Konstantin Frank Rkatsiteli / 2014 / Finger Lakes / $**

Dr. Frank may be the only US winery making varietal wine from this unpronounceable Georgian grape, but they do it very well. This graceful white recalls fresh herbs and peaches.

○ **Dr. Konstantin Frank Reserve Riesling / 2014 / Finger Lakes / $$**

One of the classic wines of the Finger Lakes region, this reserve Reisling is a pleasure when young but has a surprising potential for long-term aging as well.

FOX RUN VINEYARDS

A familiar stop on the Seneca Lake wine tourist route—not least for its annual Garlic Festival—Fox Run has moved production from its original Civil War–era dairy barn (it now houses the tasting room) into sleeker digs, but founding owner Scott Osborn and winemaker Peter Bell haven't deviated from their original conviction that European-style grapes are the present and future for the Finger Lakes. The 55 acres of vineyard here were planted beginning in 1984, and the decades of familiarity with the soils are yielding results like the Geology Series Rieslings, which highlight distinctive vineyard blocks. Fox Run also makes fine rosé, a notable Bordeaux-style blend and a lineup of fortified and dessert wines.

○ **Fox Run Reserve Riesling / 2011 / Finger Lakes / $$**

Peter Bell uses a single block of grapes for this lovely Riesling, with scents of white peach and honeysuckle.

● **Fox Run Cabernet Franc / 2014 / Finger Lakes / $$**

Spot-on Cabernet Franc from one of the top Finger Lakes producers: ripe raspberry fruit entwined with the tea leaf and olive notes typical of the variety.

HEART & HANDS WINE COMPANY

The husband-and-wife team of Tom and Susan Higgins opened this 2,000-case boutique winery on Cayuga Lake in 2008. Winemaker Tom's roundabout path to Heart & Hands (the name refers to the traditional Irish wedding ring, the Claddagh) took him through the tech industry, France and Josh Jensen's seminal California Pinot Noir winery, Calera (see p. 158). Susan, who works in management consulting, oversees the winery's business and operations side. The Higginses specialize in Riesling and Pinot Noir, including a noteworthy Barrel Reserve Pinot. Both varietals have helped propel this artisan brand to the top rank of Finger Lakes producers.

● **Heart & Hands Pinot Noir / 2013 / Finger Lakes / $$**
A blend of grapes from Tom Higgins's various vineyard sources, his most affordable Pinot is delicate and fragrant.

● **Heart & Hands Elaine's Vineyard Pinot Noir / 2013 / Finger Lakes / $$$** This is an impressive single-vineyard Pinot Noir, full of black cherry and tea leaf character.

HERMANN J. WIEMER VINEYARD

One of America's premier Riesling sources, and arguably the Finger Lakes producer best known to wine lovers outside the region, this Seneca Lake estate was founded by German émigré Hermann J. Wiemer in the late 1970s. Wiemer was uniquely positioned to bring fine Riesling to the Finger Lakes: His family had been making wine in Germany for more than 300 years, and his father's work at Bernkastel's Agricultural Experiment Station taught the younger Wiemer the benefits of grafting vinifera wines onto American rootstock. By the time Wiemer retired in 2007, turning over the winery to his assistant Fred Merwarth, his project had gained acclaim for its superb Rieslings, as well as estimable Chardonnays and refined reds.

○ **Hermann J. Wiemer Dry Riesling / 2014 / Finger Lakes / $$**
Certainly one of the best Finger Lakes (and US) Rieslings for the price, the winery's basic dry bottling is streamlined and evocatively aromatic.

○ **Hermann J. Wiemer HJW Vineyard Riesling / 2014 / Finger Lakes / $$$** Sourced entirely from Hermann Wiemer's original vineyard (planted in 1976) on Seneca Lake, this wine proves that the Finger Lakes can hold its own against any Riesling region in the world.

LENZ WINERY

One of the first wineries on Long Island's North Fork, Lenz claims some of the region's oldest vines, with the earliest dating to 1978; all of its bottlings come from the winery's 70 estate acres. Winemaker Eric Fry arrived in 1989 and has been making graceful estate wines vinified in his own style ever since. Fry won't sell wines until he judges them ready to drink, meaning that Lenz's reds, whites and sparkling wines are often a few vintages behind those of its neighbors. Fry's confidence also shows in the winery's tradition of hosting blind tastings for industry professionals, pitting Lenz Old Vines Merlot, for example, against Château Pétrus.

○ **Lenz Old Vines Gewürztraminer / 2010 / North Fork of Long Island / $$** Made in a dry style, this supple Gewürztraminer emphasizes the variety's spice aspects over its sometimes cloying floral character.

● **Lenz Estate Selection Merlot / 2013 / North Fork of Long Island / $$** Soft, rich, loaded with black cherry fruit character, Lenz's flagship Merlot deserves its impressive reputation.

MACARI VINEYARDS

The Macari family has owned its 500-acre waterfront domain in Mattituck on Long Island Sound for decades, but they put in wine grapes only in 1995. (Today's 200 acres of grapes share the biodiverse estate with cattle, Spanish goats and a roaming menagerie.) Joseph Macari, Jr., farms the land biodynamically, and has it planted to an expansive collection of grapes, from Bordeaux blending varieties to Grüner Veltliner and Viognier. The winery also sources Riesling from the Finger Lakes. Napa Valley native Kelly Urbanik has handled winemaking duties since 2006 with consulting help from Austria's Helmut Gangl. Wine tourists can taste Macari wines at the Mattituck estate and at a smaller tasting room in Cutchogue.

○ **Macari Reserve Chardonnay / 2013 / North Fork of Long Island / $$** Luscious and rich, but neither overblown nor over-oaked, this layered white speaks to Macari's reputation as one of Long Island's top (if not *the* top) Chardonnay makers.

● **Macari Bergen Road / 2010 / North Fork of Long Island / $$$** A Merlot-based, Bordeaux-style red, Macari's top wine is made only in the best vintages. The 2010 shows fine tannins that support red cherry and violet flavors.

RAVINES WINE CELLARS

Morten Hallgren is yet another accomplished Finger Lakes winemaker to emerge from Dr. Konstantin Frank's cellars (see p. 266), but he may be the only one who grew up on a wine estate in Provence and got his enology degree from France's prestigious Montpellier SupAgro. He and wife, Lisa, staked out 17 acres above Keuka Lake in 2000, and have built a reputation as one of the region's top wineries. Though Ravines has scored successes with Bordeaux reds and Pinot Noir, its dry Rieslings—including a single-vineyard wine from the old vines of Argetsinger Vineyard—are what have captured the attention of consumers and the wine press.

○ **Ravines Argetsinger Vineyard Dry Riesling / 2012 / Finger Lakes / $$**
Possibly the best Riesling made in the Finger Lakes, Ravines's bottling from the Argetsinger Vineyard is potently mineral in character, and able to age for years.

● **Ravines Pinot Noir / 2013 / Finger Lakes / $$**
A fragrant Pinot typical of the Finger Lakes style: delicate, spicy and hewing more toward France than California.

RED NEWT CELLARS

It says something about both the quality revolution in the Finger Lakes and the camaraderie in the wine business around Seneca Lake that Tierce—a joint-project Riesling by Red Newt's proprietor David Whiting, Anthony Road consultant Johannes Reinhardt (see p. 264) and Fox Run's Peter Bell (see p. 266)—was served at President Obama's second inaugural lunch. For New York wine lovers, Red Newt's self-proclaimed "Lifechanging Riesling" is a benchmark in itself. In recent years, Whiting has shifted his focus from the winery, in Hector, to its well-known bistro, and brought in Kelby Russell, formerly of Fox Run, to man the cellar, which also turns out noteworthy Gewürztraminer and Pinot Gris.

○ **Red Newt Cellars "Circle" Riesling / 2013 / Finger Lakes / $**
Anyone with doubts about sweet (well, very lightly sweet) Riesling should try this one. Its touch of sweetness perfectly balances the bright acidity and only intensifies the vivid fruit.

○ **Red Newt Cellars Sawmill Creek Vineyards North Block Riesling / 2012 / Finger Lakes / $$** The winery's single-vineyard Rieslings are all impressive, but in 2012 the winner may be this laser-focused effort.

SHAW VINEYARD

This is the kind of personal-scale, unpretentious operation that is moving the ball forward these days in the Finger Lakes. Owner Steve Shaw was a hands-on farmer first, growing grapes for many years, and his packed-to-the-walls, barn-like winery on Seneca Lake reminds you of wine's agricultural roots. (Shaw Vineyard, he says, "does not hide the winemaking process.") When he built his own winery and launched this label in the early 2000s, he was ready with new energy and new ideas, including designing custom-made equipment for handling cool-climate grapes. Shaw places particular emphasis on his reds, many of which receive long, extended barrel aging.

○ **Shaw Vineyard Dry Riesling / 2013 / Finger Lakes / $$**
Citrus peel and an intriguing resinous-beeswax note announce the character of this poised, light-bodied white.

● **Shaw Vineyard Keuka Hill Reserve / 2007 / Finger Lakes / $$**
Steve Shaw's long-aging approach to his reds (they stay in barrels for four years) is unusual, but the results are impressive. This Bordeaux-style blend is supple and nuanced, and not at all over-oaky.

SHINN ESTATE VINEYARDS

After founding one of New York City's first committed, seasonal, locavore restaurants (Home) in the early 1990s, Barbara Shinn and David Page bought a homestead in Mattituck on the North Fork of Long Island in 1998 and spent two years preparing the land before planting a 20-acre vineyard (and opening the well-known Farmhouse bed and breakfast). Their talented winemaker, Patrick Caserta, has made some notable wines—particularly Merlots and Bordeaux-blend reds and a roster of well-crafted whites—from the biodynamically farmed, alternatively powered property. Page is also a skilled distiller, producing microbatches of eau-de-vie and grappa from the estate's alembic pot still.

○ **Shinn Estate Vineyards First Fruit Sauvignon Blanc / 2014 / North Fork of Long Island / $$** A favorite of *Top Chef* star Tom Colicchio, this herbal, melony Sauvignon Blanc is a perfect summertime white.

○ **Shinn Estate Vineyards Haven / 2013 / North Fork of Long Island / $$$** The Sauvignon Blanc and Sémillon in this complex white spend extended time macerating on the skins, giving the wine a light orange hue and intriguing fig and melon notes.

SPARKLING POINTE

This well-funded, high-tech Southold winery is serious about putting Long Island on the méthode champenoise sparkling wine map. Proprietors Tom and Cynthia Rosicki's sparkling wine facility produces seven cuvées, headlined by the *tête de cuvée* Brut Séduction, which is aged on the lees for eight years in the bottle, longer than most Champagnes. In charge of the cellar is Long Island veteran Gilles Martin, a Frenchman with an advanced degree in enology and a résumé that includes a long stint at California sparkling wine powerhouse Roederer Estate (see p. 185). Esteemed viticulturist Steve Mudd manages Sparkling Pointe's 40 sustainably farmed estate acres planted to the three traditional Champagne grape varieties: Pinot Noir, Chardonnay and Pinot Meunier.

○ **Sparkling Pointe Brut / 2013 / North Fork of Long Island / $$**
Made from the classic trio of Champagne grapes, this Long Island sparkler also has the bright intensity followed by creaminess that's a feature of good Champagne.

WÖLFFER ESTATE VINEYARD

The charismatic international entrepreneur Christian Wölffer created a kind of high-style fantasy domaine on Long Island: a lovely vineyard and winery in the heart of the Hamptons, with a sprawling stable and equestrian facilities. After his death in 2008, his winery team has carried on, led by talented winemaker and partner Roman Roth (German-born, like Wölffer, and one of Long Island wine's leading lights) and vineyard manager Richard Pisacano. Wölffer's rosé is a popular local hot-weather drink, but the real glories of the place are its Bordeaux-style reds (including the Merlot bottling from Roth's Grapes of Roth project), a very fine Chardonnay and often exceptional sparkling wine.

● **Wölffer Estate Rosé / 2015 / Long Island / $$**
Bottles of this pale pink rosé are an inescapable sight in New York's Hamptons during the summer months. There's a reason, though, for the wine's ubiquity: It's quite good—fresh, lively and endlessly refreshing.

● **The Grapes of Roth by Wölffer Estate Merlot / 2011 / Long Island / $$$** The name of this brooding red is a play on winemaker Roman Roth's own name. Notes of leather and toasted oak accent the wine's ripe, dark berry fruit.

Producers/ Other Northeast

HERMIT WOODS WINERY / New Hampshire

What happens when you combine local ingredients—like berries, flowers and honey—with traditional winemaking techniques like fermentation until dry and extended barrel aging? If you are the three partners in this venture, you have a hit on your hands. What began as a home-winemaking operation at partner Bob Manley's house has now moved into a sleek, blond-wood store and tasting bar on Main Street in Meredith. Though the 2,400-case winery does produce some grape-based wine (largely from hybrid varieties), its signature bottling is Heirloom Crabapple. Other offerings include berry wines, day lily wine with rhubarb and honey and a range of sparklers.

● **Hermit Woods Petite Blue / 2014 / New Hampshire / $$**
A dry red wine made from wild blueberries may sound odd, but this is serious stuff: in weight and style similar to good Pinot Noir, yet with the scent of fresh blueberries.

● **Hermit Woods Lake House Red / 2013 / New Hampshire / $$$**
A mélange of wild raspberries, blackberries, elderberries and blueberries (but no grapes) goes into this delicious dry red.

NEWPORT VINEYARDS / Rhode Island

John and Paul Nunes are among the largest grape growers in New England. Their 60 vineyard acres on Aquidneck Island are surrounded by Narragansett Bay and warmed by the Gulf Stream, with constant breezes that help protect the vines from the fungi and rots that beset so many humid-climate vineyards. Their vineyard parcels include the historic Nunes farm once owned by their great-grandfather; the brothers purchased it in 2002 from their family and gave it a makeover. Winemaker George Chelf has drawn particular praise for his Rieslings and sparkling wines. A multi-million-dollar renovation completed in 2015 added a new tasting room, event space and restaurant.

○ **Newport Brut Cuvée / 2011 / Rhode Island / $$$**
Citrusy and vivacious, this sparkler may not be as complex as Champagne, but with a good chill it's definitely appealing.

UNIONVILLE VINEYARDS / New Jersey

In the rolling hills of Hunterdon County—out where it's easy to see why New Jersey is called the Garden State—Unionville manages five vineyards of diverse wine grapes in the midst of the nation's most densely populated state. Indeed, it was a desire to curb development that led to the 1980 purchase of the 19th-century farm in Ringoes that is at the winery's core. Unionville is surprising doubters with the quality of its wines, which span a considerable array of reds and whites. UC Davis–trained winemaker Cameron Stark has bottled some impressive wines, among them the Amwell Ridge Viognier and, from the Pheasant Hill Vineyard, the winery's signature Chardonnay and one of the Northeast's premier Syrahs.

○ **Unionville Amwell Ridge Viognier / 2013 / New Jersey / $$**
Winemaker Cam Stark keeps just this side of Viognier's potentially over-the-top richness with this lemon curd–and–peaches white.

● **Unionville Amwell Ridge Counoise / 2013 / New Jersey / $$**
Floral and delicate, this unusual varietal red (Counoise is typically a blending grape) is equally good at room temperature or with a light chill.

Southeast

The top wineries in the Southeast, particularly in Virginia and Maryland but also farther south in North Carolina and even Georgia, have proven that the challenges to viticulture here–including uncertain rainfall patterns and vine diseases encouraged by a hot, humid climate–can be overcome in great style. Wine lovers who haven't sampled the region's offerings in recent years will be impressed by their quality; at their best, Southeastern wines can be astonishingly good. As pioneering winemakers in various micro-climates around the region learn how to unlock the potential of their specific vineyards, the future of winemaking in the Southeast looks bright indeed.

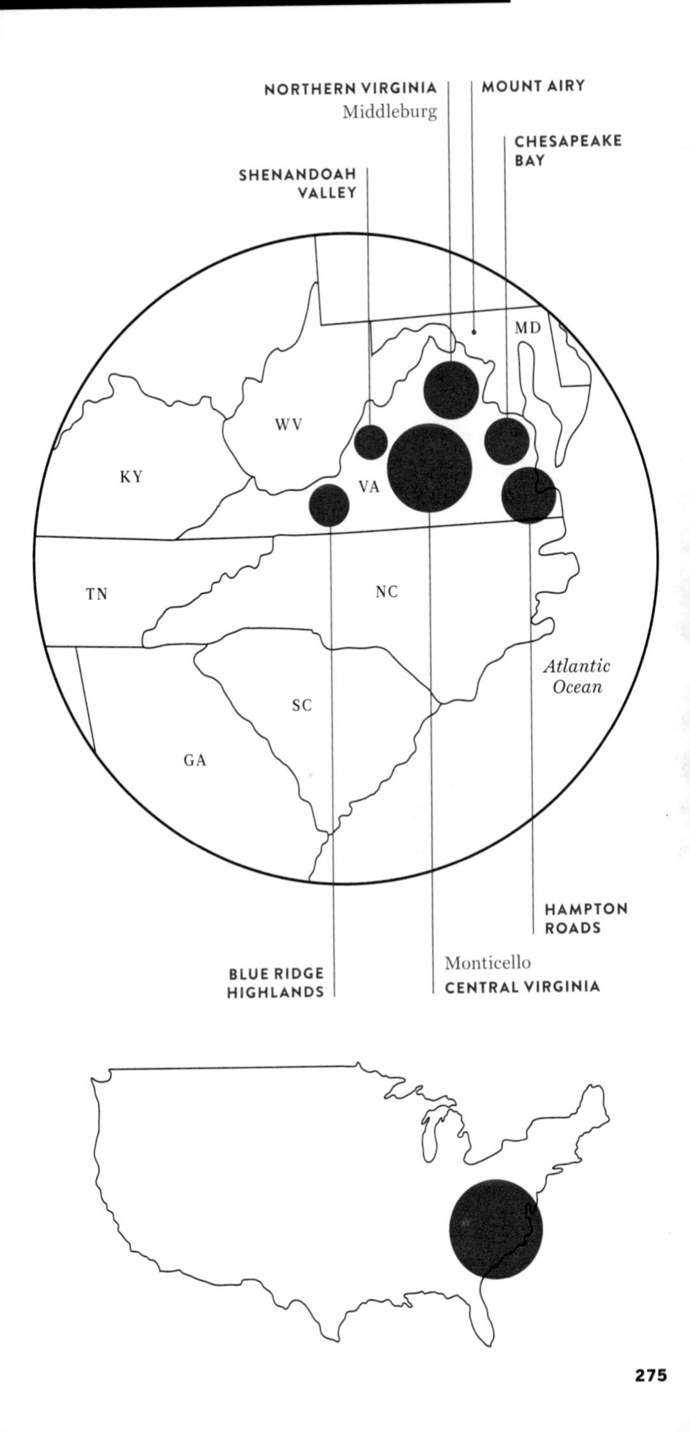
NORTHERN VIRGINIA
Middleburg
MOUNT AIRY
CHESAPEAKE BAY
SHENANDOAH VALLEY
MD
WV
KY
VA
TN
NC
Atlantic Ocean
SC
GA
HAMPTON ROADS
Monticello
CENTRAL VIRGINIA
BLUE RIDGE HIGHLANDS

Virginia

CLAIM TO FAME

Virginia has come very far, very fast in terms of wine, and now may even vie with New York for the title of finest wine-producing state east of the Mississippi. Diligent, homegrown winemakers, plus wealthy outside investors, plus a dose of Old World expertise (from world-class European consultants) are all coming together in Virginia to produce delicious wines from classic Bordeaux varieties (Cabernet Sauvignon, Merlot and Cabernet Franc), from Viognier and Chardonnay, and from America's often very fine native Norton grape. It doesn't hurt that Virginia also has a number of high-profile celebrity figures, such as Dave Matthews, Donald Trump and AOL co-founder Steve Case, raising consumer interest with their wine projects here. Though wineries are scattered around the state, the majority are located east of the Blue Ridge Mountains, around Charlottesville (particularly in the Monticello AVA) and north toward Washington, DC. As a general rule, Virginia's wines are medium-bodied and elegant, with higher acidity than California's rich, full-bodied wines.

KEY GRAPES: WHITE

CHARDONNAY This is Virginia's most widely planted grape, and wineries here produce some notable examples, often in a full-bodied, robust style.

VIOGNIER The exotically floral, mouthwatering wine of the northern Rhône has made itself right at home here. Virginia's Viognier bottlings are typically lighter-bodied than West Coast versions, and the best of them can rival those produced anywhere else in the United States.

KEY GRAPES: RED

CABERNET FRANC This softer, spicy, herb- and violet-perfumed parent of Cabernet Sauvignon is made into some of Virginia's top reds, particularly in the Monticello AVA.

CABERNET SAUVIGNON Cabernet Sauvignon thrives in Virginia's warmth, and is produced in a range of styles here.

MERLOT Robust, spicy Merlot and Merlot-driven blends like Barbourville's famous Octagon are among the state's most sought-after wines.

NORTON This American-born, Virginia-bred grape, all but forgotten after Prohibition, is enjoying a revival, thanks partly to champions like Jennifer McCloud at Middleburg's Chrysalis Vineyards and partly to its clean, fruity, generous flavors.

Producers/ Virginia

ANKIDA RIDGE VINEYARDS

Winemaker Nathan Vrooman is looking to alter the paradigm here as he boldly makes Pinot Noir where no Pinot has gone before. Planted in 2008, Ankida Ridge's sustainably farmed vineyard is in a unique spot, on granite soil 1,800 feet up on the eastern slope of the Blue Ridge Mountains. Ubiquitous vineyard consultant Lucie Morton called it "Little Burgundy," and the concept stuck. For a relatively new operation in a new *terroir* for the so-called heartbreak grape, these wines have enjoyed great early success, as have the Chardonnays. The winery also produces a line of non-estate-grown wines, called Rockgarden.

○ **Ankida Ridge Chardonnay / 2013 / Virginia / $$$**
Aging in all-neutral oak gives this wine a clarity and streamlined expression that more New World Chardonnays would do well to emulate.

● **Ankida Ridge Pinot Noir / 2012 / Virginia / $$$**
Dry spice notes and crisp cherry fruit give this Pinot a European sensibility—not atypical of Virginia wines overall.

BARBOURSVILLE VINEYARDS

In 1976, defying advice to plant tobacco instead, Gianni Zonin, of the Veneto's prominent wine-producing family, bought this 19th-century estate near Charlottesville, in the Piedmont of the Blue Ridge Mountains, and accomplished what the property's onetime neighbor Thomas Jefferson could not: produce fine wine. Winemaker Luca Paschina hails from the other Piedmont—the one in northwestern Italy—and he has not just turned Barboursville into a success in its own right, he's helped make it a leader for the Virginia wine industry. Paschina creates a galaxy of bottlings from French- and Italian-descended grapes, most famously the high-end red Bordeaux blend, Octagon.

○ **Barboursville Vineyards Vermentino Reserve / 2014 / Virginia / $$**
People may plump for Viognier as Virginia's signature grape, but this crystalline, minerally Vermentino makes a strong case for this Italian coastal variety as an alternative.

● **Barboursville Vineyards Octagon / 2013 / Virginia / $$$**
Luca Paschina's flagship Bordeaux-style blend has probably won more awards than any other Virginia red wine. Classically proportioned, able to age effortlessly, it's a world-class wine.

BOXWOOD ESTATE WINERY

Former Washington Redskins owner John Kent Cooke recruited famed Bordeaux consultant Stéphane Derenoncourt to help make the wines at his Virginia estate in Middleburg's horse country. Cooke's daughter Rachel Martin manages the winery; winemaker Josh Gerard oversees the now nearly 20-acre vineyard, which consultant Lucie Morton began planting in 2004 with a focus on the five main Bordeaux red grapes. The farming practices combine old-fashioned hands-on vineyard care with high-tech touches such as a GPS system that records vineyard maintenance. The estate aims to top out at a boutique-size 5,000 cases, bottling three red blends and a rosé.

● **Boxwood Estate Boxwood / 2014 / Middleburg Virginia / $$**
This left bank Bordeaux–style red (i.e., Cabernet Sauvignon leads the blend) is impressively tannic in its youth but opens up after a year or two; 2014 should be no exception.

● **Boxwood Estate Topiary / 2014 / Middleburg Virginia / $$**
Topiary is the winery's "right bank" cuvée, made with equal parts Cabernet Franc and Merlot. Deep, dark and smoky, it's approachable upon release.

GLEN MANOR VINEYARDS

Near the scenic Skyline Drive, on the western slope of the Blue Ridge Mountains, Jeff White planted six acres of a more than 100-year-old, 212-acre family farm to wine grapes in 1995, and launched his own wine brand in 2007. A veteran of the well-regarded nearby Linden Vineyards, White uses his now 14.5 vineyard acres to make small lots of wine with a Bordeaux bent, including the flagship Cabernet Sauvignon–driven Hodder Hill bottling and the more right bank Merlot–Cab Franc (with a small amount of Petit Verdot) St. Ruth blend. One intriguing specialty here is Petit Manseng, a white grape of southwestern France that White crafts in both off-dry and late-harvest styles.

○ **Glen Manor Sauvignon Blanc / 2015 / Virginia / $$**
Virginia's climate is tricky for Sauvignon, but Jeff White has a knack for the grape. His 2015 bottling is characteristically bright and lively.

● **Glen Manor Hodder Hill / 2013 / Virginia / $$$**
This Cab-centric blend is crafted in a restrained, more Old World style: Think red fruits, spicy tannins and a long life ahead in the cellar.

KING FAMILY VINEYARDS

When polo aficionado David King acquired this Crozet property in 1996, his first priority was not winemaking, but creating a field for the polo matches that are now played here every Sunday from Memorial Day until mid-October. King went about building his winery with the same determination he applied to chasing a polo ball. Since its first vintage in 2000, King Family Vineyards has grown into a 10,000-case operation, with the core of its offerings from the estate's 31 vineyard acres. Beaune-trained French winemaker Matthieu Finot brings a world-wine-traveler's perspective to the cellar here, and has found particular success with the winery's flagship Meritage blend.

○ **King Family Vineyards Viognier / 2014 / Monticello / $$**
This is spot-on Viognier, lemon-zesty with ripe peach notes underneath—and more proof that Virginia's inclination toward this difficult variety isn't delusional.

● **King Family Vineyards Meritage / 2013 / Monticello / $$$**
Merlot forms the backbone of this elegant blend. As with many top Virginia reds, it walks an interesting line between California ripeness and Old World subtlety.

LINDEN VINEYARDS

Owner/winemaker Jim Law is not only one of Virginia's Chardonnay masters (he makes very fine Bordeaux-style reds as well), he's also one of the state wine industry's longtime leading lights. Law planted his Hardscrabble Vineyard high in the Blue Ridge way back in 1985—an eternity ago in Virginia wine time—and today his 4,000-case production consists of wines sourced from old-vine Hardscrabble, as well as the Avenius and Boisseau vineyards, or a combination of all three plantings. Law's sought-after Chardonnays are typically barrel-fermented and often held back well beyond other wineries' release dates for added maturation.

○ **Linden Late Harvest Vidal / 2010 / Virginia / $$**
The usually nondescript Vidal variety hits remarkable heights in this unctuous, wildflower honey–scented dessert wine.

○ **Linden Avenius Chardonnay / 2013 / Virginia / $$$**
Jim Law's mastery of Chardonnay should be immediately apparent to anyone taking a sip of this complex, precise white.

MICHAEL SHAPS WINEWORKS

An alumnus of Virginia's Jefferson Vineyards and King Family Vineyards (see p. 279), Michael Shaps founded his own winery in 2007 outside Charlottesville. The Burgundy-trained vintner (Shaps is also the owner-winemaker of Maison Shaps in Meursault, France) brings an Old World artisan-wine approach to the small-lot wines he bottles under the Michael Shaps and Virginia Wineworks labels. As the owner of the custom crush facility where he offers contract winemaking services in addition to making his own wines, Shaps has a unique opportunity to see what's working for others in Virginia. His Petit Verdot and Viognier bottlings have been especially well received, and he has developed a smooth hand with the rough, tannic Tannat grape, which he believes is a comer.

○ **Michael Shaps Petit Manseng / 2014 / Monticello / $$**
Petit Manseng, native to southwest France, is typically used for sweet wines; Shaps turns it into a thrillingly intense, bone-dry, tropical-fruited white.

● **Michael Shaps Tannat / 2013 / Monticello / $$$**
Tannat's thick skin can make it fiercely tannic; it also makes the grape well suited to Virginia's humid climate. Shaps's version is powerful but not harsh, with lots of ripe dark fruit.

RDV VINEYARDS

In a state marked by ambitious, well-heeled winery owners, Rutger de Vink stands out, not least because he brought in a dream team of consultants from Bordeaux, headed by enologist Eric Boissenot. The lovely RdV winery in Delaplane turns out two very pricey (for Virginia) Bordeaux-style blends—Lost Mountain and Rendezvous—both of which have been taken up not just by local fanciers, but by the wine press. Enthusiastic and photogenic, de Vink may well turn out to be the Virginia wine industry's first national star.

- **RdV Vineyards Lost Mountain / 2012 / Middleburg Virginia / $$$$**
  This is considered by some to be the best red wine made in Virginia. The Cab-based blend is rich without being overripe, with finely tuned tannins and a long, complex finish.
- **RdV Vineyards Rendezvous / 2012 / Middleburg Virginia / $$$$**
  The flip side of Lost Mountain, this Merlot-driven red offers equal poise and complexity, with plummier fruit and tannins that are more plush than linear.

Producers/ Other Southeast

BLACK ANKLE VINEYARDS / Maryland

Sarah O'Herron and Ed Boyce followed their winemaking dream—to Black Ankle Road in Mount Airy—in a very particular and conscientious way. The wines they produce are all sourced from their sustainably farmed property (the first grapes came in in the mid-2000s), where even the buildings are sustainably constructed with materials from the estate. Their 42 planted acres yield a bevy of small-lot wines, from relatively big-bodied reds, including Syrah and Bordeaux blends, to aromatic whites like Albariño, many of which are sold out pre-release.

- **Black Ankle Feldspar / NV / Frederick County / $$$**
  This nonvintage Cabernet-centric blend has personality to spare: dark fruit, elegant tannins and a long, insistent finish.
- **Black Ankle Leaf-Stone / 2012 / Frederick County / $$$**
  Notes of peppery spice and leather underpin the flavors of this impressive, medium-bodied Syrah.

Midwest

Thanks to the dedication and growing skill of its vineyardists and winemakers, the Midwest is home to substantial wine industries in Michigan, Missouri, Ohio and Illinois. Midwestern vintners persevere despite sometimes difficult weather conditions, including winter freezes and, in warmer areas, challenging rainfall and humidity patterns. Many wineries have built their followings on hybrid and native varieties, such as Norton (Missouri's official grape) and Chardonel, that are better adapted to local conditions. On the other hand, Michigan's successes, especially with Riesling, illustrate how the region's wines can also appeal to drinkers conditioned to appreciate European wine grapes.

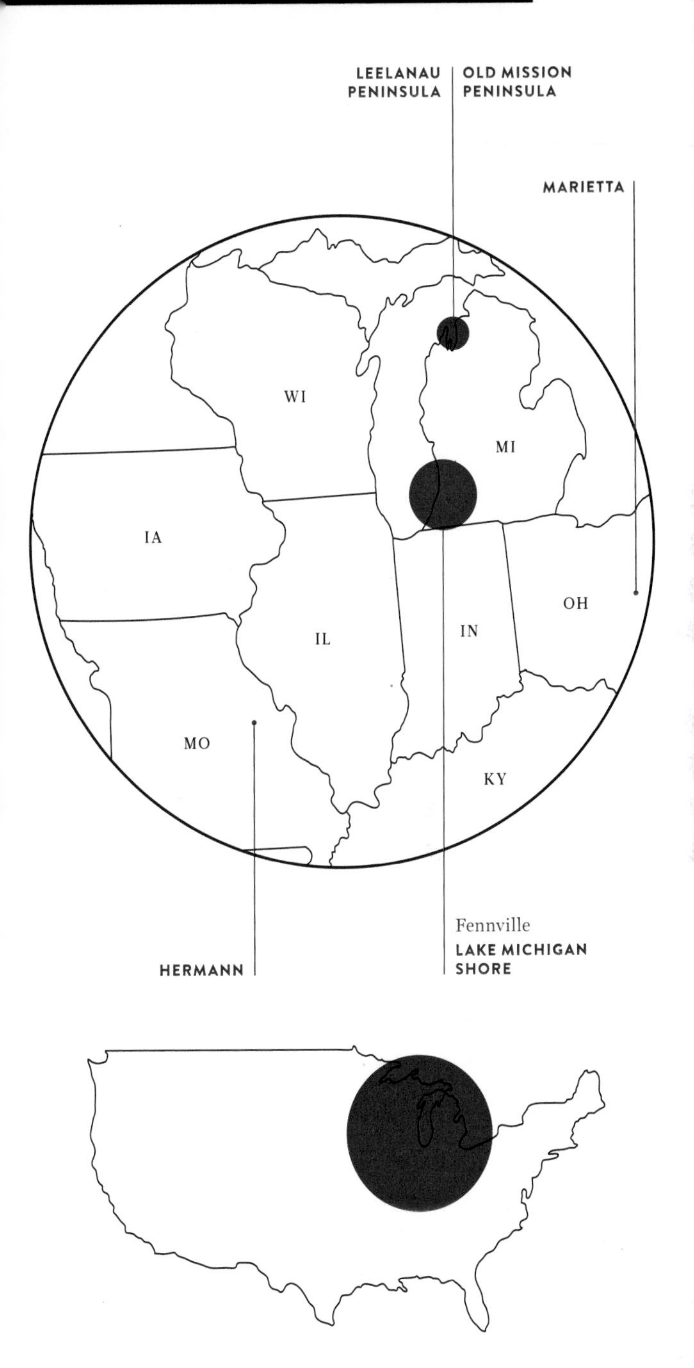
LEELANAU PENINSULA
OLD MISSION PENINSULA
MARIETTA
WI
MI
IA
OH
IL
IN
MO
KY
Fennville
LAKE MICHIGAN SHORE
HERMANN

Michigan

CLAIM TO FAME

Tasting is believing: The best of Michigan's 120 wineries are producing head-turning wines that are slowly making their way, through word-of-mouth and wine clubs, into the hands of wine lovers outside the region. Centered around two side-by-side peninsulas jutting into Lake Michigan—Leelanau and Old Mission—this is a small but energized wine business, where European vinifera grapes account for over two-thirds of all wine-grape acreage in the state and nearly all of the new plantings. Climate is a challenge here, with its brutal winters and relatively short summer growing seasons. Conditions are somewhat moderated by Lake Michigan's tempering influence, but even Riesling, the European grape that succeeds best here, faces weather far more extreme than in the Old World vineyards of its origin. The sometimes rocky, south-facing vineyards of the Leelanau Peninsula tend to produce crisp wines with vibrant acidity—more Mosel, perhaps, than Alsace—while the more clay-influenced soils of the Old Mission Peninsula give the wines more softness and juicy, floral character.

KEY GRAPES: WHITE

CHARDONNAY Michigan Chardonnay tends to be on the crisper, fresher side, even in barrel-fermented bottlings. In the hands of top producers like L. Mawby, the grape can make very tasty sparkling wine.

GEWÜRZTRAMINER Michigan may be known for its Riesling, but that is not the only Alsace/German grape that excels here; the state's crisp, aromatic Gewürztraminers are also gaining a fine reputation and are on the rise.

RIESLING This is the state's most successful grape. Sommeliers have long known that Michigan's Rieslings can compete in blind tastings with the finest examples in America.

KEY GRAPES: RED

CABERNET FRANC In warm, relatively dry vintages, Cabernet Franc produces delicious wines here, whether by itself or blended with Merlot.

PINOT NOIR This grape is finicky and difficult to grow under the best of circumstances, but Michigan's ambitious winemakers are working to make Pinot Noir thrive here.

Producers/ Michigan

BLACK STAR FARMS

Black Star Farms bills itself as an agricultural destination, which seems fair enough: It operates two wineries and three tasting rooms, an eau-de-vie and grappa distillery, the stylish Inn at Black Star Farms and much else. With the retirement of Donald Coe in 2016, his co-founder, Kerm Campbell, and the latter's wife, Sallie, are now full owners of Black Star. The 25,000-case wine operation sources more than half of its grapes from the Campbells' own vineyards; the rest come from a group of growers that acts as a sort of cooperative with ownership interest in the winery. Though Riesling and Chardonnay are mainstays here, Black Star has scored notable successes with its reds as well.

○ **Black Star Farms Arcturos Dry Riesling / 2013 / Old Mission Peninsula / $$** Floral on the nose, this graceful, aromatic dry Riesling, brimming with peach and lime zest character, should easily convince any doubters about the potential of Michigan Riesling.

● **Black Star Farms Arcturos Pinot Noir / 2013 / Michigan / $$** Notoriously finicky Pinot Noir does surprisingly well on Michigan's Old Mission Peninsula, here producing a lightly smoky, herbal, cherry-inflected red.

CHATEAU DE LEELANAU VINEYARD AND WINERY

Located at the gateway to Leelanau wine country, north of Traverse City, Chateau de Leelanau was acquired in 2009 by Matt Gregory and members of the Gregory clan as an extension of their two-generation farming and orchard operation; it is now co-owned by Matt and former Cincinnati Bengal football player Kyle Cook. The winery's offerings range from a sparkling Chardonnay-and-peach blend (Peach Fizz) to cherry wine and caramel apple hard cider. About half of Chateau de Leelanau's wines are blends, some named for local farms, but the flagship wine is a varietal white made from the Bianca grape, an obscure Hungarian cross between Bouvier and Villard Blanc.

○ **Chateau de Leelanau Bianca / 2011 / Leelanau Peninsula / $$**
Winemaker Matt Gregory's signature wine, made from the Hungarian hybrid grape Bianca, is reminiscent of Sauvignon Blanc with its bright acidity and ripe grapefruit notes.

● **Chateau de Leelanau Hawkins / 2012 / Leelanau Peninsula / $$**
The Regent grape variety—an odd hybrid of Sylvaner, Müller Thurgau and Chambourcin—is the source for this intensely colored, peppery, blackberry-fruited red.

CHATEAU FONTAINE

This operation is a family affair, from Lucie and Dan Matthies, who put wine grapes into a south-facing potato field and cow pasture on the Leelanau Peninsula in the 1987; to their son Doug, who manages the now 30 acres of grapes; to his aunt Sally, who painted the distinctive sunset labels. The family faced a steep learning curve—the first wines were made from a home-winemaking hobbyists' kit—but today Doug runs Big Paw Vineyard Services to share their acquired expertise with other area growers and winemakers. While Chateau Fontaine may be best known for its varietal whites, particularly Riesling and Gewürztraminer, its multigrape blends are very popular as well.

○ **Chateau Fontaine Riesling / 2014 / Michigan / $**
Crisp and focused, with pear-peach fruit notes and bracing acidity, this is regularly one of Michigan's top dry Rieslings.

○ **Chateau Fontaine Pinot Blanc / 2014 / Leelanau Peninsula / $$**
Not much Pinot Blanc is grown in Michigan (or in the entire US, for that matter), but Chateau Fontaine's version nails the variety's appeal, with lemongrass and melony fruit notes and excellent balance.

CHATEAU GRAND TRAVERSE

Chateau Grand Traverse and its owners, the O'Keefe family, deserve credit for helping to bring the Old Mission Peninsula—a strip of land jutting into Grand Traverse Bay—to prominence. Today Chateau Grand Traverse is the largest commercial winery in northern Michigan. Founder Ed O'Keefe is hard to intimidate—he was a Green Beret—so he wasn't deterred in the 1970s when most people believed that vinifera grapes wouldn't grow so far north. The winery is run by his son Eddie now, with the winemaking handled for many years by German-born Bernd Croissant, who shows a particularly sure hand with whites: his outstanding Rieslings are fruit-forward and crisp.

○ **Chateau Grand Traverse Dry Riesling / 2013 / Old Mission Peninsula / $** Grand Traverse's exclusive focus on *Vitis vinifera* grapes pays off with this spot-on Riesling, full of tree fruit and citrus flavor, ending on dusty mineral notes.

● **Chateau Grand Traverse Gamay Noir Reserve / 2012 / Old Mission Peninsula / $$** Pinot Noir does well in northern Michigan; it stands to reason that Gamay would, too, and this light-bodied, cherry-peppery red (think good Beaujolais Villages) proves it.

L. MAWBY VINEYARDS

Larry Mawby wasn't the first person to associate sparkling wine and sex, just the first to feature the word "sex" on his labels. And yes, Sex does sell. This Leelanau Peninsula winery produces about 18,000 cases of bubbly a year, under two labels. The L. Mawby wines—in 10-plus bottlings and sweetness levels—are made using the traditional French méthode champenoise, and are composed of traditional grapes: Pinot Noir, Chardonnay and Pinot Gris with some Pinot Meunier thrown in. The more affordable M. Lawrence sparklers—including the Sex Dry Rosé and Detroit, a "Floral Hip-Hop Diva"—are produced by the bulk-fermented Charmat method.

○ **L. Mawby Tradition Brut / NV / Leelanau Peninsula / $$**
Made from Pinot Noir and Chardonnay grapes in the same manner as classic Champagnes, this sparkler could go head-to-head with many of those wines without a problem.

○ **L. Mawby Talismøn Brut / NV / Leelanau Peninsula / $$$**
Light gold in hue, with distinctive bready and earthy aromas, Mawby's single-vineyard top cuvée gains additional complexity from extended aging in the bottle.

ST. JULIAN WINERY

This southwestern Michigan winery, the state's oldest, has a long, colorful history. Founder Mariano Meconi flourished as a winemaker in Prohibition-era Ontario, Canada, but moved his Meconi Wine Company to Detroit after repeal. Later renamed for the patron saint of Meconi's home village in Italy, St. Julian continues to grow and innovate. It still produces the old stalwarts that brought it fame, like Sholom Kosher Wine, Solera Cream Sherry and a roster of sweet fruit wines, but under third-generation owner David Braganini and winemaker Nancie Oxley, St. Julian is placing new emphasis on the top end, bottling estimable varietal wines under the Braganini Reserve label.

○ **Braganini Reserve Late Harvest Vidal Blanc / 2014 / Lake Michigan Shore / $$** In this impressive dessert wine, the not-always-impressive Vidal grape turns into a silky smooth, apple-and-caramel elixir.

● **Braganini Reserve Meritage / 2013 / Lake Michigan Shore / $$** St. Julian's top bottling is a barrel selection of its best Cabernet Franc, Merlot and Cabernet Sauvignon lots; think dark cherry fruit plus a mocha note from oak.

Producers/ Other Midwest

MARIETTA WINE CELLARS / Ohio

Allen and Mary Jane Phillips opened their winery in the historic Ohio River town of Marietta in 2000. It has not been an easy path for them, what with floods and then an arson fire in 2010 that burned down the shop and winery. But the Phillipses have persevered, reopening in a nearby location that, like the first, has become a community center—a place to have lunch, buy wine and wine-related gifts and enjoy live music at Wine Down Time every Friday evening. The label includes nearly 30 wines in all, ranging from dry European-style varietals to bottlings of sweet native grapes like Niagara and Concord.

○ **Marietta Wine Cellars Riesling / NV / America / $** Lightly fruity, with bright acidity, this appealing Riesling is one of Marietta's handful of dry whites.

STONE HILL WINERY / Missouri

The town of Hermann, Missouri, now the heart of the state's wine country, was founded by German settlers in 1837. Ten years later, Stone Hill Winery opened its doors there. By the time Prohibition shut down Missouri's wine industry, Stone Hill was the second-largest winery in the US—with the nation's largest series of vaulted cellars—and had won medals at tastings as far away as Vienna. Jim and Betty Held bought and began revitalizing the lovely but run-down estate in 1965. Their sons, Jon and Thomas, run the operation today and continue to champion Missouri viticulture. Stone Hill's seven vineyards, totaling 182 acres, are planted mostly to French-American hybrids such as Vidal, Chardonel and Vignoles, but with a special focus on the indigenous American Norton grape, which yields its top red wines.

○ **Stone Hill Winery Reserve Chardonel / 2013 / Hermann / $$**
This intriguing cross between Chardonnay and Seyval, given extended barrel aging on lees, results in a full-bodied white suggestive of Chardonnay with unusual tropical fruit notes.

● **Stone Hill Winery Norton / 2013 / Hermann / $$**
A benchmark Norton and one of the best wines made in the US from native grapes, Stone Hill's flagship bottling is dark and spicy, with wild blackberry notes, suggesting an American cross between a Côtes-du-Rhône and a Cahors Malbec.

Southwest

With its long, generally dry, low-humidity growing seasons, the Southwest is decidedly a wine region to watch. Texas has already made great strides, bottling wines that are worthy of national attention. Arizona is emerging as a budding fine-wine star thanks to bold-flavored, earthy reds from Bordeaux, Rhône and Italian varieties. Colorado offers excellent high-altitude vineyards of its own: The very dry Grand Valley AVA produces some of the state's best full-bodied reds, while the cooler, higher West Elks AVA is the spot for Gewürztraminer, Riesling and Pinot Noir. The remarkably well-priced, Champagne-method sparkling wines from the French-born Gruet family have put New Mexico's nascent wine industry on the map.

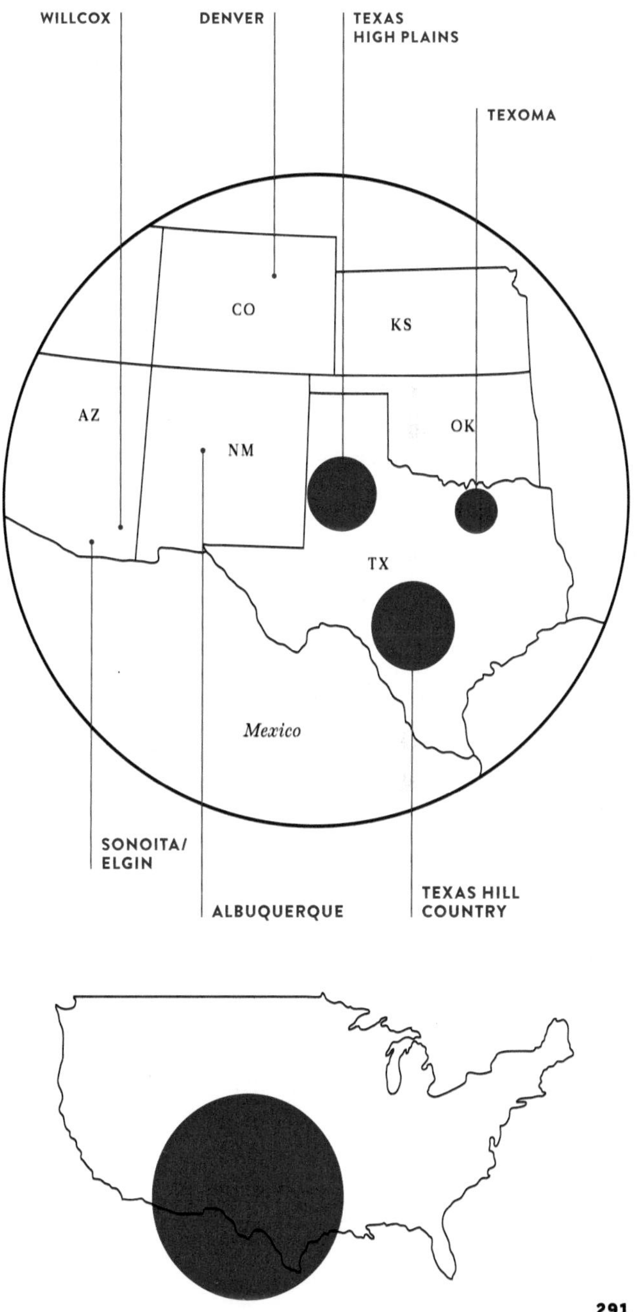
WILLCOX
DENVER
TEXAS
HIGH PLAINS
TEXOMA
CO
KS
AZ
NM
OK
TX
Mexico
SONOITA/
ELGIN
ALBUQUERQUE
TEXAS HILL
COUNTRY

Texas

CLAIM TO FAME

Home to some 350 wineries, Texas is now the nation's fifth-largest wine-producing state. It boasts a substantial wine tourism industry—centered around the Texas Hill Country town of Fredericksburg (both the region and the town are AVAs)—and is a hot-bed of experimentation with grape varieties in various climate conditions. Many top Texas wineries around the state rely on the remote High Plains AVA around Lubbock to actually grow their grapes. The semi-arid High Plains region, with vineyards at altitudes of up to 4,000 feet, accounts for about 85 percent of the state's wine grapes, including a wealth of European vinifera vines. But Texas is also a stronghold of hybrid and native grape varieties, which are better suited to more strenuous growing conditions. There are many fine—and expensive—wines being made in Texas today, with the promise of more to come.

KEY GRAPES: WHITE

BLANC DU BOIS A relatively recently crossed hybrid from Florida, Blanc du Bois has found a home in Texas, where it is made into fruity, dry or semi-sweet wines.

CHARDONNAY Spring frosts and vine pests make Chardonnay a challenging grape to grow in much of Texas, but its popularity encourages producers to persevere.

MUSCAT CANELLI (MUSCAT BLANC) In Texas, this variety is the source of fruity, light, off-dry, crowd-pleasing wines with exotic floral notes.

VIOGNIER Texas wineries turn out rich Viogniers with classic stone-fruit and floral perfume aromas.

KEY GRAPES: RED

CABERNET SAUVIGNON Texas produces some fine examples of Cabernet Sauvignon. Like other Bordeaux red wine grapes, it fares better in this hot climate in vineyards above 3,000 feet.

LENOIR (BLACK SPANISH) Used in Texas to make rich, fortified wines, this disease-resistant hybrid is also getting star turns these days as a dry red.

MERLOT Lively, rich, juicy Merlot and Merlot blends come from vineyards at high altitude here.

TEMPRANILLO Plantings are still modest, but this Spanish grape, like Italy's Sangiovese, can handle hotter climates without losing structure and definition. Both varieties have great potential here.

Producers/ Texas

BECKER VINEYARDS

Quarter horses and a 19th-century bar from a San Antonio saloon set the Lone Star vibe at this Texas Hill Country property (it also features acres of lavender and orchards). Endocrinologist turned vintner Richard Becker and his wife, Bunny, founded their winery in 1992, qualifying them for pioneer status. Over the years, Becker Vineyards has grown into a 100,000-plus-case operation with three estate vineyards; it also buys more Texas grapes than any other winery in the state. Bordeaux-based reds and Viognier are the biggest stars in the expansive portfolio, though winemaker Jonathan Leahy constantly experiments.

○ **Becker Vineyards Reserve Viognier / 2014 / Texas High Plains / $$**
This full-bodied white stays just this side of Viognier's tendency toward over-the-top flamboyance; rather, it's floral and melony, with enough acidity to lift the ripe fruit.

● **Becker Vineyards Chevaux Noir / 2014 / Texas High Plains / $$$**
An homage to Bordeaux's classic Cheval Blanc, this similar blend—Merlot and Cabernet Franc—is powerful and structured, with a distinct tobacco note.

BENDING BRANCH WINERY

Robert W. Young (a physician and vintner) and viticulturalist John Rivenburgh (who departed the project in 2016) planted their first vines near Comfort, Texas, in 2009. They were determined to farm organically and sustainably, and to focus on warm-climate vinifera grapes. The operation's current 20 vineyard acres are planted to more than a dozen varieties. The emerging star from amid an experimental welter that includes such off-the-beaten-track grapes as Souzão and Picpoul Blanc has been the red Tannat variety, which seems particularly suited to the Hill Country *terroir*. The ambitions of this already well-regarded winery can be gauged from the relatively stiff prices of its higher-end offerings, such as the Chloe Cuvée red blend and the Petite Sirah Reserve, both sourced, as are other Bending Branch bottlings, from California.

● **Bending Branch Texas Tannat / 2012 / Texas / $$**

This full-bodied, formidable red shows the promise of the thick-skinned Tannat variety in Texas's unpredictable climate; tannic now, it's worth cellaring for a few years.

BRENNAN VINEYARDS

Dr. Pat Brennan enlisted his wife, family and friends in the marathon effort to plant Brennan Vineyards' first 5,000 vines over the course of a long weekend in 2002. The three main vineyards—Comanche (for such grapes as Viognier, Cabernet Sauvignon and Syrah), Newburg (for Mourvèdre and Nero d'Avola) and Blue (for Cabernet Sauvignon and Viognier)—are situated in the rolling hills near the junction of the Hill Country and Texas High Plains growing areas, though the winery sources from a number of growers as well. Viognier is Brennan's signature wine in a portfolio that includes the everyday-drinking Austin Street bottlings and the main Brennan Vineyards premium label.

○ **Brennan Vineyards Lily / 2013 / Texas / $$**

A Rhône-style white blend made with Viognier, Roussanne and a surprisingly high percentage (47 percent) of Muscat of Alexandria, this is unsurprisingly floral (given the Muscat) but also balanced and full of complex stone-fruit flavors.

● **Brennan Vineyards Super Nero / 2012 / Texas / $$$**

A signature grape of Sicily, Nero d'Avola seems to grow equally well in Texas's similarly hot climate. Winemaker Todd Webster fashions it into a fruit-forward, spicy red that's hard not to like.

DUCHMAN FAMILY WINERY

A pair of doctors, Lisa and Stan Duchman, founded this star-quality winery that helped put Driftwood, Texas, near Austin, on the wine map (some are now calling it the "Napa Valley of Texas"); their stone-clad villa is on many tourists' itineraries as well. The emphasis here is on Mediterranean-style wines, including semi-obscure (to most Americans) varieties like the Greco-Italian red Aglianico and the crisp white Vermentino, along with a slew of others. Following their motto, "100% Texas Grapes. 100% Texas Wine," the Duchmans and winemaker Dave Reilly scout grapes from around the state, many from top vineyards in the cooler climes of the Texas High Plains AVA.

○ **Duchman Family Winery Viognier / 2014 / Texas High Plains / $$** Made in a crisp, bright style, unlike the opulent, often heavy style favored by California, this High Plains Viognier is aromatic and elegant, and a steal at the price.

● **Duchman Family Winery Montepulciano / 2012 / Texas High Plains / $$** Dave Reilly's interest in Italian varieties pays off with this plummy, structured red. The inviting fruit gains complexity from tobacco and pepper notes.

FALL CREEK VINEYARDS

Created in 1979 by businessman and rancher Ed Auler and his wife, Susan, with the late, iconic André Tchelistcheff as an early consultant, this Texas Hill Country producer is a centerpiece of the state's wine establishment: Fall Creek wines have been poured at four Presidential inaugurations and numerous state dinners. Although now almost 40 years old, the operation has been as dynamic as a startup in recent years, opening a second visitors' facility in the emerging wine center of Driftwood to complement its winery and tasting room in Tow, and hiring Sergio Cuadra from Chile as winemaker in 2013. Formerly of Concha y Toro and Anakena, Cuadra oversees an extensive lineup capped by an impressive flagship: the Meritus red blend.

● **Fall Creek Salt Lick Vineyards Tempranillo / 2012 / Texas Hill Country / $$** Another argument for Tempranillo becoming one of Texas's mainstay red grapes, this rich red has classic cherry-plum Tempranillo fruit character with firm but ripe tannins.

● **Meritus / 2012 / Texas Hill Country / $$$** Polished and complex, this ageworthy Cabernet Sauvignon–Merlot blend is made only in top vintages.

MCPHERSON CELLARS

Kim McPherson has Texas wine in his veins: His late father, Dr. Clinton "Doc" McPherson, was one of the founders of modern winemaking here. After graduating from UC Davis, Kim worked in various Texas cellars before opening his winery in downtown Lubbock in 2008. He focuses on Rhône, Italian and Spanish varietals sourced from a number of top vineyards in the High Plains AVA, including his family's Sagmor. Wine tourists who don't have Lubbock on their itineraries should note that McPherson partners with Brennan (see p. 294) and Lost Oak in the Four Point tasting room and wine center in the Hill Country wine town of Fredericksburg.

○ **McPherson Reserve Roussanne / 2014 / Texas High Plains / $$**
Roussanne's alluring white peach–nectarine character is on full display in McPherson's reserve bottling.

● **McPherson Les Copains / 2013 / Texas / $$**
This Côtes-du-Rhône-inspired blend of Cinsault, Syrah, Carignane, Mourvèdre and Grenache does a remarkable job of proving the unlikely premise that Lubbock, Texas, and the Rhône Valley are not that different after all.

PEDERNALES CELLARS

This winery is a Kuhlken family operation: Jeanine and Larry planted the estate vineyard in 1995; their son David is the winemaker. They bottled their first wines in 2006 and began scoring hits with head-turning Tempranillos and juicy Viogniers. The winery, located in Stonewall, on the US 290 "Wine Road," also turns out a number of other Spanish- and Rhône-style wines sourced from its own Hill Country estate vineyard and from top High Plains growers like Bingham, Newsom and Reddy. Pedernales bills itself as "Texas's premier boutique winery," and its headliners, like the Family Reserve red and the reserve Tempranillos, have prices to match the claim.

○ **Pedernales Viognier Reserve / 2014 / Texas / $$$**
Citrus and stone-fruit notes lead off this impressive white's flavors; if true to form, in a couple of years it will start to offer enticing nut and caramel notes as well.

● **Pedernales Tempranillo Reserve / 2014 / Texas / $$$**
This layered, cherry-inflected Tempranillo is good evidence of Texas's capacity to produce wines that can compete with top bottlings from California (or, in this case, Spain).

Producers/ Other Southwest

CALLAGHAN VINEYARDS / Arizona

The French newspaper *Le Monde* has called this winery in Elgin, not far from Tombstone, one of the most interesting in America, a sentiment echoed by US critics. Yet Callaghan Vineyards isn't as well known to general drinkers as it should be, given the expert winemaking of Kent Callaghan and his team. Perched 4,850 feet up in the high desert of southern Arizona, within the state's only AVA, the winery has undergone a long learning curve since its founding in 1990. Today it turns out a roster of deep, full-textured wines, with a specialty in Spanish and Rhône reds.

● **Callaghan Vineyards Mourvedre / 2013 / Sonoita / $$**
A lighter, more aromatic take on Mourvèdre, this red is high-toned and savory—unusual at first, but eventually compelling.

● **Callaghan Vineyards Caitlin's / 2013 / Sonoita / $$$**
Petit Verdot is the heart of this top-line red (the rest is Merlot and Cabernet Franc). Ink-dark and spicy, it offers plenty of black cherry and blackberry fruit, and no lack of tannins.

DOS CABEZAS WINEWORKS / Arizona

Todd Bostock saw the potential of Arizona wine while working at the original incarnation of Dos Cabezas, founded in the 1990s by Arizona wine pioneer Al Buhl. In 2006, Bostock, with his wife, Kelly, and his parents, bought the winery and relocated it to Sonoita, near the family's 15-acre Pronghorn Vineyard, planted at 4,800 feet to an evolving array of varieties. While the winery's spicy El Campo Tempranillo-Mourvèdre blend is made from Pronghorn grapes, Dos Cabezas also sources quality fruit from its 4,300-foot-high Cimarron Vineyard in Cochise County.

● **Dos Cabezas WineWorks Águileón / 2012 / Arizona / $$**
Todd and Kelly Bostock's take on the wines of Rioja, this Tempranillo-based blend is deeply colored but brighter and more red-fruit-driven than the El Norte bottling.

● **Dos Cabezas WineWorks El Norte / 2012 / Arizona / $$**
A Syrah-driven, Rhône-inspired blend, this spicy, cherry-rich red calls out for a rich winter dish like cassoulet.

GRUET WINERY / New Mexico

Central New Mexico's high desert is home to one of America's favorite sparkling wine brands. The Gruet family, founders of France's G. Gruet et Fils Champagne house, planted their pioneering Albuquerque-area vineyard in 1984, and released their first New Mexican sparkling wine in 1989. At altitudes of over 4,200 feet, Gruet's vineyards experience warm days and big temperature plunges at night, which help lock in the grapes' acidity. The apple-and-citrus-driven basic brut and toasty Blanc de Noirs in particular are among the best-value sparkling wines made anywhere. Now that Gruet is part of the portfolio of Washington state's Precept Wine, its wines are likely to enjoy even wider distribution.

○ **Gruet Blanc de Noirs / NV / America / $$**

Primarily Pinot Noir, pale orangey-pink in hue and full of appealing raspberry and pear character, this Blanc de Noirs bottling is one of the unquestionable steals in American sparkling wine.

○ **Gilbert Gruet Grande Reserve / 2007 / New Mexico / $$$**

The winery's tête de cuvée blend is aged for six years before release, giving it distinctive brioche-and-toast notes and a creamy texture.

THE INFINITE MONKEY THEOREM / Colorado

Working out of a warehouse in Denver's River North arts district and a second facility in Austin, Texas, the English-born, Australian-trained vintner Ben Parsons has become a quirky ambassador for urban wines. He is also on a mission, he has said, to strip away pretense from wine, which involves, among other things, turning out cheeky creations such as his Moscato Can, a fizzy Muscat rosé in a single-serving can (there are also kegs and refillable growlers). More serious wines—well, serious for wines with a picture of a chimp on the label—like the 100th Monkey blend have gained Parsons a following for offering quality, and a lot of complexity, for the price.

● **Cabernet Franc / 2014 / America / $$**

This tobacco-inflected red isn't wildly complex, but it's definitely packed full of ripe, dark cherry fruit.

● **The Infinite Monkey Theorem The Blind Watchmaker / 2014 / America / $$** A blend of Syrah and Merlot, this easy-drinking, juicy wine brims with black- and raspberry flavor.

SAND-RECKONER VINEYARDS / Arizona

The Willcox area of southeastern Arizona is gaining a critical mass of fine winemaking thanks to projects like this one. Rob Hammelman—a peripatetic winemaker whose résumé includes an Australian enology degree and cellar work in France's Gigondas region—founded this boutique winery with his wife, Sarah, in 2010. That year, the couple acquired their 12-acre, 4,300-foot-high farm, whose sandy loam soils and limestone bed are well suited to grape development. (The winery name references the site's sandy soil, as well as a 3rd-century BC thought experiment by Greek scientist Archimedes—in case you wondered). Though the Hammelmans' plantings are nearly all warm-weather red varieties like Syrah and Sangiovese, the surprise early break-out wine has been a flowery, complex, age-worthy Malvasia Bianca.

○ **Sand-Reckoner Malvasia Bianca / 2014 / Arizona / $$**
Floral and perfumed, but not too much so, this exotic white shows that an unusual grape, grown in a very unusual place (southeastern Arizona), can create a wine far, far better than anyone might reasonably expect.

● **Sand-Reckoner r / 2013 / Arizona / $$**
Rob Hammelman's "r" bottling is his ode to the red blends of the southern Rhône: dark-berried, full-bodied and savory.

Pairing Guide

These days the adage "White wine with fish and red with meat" seems to have been replaced with "Drink whatever you like with whatever you want." Both approaches have advantages, but neither is an absolute. The truth is that there is no one principle for creating perfect wine matches beyond the fact that you want to bring together dishes and wines that highlight each other's best qualities rather than obscure them. To help make delicious matches at home, the following pages provide five basic strategies for matching and tips for pairing based on the main course and cooking technique. The specific bottle recommendations are all from this guide.

WINE-PAIRING GUIDELINES

THINK ABOUT WEIGHT One simple approach to pairing wine and food is to match lighter dishes with lighter wines and richer dishes with richer wines. We all know that a fillet of sole seems "lighter" than braised beef short ribs. With wine, the best analogy is milk: We know that skim milk feels lighter than whole milk, and wine is similar. So, for instance, Cabernet Sauvignon or Amarone feels richer or heavier than a Beaujolais or a crisp rosé from Provence.

TART GOES WITH TART Acidic foods—like a green salad with a tangy vinaigrette—work best with similarly tart wines: a Sauvignon Blanc, say, or a Muscadet from France. It might seem as though a richer, weightier wine would be the answer, but the acidity in the food will make the wine taste bland.

CONSIDER SALT & FAT Two things to keep in mind about how your palate works: First, salt in food will make wine seem less sour, softening the edge in tart wines; and fat in a dish—whether it's a well-marbled steak or pasta with a cream sauce—will make red wines seem lighter and less tannic.

SPLIT THE DIFFERENCE In restaurants, a group of people will rarely order the same entrees; instead, someone will order fish, another person a steak, a third the pasta with duck ragù, and so on. In instances like this, go for a wine that follows a middle course—not too rich, not too light, not too tannic. For reds, Pinot Noir is a great option; for whites, choose an unoaked wine with good acidity, like a dry Riesling or a Pinot Gris from Oregon.

MOST OF ALL, DON'T WORRY Pairings are meant to be suggestions. Play around with possibilities and don't get caught up in absolutes. After all, Cabernet may go well with a cheeseburger, but if you don't like cheeseburgers, that doesn't matter at all.

Pairing Chart

	DISH	BEST WINE MATCH
CHICKEN	STEAMED OR POACHED	Medium white or light red
	ROASTED OR SAUTÉED	Rich white or rosé
	CREAMY OR BUTTERY SAUCES	Rich white
	TANGY SAUCES MADE WITH CITRUS, VINEGAR, TOMATOES	Medium white
	EARTHY FLAVORS LIKE MUSHROOMS	Medium red
	HERBS	Light, crisp white
PORK	GRILLED OR SEARED, LEAN	Medium red
	GRILLED OR SEARED, FATTY	Rich red
	BRAISED OR STEWED	Rich red
	SWEET SAUCES OR DRIED FRUIT	Medium white
	SPICY INGREDIENTS	Medium, off-dry white or lighter red
	CURED OR BRINED	Medium white or rosé

GREAT VARIETIES	BOTTLE TO TRY
Chardonnay (lightly oaked or unoaked), Riesling, Gamay	2014 Chateau Ste. Michelle Eroica Riesling / p. 233
Chardonnay, Rhône-style white blend, rosé	2015 Wölffer Estate Rosé / p. 271
Chardonnay, Rhône-style white blend	2012 Au Bon Climat Nuits-Blanches au Bouge Chardonnay / p. 153
Chenin Blanc, Sauvignon Blanc, Sémillon	2015 Spottswoode Sauvignon Blanc / p. 81
Cabernet Franc, Gamay, Norton, Pinot Noir	2013 Radio-Coteau La Neblina Pinot Noir / p. 136
Pinot Grigio, Sauvignon Blanc, Tocai Friulano	2014 Matthiasson White Wine / p. 60
Cabernet Franc, Sangiovese	2013 Lang & Reed Two-Fourteen Cabernet Franc / p. 54
Merlot, Rhône-style red blend	2013 Tablas Creek Vineyard Esprit de Tablas / p. 189
Grenache, Petite Sirah, Syrah, Rhône-style red blend	2014 Dashe Les Enfants Terribles Grenache / p. 107
Chenin Blanc, Pinot Gris, Riesling (medium-bodied)	2014 Sineann Pinot Gris / p. 217
Riesling, Gamay, Pinot Noir (lighter-style)	2014 Edmunds St. John Bone-Jolly Gamay Noir / p. 164
Albariño, Sauvignon Blanc, Sémillon, rosé	2014 DeLille Cellars Chaleur Estate Blanc / p. 236

	DISH	BEST WINE MATCH
BEEF	GRILLED OR SEARED STEAKS, CHOPS, BURGERS	Rich red
	BRAISED OR STEWED	Rich red
	SWEET SAUCES LIKE BARBECUE	Rich, fruity red
	SPICY INGREDIENTS	Medium red
LAMB	GRILLED OR ROASTED	Rich red
	BRAISED OR STEWED	Rich red
	SPICY INGREDIENTS	Lighter or medium red
FISH	GRILLED	Medium white, rosé or light red
	ROASTED, BAKED OR SAUTÉED	Medium white or rosé
	FRIED	Light or medium white, rosé or light red
	STEAMED	Light or medium white
	SPICY INGREDIENTS	Light or medium white
	HERB SAUCES	Light or medium white
	CITRUS SAUCES	Light or medium white
	SHELLFISH, COOKED	Medium or rich white
	SHELLFISH, RAW	Light white

GREAT VARIETIES	BOTTLE TO TRY
Cabernet Sauvignon, Syrah	2013 Gramercy Cellars Lagniappe Syrah / p. 241
Syrah, Zinfandel, Bordeaux-style red blend, Rhône-style red blend	2011 Bonny Doon Vineyard Le Cigare Volant / p. 156
Grenache, Zinfandel	2014 Nalle Zinfandel / p. 132
Barbera, Cabernet Franc, Sangiovese	2013 Terra d'Oro Barbera / p. 191
Cabernet Sauvignon, Merlot, Syrah, Bordeaux-style red blend	2013 Blackbird Vineyards Arise / p. 24
Grenache, Syrah, Zinfandel	2014 Robert Biale Vineyards Black Chicken Zinfandel / p. 72
Barbera, Pinot Noir, Sangiovese	2013 Ken Wright Cellars Pinot Noir / p. 212
Chardonnay, Pinot Gris, rosé, Pinot Noir (lighter-style)	2015 Lynmar Estate Rosé of Pinot Noir / p. 127
Chardonnay (lighter-style), Pinot Blanc, Pinot Gris, rosé	2014 The Eyrie Vineyards Pinot Blanc / p. 211
Pinot Blanc, Pinot Gris, Riesling (fuller-bodied), rosé, Gamay	2015 Trefethen Dry Riesling / p. 87
Chardonnay (lightly oaked), Sauvignon Blanc, Sémillon	2013 Stony Hill Chardonnay / p. 84
Pinot Gris, Riesling (off-dry), Sémillon	2014 Charles Smith Kung Fu Girl Riesling / p. 233
Pinot Gris, Sauvignon Blanc, Sémillon	2015 Behrens Family Winery La Danza / p. 23
Pinot Gris, Sauvignon Blanc	2014 Honig Sauvignon Blanc Reserve / p. 48
Albariño, Chardonnay, Viognier, Rhône-style white blend	2014 àMaurice Cellars Viognier / p. 227
Albariño, Chardonnay (lightly oaked or unoaked), Pinot Gris	2014 Marimar Estate Albariño / p. 129

	DISH	BEST WINE MATCH
GAME	VENISON	Rich red
	DUCK OR GAME BIRDS, ROASTED OR PAN-ROASTED	Medium red
	DUCK OR GAME BIRDS, RAGÙ OR STEW	Medium or rich red
PASTA	BUTTER OR OIL	Medium white or rosé
	CREAMY, CHEESE SAUCES	Medium white, light or medium red
	TOMATO-BASED SAUCES	Medium red
	SPICY SAUCES	Medium white, light or medium red
	MEAT SAUCES	Rich red
	FISH AND SEAFOOD SAUCES	Medium or rich white
EGGS	PLAIN OR WITH HERBS	Sparkling
	WITH CHEESE (QUICHE)	Sparkling, medium white or rosé
SALADS	TART DRESSINGS LIKE VINAIGRETTE	Light white
	CREAMY DRESSINGS	Medium white
	PASTA & OTHER STARCHY SALADS	Rosé or light red

GREAT VARIETIES	BOTTLE TO TRY
Cabernet Sauvignon, Merlot, Syrah, Zinfandel, Rhône-style red blend	2014 Bedrock Wine. Co. The Bedrock Heritage / p. 101
Pinot Noir, Rhône-style red blend	2013 Hirsch Vineyards San Andreas Fault Pinot Noir / p. 118
Merlot, Sangiovese, Syrah, Bordeaux-style red blend	2012 Andrew Will Two Blondes Vineyard / p. 227
Pinot Blanc, Pinot Gris, rosé	2014 Elk Cove Vineyards Pinot Gris / p. 209
Chardonnay (lightly oaked), Rhône-style white blend, Barbera, Rhône-style red blend	2014 Terre Rouge Enigma / p. 191
Barbera, Cabernet Franc, Sangiovese, Super Tuscan-style red blend	2012 Brian Carter Cellars Tuttorosso / p. 230
Pinot Grigio, Charbono, Sangiovese, Rhône-style red blend	NV Thackrey & Co Pleiades XXIV / p. 192
Merlot, Syrah, Zinfandel, Rhône-style red blend	2013 Donkey & Goat Fenaughty Vineyard Syrah / p. 163
Pinot Blanc, Sauvignon Blanc, Sémillon	2014 Kamen Sauvignon Blanc / p. 121
Dry sparkling wine	2011 Domaine Carneros Brut / p. 36
Dry sparkling wine, Riesling, rosé	2015 Balletto Rosé of Pinot Noir / p. 100
Albariño, Pinot Grigio, Sauvignon Blanc, Vermentino	2014 Barboursville Vineyards Vermentino Reserve / p. 278
Chenin Blanc, Pinot Gris, Sémillon	2014 Pine Ridge Chenin Blanc–Viognier / p. 68
Rosé, Gamay, Pinot Noir (lighter-style)	2012 Chateau Grand Traverse Gamay Noir Reserve / p. 287

Recipes

HALIBUT WITH PARSLEY-LEMON SAUCE & PINOT GRIS

Total **40 min;** Serves **4**

Pinot Gris wines from Oregon are a bit less rich and have a little more acidity than Chardonnays tend to. They go fantastically well with meaty fish like these luscious halibut steaks.

- **¼ cup extra-virgin olive oil**
- **2 large shallots, thinly sliced**
- **1 cup water**
- **½ cup heavy cream**
- **4 cups loosely packed parsley**
- **2 tsp. fresh lemon juice**
- **Kosher salt and pepper**
- **Four ½-inch-thick halibut steaks (1½ lbs.)**

1. In a medium saucepan, heat 2 tablespoons of the olive oil. Add the shallots and cook over moderate heat until softened, about 5 minutes. Add the water and simmer until reduced by half, about 6 minutes. Add the cream and simmer until reduced by one-third, about 6 minutes. Let cool for about 10 minutes.

2. Stir the parsley into the saucepan. Transfer the sauce to a blender and coarsely puree. Return the sauce to the saucepan. Stir in the lemon juice, season the sauce with salt and pepper and keep warm.

3. In each of 2 large nonstick skillets, heat 1 tablespoon of the remaining oil until shimmering. Season the halibut with salt and pepper and cook over high heat, turning once, until browned and just cooked, about 4 minutes. Transfer the halibut to plates and serve with the parsley sauce.

SCALLOPS WITH THAI CHILE SAUCE & OFF-DRY RIESLING

Total **25 min;** Serves **4 as a starter**

An off-dry Riesling's tart acidity and light sweetness complement any Asian cuisine that balances sweet, spicy and tangy flavors. The varietal pairs beautifully with these succulent seared scallops topped with a vibrant Thai chile sauce.

- **¼ cup plus 3 Tbsp. olive oil**
- **2 Tbsp. minced cilantro**
- **2 Tbsp. chopped roasted peanuts**
- **2 Tbsp. fresh lime juice**
- **1 Tbsp. thinly sliced red Thai chiles**
- **1 Tbsp. minced fresh lemongrass**
- **Kosher salt**
- **12 sea scallops**

1. In a small bowl, stir ¼ cup of the olive oil with the cilantro, peanuts, lime juice, chiles, lemongrass and ½ teaspoon of salt.

2. In a large skillet, heat the remaining 3 tablespoons of olive oil. Season the scallops with salt and cook over high heat, turning once, until golden, 3 minutes. Transfer to plates, spoon the chile sauce on top and serve.

WHOLE ROAST CHICKEN WITH 40 BRUSSELS SPROUTS & OAK-AGED CHARDONNAY

Active **10 min;** Total **1 hr 15 min;** Serves **4**

Roast chicken can go with almost anything. A full-bodied white, like an oak-aged Chardonnay, would be fabulous with this dish's warm caraway spiciness and lemony tang.

One 4-lb. chicken

2 Tbsp. extra-virgin olive oil

Kosher salt and pepper

40 brussels sprouts (1½ lbs.), trimmed

2 Tbsp. unsalted butter, cubed

1 tsp. caraway seeds

2 Tbsp. fresh lemon juice, plus lemon wedges for serving

1. Preheat the oven to 450°. Rub the chicken with the olive oil and season with salt and pepper. Place the chicken in a roasting pan and roast until an instant-read thermometer inserted in the thickest part of each leg registers 165°, about 30 minutes.

2. Add the brussels sprouts, butter and caraway seeds to the pan and roast for 20 minutes longer, until the chicken is cooked through. Sprinkle the lemon juice over the sprouts and let the chicken rest for 15 minutes. Carve the chicken, toss the brussels sprouts and serve with lemon wedges.

TRIPLE-DECKER BAKED ITALIAN CHEESE SANDWICHES & DRY ROSÉ

Active **30 min;** Total **2 hr 45 min;** Serves **8**

Some cheeses go better with white wine, some with red; yet almost all—like this rich baked cheese sandwich—pair well with dry rosé, which has the acidity of white wine and the fruit character of red.

8 plum tomatoes, halved lengthwise

¼ cup extra-virgin olive oil

Kosher salt and pepper

1 tsp. thyme leaves

2 white Pullman loaves—ends discarded, each loaf cut into twelve ½-inch-thick slices

1 lb. sliced provolone cheese

1 lb. Fontina cheese, coarsely shredded (about 5½ cups)

½ cup freshly grated Parmigiano-Reggiano cheese

1. Preheat the oven to 325°. On a large rimmed baking sheet, toss the halved tomatoes with 2 tablespoons of the olive oil and season with salt and pepper. Bake the tomatoes cut side up for 1½ hours, until soft and starting to brown. Sprinkle with the thyme leaves and bake for about 30 minutes longer, until the tomatoes are very tender and slightly shriveled but still juicy. Let cool.

2. Increase the oven temperature to 375°. Brush 16 bread slices with the remaining 2 tablespoons of olive oil; arrange 8 of the slices oiled side down on a large rimmed baking sheet. Top with the provolone and the unbrushed bread slices. Cover with the tomatoes, 4 cups of the Fontina and the remaining 8 bread slices, oiled side up. Press gently on the sandwiches and bake for about 15 minutes, until the bread is toasted and the cheese is melted.

3. Preheat the broiler. Toss the remaining Fontina with the Parmigiano-Reggiano and sprinkle on the sandwiches. Broil 3 inches from the heat for about 1 minute, until the cheese is melted. Transfer the sandwiches to plates and serve.

SAFFRON LINGUINE WITH HERB OIL AND SHAVED MANCHEGO CHEESE & SYRAH

Total **35 min;** Serves **4 as a starter**

Sharp cheeses such as Manchego and pecorino stand up to lusty Syrah. Fresh herbs and toasted almonds add complexity and texture to the pairing.

- **½ cup chopped flat-leaf parsley**
- **¼ cup chopped mint**
- **¼ cup extra-virgin olive oil**
- **1 tsp. chopped tarragon**
- **½ tsp. chopped thyme**
- **1 tsp. fresh lemon juice**
- **2 Tbsp. unsalted butter**
- **1 large garlic clove, minced**
- **Pinch of saffron threads**
- **½ lb. linguine**
- **¼ lb. Manchego or young pecorino cheese, shaved with a vegetable peeler**
- **½ cup sliced almonds, toasted until golden**
- **Freshly ground black pepper**

1. In a blender, puree the parsley with the mint, olive oil, tarragon, thyme and lemon juice. Scrape the herb oil into a bowl.

2. Melt the butter in a large skillet. Add the garlic and saffron and cook over low heat until fragrant, about 1 minute.

3. Cook the linguine in a pot of salted boiling water until al dente. Set the skillet with the garlic over moderately high heat and add ½ cup of the pasta cooking water. Drain the pasta, add it to the skillet and toss well. Transfer the pasta to warmed shallow bowls. Top with the cheese shavings, toasted almonds and herb oil. Sprinkle the linguine with pepper and serve at once.

MAKE AHEAD The herb oil can be refrigerated for up to 1 day. Let it return to room temperature before serving.

GRILLED LAMB LOIN CHOPS WITH POMEGRANATE RELISH & PINOT NOIR

Total **30 min;** Serves **4 to 6**

Lamb's innate gaminess and the bright juiciness of pomegranate seeds make this a perfect dish to pair with a Sonoma or Central Coast Pinot Noir.

Eight 7- to 8-oz. lamb loin chops, cut 2 inches thick

Kosher salt and pepper

1½ cups pomegranate seeds (from 2 pomegranates)

1 lightly packed cup mint, chopped, plus whole leaves for garnish

1 shallot, minced

3 Tbsp. extra-virgin olive oil

2 Tbsp. sherry vinegar

1. Light a grill or heat a cast-iron grill pan. Season the lamb chops with salt and pepper and grill over moderate heat, turning occasionally, until lightly charred all over and an instant-read thermometer inserted in the thickest part of the chops registers 130°, about 15 minutes. Transfer to a platter and let rest for 5 minutes.

2. In a medium bowl, mix the pomegranate seeds with the chopped mint, shallot, olive oil and vinegar; season with salt and pepper. Serve the relish with the lamb chops, garnished with mint leaves.

SWEET-AND-SPICY GRILLED BEEF SHORT RIBS & ZINFANDEL

Total **45 min;** Serves **4**

Zinfandel's rich fruitiness and peppery notes are terrific with substantial dishes that combine sweet and spicy flavors, like these delectable grilled short ribs.

¼ cup packed light brown sugar
1½ Tbsp. kosher salt
1 Tbsp. paprika
1 Tbsp. chili powder
1 tsp. garlic salt
1 tsp. dried oregano
1 tsp. black pepper
3¾ lbs. flanken-style beef short ribs, sliced ⅓ inch thick
Canola oil, for oiling the grate
Lemon wedges for serving

1. In a medium bowl, mix all of the ingredients except the short ribs, oil and lemon. Rub the mixture all over the short ribs and let stand for 20 minutes.

2. Light a grill and oil the grate. Grill the ribs over high heat, turning once, until nicely charred and nearly cooked through, about 6 minutes. Transfer to a platter and serve with lemon wedges.

MAKE AHEAD The spice rub can be stored in an airtight container for up to 1 month.

SERVE WITH Coleslaw.

BLACKBERRY-GLAZED PORK CHOPS & CABERNET SAUVIGNON

Total **45 min;** Serves **4**

California Cabernets often have a blackberry character that makes them amazing with these juicy pork chops.

- **½ cup blackberry preserves**
- **2 Tbsp. barbecue sauce**
- **1 Tbsp. Dijon mustard**
- **Four 12-oz. bone-in pork loin chops (with the tenderloin), cut 1½ inches thick**
- **Kosher salt and pepper**
- **1 lb. Broccolini**
- **2 Tbsp. extra-virgin olive oil**

1. Light a grill or heat a grill pan. In a small bowl, whisk the preserves with the barbecue sauce and mustard. Season the pork chops with salt and pepper and grill over moderate heat, turning occasionally, until lightly charred and nearly cooked through, about 15 minutes. Brush the chops with the blackberry glaze and cook, turning and glazing frequently, until an instant-read thermometer inserted near the bone registers 140°, about 5 minutes longer. Transfer the chops to a carving board to rest for 5 minutes.

2. Meanwhile, in a large bowl, toss the Broccolini with the olive oil and season with salt and pepper. Grill over moderately high heat, turning, until lightly charred and crisp-tender, 3 to 5 minutes.

3. Serve the pork chops with the Broccolini, passing any remaining glaze at the table.

MAKE AHEAD The blackberry glaze can be refrigerated for up to 1 week.

Index of Producers

D

E

F

G

H

I

J

K

L

M

T

U

V

W

Y